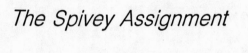

The Spivey Assignment

Other books by Philip Rosenberg

The Seventh Hero: Thomas Carlyle
and the Theory of Radical Activism

Contract on Cherry Street

Point Blank (with Sonny Grosso)

Badge of the Assassin (with
Robert Tanenbaum)

PHILIP ROSENBERG

THE SPIVEY ASSIGNMENT

A Double Agent's
Infiltration of the
Drug Smuggling
Conspiracy

Holt, Rinehart and Winston
New York

Published by Holt, Rinehart and Winston, 383 Madison
Avenue, New York, New York 10017.
Published simultaneously in Canada by Holt, Rinehart and
Winston of Canada, Limited.

Library of Congress Cataloging in Publication Data
Rosenberg, Philip, 1942–
    The Spivey assignment.
    1. Spivey, Larry. 2. Narcotic enforcement agents—
Georgia—Biography. 3. Undercover operations.
4. Smuggling—Georgia. I. Title.
HV5805.S64R67   364.1'57'0924 [B]   79–10085
ISBN 0–03–044371–7

First Edition

Designer: Amy Hill
Printed in the United States of America
10 9 8 7 6 5 4 3 2 1

Acknowledgments

T he following story is based on actual cases in which Larry Spivey participated during his brief career as an undercover agent for the Georgia Bureau of Investigation. In a few instances it has been necessary to deviate from the facts where a full recounting of the actual events would compromise the identity and the safety of an informant or jeopardize an ongoing investigation. Otherwise, I have tried to stay as close to the facts as possible. My primary source in the writing of this book was extensive interviews with Mr. Spivey, whose phenomenal memory for detail, aided by the investigative summaries he prepared while the cases were in progress, gave me a wealth of materials to work with.

I have taken the liberty of changing many of the names, for it seemed to me no valid public interest would be served by calling the identities of certain individuals to national attention. My purpose in writing this book, and Mr. Spivey's in wanting his story told, was to throw some light on the drug smuggling problem in America today, and to give the reader a vivid sense of the monumental task facing law enforcement personnel. For this purpose, the names of individual criminal entrepreneurs, many of whom are already paying for their crimes, seemed irrelevant. On the other hand, the real names of most of the people on the law enforcement side have been used, for it seemed to both Mr. Spivey and me that some sort of public recognition was due them for their selflessly heroic, often dangerous, and invariably unacknowledged work. Caught in a crossfire between opposing forces in a paradoxical society, which openly tolerates the use of certain drugs it nevertheless insists on declaring illegal, narcotics agents are roundly damned on the one hand for interfering with the rights of citizens to smoke, snort, or ingest the chemicals of their choice, while on the other hand they are mocked for their failure to win the war against drugs.

Both Mr. Spivey and I would like to thank Deputy Director Tom McGreevy and Inspector Phil Peters of the Georgia Bureau of Investigation, as well as the entire staff of the GBI's Controlled Substances Section. On my part, I owe them my warmest thanks for their cooperation in the writing of this book. Mr. Spivey's debt of gratitude runs deeper. He has asked me to say that in his opinion there is no finer law enforcement agency anywhere; the men and women of GBI whom he has met and worked with are among the best in their business, utterly unrivaled in their intelligence, dedication, and complete incorruptibility.

We would both like to thank our agents, Julia Coopersmith and Bob Dattila, without whom this book could not have come into existence. We owe them far more than their commissions reflect. I want to express my deepest appreciation to my wife Charlotte, whose solid instincts about what works and what doesn't again produced a number of valuable suggestions. Wanda Huttner and the staff at Star-Pack, Inc., again must be thanked for their diligence in preparing finished manuscript, often against almost impossible deadlines. And I would especially like to thank my son Mark, who put up with a lot, and who generously let us play with his electric trains when we needed some diversion.

The Spivey Assignment

Prologue

aptain Ramón Guterez stood in the dark wheelhouse of the Panamanian freighter and pulled the sleeve of his turtleneck sweater back to reveal the luminous dial of the skin diver's watch on his left wrist: 3:06. The freighter was anchored four miles off El Pájaro, Colombia, in the Caribbean Sea. Behind the captain, half a dozen loaded Uzi submachine guns hung on pegs at the rear of the wheelhouse. Guterez stretched until his elbows almost touched behind his back, then let out his breath slowly. He massaged his stomach with his right hand, which came to rest on the butt of the .45 holstered on his hip.

For a man in his early fifties, Captain Guterez was in good shape. Other than a slight roll of loose flesh where the black turtleneck was tucked into his blue trousers, there was no discernible fat on his body. The army belt and holstered gun rode almost casually on his side. He fumbled in his pants pocket and came out with a pack of Luckies and a Zippo lighter. Shaking out a cigarette, he pulled it from the pack with his lips, lit it, and strode purposefully from the wheelhouse out onto the open wing of the bridge. The ship had drifted around with the outgoing tide as it rode at anchor so that the bow now faced the distant shore. The captain watched as the moon slid silently into the glass-black water. In a little over an hour the sun would be rising neon yellow over the still invisible hills.

Below him, a small barge tied alongside the freighter rode up and down on the swells, nuzzling against the port side of the ship. On the loading platform forward of the bridge, the port boom was swung out over the lighter while the starboard boom hung poised above the open number two hold.

From where he stood on the bridge, Guterez could see half a dozen Indians working by a dim light in the hold of the ship. A fully loaded net suspended from a weighted hook at the juncture where the cables from the two booms came together descended slowly toward them. On the deck above the open hold stood an almost naked man, the sweat on his brown skin glistening like fireflies in the starlight. He made a clockwise circular motion with a red flashlight, and the hook stopped. Two of the Indians in the hold slipped the ropes of the net over the point of the hook, letting the net fall free. The dozen bales it contained rocked as they sought equilibrium on top of the bales already layering the hold.

Working quickly, using hands and stevedore's hooks, the two Indians swung the bales over to two other men, who stacked them. In a matter of minutes the net was empty, and one of the men in the hold gathered up the four corners, hung the empty sling back on the hook, and stepped clear.

The brown-skinned man on the deck made a counterclockwise motion with the red wand, and the winches whined, sucking the net out of the hold to a point directly under the tip of the starboard boom. The starboard winch gave slack, which was taken by the port boom, drawing the empty sling over the deck until it hung above the bobbing lighter. A toothless Indian, openmouthed and wide-eyed in the near darkness, reached to catch it as it descended neatly toward him.

Watching from the bridge, Captain Guterez nodded with satisfaction. The barge was more than half empty, and the number two cargo hold was almost full. He took a final drag on the cigarette, flipped the butt over the side, and, without waiting to watch it arch its way into the water below, turned to the wheelhouse. Inside, he rang the engine room on the engine order telegraph. Through the copper tubing next to the telegraph a voice answered in Spanish.

"*Sí, Capitán?*"

"*Cuarenta cinco minutos.*"

"*Sí, Capitán.*"

They would be getting under way in forty-five minutes. During the daylight hours the ship would cruise down the coast of Colombia and back, keeping out of sight of land and clear of all normal shipping lanes. It would return after dark to fill the number three hold with the remaining bales of marijuana and to bring aboard the cocaine.

One

L arry Spivey knew he wasn't a violent man, but he hadn't figured out any other way to explain why violence followed him around the way a rattlesnake follows a hare. He was born in Augusta, Georgia, but raised in Izmir, Turkey, where his father was a tobacco exporter. He was only seven years old when he witnessed his first public hanging.

He went with a group of his Turkish playmates, getting there early to be in front of the grown-ups who would pack the sun-parched square. They drank sodas and joked lightly, their laughter filled with nervous excitement. Then the crowd parted, and the man was led out to the rickety gallows in the center of the square. He was an old man, grizzled and lean, with arms like sticks and a chest so hollow his ribs seemed to have been painted on his naked skin. His head had been shaved a few days earlier and was covered with stubbly black hair that made his gaunt face look like a coconut. His eyes looked dead already.

Larry watched, hardly knowing what to expect, as the uniformed executioner shoved the old man up the three shallow steps to the platform, then onto the wood crate set atop it. With a shocking lack of ceremony that etched the sheer brutality of the moment in Larry's mind forever, the hangman dropped the noose over the man's head, tightened the knot, and drew up the slack. Then he kicked out the crate, and the old man was dangling by his neck, neither alive nor dead. The Turkish boys had told Larry garish stories of the dying convulsions of hanged men, and he had expected to see a body hurtling through space until it jerked to a violent halt, at the end of its rope. He had expected anything but the harrowing banality of such uneventful death.

Three years later, in the same public square, a boy Larry's age fell into a pit of unslaked lime. He had been sitting in a tree, watching a camel fight, when the branch broke. Larry didn't see him fall, but he heard him shriek and saw the crowd surge toward the lime pit. The boy was pulled free, wailing in agony, a few words intelligible in his cries. He seemed to be apologizing for drawing so much attention to himself. He was carried to the cistern by two men. His clothes had been torn from him, and his skin was smoking like smoldering wood. The men ladled water onto his cooked flesh, laid him on a blanket, and carried him away, his abject cries fading slowly from the square.

Larry ran home, pulled some clothes and comic books from his closet, and pleaded with his father to take him to the hospital. The boy was dead when they got there. Clutching his pathetic gifts to his chest, Larry rode home next to his father, feeling alone, shocked, and unspeakably afraid.

These were among the memories he brought back to America with him in the summer of his thirteenth year. For three years he attended a private school in Georgia, while his parents remained in Turkey. When he graduated three months before his seventeenth birthday, he cajoled his mother, who had come over on the *Constitution* for the summer, into signing the parental consent form the navy required for underage enlistments.

He stayed in the navy four years, compulsively seeking the most dangerous assignments available in peacetime. He volunteered for underwater demolitions training. He served on counterinsurgency patrols in the mountains of Laos when a navy intelligence team was rushed into the country to hold the line until the army's Military Advisory Group could be mobilized. He was in Guantánamo Bay at the time of the Cuban Missile Crisis.

He came out of the navy in June 1963, twenty-one years old, with no more roots than a Kurdish nomad. He drifted about the Southeast, working on paving crews in Florida and Georgia, doing a little singing at a nightclub in North Augusta, South Carolina, working off and on as a disc jockey for Elvis Presley's old Tupelo buddy Bob Ritter, who managed radio station WGUS in Augusta. Once he even joined four anti-Castro Cubans on a gun run from Miami to the Camagüey Peninsula in a thirty-eight-foot custom inboard. He married a twenty-year-old moonshiner's daughter and had five kids. After the third was born, he called his father to tell him he was married and to wish him a Merry Christmas.

Gradually Larry's life began to take on settled habits. In the navy he had piled up sixty-three hours of college credits, and he had been adding to them slowly even during the worst years. Before long he had enough credits to move to Atlanta, where he worked on a construction gang while completing his senior year at Georgia Tech. When he graduated from Tech, he went to work for a construction company in Jacksonville that did an annual business of over $35 million.

Larry rose quickly, impressing his boss with his almost combative aggressiveness and his radical openness to new ideas. In an industry dominated by the rule-of-thumb calculations of experienced engineers, Larry pioneered the computer programming of construction projects. He put together a program for a large corporation's headquarters in Florida that told him what hour of what day every door would be hung, every toilet and light bulb installed in the three-story office and warehouse complex. The job came in twenty-nine days in front of the deadline and $400,000 under the bid; Larry got his picture on the cover of an engineering magazine. He went into business for himself.

Work came in slowly at first. He won a contract to rebuild a 120-year-old church lovingly crafted by slaves out of twelve-foot oak beams and handmade bricks. When downtown Fort Valley, Georgia, was gutted by fire, Larry was given the job of rebuilding it. His reputation as a young and imaginative builder began to spread throughout the Southeast, and his business grew almost too fast for him to keep track of it. When he took stock on his thirty-first birthday, he was worth nearly $2.5 million. And he was single. His marriage to Sue had long since shivered into separation and divorce.

He worked out of Marietta and kept an apartment there for entertaining. He lived on a farm in Greene County, commuting the 140-mile round trip each day in his own single-engine Grumman Traveler. He collected guns and airplanes. He branched out from construction to land development; he branched out into refrigeration; he branched out into aerial photography. He bought three thousand acres of cattle land outside Eagle Pass, Texas, and became a weekend rancher.

The South was booming, and Larry Spivey boomed with it. Not since the days of the railroad barons had the country seen such a crop of young millionaires. He went into partnership with James Bentley, a former comptroller general in the Maddox administration who had run unsuccessfully for the gubernatorial nomination against Jimmy Carter in 1970. His social circle included celebrities such as Ted Turner, the headstrong playboy who raced yachts and owned the Atlanta Braves. Even an occasional personal setback couldn't dent the euphoria of his having the world by the tail. For one giddy year he carried on an erratically passionate affair with his secretary Charlene that ended when she gave notice she was quitting to marry a fifty-three-year-old Greek who owned half a dozen Chrysler dealerships. He knew she wanted him to forbid it, to take her away himself, but he refused to be maneuvered into anything. His sense of himself was too triumphant to permit him to do anything except let her go. She married the Greek in a Las Vegas chapel and sent Larry a picture of the wedding. That was in the fall of '73.

In the summer of '74 Charlene divorced the Chrysler dealer and came back to Larry. At just about the same time, W. T. Grant's announced it was closing all its stores. The two together added up to a kind of good-news-bad-news joke, except there was something rather dubious about the quality of the good news. But there was no doubt at all that the bad news was devastating. Larry had built twenty-two shopping centers with Grant's as the principal lessor. All the minor leases—the restaurants, the boutiques, the bicycle shops—were conditional on the presence of the big department store. It was going to be a wipeout.

For the rest of the summer and into the fall, Larry fought to salvage what he could. In August a chain of steak-and-burger restaurants with outlets in sixteen of his centers exercised its right to terminate its leases. Without Grant's to pull a steady flow of shoppers, the restaurants couldn't do enough business to keep open. Then a dry cleaner closed nineteen stores on him. The cancellations came faster and faster, feeding on themselves the way a block-busting operation explodes through a neighborhood.

In October Larry sold the ranch in Texas. In November he got rid of the farm in Greene County and closed the office. Then the damnedest thing happened. Charlene asked him to marry her.

"You've got to be crazy," he said. "I'm going bankrupt."

"There's bankrupt and there's bankrupt," she answered slyly, her dark eyes laughing with abandoned gaiety. Her black hair shone like a sparkler as she tossed her head, and he knew it wouldn't do any good to explain. Nevertheless, he tried to tell her the difference between a personal and a corporate bankruptcy, and when it was clear that she either wasn't listening or didn't understand, he accepted her proposal. They were married in March.

Things went from bad to worse. The bottom came up to meet him on June 18, when Don Gilson, his lawyer, called him to his office to tell him the party was finally over. "You're not going broke anymore," Gilson said.

"You are broke. It's filing time. I hope you at least had the sense to sell the airplanes."

"Yeah."

"What'd you get for them?"

"Nothing."

Gilson shook his head. "Figures," he said.

The planes and Larry's interest in the engineering business had been sold to his partner, who couldn't pay for them. He gave what he could for the business, which wasn't worth much by that point, but all he could offer for the planes was "wet time"—flying time with fuel. Then Larry swung a deal with Jack Winter, the pilot he had laid off when he went out of the aerial photography business. Winter had been an air force fighter pilot who had flown F-4 Phantoms. When Larry fired him, he leased a small airstrip outside Marietta and set up as an instructor, borrowing aircraft from his friends whenever he got a student or a charter. When he heard that Larry had a couple of hundred hours of wet time and no place to go, he offered to buy the time for cash. It was a good deal for both of them. It gave Winter reliable access to an airplane, and it gave Larry walking-around money.

Larry explained the arrangement to Gilson, who listened absently, spreading papers on his desk. When Larry finished speaking, the lawyer had three sets of forms lined up across his blotter. He tapped the first one with his forefinger and said, "This is where you list all your creditors and the amounts you owe them. And I mean all of them. I take it you know what the word *all* means?"

Larry nodded dumbly, and Gilson's finger jumped to the second stack. "On this one you list all the assets you don't intend to keep."

Third stack. "Here's where you list all the assets you wish to retain. With the court's permission. Under the Federal Bankruptcy Act, the court will allow you to keep fifteen hundred dollars' worth of assets. Take these home and work on them. If you need any help, call me. Any questions?"

Larry had one. "Do you handle divorces?" he asked. He could see one coming.

Two

"D amn, if that ain't the most pee-culiar thing," state game warden Chick Ware muttered to himself. It was the twelfth vehicle he had seen that afternoon coming or going on the one-lane gravel path that cut off Georgia Highway 99 into the marshes. Ain't no call for that many folks to be trucking down to Southern's Bluff, he thought as another way of reminding himself how "pee-culiar" the whole thing looked. Normally it took either a direct order or a flagrant and conspicuous violation of a major law to motivate Chick Ware to interrupt his hypnotic patrolling of the woods and marshes along Highway 99. After twelve years as a warden, he was still a decade shy of filling up the citation book he had been issued when he came on the job.

But a dozen vehicles, a couple of dozen folks at Southern's Bluff beat anything he had ever seen. Ain't nothing but sand ticks down there, he thought. Sand ticks, gnats, and mosquitoes the size of hummingbirds.

Ware pulled onto the loose shoulder to consider, then tried to raise some help on the radio. He never had been able to make the contraption work, so he gave up and drove to Crescent, where he called from the pay phone at Sol Armis's Flying A station.

Well before sunset, forty-two customs agents converged on Crescent, Georgia, raising the population of the tiny hamlet by half. Chick Ware was in his glory as his creaky Plymouth led a carful of agents to the inconspicuous clearing where the tiny gravel road broke through the stunted pine-woods that ran the length of Highway 99. "Let's have a look," said Lorin Cleaver, the district director of the Savannah patrol office.

Leaving their own car and the sulking 285-pound warden at the clearing, the customs agents, armed with flashlights, shotguns, and a portable two-way radio, set off down the rutted gravel path on foot. Short grass as thick as the bristles on a brush sprang in unexpected clumps along the way. With every step the agents took, the piney woods got thinner and thinner, the soil underfoot more sandy. Finally, the forest faded into a soggy marsh that soon became a full-fledged swamp.

Circling away from the path, the agents stumbled through the marsh until they found themselves standing on the spongy bank of the Sapelo River. Then, taking cover in the thick, reedlike grass that began just a few strides from the water's edge, they followed the river downstream until they came to the edge of a clearing where the gravel path ended in the streambed.

That fool of a game warden sure lucked into something this time, Cleaver thought as he studied the clearing. Seven campers, a van, and a Buick Riviera were parked in the clearing. A small houseboat was moored along the bank of the river. Just at first glance Cleaver saw a dozen men and figured there would be a dozen more, counting the ones he couldn't see inside the campers and the ones who would be coming in on the boat he knew they all were waiting for.

He had seen operations like this before, but never this big. He knew how it worked. Somewhere offshore in international waters, a large freighter was at this moment just about finished off-loading a couple of tons of marijuana onto a boat small enough to navigate the shallow Sapelo River. The men in the campers were the buyers, who already had paid the owner of the Buick Riviera for their consignments. The big buyers would be taking away more than a million dollars' worth, paying for it in cash. The money was out of Georgia by this time, having left the landing with a henchman when the pot boat put out for its rendezvous with the freighter.

Cleaver and the three other agents drew back from the lip of the clearing to plan their strategy. They radioed back to Crescent and ordered the men there to deploy themselves along Highway 99 at the mouth of the gravel road. Then it was a matter of waiting.

Darkness settled in like a cat on a windowsill, winding inward from the edges of the horizon. The four agents sat stoically on the wet ground as the insects stormed maliciously and the thin, loose-packed soil surrendered its warmth. The temperature, which had been in the mid-eighties, dropped sharply. "As soon as I get back to Savannah," one of the agents whispered self-pityingly, "I'm gonna find me one of them fancy poodle barbershops and sign up for a tick dip."

"Tick dip, hell," another scoffed. "I'm gettin' a transfusion. I ain't gonna have enough blood in me to fill a teacup."

From the pot smugglers' camp in the clearing an occasional shout drifted across the intervening silence. Hours passed, lit only by a waxy half-moon and the reddish glow of the drug dealers' cigarettes. Cleaver wondered what they were smoking. Midnight came and went.

Suddenly there was movement in the clearing and a bright light on the river. A small inboard-outboard with a searchlight mounted in the bow cruised up the river, followed by a sixty-five-foot shrimp boat, which tied up alongside the moored houseboat. One by one, the parked campers turned on their headlights to illuminate the area.

Not a bad idea, Cleaver thought. The shrimp boat lay so low in the water that it couldn't go more than a few yards from the middle of the channel without running aground. They were going to off-load across the deck of the houseboat, which would serve as a makeshift pier.

Figuring it would take at least three or four hours to unload the shrimp boat, Cleaver decided to let the smugglers work up a sweat for an hour or so before taking them down. "Boat's in," he radioed to the backup cars on 99. "Sit tight till I give the word."

The unloading went slowly as the marijuana, packed in bales that seemed to run from as small as fifty pounds to as much as seventy-five, was hand-carried from the shrimp boat to the houseboat to the shore. For his own amusement Cleaver counted, and when the hundredth bale was safely stowed in one of the campers, he punched the button on his radio and said, "Let's hit 'em!"

Thirteen government cars rolled down the gravel pathway, lights off, steering by moonlight. The fourteenth positioned itself broadside at the end of the path in case any of the smugglers slipped through. As the first car in the convoy moved into the clearing, it swerved sharply to the left and its lights came on. Car after car followed, fanning out in a huge arc that covered the inland side of the clearing like a row of posted sentries. Agents tumbled from the cars, lost their footing in the loose soil, scrambled for the landing with shotgun barrels glinting in the light of their own headlights behind them.

"They just took off like a covey of quail," Cleaver said later. There was no resistance, not a shot fired. Just flight. Eighteen of the drug dealers were caught in the first scrimmage, flopping in the sand like fish yanked from the water, tackled by middle-aged customs agents who hadn't been in a game like this since high school. Five of the smugglers made it to the swamp, where Cleaver figured they'd keep till morning since he wasn't about to risk sending any of his men in after them. So far the slate was clean, and he wanted to keep it that way. Except for mosquito bites, none of his agents had been hurt.

With daylight, the five fugitives began to straggle in, surrendering at the clearing or on the highway in ones and twos. "They had them a nice night thrashing around out there," one of the agents commented. "I guess jail was startin' to look mighty appealin' by then."

The marijuana was loaded back onto the shrimp boat and taken to Savannah, where customs agents weighed and labeled each bale. When the adding machine ran up the tally, it came to an even thirty-six thousand pounds. Eighteen tons. All of it high-grade Colombian grass.

From Washington, Cleaver learned that a year and a half earlier customs agents in Nogales, Arizona, had seized a nineteen-ton load.

"Shit," he moaned. "We damned near had ourselves a record."

A gentle offshore breeze came up with the sun as the sloop *Odessa* rounded Hilton Head Island. Arleigh Richmond gave orders for a starboard tack that would swing it through the north channel before the Savannah beaches started to heat up under the flaming June sun.

Richmond moved to the starboard rail and studied the horizon tensely. As he watched, a small vessel broke from the mouth of the channel and headed out into open water, bearing straight for the sloop. Richmond took a few steps forward to get a better look, pulling the Smith & Wesson .357 Magnum from his waistband.

"What is it?" Rita Braverman asked, joining him at the rail. In her hands she held two mugs of steaming coffee. She passed one to Richmond, who took it without answering.

Richmond took his eyes off the fast-approaching powerboat to glance at the girl, but she seemed unaware of his attention. Her head was bent to the mug, her lips pursed as she sucked at the surface of the hot coffee. She looked bright and fresh, despite a sleepless night in which she had worked as hard as any of the men loading three tons of high-grade marijuana into the hold below the deck.

The low sun stood behind the sloop, catching the windscreen of the approaching powerboat and throwing the light back with a blinding glare.

Squinting into it, Richmond could make out the shape of a man in a blue windbreaker standing on the prow of the powerboat. The man waved both arms. Arleigh Richmond replaced the Smith & Wesson in his waistband.

The twenty-four-foot powerboat roared past the graceful sloop, cut a neat, tight circle directly astern of it, and charged forward to lead the way into the channel.

Less than an hour later the *Odessa* was gliding serenely in the narrow passage between the mainland and Sandfly Island. Expensive beachfront property stretched back from both shores, the houses widely separated, each with its own idiosyncratic architecture—here a glass igloo, there a squat, turreted weatherboard fort bristling with open porches, the plaything summer homes of some of Georgia's richest families. Taking a starboard tack, the sloop hugged the Savannah shore, making for a long aluminum pier, where a portly man of about sixty waited for it to tie up. He was wearing leather sandals over white calf-length socks, baggy bermuda shorts, and a bright print shirt.

Arleigh Richmond leaped to the pier and motioned for Rita to accompany him. The portly man, Gerald Haney, led them across the loose, sandy beach, over a shallow rise bristling with sea oats, and around the house to where two vans and two camper pickups were parked side by side. Rita climbed in behind the wheel of a gray Dodge van and drove it to the pier, handling it skillfully in the tricky sand. When it was loaded, she would return it to the front of the house and bring the next truck around. The marijuana was packaged in fifty-pound burlap bales, each of which contained two hundred identical blue plastic bags.

At upwards of $40 an ounce for the "manicured" Colombian grass, each four-ounce plastic packet was worth, conservatively, $160 on the street; each bale, $32,000; each truckload, $960,000. The entire haul, taken off the freighter in the moonless hours after midnight, would bring a solid $3.25 million.

By three o'clock, all four trucks were fully loaded and the shipment began to move out. Ferlin Lane, a twenty-two-year-old Black, went first in a Chevy van. Wayne L. Reynolds followed twenty minutes later in the gray Dodge, taking Rita with him. Shortly after four, Arleigh Richmond and his brother Glenn rolled out in the last two trucks, a pair of camper pickups. For the first few miles each vehicle took the same route, the only one that would get them out of the beach area—U.S. 80 into Savannah. Thereafter they took different routes, the Richmond brothers heading straight for Atlanta, a steady five-hour drive through flat timberland on

Interstate 16, Reynolds and Lane checking in for the night at two different motels in downtown Savannah.

A few minutes before eight o'clock that evening, when the sun was still a good hour above the horizon, a pair of jumpy federal agents attached to the Drug Enforcement Administration slammed their way through the door of Room 118 at the Magnolia Motor Lodge on Drayton Street in Savannah and placed Ferlin Lane under arrest. They took him out to their car in handcuffs and shoved him into the back seat. One of the agents leaned in through the front window for the microphone under the dash.

"We just popped the nigger," he said. "What are y'all fixin' to do?"

"Aw, Jesus Christ," the answer came back. "Take him in. We'll bag the other pair."

Ten minutes later, four agents shouldered through a motel room door a few blocks away on Bay Street and arrested Wayne Reynolds and Rita Braverman. The woman was asleep in one of the twin beds when they came in; the man was sitting on the other bed in his underwear, watching "All in the Family." No weapons were found in the room.

Shortly after ten o'clock, two federal agents knocked on the door of the Haney summer house, identified themselves to Mrs. Haney, and asked to see her husband. She led them into the spacious, high-ceilinged living room.

"Gerald Haney," one of the agents said, reaching into his pocket. "We have a warrant for your arrest."

Haney set his drink on the low parquet table in front of him and rose slowly. "I don't understand, Gerald," his wife was spluttering. "What is the meaning of this?"

"It means I'm under arrest, my dear."

"But there must be some mistake," she pleaded, turning in mid-sentence to face the two agents.

"Yes," her husband agreed amiably. "There must have been some mistake. Please call my attorney and let him know about this. Shall we go, gentlemen?"

Halfway across the state of Georgia, three teams of federal agents staking out the two-story Marriott at the intersection of I-285 and the Chamblee-Tucker Road on the northeast edge of Atlanta learned that the arrests had been made in Savannah. Arleigh and Glenn Richmond, the objects of their surveillance, were relaxing in their room with cigars and a bottle of I. W. Harper, Arleigh's .357 Magnum on the night table beside the bed.

He didn't even have a chance to reach for it when the door flew off its hinges and landed like a gangplank on the rust-colored carpet. He was looking down the barrels of at least three shotguns and God knew what else, and he heard a voice say, "Stay cool, motherfuckers. Don't even twitch."

In the cockpit of the B-25 Andy Plott pulled his trench coat tightly closed and cursed himself for not having worn something heavier. What kind of idiot, he asked himself, flies an airplane in a raincoat? He reached forward to turn up the heat in the already overheated cockpit.

"Jesus Christ," Bill Flanagan groaned from the copilot's seat, "you're going to cook us. You sick or something?"

Plott didn't answer. He had been shivering uncontrollably ever since he had shaken the feds who had risen after him out of Jacksonville. The whole trip had been a nightmare, and he didn't understand what had gone wrong. He'd been tailed on the way down and tailed on the way back, and he knew that that much attention couldn't be luck.

Ten months earlier the Georgia Bureau of Investigation had caught Plott and a man named Denver Rice attempting to bring in six tons of marijuana in a Convair Constellation. When no indictment was handed down, Plott knew what it meant. GBI wasn't satisfied with six tons of grass. They were lying back, figuring they could use him to get the money-men who were running the operation.

Well, fuck them, Andy Plott had said to himself when he agreed to fly the B-25 to Colombia for a four-ton rip. And that's what he said to himself again as he lowered the powerful bomber to within a few hundred feet of the densely wooded hills southwest of Dawsonville in Dawson County, Georgia. "Everything set back there?" he asked Flanagan. "Drop zone's coming up."

Flanagan glanced aft and grunted an affirmative while Plott studied the black terrain below him, looking for the marker lights that would signal the borders of the drop zone. He had circled around and was coming in from the northwest now at a heading of 160. The marker lights came up on schedule just where they were supposed to be. Plott clicked on his landing lights, dropped to two hundred feet, and reached for the pilot's override on the bomb-release switch. He felt a rush of air as the bomb-bay doors slid open, a slight but reassuring hop as sixteen hundred pounds of cargo tumbled onto Dawson County.

The grass was stacked in two-hundred-pound bales, forty of them. The first eight bales had been wrapped in two cargo nets and positioned on the bomb-bay doors. In planning the operation, Flanagan had boasted he could drop the whole load at once by modifying the bomb racks; but it hadn't worked out that way, and so they were going to have to make five passes over the forty-acre field.

While Plott circled for a second approach, Flanagan went aft to load eight more bales into two more nets. Five minutes later the bomber was bearing in on the field again. Plott released the switch but felt nothing.

"Sorry, man," Flanagan called, "this shit's bulky. Got wedged in. I'll get it next time." He was using a stevedore's hook to pry the jammed nets free.

Plott pulled back on the control yoke and the B-25 eased above the hills that rose on the far side of the field. He circled for a third approach while Flanagan struggled to get the bales into position. "Stand clear, bombs away," the pilot shouted as they came up on the lights.

Nothing happened. Plott saw the first light race under him, and he felt nothing. A few seconds later the marker at the far end of the strip was gone, and still he felt nothing. "What the fuck's going on?" he shouted, turning to look over his shoulder into the darkened cargo hold.

There was no time for Flanagan to answer. The B-25 ripped into the side of a hill just outside Silver City, Georgia, and burst into flame.

The first man on the scene was Buster Harris, a ranger with the Georgia Forestry Commission. "It just flew into the mountain," he said. "It hit the trees about thirty-five or forty feet up, and that was it."

The ranger struggled to pull a still burning body from the wreckage but was driven back by the flames. The stench of burning marijuana hung in the woods the way cigar smoke clings to a beard.

Agents Paul Carter, Mike Eason, and George Clardy of the Georgia Bureau of Investigation arrived on the scene well before morning. They didn't know yet who had been on the plane but were hoping against hope it wasn't Andy Plott. So far he was the only connection they had to a smuggling ring that was annually inundating the Southeast with hundreds of millions of dollars' worth of marijuana and cocaine. If he had gone down in that wreck, ten months of hard investigative work had gone down with him.

The three agents presented their credentials to the Dawson County sheriff's deputy standing guard at the roped-off site. Another deputy arrived and conducted them to a small clearing where the two charred bodies had been laid. They had been covered with a single bed sheet thrown so carelessly over them that two bare feet poked incongruously beyond the edge of the covering. The rubber soles of the shoes had melted, and the leather had curled back to expose the blackened flesh. As the deputy reached forward to remove the sheet, Mike Eason stopped him. "Don't bother," he said. "That's Andy. Nobody's got feet as small as Andy. Smallest feet in the world."

Treat Mountain stands halfway between Cedartown and Cave Spring in rural Polk County, Georgia, where the winding country roads know only the shuffling crawl of a dirt farmer's Model A pickup, the whoosh of a moonshiner's custom Fury.

"Stay cool and listen, man," Ron Agee said, standing in the crisp morning pine shade on top of the mountain. "I know the book says five thousand feet, and I'm telling you I don't need five thousand. Just make damned sure there's three thousand clear by midnight, hear?"

The man on the bulldozer shrugged, gazing across the top of the low, breast-shaped foothill to gauge the distance. "It's your ass," he said.

Ron Agee was a twenty-seven-year-old adventurer, entrepreneur, and self-taught pilot from Fort Lauderdale, who liked to boast he could fly anything from a Chinese box kite to an Apollo moon lander. Those who had seen him fly knew it was true. When Andy Plott ended his last Colombia-to-Georgia pot run against the side of a hill in Dawson County, Agee signed on as his replacement.

Racing his black Porsche from Treat Mountain through Cedartown, Rockmart, Yorkville, Dallas, and Powder Springs, Agee reached the general aviation terminal at Atlanta's Peachtree-DeKalb Airport a little after eight. Fifteen minutes later he took off in his own twin-engine Twin Beech D-18 for Boca Raton, where he switched to the DC-4 he had picked up for $16,000 at an army surplus auction in Tucson, Arizona. For the past month and a half he had been practicing touch-and-goes in the mammoth, four-engine, forty-ton transport, now fueled with just a hair under three thousand gallons of gasoline. Agee filed a flight plan for Key West and took off for the south with his copilot Gene Ehrlichman.

While the DC-4 cruised comfortably at eight thousand feet, the twelve-man crew Agee had left behind in Georgia raced against the midnight deadline to flatten the top of Treat Mountain. Three bulldozers bit into the earth, uprooting the smaller stumps and leveling the terrain around the larger ones. Attacking the trees with heroic fanaticism, the wood-chopping crew managed to keep ahead of the dozers, stretching the two-hundred-foot-wide runway to three hundred, then four hundred feet in length. At one-thirty they broke for lunch, slouching toward the shade for shelter from the broiling August sun.

Two hundred miles to the south of them, a stationary front anchored over the Gulf of Mexico for the past forty-eight hours broke loose from its moorings and headed for land. Moving slowly at first, it lumbered over Mobile Bay, sliced across the western tip of Florida, and picked up speed as it rolled up Alabama. By three-thirty the skies above Treat Mountain were prematurely dark. By four o'clock the rain was falling so hard the dozer drivers didn't have more than twenty feet of visibility with their headlights on.

The gritty clay soil drank the water as fast as it came until the mountaintop wore a thin covering of slippery mud that deepened with every passing minute. Soon the dozers were up to their hubs in the goo, as soft as butter in a churn. Pine stumps covered in the afternoon's work now lay bare again as the soil so carefully mounded over them washed down the sides of the mountain. One man drove to Cedartown, twelve miles away, to call the weather service for a prediction. The storm wasn't expected to pass before midnight.

There was no hope now of readying three thousand feet of runway for Agee's return. Even a thousand feet was questionable, but what was the point? A ninety-three-foot aircraft with a stall speed of ninety miles an hour could no more land in a thousand feet than a timberwolf could sleep in a matchbox. Still, the work went on.

At eight o'clock Ron Agee's DC-4, making its return flight from Colombia, cruised over the beach just north of West Palm Beach, Florida, at an altitude of fifteen hundred feet. Banking slightly to the right, it followed the Florida coastline straight to the Georgia border, then circled to the west in order to come up on Treat Mountain without penetrating the Atlanta terminal control area. The swollen rivers only a few hundred feet below him, glinting silver in the horizontal sunshine, gave Agee his first intelligence of heavy rain.

Somewhere over Mitchell County, less than an hour behind the storm, he swung to the northwest, crossed into Alabama, and spiraled around to come in on the mountain from the north. Shortly before ten o'clock he raised his ground crew on the radio. To prevent interception of their communications, they were using CBs with two crystals reversed to put them on the Civil Air Patrol frequency.

"Set the lights," Agee radioed. "I'm coming in as soon as you're ready."

"We got a problem, Ron," the transmission came back. "We came up short."

"How much you got?"

"It rained all day."

"How much?"

"Maybe a thousand."

For a few seconds there was no answer. Then Agee said, "I'm coming in to take a look."

The DC-4, its landing lights on, roared over Treat Mountain. In the cockpit, Agee's lips tightened to whiteness when he saw the pathetically small clearing, its freshly denuded earth so wet it glittered under the bright beacons as though lit from below.

"What the fuck do you call that?" Agee radioed down.

"I told you. It rained all day."

"Forget it," Agee snapped. "How long's it gonna take you to string the lights?"

"You're crazy."

"I said how long?"

"Half hour. But you can't land here."

"String 'em. You've got till midnight. I gotta burn off some of this fuel."

On the ground the fatigued workers looked at each other in amazement. "I dunno," one of them muttered with skeptical admiration. "If it was me, I'd th'ow the fuckin' grass outta the plane and forget the whole thing. That guy's got balls like a fuckin' elephant."

Agee raced over the Georgia countryside with the mixture at full rich, the throttle all the way out, and the props pitched for maximum fuel consumption. Beside him in the cockpit, Ehrlichman, riding in the copilot's seat, pleaded with him to change his mind. But the pilot didn't even seem to be listening. "Look," he said at last, "you want to leave, leave. If not, shut up."

Shortly before midnight two strings of hundred-watt bulbs connected to a portable generator lined the first three hundred feet of the short, sloppy runway. One of the workers climbed to the top of a forty-foot pine at the upwind edge of the runway, carrying a five-cell flashlight to give Agee a target for his final approach.

"Ron?" the man with the radio asked.

"Yeah?"

"You sure you wanna do this?"

"Yeah."

"Man, you got a lotta balls."

"Balls, hell," Agee laughed. "I'm outta gas."

It was hardly an exaggeration. By the time the bulky transport had circled into the wind for its final approach, it was down to a thimbleful of fuel. Skimming only a few hundred feet above the treetops, it whooshed silently over a two-lane county road where Luke Morin's battered pickup was threading its way carefully through the clots of ground fog that always formed after a good summer rain. Suddenly, for just the briefest moment, everything—Morin, the road, the truck—was bathed in a sea of brilliant light that passed so quickly Morin couldn't catch even a glimpse of the supernatural aircraft. He had enough presence of mind to check his watch. It was exactly 11:57. He raced to a pay phone seven miles away and dialed the Polk County sheriff's office to report a UFO.

Eleven fifty-seven was also the moment Ron Agee first saw the thin finger of light poking vertically into the black sky. He centered the nose of the plane on it and deliberately feathered all four props. Goddamn, he thought with wondering detachment, I'm flying a fifty-ton glider. Dead ahead, he could make out the small stand of pine that was the source of the light shaft that seemed to be drawing the plane toward it. Strung out behind the trees were the twin rows of rapidly approaching landing lights.

The DC-4 sank sickeningly as it lost airspeed. Biting almost through his lower lip, Agee fought the controls of the dangerously sluggish machine. Then the nosewheel struck the tallest pine, knocking the man with the flashlight out of his perch. He cried out in pain and tumbled through the branches to the ground. Above him, the props and main gear of the aircraft sheared off the tops of the surrounding trees. Like a monstrous chicken hawk, the DC-4 swooped for the clear ground ahead.

The wheels first touched the mud about fifty feet from the start of the runway. Agee clamped the brakes tight, but it didn't matter because the plane wasn't rolling at all. It swam through the viscous ooze, its back end whipping like a horse's tail, the wheels plowing the mud, sinking deeper and deeper as the aircraft discharged its awesome momentum into the soft, receptive mountain. When it finally wallowed to a stop, it had used less than half the tiny runway. The distance covered on the ground was barely 430 feet.

Ron Agee scrambled from the cockpit in triumph as the ground crew rushed to embrace him. A few seconds later Ehrlichman tumbled down the ladder, landing on his backside in the mud. He scrambled to his feet and ran at Agee hysterically screaming curses and threats, his arms waving wildly. Two men restrained him and led him off toward the woods to calm down. From there he watched as Agee supervised the unloading of more than $15 million worth of marijuana, hashish, and cocaine.

In less than an hour three vans and a station wagon had been fully loaded. Following the dozers, they picked their way down the north slope, leaving the mountain once again deserted. All that remained behind was the hulking DC-4, its wheels locked in the mud like a prehistoric reptile stoically awaiting a slow death in the slime.

A little before two o'clock two Haralson County deputy sheriffs, just coming off duty, were driving on a dirt road when they were passed by a van and a station wagon traveling in the opposite direction.

"Whaddya say?" the driver asked.

"Beats going home," his partner said, chuckling.

The driver did a quick bootleg turn, easily overtook the two vehicles, and motioned both to the side of the road. With guns drawn, the deputies walked slowly to the rear of the van. One of them reached up and jerked open the rear door. He found himself facing three men sitting on boxes which later turned out to contain ninety pounds of hashish.

"Get your ass back to that radio and see if you can scare us up a search warrant," he told his partner. "Looks like we got ourselves a pack of moonshiners."

Three

acing bankruptcy and divorce, only a sentimentalist would have wasted much time contemplating the future. Rich and influential little more than a year ago, only an egotist would have indulged himself in contemplating the past.

Larry Spivey was neither egotistical nor sentimental. So he sat in the empty dining room of Denny's restaurant contemplating the scrambled eggs on his plate so intently that he didn't even notice when another man entered the room.

"Spivey! Glad I ran into you," Gus McClellan's voice boomed loud enough to be heard in the parking lot outside. McClellan yanked a chair from under the table and lowered himself into it.

"Sit down," Larry said needlessly, rifling through his memory to place the amiable behemoth who was already reaching for a piece of his toast. Gus Something. Lives just outside town, makes horseshoes and scrap metal constructions he calls things like Seagull and Endogamy. There was a party. Charlene knew his wife. Coke and grass. We left.

"Actually," McClellan was saying, his voice softer now, almost a whisper, "it wasn't an accident, my running into you like this."

"No?"

McClellan peeled the plastic lid back from a little square container of grape jelly and squeezed the contents of the packet onto the triangle of toast. "Heard you're a little down on your luck," he said.

"That's one way to put it."

"Filing for bankruptcy."

"Already filed."

"Split up with Charlene."

"Uh-huh."

"Where you staying?"

"The Scottish. . . . What the hell is this?"

"Just making conversation. You gonna eat those potatoes?"

"Help yourself."

The hash browns disappeared as quickly as the toast. "No," McClellan said, wiping grape jelly from his beard with a napkin from the next table, "it's no accident, running into you like this. Been looking for you. Got a business proposition."

Larry smiled ruefully, finding wry amusement in the fact that it had come to this. A business proposition from an overweight blacksmith who seemed to own only one shirt. But it had come to this, so he gestured for McClellan to continue.

The big man reached into the pocket of his plaid flannel shirt for a cigar, lit it, and leaned forward, elbows on the table. "I got a connection in Guatemala," he said.

"A what?" Spivey asked incredulously, even though he had not misunderstood.

"A connection. Grass."

"What makes you think I'm interested in anything like that?"

"You got an airplane."

"Lots of people—"

"And you're broke."

"That makes a little more sense," Larry had to admit, bored and curious enough to want to hear the scheme. Already he could see McClellan grinning in some South American jungle while a pack of *mestizo* con men with gold teeth pretended they didn't speak English and picked him clean.

"I knew you were the guy," McClellan said.

"I didn't say that."

"All we need from you is the plane and fifteen grand."

Larry laughed. "This has got to be some kind of a joke," he said.

"Do I sound like I'm joking?"

"As a matter of fact, yeah. I'm on the cuff for the toast you just ate."

McClellan's voice became urgent, like that of a man asking for a job. "Listen, Larry," he said, speaking slowly at first, then with breathy rapidity. "The stuff's not gonna cost us more than twenty-five, thirty bucks a pound. We get four hundred pounds, and it goes for forty bucks an ounce. And you know what, there's twenty ounces to a pound, no kidding. That's the way they figure it, know what I mean. Believe me, Larry, I worked it all out. It's three hundred and sixty thousand dollars."

"No way, Gus."

"Just fifteen grand."

"See you around, Gus."

McClellan didn't take a hint well. Although he shambled out of Denny's, he was back again two weeks later with a more refined version of his offer. This time he brought reinforcements—Jack Winter, Larry's former pilot, who was buying the wet time in Larry's former planes, and an uncivilized little tough guy named Johnny Harrel. They showed up unannounced at Larry's motel and drove him to the Steak and Ale, a chain restaurant on Route 41 in Marietta. Winter sat alone in the back seat, wearing the sheepish expression of a puppy standing over a puddle in the living room. When Larry asked him how he had got mixed up in a thing like this, the ex-fighter pilot answered with a self-deprecating shrug.

Harrel did most of the talking, hinting at powerful underworld connections. "For you guys this is gonna be a lot of money," he said as McClellan's Impala pulled into the restaurant parking lot. "For my people it's a nice piece of change. We'll all do all right, what do you think?"

"I think you ought to get yourself a new tailor," Larry said, sliding out of the front seat.

Harrel eyed him fishily. "Huh?"

"You're missing the whole point of a concealed weapon," Spivey explained. "That bulge, it's not very subtle."

Harrel said, "Maybe I'm not a subtle guy. Maybe that's the way I like it."

Gus McClellan guffawed loudly, as though the pugnacious little man had said something very funny. But there was nothing funny about Johnny Harrel, once you got past the way he looked. He stood only five feet five inches tall and had thick orange-red muttonchop whiskers like an orangutan. He swaggered when he walked, and he bragged a lot, but he was undoubtedly telling the truth: He was not a subtle guy.

He led the way into the Steak and Ale, snapping his fingers for the maître d' and then waving Spivey, McClellan, and Winter to their corner table like a school crossing guard. He sat facing the door and unbuttoned his jacket ostentatiously.

"Gus tells me you're hung up for the money," he said.

"No," Larry corrected, still not sure why he was there. "Gus left out the part where I told him he could take his marijuana and blow it out his ass."

McClellan, who laughed at the oddest times, laughed again but stopped himself when he saw that Harrel wasn't amused. Harrel said, "Because money's not a problem."

"I'm happy for you."

"You a wiseass or something?" Harrell asked.

"No, no," McClellan cut in, waving his pawlike hand. "It's just the way he talks."

"Because I don't like wiseasses."

"I'll tell you the truth, Harrel," Spivey said. "I've got a lot of problems right now. And whether or not you like me isn't at the top of the list."

Harrel said, "Maybe it should be."

Spivey stood up to leave, but McClellan grabbed his arm. "C'mon, Larry," he pleaded, "just listen to what he's got to say. Can't hurt to listen."

There was an edge of something that sounded almost like panic in his voice, and Larry realized that the likable gorilla already knew he was in over his head. Probably he had made somebody promises it would be dangerous not to keep. At Denny's he had been talking about adventure, a couple of guys larking around like smugglers. But now that Harrel and whoever he fronted for were in it, the whole picture had changed. Larry glanced at McClellan, trying to read the big man for a sign of the fear he thought he had heard. But the wide, round face was a blank, all traces of expression swallowed up in the thick black beard as though it were a disguise. Larry sat down again, mostly for McClellan's sake.

Harrel snapped for a waiter and the four men ordered. "S'long as everybody understands the rules," he said when the waiter was gone, "no reason we can't all work together. The thing is we're partners. Nobody's marrying anybody, if that's what you're thinking."

It hadn't been. Up till then.

"We each make a contribution, see?" Harrel continued. "Gus has the connection; you got the plane; Jack here can fly it. My organization puts up the money. Simple?"

"Simple."

"So you're in?"

"No."

Jack Winter, who hadn't uttered a word so far, said, "Larry, I think you better think it over."

24

It was the second veiled threat of the evening and the second time Larry got up to leave. This time no one reached to stop him. He left the restaurant and walked back to his motel, hiking along the shoulder of 41 with his hands deep in his pockets and his shoulders hunched against the evening chill. Big semis rumbled past him, coming up like a roll of timpani, shaking the earth. It was three miles to the motel, but he needed time to think.

How the hell does a simple guy like Gus McClellan get himself into a thing like this? he wondered. Then he realized he was in as deep as McClellan. Walking out on them hadn't changed that. Winter had access to Larry's AeroCommander and could fly it to Guatemala or Colombia or Tierra del Fuego for that matter.

All I need, he thought, is for them to get busted in my plane. It was quite a prospect—broke, divorced, and spending the next twelve to twenty years in a cell with those two idiots. And What's-his-name, the dwarf baboon with the shoulder holster—of course, nothing would happen to him. Winter and McClellan were already scared silly; they'd face a firing squad sooner than finger him.

The way Larry added it up, it almost seemed there was no percentage in staying out since he was in anyway. Except for one thing. Harrel frightened him, though not in the same way he frightened the other two. Larry didn't doubt for a second that Harrel was dangerous, the kind of guy who would kill a man to do a friend a favor, but that wasn't the problem. Larry had always been able to take care of himself. The frightening thing about Harrel was what happened to you when you worked for him. Not what he might do to you, but what you did to yourself. In the car on the way to the restaurant McClellan had said, "Now we got some muscle behind us, we can take care of anybody that gets in the way." Gus McClellan said that, and he said it as if he liked the idea.

Larry got back to his motel and stretched out on the twin bed. For twenty minutes he didn't move. Then he reached for the phone and called the Georgia Bureau of Investigation, asked for the narcotics desk.

"Controlled Substances. Agent Carter."

"I wanted Narcotics."

"I can handle it. What can I do for you?"

"I've been approached to fly marijuana into the country."

"All right. Let's take it from the beginning. Who are you, and who approached you?"

"Not so fast. I don't want to finger anybody. I just don't want to be involved, that's all."

"I can appreciate that. What do you want from us?"

"I wish I knew."

"Look," Carter said. "Maybe we should get together, talk about it. Just give me your name."

He was smooth and reassuring. Larry knew he was being maneuvered, but he admired the skillful way Carter did it. "Spivey. Larry Spivey," he said.

"You free now? Where are you?"

"Marietta."

"Fine. You know the Denny's on Delk Road?"

"You're kidding," Larry said, taken off guard. "That's where they approached me. I'm just across the street from it. Couldn't we find someplace else, someplace a little more . . . ?"

"Obscure?"

"Yeah."

"Too hokey. If you meet somewhere under a bridge, people start wondering why. Best way in the world to attract attention. As long as you don't know me, then the people you know don't know the people I know. Take my word for it."

"Okay. Half an hour then. How'll I know you?"

"You'll know."

A tall, lanky man with long blond hair as curly as an Afro stood at the doorway to the dining room, scanning the tables. He was wearing a mustard-colored leisure suit and a flowery print shirt open at the throat. A coke spoon on a gold chain hung from his neck. He wasn't what Larry had expected; but Larry nodded in his direction, and he strolled across the room and slid into a chair.

Carter ordered pecan pie and coffee, Spivey just coffee. After a few minutes of getting acquainted, Carter said, "Where do you want to start?"

Without mentioning any names, Larry told him about McClellan's first approach, about his return with a "gangster type," and about his own fears that his airplane would be used with or without his consent. "I don't actually own the plane anymore," he explained. "But they'd be taking it out on my time. And I don't trust them, that's the bottom line. I know how these things work."

"You do?" There was a slight mocking tone in Carter's question, but it wasn't offensive.

"I think so. If they got arrested, there'd be a lot of pressure for them to name names. And they're not about to mention the guy with the gun."

"Johnny Harrel?"

"How did you know?"

Carter gestured with his hands. It meant: I know a lot of things that would surprise you.

Larry said, "Well, then you get my point. I think the name they'd give you would be mine."

"So you just want to go on record that you're not involved?"

"Something like that."

Carter put down his half-empty cup and reached for the check the waitress had left when she brought the coffee. "You're on record," he said so tersely he sounded bitter. "Anything else I can do for you?"

"Nothing I can think of. What's your problem?"

Carter smiled. "You in a mood for listening?" he asked.

"Sure."

Talking rapidly, with electrifying leaps from story to story, from point to point, Carter launched into a ten-minute lecture on the drug industry in Georgia. He told about the seizures at Savannah and Atlanta, about Southern's Bluff and Andy Plott crashing in a B-25 and the Polk County pot plane on Treat Mountain. "This is all in the last couple of months," he said. "Maybe you read about some of it in the papers?"

"Yeah. Sounds like you guys are pretty much on top of it."

"Bullshit. That's what everybody thinks. Between the crash and the seizures, there's something like thirty million dollars' worth of drugs that didn't get through. And it hasn't made a dent. We just got lucky a couple of times, that's all. Most days we're just pissing into the wind."

He went on to explain that Georgia had become the drug capital of the Southeast. Its hundred-mile coastline was dotted with literally thousands of coves and inlets that made it virtually unpatrollable. By air, its location on the Atlantic coast and its remote and undeveloped areas made it the natural end point for drug runs from South America. "In New York," he said, "they seized a hundred pounds once, and they made a movie about it. *The French Connection.* It was a big deal. Down here we got stuff coming in by the ton. We keep hearing stories about a freighter that comes up from Colombia. Carries coke, hash, and grass, about a hundred tons of it each trip. Figure it out yourself."

"I get the picture. What's the point?" Spivey asked, although he thought he knew already.

"The point is we've never been able to get a man on the inside. Sure, we get a stool pigeon every once in a while. We bust a guy and turn him around. But we never get anyone bigger than the mules, and the mules can't give us anything except other mules. We need someone inside the organization."

"And you think it's me?"

"You're perfect," Carter said. "The CIA couldn't make up a guy with your credentials. You're used to having big money, you're broke, and you're losing your wife. Nobody's gonna wonder why you're going in. Besides, they approached you. You're also the kind of guy who can work his way up past Johnny Harrel to whoever runs him. And then past that guy. Throw in the fact you've got combat experience in the navy and you know your way around guns, so you should be able to handle yourself okay. Larry, you're perfect for it. We really need you."

Spivey laughed, flattered and more than a little excited for the first time since the financial empire he had put together for himself had started to fall apart. He knew it wouldn't take much more from Carter to push him into the decision that would change the rest of his life, so he said, "All right, that's why you want me to do it. Why do I want to?"

"Money?" Carter asked. "We can't offer you much. The best we could do is make you a special agent, eight-sixty a month. But that's not what you were asking, is it?"

"No."

"The reason you're gonna do it," Paul Carter said, with an absolute certainty that came from knowing he had sized up his man, "is that you're thirty-three years old and right now you've got nothing better to do."

Four

The next six days passed quickly, disappearing in a fog of numb, unmarked time. Saturday and Sunday were uneventful, a period for brooding about the decision he had made. Slowly the realization grew in him, despite his weakening attempts to deny it, that everything he had done with his life was suddenly behind him. On Monday he would start the process of becoming an undercover agent, and once the machinery had been set in motion, there would be no stopping it. It would no more matter that he had once been wealthy than it would matter that he was now bankrupt.

Those were terms from the real world of blueprints and leases and social contacts he was leaving behind. In the months to come, he would be living in a nightmare fantasy where there were no rules, no laws, no understanding, only the tenuous intermeshing of "connections," the whole of it, every waking and sleeping moment, based on deception and duplicity. He knew that in a matter of days he would be asked to call Winter or McClellan to tell them a lie, that he would be one of them. What he didn't know was where it would end, how difficult it would be to reorient himself to openness after having been undercover, whether a double agent's psyche can ever find its way back to singleness.

He remembered a joke. An old, incredibly wise professor asks the first student, "If two men come down a chimney, and one of them is clean and the other is dirty, which one washes himself?"

The first student answers confidently, "The one who is dirty."

"No," the professor explains, "because the one who is dirty looks at the one who is clean and thinks that he too is clean. And the one who is clean looks at the one who is dirty and thinks that he too is dirty."

The class gasps in awe, and the professor turns to the second student. "Have you learned anything?" he asks. "Two men come down a chimney. One is clean, and one is dirty. Which one washes himself?"

"The one who is clean because—"

The professor cuts him off. "You are a fool," he sneers. "A clean man would not wash himself."

He turns to the third student. "Pay attention," he demands. "Two men down a chimney. One clean, one dirty. Which one washes?"

The third student hesitates. He starts to say "the clean one"; he starts to say "the dirty one." He gives up, baffled. The professor stares at him with contempt. "Imbecile!" he taunts. "How can two men come down the same dirty chimney and one of them be clean?"

That was what Larry Spivey wondered, frightened of what the answer would be, but determined—with an almost fanatic determination that he exercised the way an athlete exercises his muscles—to find out for himself.

The call to McClellan was placed on Thursday, after four days of intensive training in everything from the art of wearing a concealed microphone to the procedures for filing case reports. School ended when Inspector Phil Peters, the head of the Georgia Bureau of Investigation's Controlled Substances Section, strode to the desk at which agents George Clardy and Mike Eason were briefing Larry on various niceties of the rules of evidence. Peters held a thin sheaf of papers rolled like a baton in his left hand. "Spivey," he asked, "you ready to get to work yet?"

Larry thought he had been working. "Yes, sir," he answered reflexively. Something about Phil Peters's bearing made the right answer automatic.

"Then come with me," the inspector ordered, turning from the desk and walking quickly toward his own office, a small square of space marked out from the squad room by floor-to-ceiling partitions. A short man, five-eight or five-nine at most, stocky and well muscled, with close-cropped curly black hair, Peters had been a cop in GBI since his twenty-first birthday. Thirty-two now, he already had the distinction of having been Georgia's first narcotics agent and its youngest inspector. In the course of a brilliant career as a state cop, he had succeeded in working his way up to a desk job, which he hated. Just a few weeks earlier, in August, he had reached a decision to demand that he be put back in the field, even if it meant a demotion. But he was saved the necessity of doing so by GBI Director Beverley Ponder, who on September 1 created the Controlled Substances Section to deal with the alarming increase of drug traffic. Peters was put in charge of it.

Every agent in the unit was handpicked by Peters, their names culled from a mental list he had been compiling over the years while he waited for the chance to put his ideas about counterattacking the drug dealers into action.

"You know what we want, don't you, Spivey?" Peters asked, moving around behind his desk. He pulled open a file drawer and threw the roll of papers into it.

"Contact McClellan, tell him I'm in. Then we take it from there."

Peters shook his head. "Not quite," he said. "We think you can give us more. Your friend McClellan is an amateur, hardly worth bothering with. I've got a lot more interest in Harrel, the monkey with the gun. But let's not stop there. He's a front man, and we want the guy he's fronting for. Tell McClellan you can't work with Harrel, tell him he's got to get you to the man who runs Harrel or they don't get your airplane. Think you can handle it?"

Larry considered and nodded confidently. "I think Gus will buy it," he said. "But I don't know if he can pull it off."

That struck Peters as a reasonable answer. He lowered himself into his chair and motioned for Larry to take the seat opposite the small metal desk. "This is in the nature of a peptalk, Spivey," he said, his tone softening to something that had more authority, less command. "I think you're the kind of guy that doesn't need it, but there's no charge, so listen a minute. Carter already told you how valuable he thinks you can be to us. I agree. You've got a credibility with the other side that we couldn't manufacture. But if you're gonna make the most of it, you gotta think big. Whatever you're doing, you gotta be looking around the next corner. I want you to take it as far as it goes, and that's somewhere out past the man who runs the man who runs Harrel. Now how do you reckon you do that?"

He leaned back in his chair as he drawled the final question, which came out slightly mocking and folksy. Larry had noticed that Peters's accent seemed to fade and thicken at will. Right now he was very much the old country boy.

"Work my way up, I guess," Larry offered tentatively. "Same as any business. Make myself important to them."

Peters nodded. " 'Cept for one thing," he said. "They gotta think they need you for the deal, but there's a catch. They can't ever really need you. If they do, we got a shit case. Take this one. McClellan wants your airplane. You gotta tell him he can have your airplane, right? That's what gets you in. But you can't let him have your airplane."

Larry was puzzled. "Why not?" he asked.

"Because that's entrapment. You're our agent now. If an agent provides any essential service without which the criminal enterprise could not advance, that's entrapment, and the perpetrators beat the case."

It was going to be trickier than Larry had imagined. "If I can't provide them with the aircraft," he asked, "then what the hell am I doing there?"

Phil Peters shook his head and smiled broadly, but it wasn't a warm smile. "Beats me," he said. "You'll think of something."

Dan Gordon was a successful insurance executive, widely known in the Atlanta business community. Blond and good-looking in a country-club sort of way, he dressed stylishly and had the impeccable manners of a European aristocrat. "I understand you haven't been able to make a satisfactory adjustment with my associate Mr. Harrel," he said, looking straight into Larry's eyes. He poured the wine as he spoke.

"I said I wouldn't work with him," Larry answered. "If you want me in, keep him away from me. That means now and later."

Gordon raised his wineglass toward his eyes and studied its lip distractedly for a moment. "Perhaps if you told me the nature of the problem," he suggested softly.

Larry knew he was being baited. "It's just the way it's going to be," he said, refusing to rise to it. "If not, I've got places I'd rather be."

The five men were in a private dining room of a restaurant in Druid Hills, an Atlanta suburb. They had just spent the better part of an hour making small talk over drinks and appetizers. When their dinners had been brought in, Gordon had dismissed the waitresses with instructions not to return until summoned. He considered Larry's ultimatum expressionlessly, knowing that in better times he would have had Harrel throw Larry out. But then, in better times he wouldn't have been at such a meeting in the first place. He was backed into a corner. In the past couple of months he had lost two major supply lines, the first when Andy Plott's B-25 crashed, the second when Ron Agee was arrested after the Treat Mountain landing. His buyers were screaming for delivery, and he was desperate for any kind of run that would tide things over. Normally he kept a wide distance between himself and the smuggling business, leaving everything but the profits to underlings like Harrel. But Spivey insisted on meeting him, and Spivey had a plane; this meant that for the time being Gordon would have to play by a set of rules he didn't like.

"Personality clashes are inevitable in any business," he said in a tone of comfortable generalization. He took a sip of the wine and savored it thoughtfully before going on. "Usually there are ways around them. I can give you my assurance, Larry, that your contacts with Mr. Harrel will be kept to an absolute minimum. Is that satisfactory?"

Larry agreed that it was, and Gordon immediately turned his attention to Winter and McClellan. The shaggy blacksmith commenced at once to outline his plan.

"My connection in Guatemala can give us all the grass we can buy," McClellan began. "He says he's got a lot of fields under cultivation in the mountains, high-altitude stuff, top quality. He says he's got an airfield up there we can use. Naturally we gotta check that out, right, Jack?"

Winter hadn't said a word since the five men had sat down at the table. The stocky ex-fighter pilot had flown combat in Southeast Asia and had lost none of his courage. But like many fliers, he was a shy man, tense and tight-lipped on the ground, where he felt literally out of his element. "Yeah, right," he said. "They got funny ideas down there about what makes an airfield."

Gordon didn't care about the details. "When can you go?" he asked.

"Fly down day after tomorrow," McClellan answered with foolish eagerness, as though he expected Gordon to be impressed by simple enthusiasm. "Figure a week there. Those guys move slow, Spanish and Indians, know what I mean? We should be ready for the run a week from Saturday."

As McClellan spoke, Winter rose from the table and picked up a flight bag he had deposited on his way in. He scooped out a large handful of maps, which he carried to an unused table against the wall of the small dining room. Motioning for the others to join him, he began to outline his flight plan.

Larry's AeroCommander would be equipped with auxiliary fuel tanks, which Winter would fill himself at the airfield he leased. When he picked up the load in Guatemala, the drug suppliers would have to refuel him for the return flight. These arrangements would have to be worked out in advance. Drawing his finger along the charts he had spread out on the table, Winter traced the route he would be flying. It ended at an unspecified location in the mountains above Guatemala City.

"Now, getting back's no problem," the pilot said confidently. "There's three systems we've got to beat. There's customs, there's the air force, and there's FAA control radar. Customs is nothing. All they've got is a few aircraft thinly scattered. Now the air force radar will pick up anything higher than a tree; there's no way they won't spot us. But all they care about is the Russians don't bomb Atlanta. I flew for them, and I know. I was with an interceptor squadron in the ADIZ, the Air Defense Identification Zone. The interceptors don't scramble for anything flying under a hundred eighty knots. So if we keep our airspeed down, they could care less. Okay?"

Gordon nodded his approval.

"Now the way you beat the air controllers is like the way a quarterback beats a zone defense," the pilot went on. "You go for the seams."

He pulled a nylon-tipped pen from his pocket and drew two intersecting arcs on a map of the southeastern United States. The center of one was at Miami, of the other at Jacksonville. They overlapped on the Florida coastline just south of Melbourne.

"This is where we come in," he said, lightly crosshatching the convex area formed by the intersection of the two arcs. "It's next to impossible to find a space between the control zones, so the trick is to hit them both. Each of the controllers figures the other one has you. I never knew it to miss."

"He's great, isn't he? I told you he could do it," McClellan brayed triumphantly, as though Jack Winter were a robot he had invented.

If Gordon was impressed, he didn't show it. "It should work," he said matter-of-factly, turning from the charts and walking back to the dining table. "I think we want to make the first run small, just to try out the system. Let's figure four hundred, five hundred pounds tops."

Winter folded his charts, as though the conversation that had just commenced didn't concern him. McClellan, though, turned to face the seated drug impresario with a look of utter disappointment on his face. He had been thinking in terms of much bigger payloads, but Larry motioned for him to keep his objections to himself.

When no one said anything, Gordon went on speaking, the point settled. "I want Johnny to go with you when you check it out. That shouldn't give Larry any problems since he won't be going. No reason for him to get mixed up with that end of it."

It sounded reasonable to McClellan, but before he could say anything, Larry pulled him to the far side of the room for a whispered huddle.

"What the hell's the matter with you?" he demanded angrily. "Can't you see he's fixing to shaft us?"

"Huh?"

"Do I have to spell it out for you? If you take Harrel, then Harrel knows who our connection is. What are they going to need us for?"

McClellan gasped. "Jesus, Larry. What are we gonna do?"

Larry left the sulking blacksmith standing in the corner and walked back to the table. "We talked it over; it's no good," he announced flatly. "Harrel stays here. We handle our end; you handle yours."

"Why?" Gordon asked.

"I think you know why. Besides, I'm a pilot, Harrel's not. It's a long flight, and Jack might want some help."

Gordon knew when there was no point in arguing. "You're pretty good," he said, grudgingly conceding the point. "Are you sure you've never done this before?"

"Are you sure you have?"

"Lots of times."

The microphone taped to Larry's body just under his belt caught Gordon's words, sent them down through the transmitter at his waist to the GBI agents taping the dialogue in a nearby parking lot. Mike Eason was monitoring the conversation through an earphone plugged into the recorder. George Clardy sat next to him, unable to hear what was going on inside but doing his best to read the changing expressions on his partner's face.

Eason looked up with a big smile. "Gordon's lawyer is gonna like this part," he reported. "His client just told Spivey he's done this lots of times."

Five

The silver and blue Aviateca jetliner dived into the dense clouds like a spoon plunged into thick cream. Seconds later Guatemala City leaped up to meet it, glowing incandescently in the slanting late-afternoon sunshine, an egg-shaped sphere of bright white space mottled with the rich red of tile roofs. Groping outward from the city, half a dozen wandering blacktop roads, as random as scratches on a phonograph record, etched the dusty, featureless green of the surrounding wilderness for a mile or two, then disappeared without a trace. The city itself, seen from the air, looked small and fragile, as though civilization itself were no more than a bright and ironic whim, as gorgeous and as evanescent as the gestures of a dancer.

Larry Spivey presented his tourist card and vaccination certificate at the airport immigration desk. "Your business in Guatemala?" the clerk asked.

"Tourist," Larry answered blandly, with no consciousness of deception, for even in Atlanta he had begun to feel as disoriented as a tourist from the moment he had convinced Dan Gordon to let him make the trip. On the flight down, he had had to make a deliberate effort to stop asking himself what the hell he was doing there, a question as natural as it was potentially dangerous for a man in his new line of work.

McClellan and Winter, the one as frisky as a child on holiday, the other as dour as a governess, took their cue from Larry and gave the same answers to the same questions, cleared immigration, and emerged from the terminal to find Larry waiting for them at the curb. He had secured a cab, a vintage DeSoto that shivered in neutral as the driver raced the engine to keep it from stalling out.

"Camino Real," Larry told him.

The driver, a tiny Guatemalan so small he had to squint at the road through the small arc of space between the dash and the top of the steering wheel, threw the car into gear and sped from the airport down a broad, bare avenue filled with harsh, sharply lined tropical shadows. At the Camino Real, a Hiltonesque high rise in the coldly modern downtown section of Guatemala City, an officious desk clerk grinned a series of ornately Latin apologies for his inability to find any record of the room reservations McClellan insisted he had phoned down from Atlanta.

Larry stepped in and tried to straighten it out with a combination of Guatemalan folding money and high school Spanish, but the clerk only nodded with that special obligingness headwaiters, desk clerks, and civil servants reserve for those they are no longer interested in serving.

A small, square-faced Mayan Indian in a dark blue business suit tapped Larry on the shoulder. "The boy is quite right. I have taken the liberty of canceling your reservations. Please come with me."

His short black hair was brushed forward, and he smiled ingratiatingly, showing two rows of small, widely spaced teeth. He wore a cowboy-style string tie around his neck.

"It might help if I knew who you were," Larry answered coldly, although something in the Indian's manner suggested his invitation did not imply a choice.

The Indian bowed slightly, a small gesture of the head and shoulders, and drew from his breast pocket a limp calling card. "I am Jefferson Juárez," he announced. "Mario requested that I meet you."

Mario was McClellan's connection. The calling card in Larry's hand conveyed no information other than the little man's full name, Thomas Jefferson Juárez Franclen. Larry handed it back, not without misgivings about the wisdom of placing himself in the hands of a man who didn't quite know how to spell his own last name. "Which way?" he asked.

"Please to follow me," the Indian said, bowing officiously and turning on his heels. He marched away across the carpeted lobby.

As Larry reached for his bag, Gus McClellan grabbed at his wrist with a sweaty hand. Suddenly he didn't seem to be enjoying himself anymore. "I don't like it," he whispered urgently.

It was like Gus to choose a phrase that at least in his own ears sounded tough and savvy when what he wanted to say was that he was afraid.

"Don't sweat it, he's just being careful," Larry reassured him. "Pay attention; maybe you'll learn something."

McClellan brightened, not because he was less afraid, but because if this was the way drug dealers did business, it was all right with him. "S'long as we ain't being shanghaied," he joked humorlessly. Winter followed unquestioningly.

Outside, Jefferson Juárez was waiting for them in the front seat of a late-model Ford. A bellhop tossed the Americans' luggage into the trunk, and the three *gringos* climbed into the back seat.

Juárez spoke in rapid Spanish to the driver, who took off with the suddenness of a spooked horse. The car sprinted the length of a broad, scorched avenue, darting in and out of the jumbled, slow-moving traffic with breathtaking carelessness. Every once in a while Larry noticed a chauffeur-driven, air-conditioned Jaguar or Mercedes, but mostly the road was clogged with pre–World War II taxis and arthritic produce trucks loaded with sickly piles of limp vegetables held in place by swaying fence slats. In the back of one, a tiny piglet squealed plaintively as it dodged a dozen dangerously rolling melons.

At the end of the boulevard the driver threw a right turn so tight and sudden that the inside wheels of the Ford climbed the curb. On the corner an old Indian waiting for a bus jumped back in alarm, dropping the chicken cradled in his arms. It squawked in panic, beating its wings against his leg as it fell.

The car raced on, flitting from garish sunlight to deep shadow, from shadow to sunlight with such rapidity that Larry almost thought he could hear the pupils of his eyes clenching and unclenching like a set of joke-store false teeth. After half a dozen of the desperately ad-lib turns that seemed to be the driver's specialty, the car bounded to a stop in front of the Colonial Hotel, which turned out to be a surprisingly gracious four-story stone building with tile floors in the main lobby.

"Perhaps you will require some time to freshen up," Jefferson Juárez suggested. "I trust you will find the accommodations to your liking."

Evening settled over Guatemala City with apologies for the day, its cool, musky breezes more than making amends. When Jefferson Juárez called for them, Spivey, Winter, and McClellan, showered and in dry clothes, were seated on the veranda of the Colonial, sipping exotic concoctions of smooth tropical juices and jagged, mule-kick rum. The three men rose to greet him.

The Indian had changed to a fresh suit identical to the one he wore that afternoon. Formerly in the ministry of agronomy in the Guatemalan national government, Thomas Jefferson Juárez was now a high-paid influence broker retained by some of the wealthiest men in the country.

Instead of taking his charges to meet Mario, as they had expected, he led them on foot down the Boulevard del Paiz, a wide avenue flanked on both sides by granite and brick government buildings. At a squarish, white colonnaded building guarded by listless soldiers impressively armed with automatic weapons, he turned suddenly and headed for the broad staircase that mounted to a bank of heavy doors. "The Ministry of National Defense," he explained.

Waving a greeting to the guard at a checkpoint just inside the door, Juárez crossed the echoing lobby to a desk, where an aide in civilian clothes handed him four security passes.

"Is this guy for real?" Gus McClellan whispered as he pinned his tag to his chest.

"He's for real all right," Larry muttered back, as impressed as he was curious. "But real what, that's the question."

Juárez had walked off already, as was his habit, expecting the others to follow automatically. They caught up with him as he turned into a long corridor leading out of the marble center hall. He opened a heavy oak door and stepped through, holding it for the Americans.

The office, richly furnished in leather and mahogany, was so large that the tall black-haired man rising from behind the desk at the far wall seemed to be in the next room. He was wearing an army uniform, and Larry counted five stars on the collar of his tunic. Jefferson Juárez introduced him as a deputy minister of defense. He introduced the Americans as investors interested in acquiring land for development into industrial parks.

The deputy minister shook hands all around, then sank back into his chair without inviting the others to sit. By way of making pleasantries, he began questioning Larry about his plans, in particular the kind of industry he intended to bring to Guatemala.

"Actually, we are not industrialists," Larry said, thinking quickly, wishing his Indian guide had warned him about the cover story in advance. But he knew a little bit about land development and a lot about the art of saying nothing without sounding vague, so he launched into a quick sales pitch about "flexible multipurpose facilities" with a "maximum range of potential users." The deputy minister nodded and smiled, wished them luck, and offered to be helpful in any way he could. The interview was over.

"What was that all about?" Larry demanded after they had turned in their passes and were once again on the Boulevard del Paiz.

"We are not an impersonal country," Juárez answered philosophically. "Affairs here are handled on a small scale, and little that goes on is unknown to the government. It is best to have friends."

It was too soon to be sure, but to Larry the Indian's answer hinted that the entire Guatemalan government was on the take. The idea of so much corruption fascinated Larry, vividly reminding him of the nature of his mission. Already he had more to tell GBI than they had bargained for when they had sent him south, and he wanted to know more.

At the Ministry of Finance, Juárez introduced the Americans to the personal secretary to the finance minister, who questioned Larry courteously for half an hour. "If there is any way we can be of assistance, please feel free to call," the minister's secretary said at the conclusion of the interview.

At a well-guarded stone mansion that turned out to be the presidential palace, Juárez outdid himself by having the president himself summoned from a state reception to spend fifteen minutes with the Americans. While a lazy ceiling fan pawed negligently at the heavy air, the president, a small but square-built and powerful man with a rich, oratorical style of speech, listened politely to Larry's presentation, which by this time had been polished smooth. "Señor Juárez has done a great deal to diversify the structure of our agriculture," the president declared. "I am delighted to see that he still concerns himself with such beneficial matters."

Larry reminded him that he and his associates were not concerned with agricultural development.

"Yes, yes, I appreciate that," the president said softly, in a tone that could have been taken for slyness.

The three Americans left the presidential palace as impressed as Juárez intended them to be. McClellan in particular was in a state of numbed shock. For him, furtiveness was the essence of drug dealing, and the idea of advertising his presence to the top government officials made about as much sense as listing himself as a marijuana importer in the Atlanta Yellow Pages.

The last stop on Jefferson Juárez's itinerary, therefore, was not calculated to ease his doubts, for he found himself one step behind Larry and the mysterious little Indian as they charged into the headquarters of the Guatemalan National Police. In a small and dirty office on the second floor, Señor Miguel Quintana, chief of the national detectives and the country's top cop, poured Chivas Regal into five plastic tumblers drawn from five different desk drawers. McClellan skulked off to a window to take what comfort he could from the whiskey while he studied the street below. "You don't think there's a chance this guy's setting us up?" he asked Winter when the pilot joined him there.

Winter didn't know what to think.

Larry, on the other hand, was fully caught up in the spirit of the game. Glibly fielding Quintana's questions as he drew comfortably on one of the chief's hefty Cuban *supremos,* he relaxed into the role Juárez had assigned him, his hunch now hardening into a certainty that no one cared about his cover story. It seemed to him the oily-skinned chief detective was hinting coyly that law enforcement was not particularly his top priority. By the time Juárez led them out of Quintana's office, the segue from headquarters to a whorehouse seemed as natural as anything else in Guatemala.

Beyond the elbow of the bar sat Mario, McClellan's connection, his face hidden in the deep shadow of a sloping broad-brimmed hat. He wore a cluster of Spanish gold coins around his neck, and his fingers, when he raised a cigarette-sized joint to his lips, were heavy with glinting rings. McClellan, who had met him on an earlier trip to Guatemala, introduced him to Larry and the pilot. Then they ordered drinks from a light-skinned girl in a transparent blouse and a long skirt slit to the thigh. When the drinks came, McClellan went off with the waitress.

Jefferson Juárez's small, widely spaced eyes moved slowly about the opulent satin-and-candlelight bordello, taking in everything. When he spotted a girl who could have been the first one's fifteen-year-old sister, he snapped his fingers, summoning her to the table. Then he presented her to Winter as a gift.

"You will forgive me for getting rid of your companions," he explained to Larry, "but we have business to discuss. Mario does not like needless complications."

"Mario doesn't seem to have much to say either way," Larry observed. "Are you running this show, or is he?"

Across the table, Mario snorted once but otherwise let the question pass. It was impossible to tell in the dim light, but Larry doubted he was out of his twenties. He also guessed he was fronting for Juárez, who posed as a facilitator in an operation that was really his own.

"Our relations are not your concern," Juárez said, his tone not as cold as his words.

"Maybe not, but I like to know who I am doing business with."

"That may be," Juárez concurred. "But we prefer that you do not know. Can you be ready to travel tomorrow?"

"I'm ready to travel now. Where are we going?"

"To El Petén. The jungle."

"You too?"

"Yes."

"What about him?"

"You will not see Mario again. He has authorized me to make the arrangements."

The road out of Guatemala City rose like a garter snake crawling from a well. Only fifty-seven air miles to the northeast, Cobán was a six-hour drive over one hundred miles of narrow, twisting, shoulderless road that offered no forgiveness for a missed turn. At twelve thousand feet, Juárez, who was doing the driving, ran into thick clouds that hugged his rented Renault and its occupants like a damp blanket. When he could no longer see the road in front of him, he leaned out his door, feeling for the blacktop with his eyes the way a donkey probes for footing on a loose trail.

Behind the clouds, the sun set with tropical suddenness, falling off the horizon like water sucked down a drain. Now the gauzy air threw the headlights back at the car, and the pace slowed to a glacial crawl. At fifteen thousand feet they reached the top of Guatemala and began a descent down the north side of the Sierra de las Minas that took them quickly out below the cloud cover into clear air. Two more hours got them to Cobán, a large village of huddled adobe houses on the edge of El Petén, the jungle.

Juárez checked them into the only hotel in town, a two-story stuccoed affair with a restaurant on the ground floor and four barely furnished rooms on the second. It was called the Cheepi-Cheepi. Juárez explained the name meant Lucky-Lucky in the local Indian dialect. Dinner was a highly spiced meat stew made from parts of the animal not usually classified as beef. Halfway through the meal, the heavy metal door at one end of the dining room was rolled upward, and the hotel owner's Mercedes was driven in and parked next to the motorcycle already standing just beyond the tables. The owner knew Jefferson Juárez well and greeted him affectionately.

After dinner Juárez drove the three Americans to a cluster of houses set on a boggy swamp a few miles to the southeast of town. At the third house in the development, he pulled off the muddy road into the yard, setting off a mean-sounding dog chained on the porch. A slender, wiry, pajama-clad man in his early fifties came to the porch carrying a .45 automatic, which he quickly lowered when he recognized Juárez. *"Buenas tardes, amigo,"* he called, disappearing into the house and taking the dog with him.

Two minutes later he came around from the other side of the house and led his guests in. Juárez introduced him as Orlando Ramón de Cortez.

On the living-room wall Larry noticed a framed color portrait of a stern white-haired gentleman in a military dress uniform ornamented with rows of bright medals and the elaborate three-colored sash of a Latin American dictator. Tucked into a corner of the picture frame was a snapshot of Orlando himself, obviously taken many years earlier. He was in military uniform, the wings on his lapels indicating air force.

"Mi padre," he explained, gesturing toward the formal portrait. His father had been president of the Guatemalan Republic until his regime was overthrown during World War II, but he managed to escape with his family through the jungles to Mexico. In 1952, after his father had died of natural causes, Orlando and his brothers were permitted back into Guatemala, where they all went into military service. Orlando joined the air force, in which he now held the rank of captain although no longer on active duty. One of his brothers currently was among the highest-ranking officers in the Guatemalan army.

While Orlando excused himself to get dressed, his wife served coffee. Then Juárez drove Orlando and the three Americans back to the hotel in Cobán. The restaurant was closed, but Juárez turned on the lights, and Jack Winter spread his aerial maps of Guatemala across a table.

"The field we have been using is here," Orlando said, laying a bony finger on the map at a point about eighty miles north of Cobán, just inside the Mexican border. "But it is much trouble to get to. It is a three-day journey and we must ferry our goods on the rivers. For a DC-Three flight, that is four tons of marijuana on the river. Much trouble and much work. There is a closer airfield we have been considering. It was built by the Germans, during the war, and they used it to fly in personnel to the radio station they set up in the mission. Unfortunately, it will require some clearing, for it has not been used since the revolution."

"When was that?" Winter asked.

"Nineteen fifty-four."

Twenty-one years was enough time for an unused airfield to revert to jungle. Winter pointed this out and insisted on seeing the field before he would agree to fly into it.

"It is a good field," Orlando tried to reassure him. "I myself have landed P-Fifty-ones on this field."

"During the revolution?" Winter asked.

"*Sí.*"

"I think we'd better eyeball it," Jack said flatly, his tone leaving no room for doubt that the point was nonnegotiable.

"As you wish." Orlando shrugged. "I will arrange it in the morning."

The meeting broke up.

Orlando called at the hotel shortly after sunrise and breakfasted with Juárez and the Americans in the hotel dining room. The owner of the hotel turned out to be his brother-in-law. "When will you be ready to travel?" Orlando asked. His false teeth fitted badly, and he had a habit of sucking on them when he talked.

"We're ready now," Larry said.

Orlando laughed. "You are going into the jungle, *amigo.* I am afraid there is going to be much rough country and much walking."

Larry wiggled his toes inside his Gucci loafers. "Is there anywhere around here we can get some tennis shoes?" he asked, knowing that hiking boots would be out of the question in a village like Cobán.

"Perhaps in the market," Orlando suggested.

An hour later they were all back in front of the hotel, with new tennis shoes, straw hats, and polka-dot bandannas. A black-haired man in his early thirties was waiting for them by a jeep parked in front of the Cheepi-Cheepi. He wore knee-high rubber boots, khaki pants, a tight-fitting striped shirt, and a planter's hat. His name was Enrico, and Orlando introduced him as his head grower. Like Orlando, he was fair-skinned, of Castilian descent.

"Enrico will be your guide," Orlando said, shaking hands all around. "Your car and your possessions will be at my house when you return."

He drove off in Juárez's Renault while Enrico, Juárez, and the three *gringos* headed off in the opposite direction in the pale green Toyota jeep, Larry in front with the driver.

The hard-packed dirt road ended at the edge of the village, where Enrico swung a hard left and stopped in front of a steeply climbing roadway of solid rock carved from the side of a mountain. Stray boulders dotted it as far up as Larry could see, but Enrico apparently knew what he was doing. He put the Toyota into four-wheel drive and began to pick his way through the debris.

For two hours it was all uphill. The temperature mounted steadily under a burning tropical sun. Along the way, the jeep passed a faded blue bus brightly decorated with bunting and fancy Spanish lettering. Its axle broken, it listed off the roadway at an incredible angle, while the passengers, mostly women and children on their way down to Cobán to do their marketing, sat stoically in their seats. A few men clustered around it, like hunters over a carcass.

The sun was straight overhead when the road leveled out on a farmland plateau, where it wound its way through several large plantations. The fields seemed to be overgrown with what looked to Larry like densely clustered mimosa bushes. Juárez explained that they were cartomomo bushes, and that this was the only place in the world where the cartomomo bean was grown. The entire crop was exported to France, where it was used as a perfume fixative.

At the west edge of the plateau the road plummeted down a steep incline into a jungle valley, then climbed out the other side. Enrico let the jeep plunge wildly, bouncing it down the rough roadbed like an avalanche on wheels. Inside, the passengers were tossed like marbles in a can, their heads and tails alternately pounding the roof and the hard, uncushioned seats. Winter moaned that he would be two inches shorter by the time they got wherever they were going, but spirits were nevertheless high. The Americans joked freely, enjoying the adventure. From time to time Jefferson Juárez treated them to choice bits of his philosophy, indulging in wonderful generalizations about everything from women to Christianity. "A woman is like a chicken," he would say, and then explain how. Or, "A woman is like an armadillo."

An orphan since early childhood, he had been named by the Catholic missionaries who had reared him and whom he now distrusted. "They have ruined the simple ways," he lamented. "They came through the country from one side to the other, using the Bible for a briefcase and Christ for a walking stick."

The jeep had just begun to climb the west slope of the valley when it was approached by an old pickup on the way down. Enrico pulled to a stop, the pickup stopping abreast of him. From the passenger seat Larry could see into the cab. The driver was a Castilian in his late thirties. An Indian sat beside him, a World War II military Thompson submachine gun cradled across his lap. Enrico spoke with the driver in Spanish for a few minutes, then drove off as Larry craned his neck for a glimpse of the departing truck. Under a tentlike canvas covering over the back of the truck, he could see two more armed Indians sitting among stacked kilo bricks of dried and compressed marijuana. It was Larry's first proof they were heading in the right direction.

Enrico drove on, crossed one more range, and slid down into a shallow valley, where he pulled off the road onto a narrow dirt track that wound down to a slender path in less than two hundred yards. He stopped the jeep and said something to Juárez in Spanish as he climbed from behind the wheel.

"From here we must walk," Juárez translated.

The jungle, which was dense, head-high scrub growing out of dry-packed soil, thickened ahead. The first half hour was an easy hike, the exercise pleasant after the four-hour jeep ride, the hot sun acting on their senses like a narcotic. On the other side of a deserted coffee plantation the path disappeared into a trackless jungle of tall trees. The jungle floor was soft, the mud occasionally ankle-deep, making the walking hard, but they were protected from the sun by a thick canopy of knitted branches.

The path wound for mile after mile up the side of one mountain and down the next, emerging from time to time to run along the shoulder of a steep slope with a sheer drop to the valley floor below. For the first few hours the only signs of human habitation were occasional fields of maize tended by unseen Indians. Enrico loped easily, taking long, comfortable strides that only Larry and Jefferson Juárez managed to match. McClellan gradually fell behind, panting loudly a few hundred yards back, while Winter dropped completely out of sight, catching up only when Enrico called brief rest stops wherever there was a fork in the path.

After three and a half hours Enrico came to a halt where a narrow trail led off to the left. "We are about halfway," Juárez said, translating Enrico's mumbled Spanish. As soon as Gus and Jack joined the others, Enrico led the way up the branch trail to a small farmyard with a thatched hut at one end. "*Agua,*" he said, motioning with his head toward a fifty-five-gallon drum under the eave of the hut. He parted the mosquito larva on the surface with his hands and scooped water into a gourd hanging from a rusty nail on a nearby post.

Larry and Juárez drank greedily, but Gus and Jack didn't like the looks of the water. Speaking in the local Indian dialect, Juárez called the old farmer from the hut and asked him if he had anything to drink.

"*Sí, agua.*"

Juárez explained that his companions did not approve of the water.

The old man nodded his comprehension and walked off, returning a few minutes later with an armful of wild jungle oranges the size of grapefruits. McClellan and Winter pounced on him, tearing just enough skin from the oranges to squeeze the sweet juice into their dry mouths. After a fifteen-minute rest Enrico showed the Americans how to make slings of their bandannas and loaded them with oranges, which they hung from their belts. *"Buenas naranjas,"* he purred proudly, as though the succulence of the wild fruit were somehow to his credit. Before resuming the forced march to his farm, he gave the old man a quetzal and asked him to send his ten-year-old boy ahead with instructions that two horses be caught, saddled, and sent back to meet the hikers. He was beginning to doubt that McClellan and Winter would make it.

They fell behind immediately, so that the other three had to stop and wait for them often on the second half of the trek. Juárez, whose knowledge of jungle lore was as encyclopedic as his knowledge of women, used the intermissions to teach Larry how to predict rain from the behavior of ants, where wild orchids grew in the bowls of seventy-five-foot trees, how a tiny two-inch fern folded itself into a tight ball at the slightest touch, then unfurled its sensitive fronds about fifteen minutes later. "The jungle has many secrets," Juárez said grandly, indulging his flair for profundities.

In the middle of a broad field of thick bushes twelve to fourteen feet high, Enrico turned to face Larry and made a broad, sweeping gesture with his hands. *"Marijuana!"* he announced triumphantly.

Only then did Larry realize that for the past five minutes he had been walking through a marijuana field. He had never known the plants could grow so large. It was impossible to estimate the size of the field because the plants were too tall to permit him to see more than a few feet to either side of the path, but it was obviously many acres.

"We have over seventy such fields from here to Chamá," Juárez said with surprising blandness. "You are fortunate, this is the harvesttime. The rains have ended and the plants are fully grown. It is now the drying season."

He turned to walk on, leaving the field quickly behind and climbing the jungle slope on the other side. A few minutes later the stillness was shattered by a sudden cry from the rear. Larry, Juárez, and Enrico turned to the sound.

"Larry! Larry!" McClellan was calling frantically. He let out a wild shout, half pig call and half rebel yell of sheer joy.

"Man, look at the foxtails! Look at the buds! Look at this *shit!*" His voice echoed up from the floor of the valley as he danced ecstatically, surrounded by more marijuana than he could see. "Whooo-eee!"

The hike continued into the darkness, which fell with the suddenness of a light bulb going out. But the moon had risen early. Translating

Enrico's Spanish, Juárez assured the Americans there were only a few kilometers to go. Quickening the pace to get out of the jungle, Enrico instructed Juárez to warn Winter and McClellan about the *barba maria,* the twelve-foot-long bushmaster snake that hunted in the jungle at night. From that point on there was no lagging.

Picking their way down the last slope, they were stopped by the sound of horses ahead. They waited until the farmer's son came up to meet them, leading two small quarter horses by their bridles. Surrendering the horses to Enrico and gratefully accepting the quetzal he was offered, the boy crumpled the note into a tight ball and ran off into the dark jungle, swinging his machete at his side. Gus and Jack mounted the horses and rode the last mile, while Larry, Juárez, and Enrico kept pace on foot.

They reached the floor of the valley around nine o'clock, passed through a series of cleared fields separated by wood fences, and finally arrived at Enrico's *finca.* Leaving the horses with four or five Indians who appeared out of nowhere to accept them, they entered a fenced-in enclosure about the size of a football field. At the far end of the field a small L-shaped wood house stood on stilts, rising above the top of a low knoll. They crossed to it, climbed the stairs to the open porch, passed through one of the three bedrooms that constituted the whole of the house, and came out on the back porch, where two slender candles burned on the plain plank table that had been set for them.

Three Indian women, each as stout as a barrel, could be seen through the slats in the thatched cookshack in the crook of the L preparing dinner, which turned out to be a tasteless black bean soup and large bowls of tasteless black bean paste and sweet banana paste, along with a generous supply of tortillas for scooping the paste. After an eight-hour hike over twenty-four kilometers of jungle trail, all five men ate eagerly.

They slept that night on low slatted bunks covered with thin coco mats.

Enrico woke them before sunrise, and they breakfasted on a single chicken wing apiece, served in its own broth with a few bay leaves, fried bananas, and more tortillas and bean paste, washed down with bitter Guatemalan coffee. Five saddled horses waited for them near the small tin-roofed shack that served as the farm's general store and warehouse. It was seven o'clock in the morning when they left the *finca,* and Enrico promised they would be at the airfield by midafternoon. As they left the farm, they were joined by two Indians on foot, carrying automatic weapons slung across their shoulders.

For two hours they rode at a comfortable pace through pleasant shadow and occasional clearings of brilliant sunshine, climbing and descending low hills that looked like a gently rolling sea. From time to time they crossed the farmyards of Enrico's *mozos,* each a small square clearing with a patch-sized maize field patrolled by curious and active chickens. At one farm the skin of a freshly killed jaguar was stretched on a wood rack to dry. By late morning McClellan and Winter both began to suffer from dysentery, and stops became frequent.

Larry was riding just behind Enrico when they rounded the side of a mountain, following a level trail that brought them out through an opening in the jungle with dramatic suddenness. Ahead of them lay the Chamá Valley, shimmering opulently in the almost vertical golden sunlight, as gorgeous and inviting as the path ahead was dangerous. For Enrico's horse already was picking her way down a steep slope of loose rock, her hindquarters dragging on the trail as she slipped sideways, her feet skidding with each delicately placed step. Small stones rolled ahead of her, like dice tumbling from a cup.

Larry hesitated a moment, awed by the lush beauty of the panorama in front of him. The valley stretched off to his right, broadening out from a narrow mouth. On the far side of it, a few hundred yards away, a foothill rose easily, probing tentatively toward the bright azure sky, three thatch-roofed huts on the side of it like stepping-stones to the top. The voice of a mother fussing at her children floated across the valley. Behind the foothills, a series of bolder mountains rose more assuredly, their peaks the steel-cold color of stone above the timberline. In the distance, a volcano sighed a column of sparkling white smoke into the still air.

Taking a deep breath, Larry coaxed his horse onto the slope, then held on as she fought to keep her footing. To his left the mountain dropped off straight into the valley three hundred feet below, as sheer as the side of a building.

Thirty minutes later all five men were safely on the floor of the valley. Turning to the right, they followed a winding trail along the base of the mountain until they came to the bank of a broad, fast-moving turquoise river. Beached on the sandy spit in front of them was a solid dugout canoe carved from a twenty-foot tree trunk, two stout bamboo poles resting in the bow.

The boatman, whose farmhouse was only three minutes away at the top of a low hill, was a fifty-year-old Indian with the lean, athletic body and the smooth skin of a well-conditioned man in his twenties.

He was playing with his children in the yard when Enrico called to him. On his shoulders was his youngest child, a naked brown-skinned boy who couldn't have been more than a year old. He set the child down and hurried to greet Enrico, who introduced him to Juárez and Larry. His name was Jesús, and his gray eyes were darkened with cataracts that would leave him blind in no more than a year or two.

Jesús poled the party across the churning river two at a time, first Enrico and one of the armed Indian guards, then Larry and Jefferson Juárez. As Larry and Juárez made the crossing, Jesús engaged Juárez in an animated conversation in the local dialect, speaking with considerable passion. He was obviously distressed about something.

"What's bothering him?" Larry asked while he and Juárez waited for Jack and Gus to be brought across.

"A jaguar is taking his dogs, his chickens, and his pigs," Juárez said indifferently. "He is having to take every living thing he owns into the house with his family at night. The jaguar is near here. He has followed it into the mountains and knows where it lives, but he has only a machete. He wonders if one of us will kill it for him."

As a young man Larry had hunted leopard and never forgot the thrill of stalking big cats. "Tell him I will try if the opportunity presents itself," he said.

When all six men were on the west bank of the river—one of the Indian guards was left behind with the horses—Enrico led them up a hill to a crumbling seventeenth-century Spanish mission that had been commandeered and turned into a German radio relay station during the war. It now housed the family and servants of the young *patrón* who supervised the operation of a nearby farm for an absentee landlord. There they rested briefly. The airfield was only four kilometers away, but by this point McClellan and Winter were rapidly becoming seriously ill. What had started the day before on the trek through the jungle as simple diarrhea that they all joked about had developed into full-blown dysentery. Both men were weak, feverish, and nauseated, with Winter's temperature soaring alarmingly.

If the airfield had been more than a half hour's hike ahead, Larry would have insisted on turning back to get medical attention for his two companions. But having come so far and suffered so much already, Gus and Jack wouldn't hear of it. Larry discussed the problem with Juárez, who prescribed an Indian folk remedy consisting of stiff doses of salt and lime. Servants from the mission graciously supplied fresh limes, coarse salt, and clear fresh water drawn from a stream above the mission. Juárez himself prepared the concoctions, which gave Gus and Jack enough temporary relief to permit them to make the last leg of the trip. They carried about a dozen limes in their pockets as they walked, and Juárez continuously reminded them to suck on them.

Thirty minutes later Juárez halted at the top of a small knoll. With a melodramatic gesture that would have served Balboa when he discovered the Pacific, he pointed triumphantly to a long, narrow stretch of land a few hundred yards away and a hundred feet below them. Apparently it had once been an airfield but had lain untouched since the guerrilla air force abandoned it twenty years earlier. The land was relatively flat but covered with head-high grass and short, pulpy trees, the shallow roots of which wove the top of the dark valley soil like lace.

Larry was bitterly disappointed, but Winter managed to sound optimistic. "It could work," he said, his voice hollow. "Let's go down and take a look."

The path descended back into the jungle. Ten minutes later the six men emerged single file from under the dense overhead canopy to find themselves in the middle of what used to be a 4,000-foot runway about 150 feet wide. On closer inspection, Larry, who had done a considerable amount of flying himself, realized it wasn't as impossible as he had at first thought, but the decision would have to be Winter's since he would be the one flying into it. While McClellan stretched out exhausted in the tall grass, Larry accompanied the ex-fighter pilot to the highest point of the sloped runway. Jack surveyed the field, grim-faced with discomfort but grunting approvingly. He concluded that the field was suitable in length, width, and configuration. Then he studied the distant mountains for a long time.

"The approach is good," he said at last. "It'll do. As long as it's cleared right and there's fuel here waiting for me."

Juárez, who had joined them in the course of their inspection, assured him this would be no problem, for he could have the entire field cleared in a matter of days. Winter wasn't satisfied.

"No dice," he said categorically. "I don't want half a dozen Indians going over it with lawn mowers and thinking they made an airfield. Once I'm up there, if this thing ain't fit to land on, I'm not gonna have a whole helluva lot of places to go. Listen, Larry, you're a pilot, you know what I'm gonna need. If you'll come down here and supervise the clearing, make sure everything's set, I'll do it. But that's the only way I'll do it."

Winter's ultimatum was exactly what Larry wanted to hear, even though the idea of returning to the jungle for a week or two didn't particularly appeal to him. It gave him an opening to solve the problem that had been plaguing him ever since Phil Peters told him he would have to find a role to play in the smuggling operation but wouldn't be allowed to provide the aircraft.

"Sure, Jack," he agreed readily. "Maybe I'll even get a chance to hunt that jaguar. But even if this thing's cleared right, I don't think the Aero-Commander can cut it. There's no way I can get it smooth enough, and it'll probably be a little too soft."

Winter saw the point at once. An AeroCommander is a high-winged aircraft with long and brittle wing struts that would snap like matchsticks on a rough jungle runway. It also had less than a foot of belly clearance. The prospect of being stuck at the top of Guatemala with the underside of his plane ripped open and his wingtips sagging on the runway didn't appeal to him. "No sweat," he mumbled. "Soon's we get back home and I get my guts straightened out, I'll try to line up another airplane. Now let's get the fuck outta here before there's nothing left of me but a little puddle of shit in the jungle."

The party turned around and retraced its steps to the edge of the river, where Enrico hailed the boatman on the other side. They remounted their horses and rode for the *finca,* Jack and Gus dangling in their saddles so limply they were practically hanging on the horses' necks. At one point Juárez, who rode well, spurred his horse ahead. Sensing his purpose, Larry quickly overtook him, leaving the others a few hundred yards behind.

"I was hoping we would get a chance to talk," the Indian began appreciatively. "Your friends, I would imagine, are quite delighted with the arrangements for the marijuana. But I daresay you strike me as a more interesting man who would welcome a more interesting proposition."

"What do you have in mind?"

"Cocaine."

"How much?"

"As much as you can buy."

"I could be in a position to buy considerable quantities," Larry said evasively, for he knew nothing at all about cocaine and had no clear conception of how much constituted a considerable quantity. "I'll have to talk to my people when I get back. I assume I can tell them you have access to such a supply."

"Indeed, yes. I suspect you are laboring under a misapprehension, for our chief of detectives, Señor Quintana, sometimes likes to play the buffoon. When you met him, he may have given the impression he does not pursue drug traffickers with great avidity. Nothing could be further from the truth. You understand, he has made a great many drug seizures. I do

52

not wish to bore you with the particulars, but I would venture to say his national police have taken possession of two hundred fifty pounds of excellent cocaine, which he has had the foresight to keep under refrigeration. When you get back to North America, you should discuss this with your people."

Suddenly the marijuana case on which Larry had been sent to Guatemala paled to insignificance next to a huge stash of cocaine and a drug network that reached high into the Guatemalan government. But before he could do anything about Quintana, he would have to work out the details of the grass deal and get back to Georgia.

They arrived at Enrico's *finca* late in the afternoon. McClellan and Winter were sent to the stream that ran behind the pasture, where they soaked obliviously until dusk, the cool water bringing down their fevers. They collapsed onto their plank beds as soon as the sun set. Larry, Juárez, and Enrico ate on the porch, conversing well into the night while the servants brought pot after pot of coffee and Enrico produced a treasured supply of stale sweet rolls he kept in a locked cabinet.

In the morning all five men rode horses back out of the jungle to the jeep, then drove to Cobán, arriving at Orlando's house just after dark. There the final agreement was reached.

They would take out two hundred pounds of marijuana on the first trip, four hundred pounds on each weekly trip thereafter. The "grass of Chamá" would cost $33 a pound, with five dollars per pound off the top for Jefferson Juárez. After the meeting, McClellan did some quick math and worked out a projected income of $60,000 on the small load, $120,000 on each subsequent run. It would pay for a lot of horseshoes.

In addition to supplying the marijuana, Orlando agreed to provide, at a steep price, enough aviation-grade gasoline for the return trip and fifty Indians to clear the field. The Indians would cost $600, half of it up front or they wouldn't work. Larry agreed to wire $300 in care of Orlando's attorney in Guatemala City, and Orlando promised to have the Indians build Larry a hut near the runway at no extra charge.

The five men shook hands all around.

"Just one other thing," Larry told Orlando. "See if you can find me a decent hunting rifle. If I get a chance I'd like to go after Jesús's cat."

"As you wish, *señor.*"

Six

The Aviateca flight from Guatemala City touched down in New Orleans in the early afternoon of Friday, October 17. Larry's plane had been tied up there since the three smugglers had flown to Guatemala a week earlier. Winter was in no condition to fly, so Larry piloted it back to Atlanta, arriving around five o'clock.

As soon as Larry taxied onto the ramp at Peachtree-DeKalb Airport, he called Dan Gordon from a pay phone in the fixed base operation lounge. Winter and McClellan stood by the phone, urging him to hurry. Neither expected to be in circulation by Saturday, so Larry set up a lunch meeting for Sunday at the same restaurant where the first meeting with Gordon had taken place. McClellan's wife Jo picked him up at the airport and offered Winter a ride home. Larry stayed behind, not wanting to keep them waiting while he parked and tied down the airplanes.

He waited until his partners drove off, then called GBI and got Billy Shepherd on the line. The supervisor of the Major Violators Squad within GBI's Controlled Substances Section, Special Agent Shepherd had supervisory authority over the new unit known as the smuggling detail, which consisted of Larry and Agents Clardy and Eason. Only twenty-eight years old, with six years in the bureau, Shepherd was an innately conservative man who still wore button-down shirts. Except for his voice, which was as high-pitched as an adolescent's, he seemed older than his years, soft-spoken, diffident, and coolly efficient. In the command structure within GBI, he reported directly to Controlled Substances Director Phil Peters.

"You made it just in time, Spivey," he said genially, his tone as close to the cop style of ragging wit as he ever let himself get. "Everybody's just about to split for the weekend. I'll see if I can talk 'em into hanging around if you wanna get on over here and tell us what you been doin' all week."

Larry asked Shepherd to send a female agent to pick him up at the airport. If any of the wrong people happened to see him, his being picked up by a woman wouldn't arouse suspicion.

Agent Jessica Dowell dropped him off at GBI headquarters a little before six o'clock. An embarrassingly fulsome hero's welcome was waiting for him when he walked into the eighth-floor squad room, where eight or ten agents had waited around for him to show up. "You didn't bring me any souvenirs?" Paul Carter teased. "Shit, Spivey, I'm the guy that recruited you."

After a few minutes, Inspector Peters strode into the squad room and put an end to the party. "Spivey," he barked with playful gruffness, "while you were honeymooning all around Latin America at Georgia's expense, we've been stuck here working. As soon as you're ready to start earning your keep, I reckon you oughta get your tail down to the conference room and let us know what you been up to. Shepherd, bring the case files."

He checked his watch as though he were dispatching a squadron of bombers, turned on his heel, and marched out of the room. Five minutes later Larry was seated in the conference room across from Phil Peters's office. Peters sat at the head of the table, with Larry to his left and Billy Shepherd to his right. Farther down the table sat Paul Carter and Special Agents Mike Eason and George Clardy.

At Peters's request, Larry led off with a forty-five-minute account of his Guatemalan trip. All five GBI officers dutifully took notes as he spoke, occasionally interrupting with questions. Larry saved the best part for last and was gratified by the sudden surge of excitement that greeted his account of Jefferson Juárez's offer to sell him 250 pounds of cocaine from the private supply of Chief of National Detectives Quintana. "Say, how much is that stuff worth anyway?" Larry asked.

"You mean you don't know?" George Clardy answered incredulously.

"A couple of hundred grand?"

Clardy did a few quick calculations on the legal pad in front of him and looked up, shaking his head. "Try a little closer to eighty million dollars," he said.

Larry was speechless, even after Clardy had explained the calculations to him. Street coke, which usually runs between 6 and 8 percent purity, sells for between $70 and $80 a gram. To be on the conservative side, Clardy based his figuring on $70 and 10 percent purity, which produced a street value of $700,000 per kilogram. Two hundred fifty pounds of pure cocaine was about 114 kilos, and the multiplication came out to $79.8 million. "There's enough coke there," he said, "to keep a heavy user stoned for something like three thousand years. Or the whole city of Atlanta for a weekend. You figure out which is more likely."

Eason asked, "How much was the French Connection?"

"Hey, let's stop playing with ourselves and get back to reality," Inspector Peters roared before anyone could answer. "We've got to get a few things straight. First, all we've got so far is a conversation with a man who says he knows a guy who says he has the stuff. That isn't even enough to open a case file with, even if it was in our jurisdiction. Which it ain't. Guatemala is a little off our beat, don't you think?"

"Then what was I doing down there?" Larry shot back.

"Trying to get a load popped in Georgia. That's what the G in GBI stands for, remember? Not Guatemala."

"Why can't we do this one the same way? I'll sell Gordon on the idea of buying the stuff. That makes it a Georgia case, doesn't it?"

Peters shook his head. "It sure does, but it would probably be entrapment. Besides, we've got to answer to the governor and the legislature. We can't go spending Georgia's money to police the whole damn world. If they try to bring that stuff in here, I guarantee you we'll go after them. But as long as they keep it down there, it's a problem for their own enforcement people."

"But Quintana is head of their enforcement people," Larry protested archly.

Peters shrugged. "Well, that oughta make it easier for them," he drawled.

Larry was bitterly disappointed, but Peters, who threw in a vague promise he would pass the information on, was giving him no choice. Larry let the subject drop, even though he hadn't yet made up his mind to let it stay dropped. He was coming to realize how strange, sordid, and complex a world he had entered when he let Gus McClellan recruit him to work one side of the street while Paul Carter recruited him to work the other.

For the next half hour Billy Shepherd picked through the case files that had been opened during Larry's absence, reporting on all that GBI had learned about Dan Gordon and his operation. The State Intelligence

Section had contributed information on an unidentified major drug smuggler who fitted Gordon's description but operated under a number of phony names. Larry apparently was the first investigator to get a line on him.

"Now that's the kind of stuff I like to hear," Peters said at the end, closing the conference. "If we get this guy the right way, we clean up a lot of cases for a lot of different folks. And that's what we're drawing our pay for."

Larry wasn't sure.

He spent all day Saturday in the GBI offices dictating a twelve-page investigative summary of his Guatemalan trip, fleshing it out with detailed observations that would refresh his recollection when it came time for him to testify in court against Gordon's drug ring. He also included a verbatim recounting of his conversation with Jefferson Juárez about Quintana's cocaine supply. It was a long shot, but he hoped having it in writing might force someone to take action.

Eason and Clardy stopped by late in the afternoon to see how Larry's work on the report was coming. The three of them repaired to the Keg, a quiet, rustic-style establishment just down the street from headquarters. Larry ordered a scotch and soda. Eason, a small, round, gnomish man with a sense of humor like a straight razor, drank Tía Marías, while Clardy filled his ample paunch with draft beer. Larry was comfortable with both men, joking easily, not unaware that his developing friendship with them was an index of how completely he had entered into his new career. After an hour or so, the conversation slowly mellowed, and Larry began to wonder out loud whether there weren't some way to do something about Quintana's coke.

"Ah, that," Eason sighed, staring wistfully at the gas fireplace in the far wall. "Now there's a bust for you. I looked it up. It's about three times the French Connection. A case like that gives you wet dreams."

"That's about all it's gonna give you," Clardy observed realistically. "It's not our table. Nothing we can do."

Larry said, "Bullshit. That doesn't make sense. What about the feds or something? Don't they have agents all over the world?"

"You mean DEA?" Eason asked.

DEA was the federal Drug Enforcement Administration, formerly known as the Bureau of Narcotics and Dangerous Drugs but renamed by the Nixon administration in an effort to apply cosmetic remedies to clean up its image as a notoriously corrupt and inefficient agency.

"I guess so," Larry said.

Clardy was shaking his head. "Stay away from them, son," he cautioned cryptically.

Larry asked him what he meant, but all he got for an answer was: "Look, it's a horseshit outfit. They steal cases; they fuck 'em up every way there is. I'm only tellin' you for your own good."

"What do I care if they steal the case?" Larry snapped. "I'm not doing anything with it anyway. If they can lean on Quintana, it's more than we can do."

"Forget it," Eason muttered boozily. "DEA sucks. They eat Kitty Litter, man."

"They'll get you hurt."

"Or killed."

"Or both. You're gonna be down there working undercover, man. That's like hanging by your thumbs. Some asshole DEA agent could blow your cover."

For the second time in as many days, Larry dropped the subject. He still knew he would have to do something about Juárez and Quintana, but obviously Clardy and Eason weren't the ones to talk to about it. They must have had some run-ins with the DEA that had soured them on the agency. He knew enough—or thought he did—to take their complaints with a grain of salt. After all, the DEA was a federal agency, just like the FBI, and he figured Clardy and Eason were simply voicing the kind of interservice hostility he knew well from his days in the navy. He swung the conversation into other areas, but the frustrating situation had dampened everyone's spirits.

They split up around eight o'clock after agreeing to meet at GBI headquarters at ten o'clock the next morning so Larry could be fitted with the wire he would wear into his noon meeting with Gordon.

The equipment supplied in the morning by GBI electronics technician Bill Ryan consisted of a battery-powered transmitter about half the size and thickness of a cigarette pack and about two feet of thin antenna wire. Ryan himself taped the transmitter to Larry's abdomen, just at the belt line, then ran the antenna up to his left shoulder, leaving a small loop of extra wire just inside his belt to prevent Larry's movements from unplugging the antenna. He sent Larry to the next room to test the equipment. "The batteries are good for six hours. You won't need that much, but just to be on the safe side, you better turn if off until you get there. Just make damn sure you turn it back on before you go in."

Eason and Clardy, in Clardy's brown Chevelle, swung in behind Larry as he pulled out of the GBI parking lot. On the expressway, Larry turned on the transmitter and asked his partners to flash their lights if they were reading him. His voice projected cleanly from the speaker of the small reel-to-reel recorder housed in an imitation leather briefcase on Eason's lap. The Chevelle's lights flashed obligingly, and Larry clicked off the machine to save the batteries. In the restaurant parking lot he clicked it back on and repositioned the swatch of tape Ryan had put over the toggle switch to keep Larry's clothing from accidentally turning off the transmitter.

The main dining area was crowded for a Sunday, an after-church collection of elderly couples and decorous, Sunday-best families with swarms of children. As Larry crossed to the private dining room Gordon had reserved for the meeting, he spotted GBI agents Joanna Lee and Leslie Neff studying their menus in a booth.

In the back room Dan Gordon, Johnny Harrel, and a third man Larry had never seen before were seated at the table. Gordon rose and extended his hand. "Larry, I want you to meet my associate Jack Bogard. Jack, Larry Spivey."

Bogard was a huge man, well over six feet in height, with the shoulders and back of a defensive end. Jesus, I don't think GBI's got a set of cuffs to fit this guy, Larry thought as his right hand disappeared into Bogard's.

McClellan and Winter arrived together five minutes later. Winter looked drawn and haggard but a shade less green than when Larry had seen him last. McClellan's clothes hung on him like loose tenting. Between them they had lost thirty-five pounds, and it showed most on McClellan, who seemed not so much thinner as hollowed out.

Johnny Harrel laughed.

"What the hell happened to you guys?" Gordon asked.

"Jungle Jim there damn near killed us trying to make Eagle Scouts out of us," Winter groaned.

"He drinks the fucking water, and we come down with Montezuma's Revenge," McClellan added.

The talk during dinner was anecdotal, with McClellan providing a colorful narrative of their adventures south of the border. As soon as the table was cleared, Winter opened his flight bag, pulled out a set of global navigation charts, and extracted the one he wanted. Spreading it out on the table, he began his briefing.

"First thing is we have this problem. We can't use Larry's AeroCommander. It isn't suitable for the field they got for us down there. I talked to a buddy of mine, and he's got a Cherokee Six we can use. It's a perfect rough-field aircraft, and I can fix it up with a fuel cell that'll give it the range we need.

"The field they got for us looks about like a pumpkin patch right now, but Jungle Jim here's gonna go down there November fifth and straighten it all up. Fifty Indians start work on it this Monday, as soon as we wire three hundred bucks to this Orlando character. Our flight's set for the tenth, so that gives Jungle Jim five days to get up into the jungle, eyeball the field, and get back out to cable us if everything ain't perfectly beautiful.

"Now when I fly down there, Gus is gonna ride shotgun. Literally. We'll be carrying about eight grand in cash, but worse than that, the aircraft's worth about a hundred grand on the black market and I ain't about to get ripped off. Believe me, it's a long fucking walk back."

He turned to Larry and lectured him like a schoolmaster. "I'm going to give you a radio receiver preset to our Unicom frequency. You monitor it between the hours of ten A.M. and twelve noon on the tenth. That's the only time you can land there, between the morning fog and the afternoon clouds. If we don't come, do the same thing the next day and the next. That's the tenth, eleventh, and twelfth. If you haven't heard from us by noon on the third day, everything goes on hold until we talk by phone. So get your ass back to civilization and call Gus. If you do hear from us, and if everything's cool on the ground, have your shirt off and in your right hand, get at the downwind end of the runway, and wave the shirt in your left hand when I make my second pass over the field. If you're not standing there waving your shirt, we don't land. We throw the artillery out the window and try to make it to Guatemala City, take our chances explaining how come we're there without filing a flight plan. Got it?"

Larry nodded.

Gordon asked how much marijuana they had agreed to buy and how much it would cost. Larry ran down the figures for him and he approved. The entire deal, including the marijuana and all expenses, would cost around $10,000. The buyers Gordon had lined up would pay $300 a pound, $60,000 for the load.

"You're going to have to inspect the goods before we accept delivery," Gordon reminded Larry. "What do you know about grass?"

"I know good shit when I smoke it," Larry lied. The only time he had ever smoked marijuana was at a party at McClellan's house. He and Charlene had left early when some of the revelers started talking about taking their clothes off. He knew it was old-fashioned not to smoke pot, but in a lot of ways Larry was old-fashioned.

"Well, you can smoke it, but that's not going to tell you all that much," Gordon said. "You've got to know what to look for. Check out the buds, that's the most important thing. There should be lots of buds. Squeeze one. The buds should be sticky. That's the resin, and that's what makes it smoke good. And check out the color. It's got to be brown, a nice mocha brown. It may even be a light gold color. That's terrific. Brown, gold, whatever it is, that's all called Gold. But not green. If it's green, everyone will think it's Mexican, and I won't be able to move it. I can get all I want of that shit, but there's no market for it."

Larry answered confidently that he expected no problems. He asked Gordon how long it would take him to sell off the entire load and how soon he'd be ready for another run.

"Twenty-four hours to move it," Gordon said. "No more than that. If everything goes right, Jack can make another run in a few days, as soon as he can get ready."

That was just what Larry wanted to hear. "Then I might as well stay down there," he said. "No sense coming all the way out of the fucking jungle just to go back in. Just have Jack bring me my share of the bread when you come back for the next load."

By staying in Guatemala, Larry was giving himself a perfect excuse for being somewhere else when the arrests were made. An undercover agent who wants to stick around for more than one case has to make absolutely sure his cover doesn't get blown when the bust goes down.

It took only a few more minutes for the final wrinkles to be ironed out, and then the meeting broke up. Gordon gave Larry $300 to wire Orlando so that work could be started on the field.

During the next two weeks, the Georgia Bureau of Investigation brought U.S. Customs into the case. A customs agent went to the friend Winter had mentioned, rented his only Cherokee 6, and flew it to another airfield, where a transponder was installed under an inspection plate in the tail of the plane. By monitoring the special blip from the transponder on their radar screens, customs agents in the air and air controllers on the ground would be able to track Winter's flight all the way to Guatemala and back.

For as long as he could, Larry put off making a decision about the cocaine stash Jefferson Juárez had alluded to. But as the time for his departure approached, he knew he would have to have an answer for Juárez. If he told him he wasn't in a position to deal for the coke, Juárez would take his business elsewhere, and the case would be gone for good. The idea of prosecuting amateurs like Winter and McClellan while highly placed traffickers like Juárez and Quintana got a pass was repugnant to him, and he knew he had to do something.

As troubled as he was by the warnings Clardy and Eason had given him about the Drug Enforcement Administration, he knew that contacting them was the only course open to him. He called Charles Dunhill, director of the DEA office in Atlanta, and set up a meeting with two of Dunhill's agents.

The meeting took place at an International House of Pancakes restaurant in an Atlanta suburb. Larry began by explaining his GBI mission to them. The agents were aghast.

"Man, it's a good thing you came to us," Josh Seton, a tall, slender blond man in his early thirties, said patronizingly. "Do you have any idea how much trouble you're fixin' to get yourself into?"

"What do you mean?"

"I mean like say you get popped by the locals. Say they're onto this whole operation and they bust the lot of you. They got the fuckin' Napoleonic Code down there, which in your case means they lock you up and throw away the key. The only ones ever could get you out is the State Department, and they're not about to. We got treaties with Guatemala that say we gotta register all agents we send down there. And you ain't registered, boy. Which makes you nothing but a drug smuggler."

Larry knew Seton was telling the truth. He also knew why GBI hadn't taken the steps necessary to protect him. If GBI had notified the State Department about his mission, the State Department would have turned it over to DEA, and DEA in turn would have denied permission for it.

"Tell you the truth, the chances of getting busted down there don't worry me too much," he said confidently. "That's what I wanted to talk to you about. The dude I'm dealing with has got some very high-class protection. He's in tight with the chief of the national detectives."

Seton's eyebrows went up. "Quintana?"

"Quintana."

"How tight?"

"Tighter than that. Quintana's got coke, two hundred fifty pounds of it. My man offered to sell it to me."

Seton let out a low whistle. The other agent with him, whose name Larry hadn't caught, was sitting sideways in his chair, his legs crossed. He showed no reaction at all.

Seton asked, "And are you gonna buy it?"

"That's what I came to talk to you about. There's no way we can make it a Georgia case. I wanted to know what you folks could do about it."

Seton considered a long time before answering. Then he said, "Look, what you told me is interesting, but it's not a whole helluva lot to go on. We can't even open a case file on the basis of an unsubstantiated second-hand allegation. We'd have to have more. You say the guy's actually willing to sell it to you?"

"That's right."

"But you haven't seen any of it?"

"Not yet."

"Well, that's what you gotta do. Then somebody's got to cut a deal to buy it. Now who do you figure that'd be?"

"Me?"

"Goes without saying. You're already in with them. I'll tell you the truth, you're fuckin' nuts if you go stickin' your neck out down there over some dipshit two hundred pounds of grass when you got one of the biggest coke loads in the world settin' right there waitin' for you to take it down. My advice is forget this GBI thing and come on over and work for us."

Larry smiled wryly as he realized that part of Clardy and Eason's predictions about the DEA was already coming true. He had met Seton less than five minutes earlier, and already the agent was trying to talk him into walking out on his own agency.

"Can't do that," he said firmly. "But I'll tell you what I can do. You notify your man down there I'm coming. That'll cover me in case anything does go wrong. But I don't want any contact with him. If Quintana's crooked, the whole national police is crooked, and I don't want anyone there knowing what I'm doing until it's done. As soon as I load up this pot shipment and get it airborne, I'll get in touch with your man in Guatemala City and work Quintana for him. I hope that's good enough for you."

"It is."

"What's your agent's name?"

"We've got a man working out of the embassy. Rick Taveras. Contact him, he's a good man. You can trust him."

Seven

Jefferson Juárez met Larry at the Guatemala City airport on the afternoon of November 5. "Señor Quintana has been relieved of duty," he said, the first words out of his mouth. "He knows there will be no more cocaine seizures, and he is eager to dispose of what he has. The police he has guarding it are men over whom he will no longer have control. Have you spoken to your people?"

"I have. First things first. As soon as the airplane leaves Chamá with our first load, we can do business. Is the field ready?"

Juárez shrugged. "Orlando has received the money you sent to hire the Indians. I assume they have been working."

In the morning Larry and Juárez drove to Cobán, where Orlando and Enrico reported that the Indians were working on the field but that no one had gone into the mountains to inspect the work. To be on the safe side, Larry cabled McClellan in Atlanta, signaling him to delay the flight three days. He spent the afternoon in the Cobán marketplace, where the three Guatemalans assisted him in purchasing supplies for his stay in the jungle. He had in his pocket eleven hundred dollars in cash Gordon had given him before he took off from Atlanta. A machete, a hammock, food, utensils, and other gear cost him a little over two hundred.

As evening descended, an army marimba band moved into the town square. After the concert, Larry's hosts led him to the fortresslike adobe air force officers' club just off the square, where Orlando de Cortez, who still held the rank of captain, was treated with almost royal deference by

64

the beady-eyed colonel who served as commandant of the base at Cobán. As the night wore on and tongues got looser, Larry came to realize that the aviation fuel Orlando was selling him at two dollars a gallon was actually "disaquisitioned" air force property.

In the morning he paid Orlando $200 for the gasoline and the $300 balance due for the completion of the clearing operation. Then Larry, Enrico, and Juárez, joined by Enrico's ten-year-old daughter Lesbia, his fourteen-year-old son Luis, and Orlando's twenty-year-old deaf-mute son Rafael, set off in Enrico's jeep.

Six horses and two mules were waiting for them at the point at the edge of the jungle where they had abandoned the jeep on Larry's first trip. They arrived at Enrico's *finca* at dusk, too late for Larry to inspect the field that day. Lesbia more or less adopted Larry, waiting on him hand and foot, plying him with oranges, coffee, and sweet rolls, practicing the English she was learning in school on him.

In the morning Larry, Enrico, and Juárez saddled horses and rode to the edge of the Senesa River. Someone had neglected to tell the boatman Jesús they were coming, and the dugout was several miles downstream, where the old man and two of his *mozos* were gathering sugarcane. Since the Indian laborers worked only half a day, quitting when the sun got high, Enrico and Juárez cleared a shady spot under a huge fig tree with their machetes and lay down. While they were waiting, Larry practiced throwing the eight-inch knife he had bought in Cobán. When a twin-engine Beechcraft appeared overhead and began to circle, Larry called to Juárez. "Take a look at that."

The Indian's catlike eyes studied the sky. After a minute he was able to read the identification number on the plane's wing. "Mexican registry," he announced indifferently, heading back for the shade. "Must be smugglers looking for a field."

Larry watched the aircraft circle lazily for ten or fifteen minutes, then head south, climbing until it disappeared.

When Jesús appeared shortly after noon, Larry asked him about the jaguar that had been killing his livestock.

"She ees gone, *señor.*" The old man grinned, showing blackened teeth. "I followed her into zee jungle, and she know I be ready for her if she come back. She no come back."

After a lunch of cold and soggy pork pastries sent down from Jesús's farm, the old man ferried the party across the river. He turned over to Larry a set of ragged and dog-eared government papers naming himself as custodian in charge of the airfield at a salary of three quetzals a month. Once a month for the past twelve years, Jesús had made the long trek to Cobán, where a government official paid him. Larry's possession of these papers gave him something like a legal right to be at the field in case a provincial detachment of *federales* asked any questions.

At the airfield four kilometers downriver from the crossing point, Larry's worst fears came true. The Indians had started work only that morning and had cleared less than five hundred feet of the four-thousand-foot runway a Cherokee 6 would need at that altitude. In many places bamboo shoots had been whacked off at an angle about two inches above the ground, leaving viciously pointed spikes sticking up in the area supposedly cleared already. Larry pointed these out to Juárez, who explained to the Indians that they would have to be cropped flush with the ground. There were forty-one Indians on the field, and easily half of them were drunk on *boch,* a homemade corn-and-sugarcane whiskey with an octane rating higher than the aviation fuel Orlando had promised to deliver.

"Be careful how you handle these Indians," Juárez warned. "Their fathers were exploited ruthlessly by the Germans during the war. The Germans promised them money. When the work was finished, the Germans killed them instead of paying them. Such memories live long. Except for Castilians like Enrico, these Indians have seen few white men since the Germans left, and they do not trust them."

"Assure them they can trust me," Larry said. "Tell them I am an American, not a German."

Juárez smiled ironically. "I am sure you will have no difficulties, for they know you will be alone here and that they can kill you if it proves necessary. Such knowledge will make them less distrustful."

Larry thanked Juárez for the reassurance and asked him to summon the chief of the work gang. Using Juárez as an interpreter, he told the Indian he would pay one quetzal per day per man.

"When do we see the money?" the Indian asked in dialect.

"Tell him he has received three hundred quetzals already, enough to pay for a week's work. If he brings more men, I will see that he is paid accordingly."

After Juárez translated, the Indian responded animatedly.

"He says he has received no money. He says it is time for his men to stop work now. He says he will not return until he has seen some money."

Larry took what was left of the roll of bills from his pocket. "How much does he want?"

"He does not want your money now," Juárez said. "He wants only to see it. He wants to know you will have the money to pay him. If you show it to him, that will satisfy him."

Larry fanned the bills out in his hand, and the Indian grinned, nodded, and withdrew.

"Tomorrow is Sunday," Juárez explained. "No work will be done. He will be back with his men Monday morning."

After dinner at the *finca*, Juárez saddled his horse and set off for Cobán, taking the keys to the jeep and a flashlight with spare batteries. At Cobán he would make the final arrangements for delivery of the fuel Winter would need for his return flight. He promised to be back by Monday.

Sunday morning Larry was awakened at sunrise by the noise in the front yard. The top half of the door to his room was open, and he could see the nearby mountains shrouded in mist. He slipped on his jeans and walked out on the porch, where he sat in the hammock to survey the scene in the yard below.

Chickens, pigs, and goats were everywhere. Indians were coming and going from the little tin-roofed store on the far side of the broad yard, chattering rapidly in their harsh, guttural dialect.

He had been on the porch less than five minutes when little Lesbia came running up with a cup of coffee. She climbed onto the hammock and sat beside Larry as he sipped at the oily, bitter brew. "Your breakfast is ready," she said when he put down his cup.

He ate the usual meal of fried bananas, tortillas, and bean paste, with more coffee and grapefruit-sized wild oranges, then took a towel, soap, and clean pants and marched shirtless and barefoot to the clear stream of shockingly cold mountain water where Winter and McClellan had soaked their fevers on his first visit. He lathered himself from head to toe at a shallow point, then waded out to deep water to rinse himself off. He dived under the surface, and when his head came up, Lesbia was standing on the bank.

"*Camchak,* Larry, *camchak.*" She giggled, pointing behind her to the house. "Papa has a horse for you!"

Larry was just pulling on his boots on the front porch when Enrico appeared in the yard, leading a smooth-skinned copper-brown mare by the reins. The animal followed skittishly with a reluctant sideways prance. Her ears were laid back, her nostrils flared, her eyes wide with fear.

"You ride well, *señor,*" Enrico said. "You would honor me and my house if you would break this mare for me."

Larry stepped down from the porch and took the reins. The mare shied from him, her breath coming in snorts. He led her down to an open area to the side of the two-acre yard. As Enrico watched from the edge of the pasture, he began to walk her, drawing her gently in a wide circle for about forty minutes, stopping every few minutes to stroke and pat her, talking softly to her all the time. He noticed that ten or fifteen Indians had gathered at the side of the yard to watch.

When the mare was completely calm, Larry patted her reassuringly with his left hand, slipped his left foot into the stirrup, and eased himself up into the saddle. Nothing happened, so he shook the reins. One ear moved slightly forward, but that was all. He took a deep breath. It was time to test her.

He hauled off and kicked her in the side, and she went straight up, back bent, and came down with all four feet together. Larry felt his teeth click together and hoped his tongue hadn't been between them. The mare crow-hopped and kicked for about two minutes, but not so violently he couldn't stay on her. He ran her a little, giving her the rein, then pulling her this way and that until she responded well. When he was satisfied, he walked her down until she was calm again, rode her to where Enrico was standing, and dismounted.

"Gracias, gracias, mucho hombre," Enrico growled gratefully. He gestured to the horse and to himself, asking the obvious question with sign language as Larry handed him the reins.

Larry nodded, and Enrico swung into the saddle and rode the mare out to the field, where he trotted her around for about five minutes.

Bored with watching Enrico ride a now tame horse, Larry turned and started back up to the house for his cigarettes. Lesbia caught up and ran beside him, her hand in his.

"Más café?" she asked.

"Sí, por favor."

When the girl brought the coffee, Larry sent her away. Alone on the porch, he caught up on his weather diary and updated the coded notes he was keeping for the investigative summary he would have to write when he got back to civilization.

Monday morning the work chief had fifty-three Indians on the field by dawn, about ten of them drunk. He called them together when Larry walked onto the field and used hand gestures to indicate he wanted to see the money again. Larry counted the Indians and counted out the bills, one quetzal at a time. Satisfied, the chief led the men back to work, or at least back to the middle of the field. Larry supervised their labors until noon; at no point were more than eight or ten working at the same time. Some were in the shade sharpening their machetes; some were talking and drinking at the edge of the field. Others were nowhere in sight. Whenever one or two new men wandered onto the field to start cutting, a pair already at work would saunter off.

Yet the work progressed with amazing rapidity. Using long branches with inverted forks to hook and gather the grass toward them, they lopped it off with their machetes, their arms swinging rhythmically, the vegetation falling before them like a field of corn bent by the wind. By the time they stopped at noon, the runway had stretched to more than twenty-five hundred feet. Larry handed out the fifty-three quetzals to the workers, who queued up to accept them.

On Tuesday morning there were sixty-five Indians, for the word had spread that the *gringo* had money. Again Larry had to count out the bills before the men would work. Again most of them were idle most of the time. But the runway was growing quickly and had reached its full length before the sun climbed to the top of its arc. A few men already had begun felling trees to give Winter a decent approach, and the work would be easily finished by ten o'clock Wednesday morning, when the plane was due in. All that remained was to finish the approach and level some of the huge anthills that still dotted the field like giant boils.

Larry paid the Indians. Four of them stayed behind to construct the hut that had been promised at the edge of the field. In four hours the five-by-ten thatch and bamboo structure was finished, and Larry paid the builders an extra quetzal apiece. He elected to spend the night in the hut to save the three-hour trip back to the *finca* and the three-hour return trip in the morning. The boatman Jesús sent a freshly killed piglet and a small supply of beans and ground corn, along with his oldest daughter, an incredibly fat teenage girl built like a cyprus stump, much thicker at the bottom than the top. The girl rolled tortillas and roasted the pig, then crossed back to her father's farm after Larry had eaten.

While Larry slept in his jungle hut, GBI Agents Mike Eason, Robert Sprayberry, Tony Gaylee, and Jessica Dowell were deployed around the Southeast Air Terminal just outside Fairburn, Georgia. Despite its pretentious name, the Southeast Air Terminal was nothing more than a twenty-four-hundred-foot paved runway that doubled as a drag strip on Friday nights. But Gus McClellan and Jack Winter were working late on the

Cherokee 6 that would be taking them on their pot run to Guatemala, and GBI had been carefully monitoring their movements.

Eason had been in the woods since eight o'clock that evening, when he had relieved Agent George Clardy. Winter and McClellan had been at work since noon. Now it was one o'clock in the morning. A few hours earlier the smugglers had taken out all but the pilot and copilot seats, and now they were disassembling the fuel lines leading to the wing tanks in order to hook up the portable fuel cell that would extend the plane's range for the flight.

Eason tensed with expectancy when Winter jumped to the hangar floor and McClellan began handing down tools. "Looks like they're packin' up," he whispered urgently into his walkie-talkie.

Sprayberry was stationed just off Highway 29, a half mile west of the airfield. Dowell and Gaylee were on a dirt road just east of it.

Exactly as Eason expected, McClellan and Winter pushed the Cherokee backward out of the hangar onto the asphalt apron, turned it around, and rolled it to the gas pumps in front of the office shed next to the hangar. While Winter dragged the gas hose into the airplane to fill the portable fuel cell they had just installed, McClellan went back to the hangar to turn off the lights and lock up. After a few minutes Winter rolled the gas hose back onto the spring-loaded drum. He and McClellan turned the plane around and pushed it onto the runway. Both men climbed into the cockpit. Through his binoculars Eason could see the red instrument lights come on.

As Eason headed back to his car on foot, Winter cranked the engine and taxied to the east end of the runway, where he turned around and began his engine run-up and cockpit check. The single-engine Cherokee trembled in place while the pilot switched the mags. He released the brakes, and the airplane lurched down the runway, gathering speed until it climbed free of the asphalt surface.

Eason was standing beside his Plymouth and reached in to snatch the microphone from the clip under the dashboard just as the Cherokee roared overhead. "GBI, this is seventy-five. Subjects are airborne. How 'bout askin' approach control if they've picked them up?"

"Ten-four, stand by."

Eason watched the pulsing running lights as the Cherokee climbed steadily away from him and banked to the right.

"Seventy-five, that's affirmative. Approach has their transponder on radar. Subjects moving north-northeast at a heading of zero-two-five."

Eason gulped. North! It didn't make sense. Guatemala was the other way. His mind raced through the possibilities, clicking them off in fractions of a second. Maybe they had spotted the transponder. Maybe they had spotted the surveillance, and this plane was just a decoy. Maybe they were flying somewhere else to switch to another one. There was no way to tell what was happening, but he knew he couldn't afford to lose contact with the airplane.

"GBI, seventy-five. Have approach try to reach them, ask them their destination."

"Ten-four."

Eason slapped the microphone against his palm while he waited, cursing under his breath. If they got rid of the transponder or switched airplanes, Customs would never be able to find them and GBI would find itself in the embarrassing position of having helped a band of smugglers by providing an agent to load their plane for them in Guatemala.

"Seventy-five, GBI. Controller says they gave him a destination of Peachtree-DeKalb Airport."

Eason leaped into the car and switched on the ignition as he acknowledged the transmission. Flinging the microphone onto the seat beside him and jerking the Plymouth into reverse, he spun it around and threw it into drive. The tires spit a spray of gravel out behind him, then caught the edge of the pavement in screaming protest as Eason raced for the intersection with Highway 29. He grabbed for the blue dome light on the transmission hump and slapped it on the dash. Still driving with his left hand, he switched on the light with his right and groped for the microphone. The needle of his speedometer was nosing toward the hundred-mile-an-hour mark when he sliced onto 29.

"Okay, folks, you heard the man. Everybody to Peachtree-DeKalb. We can't afford to lose 'em now. GBI, seventy-five, who you got in the shop there?"

"Seventy-three was here a minute ago. He just split for Peachtree."

Seventy-three was agent Paul Carter, who had been monitoring the surveillance from the reaction center and had sized up the situation as quickly as Eason. GBI headquarters was on the way to Peachtree-DeKalb Airport and about eight miles closer than Eason.

In his rearview mirror Eason saw agents Dowell and Gaylee swing onto the highway behind him. Jessica Dowell was driving, her foot mashed against the floor as she pushed her Camaro to match Eason's speed. Bob Sprayberry started a good half mile behind her, but all the work he had done on his souped-up Chevelle paid off, and he streaked past her before she could get the Camaro wound up all the way. The three cars, Eason first, then Sprayberry, then Dowell and Gaylee, careened down the deserted highway, closing on the traffic light in Fairburn.

Eason dropped off the accelerator and yanked at the wheel, throwing his Plymouth into a sideways slide as the nose came around sharply to the right. He got her straightened away just in time and gunned the engine, climbing the grade toward the railroad crossing at the crest of the low hill. He flew over the tracks without touching them, coming down hard on the downhill side.

He flashed over the expressway, eased back only a hair to make the soft left onto the on ramp, and gunned the engine, shooting onto I-85 like a rock out of a slingshot. It was two o'clock in the morning, and the expressway was deserted except for a few lumbering semis. He saw the flashing blue light from Sprayberry's Chevelle behind him and knew his team was still intact. He tried to raise Carter, who probably had a good five miles of his head start left. "Seventy-five to seventy-three, what's your twenty?"

"Comin' up on Lakewood Freeway."

Shit, Eason thought. The Lakewood Freeway was only three, three and a half miles ahead. But he wasn't surprised. Carter's new Pontiac had so many fancy antipollution devices on it, it was a wonder it moved at all.

The south half of Atlanta sped by in a blur. Eason had his siren on now but was moving too fast for it to matter. As he passed under the lighted dome of the Capitol atop the hill to his left, he saw Carter's Pontiac ahead. By this time Sprayberry was less than a hundred feet behind him, Dowell and Gaylee a couple of hundred yards farther back.

At the North Avenue overpass Eason and Sprayberry leaped past Carter, who slowed more than he had to for the hard right bend in the expressway. Dowell passed him a few seconds later, and the fast-moving convoy, with Carter now at the rear, sped on for the interchange where 85 swung to the northeast after a tricky right-left-right S-turn.

Eason let the Plymouth drift gently through the first shallow curve, then hauled it around to the left, giving it a little more gas for encouragement. The rear end floated more than he wanted it to, but he came out of it in time for the last turn.

Sprayberry was in his mirror every inch of the way, but Sprayberry was chasing the taillights in front of him more than he was watching the road. The first turn gave him no trouble; but the left that followed caught him by surprise, and he had to fight to correct the oversteer. His Chevelle drifted too far to the left, slid off the pavement, and climbed the guardrail that started at ground level and built to window height. Sparks flew from the undercarriage as the Chevelle lifted itself off the ground and ran the guardrail like a squirrel on a branch.

Eason watched in horror as he saw Sprayberry's headlights rise in the air, then yaw crazily back toward the expressway when the guardrail threw him off. But he was fighting to retain control of his own car and still had the last deep right to make. He lost sight of Sprayberry as he sailed into it, but he grabbed the microphone and screamed, "Sprayberry, you awright?"

There was no reply.

Jessica Dowell had all she could do to dodge the flying Chevelle as it came down on its chassis and scraped wildly along the pavement in front of her. Gaylee radioed a frantic warning to Carter, who managed to get his Pontiac stopped just behind the wreck.

Miraculously, Sprayberry was already climbing through the window as Carter leaped from his car and sprinted toward him. "You all right?" Carter called.

"Yeah, but I sure wouldn't want to do that again," Sprayberry called back. "Jes' he'p me outta this thing."

Carter helped Sprayberry work his chubby frame through the window opening, and the two men stood shakily on the expressway for a minute. Then Sprayberry got his shotgun from the trunk and walked back to Carter's Pontiac. They could hear Eason's voice over the radio inquiring anxiously about Sprayberry.

Sprayberry took the microphone. "Ridin' with seventy-three now. My car ain't gonna be good for a whole hell of a lot, but I reckon I'm okay."

"Well, just make sure you ain't bleedin' from somewhere, an' then get your asses down here quick. It's a big mother airport, an' I'm gonna need some help."

Eason switched off his blue light and siren as he came up on the airport. Turning right onto the airport drive, he cut his headlights and eased into the parking area where the DeKalb County Police Department kept its helicopters. The north-south runway lay only a few feet in front of him at the foot of a shallow hill. To his left he could see the landing lights of the Cherokee 6 as the smugglers' plane bore in on the runway. He sighed with satisfaction as he realized he had just won a race with an airplane from one end of Atlanta to the other.

"Seventy-five to eighty-two, get on over to Epps Aviation, it's up at the north end of the field. Cut your lights, take a position in the parking lot. I'll let you know if they're coming up your way. Seventy-three, what's your twenty?"

"Crossing Buford Highway," Sprayberry radioed back.

"Couldn't be better, seventy-three. Just drive on up the hill out behind the firehouse. Stay outta sight, and watch the west end of the field. I'm coverin' the middle."

The upwind wheel of the Cherokee stroked the pavement first, the downwind wheel was rolling a second later, and the nosewheel gentled down as the nose fell through to complete a perfect landing. Jack Winter braked the airplane firmly and turned at the first taxiway paralleling the east-west runway. Eason lost sight of him as he taxied behind the Peachtree Aviation hangar, but Carter and Sprayberry had perfect position on him.

"Seventy-three to all units. We got 'em here," Sprayberry radioed from the top of the hill. "I'm gonna move in a little closer on foot, takin' the hand unit."

He threaded his way through thick bushes until he could see the Cherokee below him barely a hundred feet away, McClellan's grunts audible in the stillness as he and the pilot pushed the airplane into position next to an old blue Ford van. Sprayberry switched off the speaker on his hand radio. "They're tying the airplane down," he whispered into it.

McClellan stood over Winter as the pilot tied down the plane. "Shit, I hope we can go tomorrow. How long do those things last?"

"Tropical depression? Could be a day or so, could be a week. How the hell would I know?"

"Shit, all that grass. It's one hell of a crying fucking shame. I mean, what the hell is a tropical depression anyway?"

"It's a storm, turkey."

"That all?"

"Yeah. C'mon, let's get home, I need some sleep."

Winter walked to the driver's side of the van while McClellan crossed to the passenger side and opened the door. "Wait a minute, Jack," he said. "I just gotta take a leak."

Sprayberry watched as the bearish blacksmith lumbered directly toward him and stopped at the bushes on the edge of the tie-down ramp. He held his breath, so close to the smuggler he could hear him urinating.

"Hey, Jack, Jack, c'mere a minute," McClellan called. "I think there's somebody up there."

"You're crazy," Winter called back. "Nothin' up there but a bunch of bushes."

McClellan shrugged, zipped up, and stepped back onto the pavement. He stooped to pick up a wooden wheel chock lying on the ground and heaved it in the direction of the shape he thought he had seen. It caught Sprayberry on the shoulder, sending the agent scurrying away in a low crouch.

"I'm crazy, huh?" McClellan shouted. "That fuckin' bush just left!"

"C'mon," Winter called urgently, starting the van. "Let's get the hell outta here!"

Larry was up before dawn, the sun still well down on the other side of the mountains, the sky dark and starless, slowly turning a milky white as the sun rose behind the cloud cover that lay thickly on the valley. He already had been through the money ritual with the Indians, who were putting the finishing touches to the field when Enrico arrived, muttering Spanish obscenities about the weather. "Señor Ramón is at the river with the gasoline," Enrico said, using the name he invariably used to indicate Orlando.

A few minutes later Orlando approached the hut. The fuel had been brought to the river on mules, and he had stayed behind to make sure none was stolen when it was loaded into the canoe and ferried across. He sent some Indians back to carry it to the field, then commiserated with Larry about the weather. "Perhaps it will burn off by the time your friend arrives," he speculated optimistically, but both men knew the prospects weren't good.

"Where is the marijuana?" Larry asked.

Orlando nodded. "Come with me, *señor.*"

He led the way over the hill to a narrow stream that forked with the Senesa. Two boatmen with dugout canoes were stationed there, one on the far bank waiting to ferry the marijuana across as soon as the plane had landed. Across the river two mules were tied in a clearing about a hundred yards in, the marijuana packed in bulging twenty-five-pound sacks, four on each mule.

Larry lifted one sack from the mule's back and untied the neck. The grass inside was brown, dark brown, exactly as Gordon wanted. He felt the stickiness of the buds and announced his satisfaction, not unaware of the irony of the situation. "We will weigh it when my friend arrives with the airplane," he said. "I have instructed him to bring scales."

The two men recrossed the river and climbed to the airfield. By the time they got there the aviation fuel had arrived in twenty five-gallon plastic containers. A team of Indians was busy emptying the containers into the two fifty-five-gallon drums set up at the downwind end of the runway. Larry noticed the air force procurement codes stenciled on the ends of the drums. Since it was only a few minutes shy of ten o'clock, Larry and Orlando went into the shed to begin monitoring the radio for a message from Winter, even though the low sky had not even begun to lift.

At noon Larry clicked off the radio and stepped out onto the field.

"Perhaps tomorrow, *señor,*" Orlando drawled, wiping at his face with a damp bandanna. He spit on the ground. "Now it lifts," he growled. "In an hour it will be clear, worse luck for us. With your permission, I send the drivers into the jungle, *señor.*"

"It's your stuff until the plane lands," Larry said. "Handle it whatever way you think's best."

In just the few minutes they had been talking, the fog had risen a few feet off the ground. Orlando squinted across the field, looking for an Indian he could send with a message for the mule drivers. He cupped his hands to his mouth to call, but Enrico startled him with a quick gesture demanding silence.

"*Hola! Una máquina!*" he growled.

Larry strained to hear, but his ears were no match for the Indian's. Then he heard it. Barely audible above the shimmering airstrip, an engine droned like a mosquito, only the treble sounds filtering down through the fog. For two full minutes the noise hung eerily overhead, impossible to locate, diffused by the fog like light through gauze.

"Perhaps your friend did not understand the arrangement?" Orlando suggested.

Larry waved off the idea. Winter knew only one way to do things—by the book. And the sound of the engine was wrong, too—too throaty and powerful, too steady, insistent, and fierce. Larry studied the sound apprehensively, trying to make sense of it by subtracting the effect of the fog and the small, furtive echoes that loafed back from the distant walls of the valley.

Then it was clear to him, and he said the word "Helicopter" at the very instant he saw a giant Huey troop carrier plummeting through a crack in the fog like a rock dropped through a sewer grate. The side door was back, and the barrels of half a dozen guns were pointing straight at him. Even before the gear touched down, an armed man leaped clear, raising his machine gun to firing position as quickly as if he had been dropped into the middle of a war. Others followed, eleven in all, some with carbines, some with Thompsons, each with a pistol at his belt.

"Who are they?" Larry asked.

"Quién sabe," Orlando muttered sullenly, hiding his fear. "Wait here, *gringo,* this is not your battle."

Larry didn't give him an argument.

By then the first men were only fifty yards away. Orlando walked toward them, his arms carefully away from his body so as not to draw fire. He was joined after a step or two by his loyal superintendent. Larry held back, studying the scene with confused detachment, coldly angry. In the distance, beyond the armed troops, two men bearing only holstered side-arms stood by the chopper, scanning the field as though looking for someone. Then Larry lost sight of them, distracted by the men closing in on Orlando only a few yards away. One of them raised his carbine above his shoulder and brought it down with the suddenness of an ax, laying open the side of Orlando's face, which was instantly bathed in bright blood.

Larry sprinted toward the fallen man until the barrel of a Thompson in his gut told him to stop and get his hands up. Someone he hadn't noticed came around behind him, jerked his arms down, and snapped on hand-cuffs. Rough hands gave him a fast, expert frisk that cost him his knife, which disappeared into someone's pocket. The two men he had spotted earlier loitering by the helicopter were now in front of him, as suddenly as if they had materialized out of the fog. One of them, a big man with a soft paunch that sagged over his belt, slapped Larry hard backhanded across the face, while the other asked in lightly accented English, "Where's the stuff?"

Larry checked his teeth with his tongue. "What stuff?" he asked.

The big man's hand came up again, but the other stopped him with a gesture. "He needs time to think," he said in Spanish.

Over their shoulders Larry saw small groups of men circling in on the hut by the runway as delicately as if they expected to find it filled with desperate *guevaristas.* From a bush behind him, he heard the sickening sounds of a man being methodically beaten, the thud of each impact accompanied by an animal grunt of exertion and followed by a lowing groan. He checked where Orlando and Enrico had been standing and saw that Enrico was no longer there. Then he heard the middle-aged superin-tendent's guts coming up even while the beating went on. Someone swore violently in Spanish and hit him again.

Larry turned to the two men. At that point he had nothing to lose, so he tried to run a bluff. "I don't know who you jokers are, but you're making a big mistake," he said coldly, trying for the right mix of outrage and bravado but learning in the process how hard it was to sound tough with your hands laced behind your butt. "I'm an American businessman," he went on, "and the gentleman over there with the hole in his face is a good friend of the defense minister. Whoever sent you here got some wrong information, and somebody's going to pay for it."

The small man smiled insolently. "I see an illegal airfield; I see fuel for a return flight; I see everything but the stuff," he purred. "Where is it?"

"You don't see shit," Larry told him. "I've got papers for the airfield in my pocket. It's perfectly legal. The fuel you're talking about is for emergency use by the government. Read the markings on the drums if you don't believe me. It belongs to your own air force."

The smile flickered on the small man's face. With a quick gesture of his head, he sent someone to check out the fuel drums, but even before the man reached the far end of the field, the small inquisitor decided to back off. He had short light-colored hair that he wore brushed straight forward. He was surprisingly fair-skinned for a Guatemalan.

"Perhaps there has been an error," he admitted, averting his eyes. "We will know better when we have investigated fully. Your companions will be flown to Guatemala City for further interrogation and medical attention. We will wait here for the helicopter to return."

He put his hand on Larry's shoulder, turned him around, and unlocked the cuffs.

Enrico, doubled almost fetal, was being shoved and carried to the chopper. He had to be lifted in. Orlando Ramón de Cortez climbed in after, walking stiffly with considerable dignity while he held a blood-soaked bandanna to his throat. Six of the raiders climbed in after them, and the big Huey roared off, leaping from the field. The little man and four Indian troops remained behind with Larry. A few hundred feet up, the Huey banked to the south and raced out of the valley.

As soon as it was gone, the small man turned to Larry and extended his hand, grinning broadly. "You must be Spivey," he said with shocking cordiality. "I'm Rick Taveras, your friendly local DEA agent. Sorry about that little show. No hard feelings, but I had to make it convincing."

Eight

Taveras put the cuffs on Larry just before the helicopter landed, then took them off again once they were safely in his car for the ride from the airport to the American Embassy, where the DEA had its offices. With a ten-day beard and still in his jungle clothes, Larry looked the part of an arrested drug dealer. In Taveras's office Larry said, "I know what you're thinking, but it's not going to work."

"It'll work," Taveras said coolly, sitting on a corner of his desk. "I told you, we didn't want to mess up your case for GBI, but it had to be. Quintana has priority."

The DEA's priorities meant less than nothing to Larry. The point was they had blown his cover. In the chopper on the way to the raid, Taveras had warned the Guatemalan troops, "Don't shoot the *gringo* unless you have to. He's one of us."

Larry figured that line ended his usefulness in Guatemala, but Taveras didn't see it that way. "Would you rather I hadn't told them?" he asked.

"If those guys in the helicopter know I'm an agent, then the whole national detectives are going to know it by morning. And that includes Quintana. There's no way I can set up a deal with anyone, thanks to you. Why the hell didn't you stay out of it like you were supposed to?"

Taveras smiled like a willful girl. "That's over and done with," he said, dismissing the incident with a wave of his hand. "There was an urgency you could not appreciate. It happened after you went up to the mountains. Quintana is out."

"I knew that already. Juárez told me."

Taveras shrugged. "I don't suppose he told you the chief has been nominated to be consul general to Florida. He'll be traveling with a diplomatic passport. Now do you understand why it was absolutely essential to get you down here at once?"

Larry understood, but the more he understood, the less he liked it. With his connection to the national detectives severed, Quintana wouldn't want to hold onto his cocaine stash any longer than he had to. He would want to move fast. And his diplomatic passport meant he could enter the United States without having to go through customs. Hundreds of pounds of cocaine were going to be dumped in the States as soon as the oily former chief detective's new appointment went through.

"How long do we have?" Larry asked.

Taveras ran his tongue over his lips and said, "A few weeks, maybe less. After that it will be too late."

What Larry had to worry about was that it was too late already. Just because Quintana no longer headed the national detectives didn't necessarily mean he didn't have friends there, friends who could inform him that the *norteamericano* buying marijuana from Jefferson Juárez was actually a narcotics agent. Taveras was willing to take that chance because it wasn't his life on the line. Larry wasn't.

"I'll set it up for you but that's all," Larry said. "Then I get out of here while my tail's still connected to my backside. If that's not good enough for you, I'll take a pass right now."

Taveras's gray eyes narrowed, measuring his man. "Get in touch with Juárez," he said. "Tell him you were busted but you bought your way out for a thousand dollars. That's the going rate. Unless he already knows otherwise, he'll believe you. Tell him you want to buy Quintana's coke, all of it, let him set up a meeting. When you come out of that meeting, we'll take it from there."

Jefferson Juárez met Larry in the lobby of the Colonial. "You had difficulties," he said, making it sound like a question.

"Some pilot spotted the field and reported it," Larry explained. "Orlando and Enrico got roughed up a little, but they didn't find the stuff. Nobody got hurt too bad." He massaged the tips of his fingers with his thumb, the international gesture for a payoff. "It's all straightened out," he said.

Juárez nodded noncommittally. "What did you want to see me about?" he asked.

80

"What the hell do you think I want to see you about?" Larry challenged. "You were supposed to have this thing wired, had the whole damn government in your pocket, the way I heard it. And the bottom line is we get popped, Orlando and Enrico get the shit kicked out of them, and it costs me a thousand bucks. You tell me, what the fuck's the situation here?"

Juárez shrugged expressively, a gesture of resignation. "We are in a transitional period," he said abstractedly. "Mr. Quintana, perhaps you know, is no longer functioning as our chief of detectives, and my contacts with the new people have not been solidified. But I assure you it will not happen again."

"Damn right," Larry snarled, raising his hand for the waiter. "No way I'm going back into those mountains. You can give your damned airfield back to the Nazis; that's about all it's good for now. If your guy with the coke is serious and wants to do business, we can talk about that, but the grass deal is off."

Juárez was off-balance, and he wasn't sure he liked the way Larry was moving. He was used to calling the shots himself. But he wanted to salvage something. "Yes," he said, "the gentleman we spoke of is interested in selling. He would prefer that the arrangements be made quickly."

Larry didn't ease off. "Don't rush me, Jefferson," he said. "My people are interested, but before I start to cut a deal, I've got to be damned sure this is for real. So far your assurances haven't been worth the time it took me to come down here. I've got to see the stuff with my own eyes, or I don't go back to my people and make myself look like any more of an idiot."

Juárez reached into his pocket for a roll of bills and slapped a ten-quetzal note on the table to pay for the drinks. "Yes, of course," he said, an unaccustomed tone of deference in his voice. "It will be done just as you wish. Come with me, we will make the arrangements."

Juárez drove to a two-story town house directly behind the presidential palace and knocked on the front door. A man with a gun at his belt opened it. Behind him, Larry could see three men playing cards at a table in the reception area. Juárez asked for Agustín.

"Agustín is not here, *señor,*" the man with the gun said in Spanish. "He may be at home."

Larry memorized the turns as they drove to Agustín's house so that he would be able to lead Taveras to it. It was near midnight when they got there, but a well-dressed middle-aged woman told Juárez that Agustín was out and wasn't expected until late. On the way back to the Colonial,

Juárez apologized for the delay and promised to call for Larry before noon.

Larry waited until Juárez drove off before he called Taveras from a pay phone in the bar. "Make sure you're not followed and meet me somewhere," he said.

Taveras picked the spot, a traffic circle about three-quarters of a mile from the hotel. Larry walked there quickly, crossing the boulevard twice to make sure he wasn't tailed. When Taveras drove up, he let him circle the block once and then motioned for him to pull over.

"What does the name Agustín mean to you?" Larry asked.

"Nothing," Taveras said. He handed Larry a flop-brimmed fishing hat and a pair of dark glasses. Following the same route Juárez had taken earlier, Larry directed him to the town house behind the presidential palace and the house where Agustín hadn't been expected until late. Taveras wrote the name Agustín and both addresses in his notebook.

"I'll check this out, let you know what we come up with," he promised. "I'll tell you one thing, though. That's not Quintana's house."

Larry wasn't surprised. The top people don't often come out in the open. It would be up to him to tie Quintana into it when he met Agustín.

"I'm going to need a test kit," he told Taveras. "And somebody's going to have to show me how to use the damn thing."

Taveras seemed surprised. "You mean you don't know how to test for coke?" he asked incredulously, as though everybody did.

"Test for it?" Larry laughed. "I don't even know what the damn stuff looks like."

A small box wrapped in brown paper was waiting for Larry at the front desk when he came down for breakfast. He ate and went back to his room, where he opened the test kit and checked it out. There was a small corked vial filled almost to the top with lime juice, a pack of matches, and a folded six-inch square of tinfoil. A handwritten note from Taveras explained what to do. It struck him that it didn't take much in the way of equipment to go into business as a drug dealer. He hid the kit at the back of a dresser drawer and went to the lobby.

Three cups of coffee later, Juárez joined him at a table, smiling confidently and pouring out assurances. He was meeting Agustín himself in the afternoon and would make arrangements then for Larry to sample the cocaine. "As soon as I know what time that will be, I will let you know," he said. He offered to buy lunch.

In the hotel dining room Juárez expounded on women and politics and life in general, his fork describing small circles in front of his eyes as he spoke. At one point he looked toward the dining-room door and then looked away, as though there were something there he didn't want to see. Larry glanced back and saw two young Americans standing just inside the door, scanning the dining room. Their hair was long, and they were wearing jeans and hand-woven peasant shirts. One of them spotted Juárez, gestured to his companion, and started for the table, his friend a step behind. Juárez was standing when they got there, trying to hide his discomfort under a mask of geniality. He made introductions, using only first names, and invited the Americans to sit.

"We've been looking all over for you," the older of the two, the one Juárez called Bradley, said. He was short with a square body and heavily muscled arms, no more than twenty-three or twenty-four years old. "We've got to talk," he said urgently, with a slight gesture in Larry's direction that meant he didn't want to talk in front of a stranger.

"Larry is one of us," Juárez assured him.

Bradley studied Larry carefully for a few seconds, unsure. But he was obviously tense and distraught. "What happened to Sidney?" he blurted out.

"Yes, I heard," Juárez said sadly. "An unfortunate accident."

Bradley and the other young American, whose name was Dick Foiles, exchanged glances. "Was it?" Bradley asked brittlely.

Juárez said nothing.

"He had twenty thousand dollars of ours when he left for El Salvador. He was on his way back. So what happened to the coke?"

"It wasn't in the car?"

"No."

Juárez permitted himself a smile. "You know how these things are. The police, you understand. Whenever there is an accident in this part of the world, everything disappears."

Bradley wasn't convinced. "Maybe. But his car was at the bottom of a ravine, his neck was broken, and his ignition switch was off. Funny way to drive, don't you think?"

Juárez checked his watch and stood. "I wouldn't know," he said coldly. "I am not a detective. If you will excuse me, I have an appointment."

As soon as he was gone, the young Americans both turned to Larry and began to bombard him with questions about Juárez. How well did he know him? Did he trust him?

"Any reason I shouldn't?" Larry asked, playing them for information. He already knew plenty of reasons not to trust Juárez and wondered whether the two kilos of cocaine that had disappeared from the late Sidney's wrecked car were now part of the stash he was arranging to buy from Quintana.

Foiles was a year or two younger than Bradley. He had large, almost colorless eyes and a slow way of talking that made him sound decidedly stupid. He said, "We cut the deal with Juárez here and sent the spade kid to pick up the stuff in El Salvador. He made it there but not back. Juárez is the only one here who knew about it besides us."

"That's right," Bradley chimed in. "The whole thing stinks. Now I'm hearing about a lot of his deals that went down the wrong way. People get hurt, ripped off, dead."

"That sounds about right," Larry concurred. He then told them a cleaned-up version of his own adventures in the mountains in which Juárez came out as the heavy.

"So you think he set you up?" Bradley asked.

"Could be," Larry answered with pointed evasiveness.

"Then how come you're still dealing with him?"

"No choice. I've got to get a deal down before I go back. Know anywhere I can get my hands on two hundred pounds of good grass?"

"One shot?" Bradley asked.

"Nope. Two hundred for the first load. If it checks out and everything runs right, we're going to want four hundred pounds a week. Have you got a connection?"

"Sure. Us," Bradley said quickly.

"Us" was a commune of 150 Americans operating out of Panajachel, on the shores of Lake Atitlán, high in the Guatemalan mountains. Bradley described the operation. They called themselves the Young Americans and had drug connections all over Central and South America.

Larry quickly calculated the angles. That night Juárez was going to take him to meet Quintana's man Agustín to set up the cocaine buy that DEA could work into a case against the former chief of national detectives. But the marijuana deal that had originally brought him to Guatemala had fallen through, and unless he could find another to replace it, he would have no case against Dan Gordon for GBI. Now Bradley was offering him a chance to complete his original mission with a bonus thrown in—an inside look at a major smuggling operation.

"What kind of shit do you have?" he asked.

"Mexican, Oaxacan tops, the best you can get."

Larry couldn't afford to take his word for it. He had a vague sense that most Mexican marijuana was green and was generally considered inferior. The exception was Acapulco Gold, and he didn't know whether Bradley was trying to con him. If he was, and if Larry fell for it, Bradley just might start wondering who this supposedly knowledgeable drug buyer really was.

"Look, man," Larry said, bluffing from his socks, "you just don't understand the market in the Southeast. All they want is Colombian shit, Colombian Gold or Colombian Red. If you can get me some Mexican Gold I can pass it off as Colombian. But there's nobody in Georgia that wants two hundred pounds of some green Mexican shit no matter how good you say it is."

Bradley's reaction told him he had been making sense. "I can relate to that," the young American nodded. "No sweat. A dude's gotta have what he can sell. I can get you Gold, all you want. What was your deal with Juárez?"

"Twenty-eight dollars a pound, and he loaded the airplane. Two bucks a gallon for fuel."

"How much fuel?"

"Hundred gallons."

"Oaxaca's closer. You won't need that much. I can get you some dynamite Gold, fifty bucks a pound, but I throw in the fuel and the security. We pay off the locals."

"How about the airfield?"

"Don't sweat it, we'll take care of that," Bradley said smugly. "Whaddya say? Anytime you're ready, you and Foiles drive up to Oaxaca, have a look for yourselves. I've gotta stay here a couple days, but I'll catch up with you soon as I can, and we'll do some dealing."

Larry knew his cover in Guatemala could blow up any minute, as soon as one of the Guatemalan troops from the helicopter raid at the mountain airstrip got word to Juárez that the *gringo* was an agent. When that happened, Larry would have to get out of the country in a hurry. Quintana would be looking for him, and the return flight ticket in his pocket wouldn't be worth toilet paper because the airport would be the first place Quintana would check.

"Tomorrow too soon for you?" Larry asked. "Pick me up at noon."

Agustín was a large, unshaven man with the size, the hair, and the voice of a grizzly bear and a smell to match. The meeting took place in his office just behind the presidential palace. The card players were gone. Juárez,

Spivey, and Agustín killed fifteen minutes with small talk before Agustín indicated it was time to do business by sliding open a desk drawer and removing a heavy plastic bag.

Larry took the kit from his pocket, hung his jacket over the back of his chair, and rolled up his sleeves. He slid the chair to the front of the desk, unwrapped the kit, and spread the contents in front of him. When he opened the plastic bag, it was the first time he had ever seen cocaine, but he did a good job of looking as if he knew what he was doing.

He studied the tiny white powderlike crystals intently for a few seconds, nodded his head almost imperceptibly, then took out his room key and scooped a small quantity of the powder out of the bag. He deposited the cocaine on the three-inch square of aluminum foil and shook the foil to spread the crystals evenly over it. With his right hand he opened a box of matches, lit one with his thumbnail, and held it under the foil. He nodded approvingly when the crystals all turned to ash precisely at the same moment. If the drug had been cut, the impurities wouldn't have oxidized at the same temperature.

He uncorked the small, flat vial of lime juice and scooped a large portion of cocaine from the bag, this time using the plastic tag attached to his key. Holding the vial over the bag to catch spillage, he tapped the drug into the juice, recorked the vial, and shook it vigorously for a few seconds. He held the vial up toward the bulb of Agustín's desk lamp and watched the suspended coke dance in the liquid like a snowstorm in a paperweight, then congeal into a solid, dense mass in the middle of the vial. After replacing the vial on the desk, he wet the tip of his index finger and coated it with a thin crust of powder from the bag. He rubbed the drug against his gum and the inside of his lower lip, then waited until he felt his mouth start to go numb. Finally, he scooped a sample on the edge of his room key and snorted it, inhaling it first in one nostril, then the other. He leaned back in his chair and relaxed, sniffing from time to time as he apparently concentrated on the effect of the drug.

"How much of this do you have?" he asked after a few minutes.

Agustín considered before answering. "A hundred kilos, maybe a little more," he said.

"The price?"

"Ten thousand a kilo."

Larry was deep enough into the role to notice that Agustín quoted the price too fast and could be talked down.

"My people won't go over eight," he said.

Agustín closed his eyes and nodded.

"And considering that Mr. Quintana is who he is," Larry went on, "we will take delivery either in Mexico or the United States."

Agustín smiled, showing black teeth. "Mexico will be fine," he said. "Manuel Robles-Arcía is deputy chief of the *policía nacional* there and a very close personal friend. Get in touch with him, you will have no problems. But you must make the arrangements yourself. We will not be responsible for security."

"Can he be trusted?"

"Indeed, yes. If you are ever in the market for some good brown *heroína,* he will be delighted to accommodate you."

Larry, by this time no longer surprised at the depths of corruption that could be so easily uncovered, took the man's name.

"Provisions will have to be made for my people to satisfy themselves as to the quality of the entire load," he said.

"As with the money," Agustín concurred.

"What about Jefferson Juárez?"

"Señor Juárez is our man, and we will take care of him suitably," Agustín said, with a slight nod in the Indian's direction.

Larry stood up, rolled down his sleeves, and put on his jacket. He carefully repacked his test kit and put it in his pocket. "I don't think it will be necessary for us to meet again. My people will designate a representative to contact Mr. Juárez and make all necessary arrangements."

Taveras picked Larry up at the traffic circle, as he had done the night before, driving completely around it twice to make sure neither of them was being followed. Larry handed him the test kit.

"This squares us," he said. "There's coke in the juice vial, and I brought up Quintana's name at the meeting, so that ties him in. I'll write it up tonight and get it to you tomorrow."

Taveras asked, "And then you're finished?"

"I'm finished right now," Larry snapped. "I told them one of our people would make the rest of the arrangements for the buy. You just tell me who you're going to use, and I'll cut him in with Juárez. Then I'm gone."

Taveras lit a cigarette. "What are you planning to do?" he asked softly.

The last time Larry had let a DEA agent know his plans he had ended up with a busted operation. "I'm not sure," he said, reaching for the door handle.

In the morning Jefferson Juárez walked into the Colonial dining room while Larry was having breakfast. The Indian seemed tense and cold. "I was picked up by the police last night," he said as he pulled out a chair for himself.

Larry didn't believe him. "What for?" he asked.

"They wanted to question me about you, about my association with you."

"I don't get it," Larry said. "That was all taken care of."

"Perhaps not," Juárez said. "They held me for a few hours. Then they let me go. Perhaps it is nothing, but I thought you should know."

He stood up.

"I have to attend to some business," he said stiffly. "I will meet you here at two o'clock."

He left the dining room as if he couldn't get out of there fast enough.

Larry waited just until he was gone, left a few quetzals on the table to pay for breakfast, and hurried to his room. The way it looked, Jefferson Juárez was setting him up to be killed. The story about being picked up and questioned by the police didn't make sense; Juárez was too well connected to get hassled by the locals. But the police probably had been to see him last night—not to question him, but to tip him off that Spivey was an American narcotics agent. The whole drug business was based on deception, double and triple thinking, and Thomas Jefferson Juárez Franclen was a master of it. Larry was new to the game, but he was starting to get the hang of how it worked.

He packed quickly, knowing he couldn't wait around for the meeting with Juárez, knowing he couldn't stay in his hotel room either. It dawned on him that it didn't matter where he went. Quintana was above the law in Guatemala. He or his men could pull off a contract murder in the Plaza de la República and walk away from it; in fact, he already had done it once, for he was reputed to be the man who had gunned down the president of the Senate two years earlier in front of eight bodyguards and seventy-five witnesses. Or so Taveras had said. At the time he said it, it sounded like an exotic and fascinating tale. Now it was turning into a nightmare.

The one thing that was clear was that Bradley and Dick Foiles, the two young Americans, were Larry's only way out. They were supposed to pick him up at twelve, and if he could get two hours of road between him and Guatemala City before Juárez returned at two o'clock, he stood a halfway decent chance of making it to Mexico before anyone figured out where he had gone. But it was still only ten o'clock, and that left a lot of time to kill. For a minute he toyed with the idea of finding somewhere to hide until noon, but thought better of it. If Bradley and Foiles showed up early, he wanted to be able to take advantage of it.

As he waited for the elevator to take him down to the lobby, he suddenly realized that the four-page handwritten investigative summary he had prepared for Taveras was still in his pocket. If he was picked up by Quintana's people, that report was going to make it damned hard to talk his way out of it. Then he figured the hell with it. There was no way he was going to talk his way out in any case. He rode down in the elevator, picked a comfortable chair with a good view of the front door, and tried to look as nonchalant as possible while he waited.

He would have felt more comfortable if he had had his gun with him, but he had left it in Atlanta because he wouldn't have been able to get it past customs into Guatemala. Rationally, he knew a five-shot Smith & Wesson wouldn't do him much good against whatever they would be sending, but when a man is waiting for some professional killers he's never seen, he's more interested in evening the odds than he is in logic.

It took a week for the clock behind the front desk to move around from ten to eleven, another month for it to inch around toward twelve.

Then Bradley and Foiles stepped through the door, ten whole minutes early. Larry crossed quickly to meet them, his suitcase in his hand.

"Look," he said, "I've got a problem. I've got two quetzals in my pocket, and I've got to get the hell out of here. Just lend me enough to cover my hotel bill. I'll pay you back when we get to Mexico."

Bradley looked dubious. "What's the problem?" he asked.

"It's nothing much," Larry lied coolly. "I've got this meeting with Juárez at two o'clock, and I want to be gone when he gets here."

Bradley nodded. "Told you you couldn't trust that guy," he said, not sounding particularly surprised.

He paid the bill, but before they had gone two blocks from the hotel in Dick's tan Chevy van, Dick started to have doubts about driving to Mexico with a guy who was broke. Within a few minutes he had talked himself into making it a matter of principle and said flatly he wouldn't go until Larry got his hands on some money.

Goddammit, Larry wanted to tell him, there's a bunch of guys fixing to kill me, and you're hassling me about a thirty-dollar hotel bill. But when you're asking a man for a ride, it's not a good idea to tell him there are hit men after you.

"All right, stay cool, man," Larry told him. "Drop me by the American Embassy. I'll have the finance officer there call my bank in Atlanta, have them clear a check. Just step on it, will you? I told you, I don't have time to fool around."

Bradley and Foiles stayed in the van while Larry went into the embassy and told the marine guard at the desk he had business with the Drug Enforcement Administration. He gave the name Allen Carter, a code name he had set up with the DEA in Atlanta before he came down to Guatemala. After a few minutes a secretary from Taveras's office came to the front desk and signed Larry in. On the long walk back to the DEA office, which was tucked in a remote corner of the spacious embassy, the secretary told Larry that Taveras was in a staff meeting with the ambassador. Larry said he only wanted to use the phone.

He placed a collect call to the Georgia Bureau of Investigation in Atlanta and got Inspector Peters on the line. "I'm leaving for Mexico right now," he said. "I think I'll be able to set up the grass deal there. But the locals down here relieved me of my cash. So I thought I'd hit the DEA impress fund for three hundred bucks. You'll have to cover it. Just wire the money to Taveras here at the embassy."

"Will do. Just take care of yourself, hear?" Peters said.

"Phil, that's what I'm trying to do," Larry said. "It gets a little hairy sometimes, that's all."

When Larry told the secretary what he wanted and why he was in such a hurry, she got Taveras out of his meeting.

"Three hundred bucks?" Taveras asked incredulously. "What the hell do you need that for?"

"To get out of here. I'm hot. Last night the locals picked up Juárez, probably told him I'm a narc."

Taveras shrugged. "Doesn't make sense," he said. "They wouldn't do that."

He picked up the phone and dialed. "Let me talk to García," he said. "García? Taveras. Any chance your people picked up Jefferson Juárez last night? You did, huh? What was that all about? Yeah, sure. Keep in touch."

He hung up the phone. Before he had a chance to say anything, Larry said, "Thanks a fucking lot. Those clowns are fixing to kill me. Unless they're dumber than I think, you just let them know where I am."

Taveras smiled condescendingly. "You're pretty new at this, aren't you, Spivey? I think you're overreacting. García says the thing with Juárez last night had nothing to do with you. Let's just stay cool. We got a good case here, no sense throwing that all out. Quintana's what we call a Class A violator, as big as they come, baby. He's got over a hundred kilos of coke —worth over seventy million on the street once it's cut back home. Can't walk away from a thing like that."

"I'm not walking, man, I'm running," Larry said. "Here's your goddamn summary. With the shit I gave you last night, it's more than enough to open your case file. You tell me who you're going to use to work Quintana, and I'll cut the dumb son of a bitch in to him. But you can bet your ass I'll do it long distance on the phone. Because I'm telling you the case is dead; they know I'm a narc."

"You're jumping to conclusions."

"You're crazy, but I'm not sticking around here and getting killed just to prove I'm right. Give me the three hundred bucks, and let me get the hell on into Mexico. I already called my boss, and he's wiring the money to you. I've got two guys waiting outside, and they're not going to wait forever."

"Where in Mexico are you going?" Taveras asked almost casually, as though they had all the time in the world to chat.

"Oaxaca."

"Oaxaca!" he exploded. "You can't go to Oaxaca. We had two agents killed there in the last year. There's bandits all over the place, and they're killing people like flies. I can't let you go to Oaxaca. Why don't you stay here and work Quintana for me? I can pay you up to a thousand bucks a week as an informant, and your people at GBI don't even have to know about it."

Larry struggled to control his anger, but he needed the three hundred and knew there was no way to reason with Taveras. He would have to tell him something he wanted to hear.

"Okay," he said grudgingly. "You say I'm overreacting. Tell you what I'll do. Give me the bread, let me go ahead and do the grass deal in Mexico for GBI. If everything stays cool down here, I'll load the plane out, let the guys back home pop it when it lands, and come back here to work Quintana for you."

Taveras considered the offer briefly, then reached for the phone. "Let me just clear it with Charlie Dunhill in Atlanta," he said as he dialed about a dozen numbers.

After a few minutes Dunhill, the top DEA man in Atlanta, came on the line.

"Charlie, Rick Taveras in Guatemala. Look, I got Larry Spivey down here, and we got a problem. He comes down here working for GBI on a pot case, and he gets himself into all kinds of trouble with the locals. So the deal falls through, and now he wants me to give him three hundred bucks so he can split for Oaxaca and try the same thing up there. The thing of it is, he tumbled to this Class A violator, and I'm trying to convince him to stay here, where it's safer, and help me put this guy down. You know how it is with these amateurs. No perspective. He'd rather pop two hundred pounds of grass than a hundred keys of coke. How about you get his boss on the wire while I hold him and tell him we can't condone this fool's going to Mexico? Maybe he can straighten the guy out, either assign him to me so he can work the coke case or order him back to Atlanta."

Taveras hung up the phone. "Your boss is gonna call you and tell you to get on the next flight to Atlanta unless you get your priorities straightened out pretty damn fast," he said smugly.

Larry's first priority was to wrap the phone cord around Taveras's neck, but the phone rang before he had a chance. It was GBI Agent Paul Carter calling for Larry.

"Just got the weirdest call, ol' buddy. What's the trouble down there?" he asked.

"Wish I had time to explain it to you," Larry said. "The bad guys are fixing to kill me, and this asshole DEA agent's doing everything he can to make it easy for them. I need some bread, gotta get outta here to Mexico. Can you wire three hundred to Mexico City, care of Bank of America? I'll check in with you when I get there."

"Will do," Carter said. "I told you you couldn't trust those bastards. Just be careful what you're getting into, hear. And watch your ass, too. Sounds like they're coming at you from both sides."

Larry hung up the phone and looked Taveras in the eye while he considered and rejected a number of choice things he wanted to tell him. But nothing he might have said would have mattered, so he turned on his heel and walked out.

Nine

The customs clerk at Pajapita stirred heavily in his sleep, then subsided. Larry prodded him again. He opened his small, round eyes and grunted unintelligibly in Spanish as he dragged himself to his feet. Larry was prepared to kill him if it proved necessary, but he hoped it wouldn't. In Guatemala even violence moves slowly, as though the lethargic cruelty of the scorpion were the national model. Quintana probably wouldn't get around to alerting the border guards about Spivey until morning.

"If he goes for a phone," Larry whispered urgently to Dick Foiles, "go get in the van and be ready to leave quietly. I'm going to have to kill him."

Foiles went pale. He had made a big concession just driving to Mexico with a guy who couldn't even pay his hotel bill. But he had been unable to resist the combination of Larry's smooth talking and promises of money waiting in Mexico. Now he was just beginning to add it all up, and he realized he had to be ready for trouble. He had no choice, so he nodded his acquiescence.

The clerk shuffled sleepily around behind the immigration counter and held out his hand for the papers Dick Foiles handed toward him. He read them cursorily, stamped the passport and vehicle ownership documents, then passed them back to Foiles, who stepped back from the counter, waiting tensely.

Larry moved up to the waist-high counter and handed the clerk his tourist card, studying the soft, sleepy face for any sign of recognition when he read the name on the card. The clerk was in his late forties, with a slender frame on which he carried too much fat. Larry knew he could take him if he had to.

But it didn't come to that. The clerk stamped the card without really reading it and placed it on a pile with several others. *"Bueno,"* he muttered drowsily, already shuffling back toward the bench on which he had been sleeping when the two Americans interrupted him. Foiles let out his breath slowly and tipped the clerk five quetzals.

"Gracias," the clerk grumbled, slipping back to sleep, but it was Foiles who was grateful. The color was only starting to come back in his face as he slipped in behind the wheel of his van to drive across the long arch-span bridge over the gorge separating Guatemala from Mexico.

Foiles pulled the van off the road on the other side of Tapachula. They were on a broad, flat plain, the star-lit silhouette of the Sierra Madre rising steeply to their right. "Man, I could use something," Foiles said, switching on the interior light and disappearing into the back of the van.

Moving with rapid purposefulness, he disassembled the back bunk until he found what he was looking for, then reassembled it and came back to the driver's seat with a small package wrapped in tinfoil. He set the package on the console between the bucket seats and returned to the back of the van, where he rumbled around through some cabinets until he found a small mirror, a single-edge razor blade, and a plastic drinking straw. Laying these items on the console, he slid into the driver's chair and folded back the tinfoil to reveal a clear plastic bag containing an ounce of cocaine.

Using the razor blade as a scoop, he shoveled less than a tenth of a gram of the powder onto the smooth, polished surface of the mirror, then took five minutes to lay out four pencil-thin lines of powder, each about an inch long. Using the same razor blade, he cut the plastic straw in half and handed half to Larry. "Mind if I go first?" he asked, rising from the driver's chair to kneel on the carpeted floor of the van behind the console.

With one end of the straw in his right nostril, he leaned forward over the cocaine, closed off his left nostril with his forefinger, and neatly inhaled one line of the coke, the straw sliding just above the surface of the mirror. He sniffed two or three times, transferred the straw to his left nostril, and repeated the process.

"Man, that's a rush," he purred with satisfaction. "That's pure *primo,* man, can't get it like that back in the States. Help yourself."

Larry knelt in the spot Foiles vacated for him, curious about what was coming. He had snorted cocaine only once before in his life, in Agustín's office two nights earlier, but got no high from it, the effect washed out in the overpowering surge of adrenaline that had kept him going through his first undercover drug buy. Now he was going to find out what it was all about.

Carefully imitating Dick's deft movements, he snorted both remaining lines, climbed back to the passenger chair, and sniffed several times, waiting for something dramatic to start happening inside his head. He had no idea what to expect, but knew only that the law he was working for put cocaine in the same narcotic category as heroin. That could only mean it was heavy stuff.

A minute passed, but he noticed no effect. He thought of asking Dick how long it took for the drug to work but didn't want to let on that he had never used it before. So he waited a little longer, mildly disappointed. Then suddenly he wasn't disappointed any more. Fuck it, he thought. If it doesn't work, it doesn't work. I'm feeling too good to worry about that.

"Jesus," Foiles said, "I wish we had some chicks. This shit makes me horny."

"I wanna drive," Larry chirped, feeling silly, elated, and restless. He thought it was because they were safely out of Guatemala.

The light from a waxy half-moon was falling along the ground, lying across the road ahead, lighting the blacktop like rich creamed chocolate. Larry was behind the wheel, at the back end of a narrow tunnel of light that moved with him, the twisted road writhing like a gigantic snake under the van. Then the moon dropped below the horizon, and the faint Mexican landscape beyond the edges of the tunnel vanished totally, as though it were no longer there.

The van sped on, swaying around the curves like an ice skater gliding freely over open space, as Larry leaned comfortably into the turns with no sense at all of the speed they were making. Something dark flicked just past his right headlight, and he realized he had almost hit a goat of considerable size. The van swerved, sobering him, and he began to pick out more animal shapes along the side of the road.

"We're gonna have goat stew in a minute," he complained. When he switched the headlights to low beam, he could see the herd on the shoulder better but lost most of the road ahead. "Jesus, why don't you get some decent lights on this thing?"

Dick Foiles reached above Larry's head and threw a switch. Suddenly it was full daylight, the road and the countryside illuminated like a fairground half a mile ahead, a quarter mile to each side.

"What the hell did you just do?" Larry gasped.

"Landing lights." Foiles laughed. "Remember, Bradley told you we didn't need an airfield. Pull over, let me show you something."

Larry eased the van onto the shoulder, and both men climbed out into the predawn darkness, for Foiles had switched off the lights. As they walked to the back of the van, Foiles began to point out the various features of his rolling airport. Two five-gallon jerry cans were mounted on steel brackets and secured by padlocked chains on each side of the van. Two more hung from the rear doors. Lashed to the luggage carrier on the roof were ten more cans in a neat row, a chain running through their handles.

"That's eighty gallons of av gas," Foiles boasted. "Hundred octane."

Larry did the computations quickly. Winter's Cherokee 6 would get six and a half hours' flying time out of eighty gallons, enough to get him twelve hundred miles. With the fuel Larry knew he would be carrying in his fuel cell, these eighty gallons would enable him to make it all the way back to Georgia nonstop.

Foiles hopped up onto one of the jerry cans on the back and called for Larry to climb up on the other. "Take a look up here," he said, pointing to a two-foot square of plywood bolted to the roof. A large pipe nut jutted up exactly in the middle of the small platform. "Know what that is?"

"I suppose you're gonna tell me it's a landing pad."

"Not quite. But close," Foiles grinned. He hopped down and opened the sliding door on the passenger side of the van. Larry followed him inside. From a large drawer the young drug smuggler removed a small square platform on which was mounted a portable weather station— anemometer, wind sock, altimeter, thermometer, and barometer. The bottom of the platform was fitted with a coupling to bolt it directly to the matching platform on the roof, which was already wired to receive it. The lines led down through the pipe to an instrument panel mounted cleverly in a small top cabinet over the sink. From there he could read out wind speed, wind direction, altitude, temperature, and barometric pressure. With a compass to give him a runway heading, the weather equipment, the landing lights, and a CB radio to communicate the information to an aircraft, he had the capability of turning any Mexican road into a reasonably safe airport complete with refueling facilities.

"There's a straight stretch of road outside Oaxaca with no power lines on either side. I'll park this baby on the downwind end, and we can have your boy refueled, loaded with grass, and on his way home so fucking fast he won't even have to shut his engine down. We don't even need security. When he comes in, he eyeballs the road ten miles each way. If there's anyone coming, he sees them. If not, he's got a cool ten minutes, and by then he's on his way home."

Larry drove on, following the flat coastal plain to Santo Domingo, an easy two hundred miles northwest of Tapachula, the van flying as the sun came up, both men flying even higher, with coke stops every half hour. To their right the Sierra Madre rose austerely, a mellow brown against the horizon, throbbing in the intensifying heat as the sun climbed quickly. Although he was as stoned as Foiles, Larry nevertheless managed to pump the young smuggler for information.

Foiles boasted about a connection to a cocaine lab in Peru, limitless contacts for marijuana and heroin in Oaxaca. He talked about himself, too. The son of a California physician, he had drifted south of the border after dropping out of medical school three years earlier. His wanderings finally took him to Panajachel, where he was inducted into the ways of the drug-smuggling commune. He didn't think he would ever go back. His only remaining ambition was to get together enough money to make a huge score out of the Peruvian lab. Like a whore who dreams of retiring someday, he didn't know what he would do then.

At Santo Domingo the Pan American Highway cut inland, climbing into the Sierras toward Oaxaca. The city itself was a Mexican village, multiplied a few score times until it had a population of about thirty thousand. By the time the van got there early in the afternoon Foiles was driving again. He let Larry off in front of the ornate five-tiered gazebo in the center of the *zócalo,* the town's main plaza, and told him to kill an hour or two. Then he drove off to visit the local jail on the outskirts of the city, as he did each time he hit town. There he would talk with the American prisoners, especially the ones arrested since the last time he had been in Oaxaca. From them he would learn where the heat was, what kind of vehicles the *federales* were driving, who could be trusted, who had sold them out, where the action was.

He picked Larry up around four o'clock and they drove to La Higuera, a shady walled-in campground just north of the city. For three dollars a night you got a parking space next to a small concrete patio, electrical and sewage hookups to your van, and the use of a common shower and toilet facilities. For a few pesos extra, Indian girls in the neighborhood would do your laundry.

Foiles hooked up at one of the last two vacancies in the camp. He and Larry cleaned up, ate sandwiches in the van, and toured the grounds. In all, there were about twenty vehicles in the camp, mostly trailers and vans, with a few automobiles next to pitched tents. Larry quickly realized there wasn't a tourist in the lot. In the evening, after the sun went down, La Higuera turned into a smugglers' jamboree. Everyone gathered around an immense motor home in the center of the park, where the most prosperous impresario in the vicinity held court around a bright campfire that danced under the stunted trees. The sweet smell of the burning wood mixed with the spiced pungency of marijuana, as joints and Thai sticks made their way from hand to hand. The talk was all drugs.

"Man, I stay clear of Iguala. Too fucking hot."

"*Federales?*"

"Shit no, bandits."

"That shit Felipe gave me was bad, man. Son of a bitch foxed me with a sample."

"Fuck Felipe. Tol' him last year if he didn't get right I do my business with José. Ain't seen him since."

"That's cool, I like that."

"No, man, no, that purple van's *federales*. Yeah, right, right, the one with the fucking Last Supper on the side. For real, man. They popped Brian out of it last week."

"Shit, man, Dallas, everyone always says Dallas. I can't get a decent price in fucking Dallas, can't move this shit at all. Last time up I dumped my whole load in Houston. Fuck Dallas."

Larry tried to take it all in, learning names quickly, trying to match names and faces with the vehicles to which they belonged, memorizing the license numbers of as many campers and vans as he could. After a few hours, his mind was so cluttered with mnemonic clues he had to sneak off to the bathroom, where he could write down everything he had learned on a tiny slip of paper he tucked into his wallet. Then he went back for more. He made several more trips to the toilet, fleshing out his miniature file with more names, more numbers, more bits of physical description.

In the morning Foiles drove him into town for meetings with the local marijuana growers. The first stop was an adobe hotel in the center of town, where a middle-aged Mexican with a .45 automatic showing under his shirt met them in the restaurant. They talked over lunch, then went around to the back of the hotel, where the grower's Ford Ranger was parked. He opened a cardboard whiskey box, removed some folded newspapers spread over the top, and proceeded to show his wares. The box contained about two dozen tightly lashed marijuana tops, each approximately eighteen inches long, not unlike the tops of tomato plants. They were a pale and faded sea green in color.

"Not green," Larry said, shaking his head. "Can't take green. Gotta have Gold."

The grower snorted contemptuously. "This is Limón," he protested. "The best."

"Can't help you. I got a buyer that's gotta have Gold. You got anything else?"

"Not this time of the year. Later we plant the poppies, we have *heroína* for you. Now it is the time for the marijuana."

Larry and Foiles left the grower standing by his truck. In the van on their way to the next meeting, Foiles told Larry he was crazy. "That's good-smoking shit, man," he groaned. "Whaddya gotta have the Gold for? It don't even smoke as good."

Larry shrugged, not unaware of the irony. It didn't matter in the least how the stuff smoked since it was destined for a GBI incinerator. But Dan Gordon had insisted on Gold, and Larry felt he had to have it. He knew McClellan would be flying down with Winter to pick up the load and would probably reject it if it wasn't what Gordon ordered.

The second grower had a plush room in a modern hotel on a hill overlooking Oaxaca. The story was the same; only this time the grower wore two automatics at his belt and the plants were Sesamia instead of Limón. Foiles explained rapturously that Sesamia was a seedless hybrid in which the THC, the narcotic in the plant, remained in the plant itself instead of being distributed in the seeds. "It's dynamite shit," he purred.

But it was green. Larry thanked the grower, and they left.

The same ritual was enacted three more times, once in the middle of the marketplace below the town square. With each rejection, Foiles became more frantic, his speech more obscene. "You fucking fussy son of a bitch, this whole trip is un-fucking-real," he snapped. "You still owe me thirty fucking bucks for the goddamned hotel in Guatemala, and I paid for the fucking gas all the way up, the fucking sandwiches. You gonna deal or ain't you?"

Larry ran out of patience. "Listen, bastard, I told you I had to have Gold before we left," he said, trying to use language he thought Foiles would understand. "You said you could get it. Don't come down on my head because you can't do what you said you could."

Foiles got the point. "Aw, shit," he said, "I introduced you to the heaviest cats I know, and they ain't got what you need. I dunno. Let's go back to the trailer park and honk some coke, get our heads straightened out. We'll figure out something."

La Higuera that night was a replay of the night before, except that the campfire was now the scene of an elaborate barbecue hosted by the owner of a large motor home. The word was out he would be supplying everyone with Thai sticks for dessert. Larry shook his head in disbelief. Here was a man—he turned out to be a retired dentist—who actually smuggled exotic strains of marijuana *into* Mexico so he could pass out samples of his favorite smoke to his friends in Oaxaca, the marijuana capital of the Western world.

Probably no group of comparable entrepreneurs in any other line of work is as boastful as small-time drug smugglers, and Larry's dossier was expanded to include the locations of the cleverly concealed hidden compartments in many of the vehicles, the quantities they would be carrying, and where they would be crossing the border into the States. At one point Foiles excused himself and was gone a little over an hour. When he got back, he told Larry he had driven into Oaxaca to call Bradley, who had been left behind in Guatemala.

"Bradley knows some heavier dudes than I do," he reported to Larry when he got back. "He says sit tight, he'll come up in a couple of days, and if he can't find you some fucking Gold, then there's no such animal."

"Sounds cool," Larry agreed. He suggested that since there was no business to be done until Bradley arrived, he could take advantage of the time by flying up to Mexico City, where he would be able to get some money to pay his debts when he got back to Oaxaca.

The Aeromexico flight landed at Mexico City's mile-high airport shortly after ten o'clock. Larry turned in his Guatemala ticket for a cash refund at the Eastern Airlines counter and checked into the Howard Johnson motel across the broad highwaylike boulevard from the airport. For the first time since he had left Guatemala City he had cash in his pocket.

From his room he called the American Embassy and asked for the deputy director of the Drug Enforcement Administration, the highest-ranking DEA officer in Mexico and the head of all DEA operations in Latin America. When he got Ray Basch on the line, he identified himself and made an appointment for two o'clock that afternoon.

With three hours to kill before his meeting with Basch, Larry went downstairs to the restaurant and ate the first decent meal he had had in several days. The creak of the dessert cart the waitress wheeled to his table when he had finished eating was as refreshing as a hot shower, the sight of the tiered ranks of custards, cakes, soufflés, and pies like a reminder of civilization at some remote colonial outpost. As he made his way through two helpings of chocolate mousse, he thought he understood why the British in India had always dressed for dinner.

In the motel gift shop he bought a small box of stationery and went back to his room, where he spread out the crimped notes he had made at La Higuera and proceeded to write up a complete investigative summary, including all the information he had on the growers he met in Oaxaca as well as the smugglers at the trailer park.

A few minutes before his appointment, Larry got out of a cab in front of the American Embassy on the Paseo de la Reforma. The civilian guards at the wrought-iron gate waved him through to a checkpoint in the portico under the building, where he stated his business to a receptionist in a bulletproof teller's enclosure. She called upstairs to the DEA office, then wrote out a pass. A marine guard on the other side of the foyer checked the pass, logged him in, and directed him to the elevator, giving him a receipt for the canvas airline bag he was carrying. Larry took his five-page investigative summary from the bag before turning it over and rode up to the fourth floor.

The DEA offices were tucked in a corner of the building behind a solid wood door secured by a push-button combination lock. Larry pushed the buzzer on the doorjamb, and a pretty Mexican-American receptionist in a pantsuit let him in.

"Allen Carter to see Ray Basch," Larry said, using the code name he had told Basch he would be using. GBI had warned him never to contact any law enforcement agency using his real name in order to prevent his identity as an undercover agent from leaking back to drug dealers he was investigating.

After a ten-minute wait, a middle-aged woman called for him and led him through a maze of corridors, punching the combination locks on every door they passed along the way. Basch's office was immense, with a six-foot desk by the far wall and a living-room-sized sitting area at the opposite end. The walls were covered with plaques, photographs, diplomas, awards, citations, and other memorabilia of a lifetime in law enforcement. Basch himself was of medium build, in his mid-fifties but solid as a rock, with coal black hair and quick, searching eyes. He came around from behind his desk to shake Larry's hand and lead him to the sofa, then took a seat in an easy chair directly facing it.

It took Larry half an hour to run down the status of his investigation to date, going all the way back to his departure from Atlanta two weeks earlier.

"It sounds like you're really on to something," Basch said warmly. "Where do we go from here?"

"Well, sir," Larry said, choosing his words carefully, "I'm in something of a bind. My only official interest is that one planeload of grass. I'd like to load it out and let our guys back home pop it when it lands in Georgia. That's the reason GBI sent me down, and obviously it's my first priority. But I realize the situation has escalated somewhat since I've been here. Mr. Quintana in Guatemala seems to be a major violator, and he referred me to a man named Robles-Arcía, a deputy chief in the Mexican police who apparently deals heroin. I realize Quintana and Robles-Arcía are much more important than my case in Georgia, and I feel an obligation not to walk away without doing anything about them. I'm willing to do whatever has to be done, and I'm sure my boss in Georgia feels the same way."

"I should hope so," Basch said, smiling benignly.

Larry nodded, encouraged to speak frankly. "Well, yes," he said. "But that's where the problems come in. We have a very solid federal liaison in Georgia. Customs is working that case with us; their air branch is going to surveil the aircraft all the way down and all the way back. But so far we haven't been getting the same sort of cooperation from DEA."

Basch's eyebrows went up, but he said nothing.

Larry went on to explain how Taveras had stepped all over the investigation, forcing Larry out of Guatemala. "I don't know if anything can be salvaged there," he said. "I suspect Quintana knows who I am, but I don't know for sure. And I don't know if he's already warned Robles-Arcía about me."

"Are you willing to find out, young man?" Basch asked. It didn't seem he meant it to sound like a dare, but it came out that way.

"Yes, I am, sir," Larry answered without hesitation. "If your people here can cover me while I go ahead with the grass thing for GBI, I'll play the string out as far as it goes with Quintana and Robles-Arcía. If I'm already burned, I'll find out soon enough."

Basch rose from his chair and crossed to the telephone on the sideboard near his desk. "Get me Taveras in Guatemala City," he told his secretary. He hung up the phone and turned to Larry. "Would you consider working for us on a full-time basis?" he asked. "We could use some men like you down here."

Larry smiled appreciatively. "Thanks," he said. "But I've already got a job."

While the call to Guatemala City was being put through, Larry handed Basch his report on the Oaxaca trailer camp. When the secretary called back, Basch asked her to step into the office. He kept Taveras on hold while he instructed her to type up copies of the report immediately, so Larry could sign them before he left the embassy. Then he punched up the lighted button on his phone.

"Taveras, this is Ray Basch. You had a man named Larry Spivey down there a few days ago. No, I don't want to hear an explanation. I want a full report. I want it truthful and complete, and I want it on my desk tomorrow. Send it by pouch."

Apparently Taveras said something on the other end of the line, but Basch cut him off. "No," he said sternly. "Don't do a thing, don't make a single move without instructions from me. You'll be hearing from me as soon as I've seen your report."

He hung up the phone. "Do you mind if I call your boss and get this all squared away with him?" he asked Larry.

After the way he had been jerked around by Taveras, Larry was relieved to be dealing with someone who wanted things done the right way.

Basch's call to Atlanta was brief and to the point. He laid out the situation for Phil Peters, told him he would be covering Larry during the marijuana deal, and asked Peters's permission to let Larry work Quintana and Robles-Arcía for the DEA. "You've got a good man here," he said graciously.

The conversation ended on an amiable note. Then Basch called the attorney general of Mexico, as he was required to do by treaty, and reported the presence of an undercover agent who would be working under the code name Allen Carter. He did not tell the attorney general Larry's real name.

"All right," he said, hanging up the phone and moving in behind his desk. "That takes care of all the details. Now how do you want to handle this thing?"

Larry shrugged, still too new at the double-agent business to know any other way than straight ahead. "I'll call Robles-Arcía, set up a meeting, and see what happens," he said. "Can you give me backup?"

Basch shook his head and studied his blotter a few seconds before answering. "Yes and no," he said. "We're here at the pleasure of the Mexican government, you understand. We work very closely with them. Robles-Arcía and his men know all my men, so I'll leave that decision up to you. I can give you a backup, but if they're spotted, it's going to blow the deal."

"No. Thanks anyway," Larry said. "If that's the way it is, I'd rather go in alone. Jesus, though, I sure wish I had a gun."

"Do you mean to tell me you are unarmed?" Basch asked incredulously.

"Yes, sir, that's exactly what I mean."

"Well, that's something we can handle," Basch assured him, reaching for his phone. "Nancy, call Finance, have them send up three hundred dollars in cash and a voucher made out to me. Then call Don and have him bring up a Walther PPK, a box of ammo, and an extra clip. Tell him I'll sign for it. And bring in Mr. Spivey's summary."

He hung up the phone and turned to Larry. "If I may offer some advice," he said, adopting a fatherly tone, "I suggest you arrange to meet Robles-Arcía in a public place. And even then, I don't have to remind you how powerful he is. If you have any indication at all that the situation isn't right, I want you to promise me you'll get the hell out. We don't want you hurt."

Larry smiled at the quaint use of the word *hurt*. He had heard it before; it was the word the bosses always used. But undercover agents never get hurt. Killed maybe, but never hurt.

While they waited for the secretary, Larry outlined his strategy to Basch, spelling out what he wanted to accomplish at his first meeting with Robles-Arcía and offering suggestions on how the DEA should handle the Quintana situation in Guatemala.

When Nancy came in, Larry proofread and approved the summary while Basch signed for the money and the snub-nosed .380 automatic. The deputy director then snapped a crisp string of orders. "Make two copies of this, and log it in. Put Mr. Spivey's original in the burn bag. File the ribbon copy under 'Special Operations, Code Name Spiggott.' Classification Top Secret. I want one copy to go to the Georgia Bureau of Investigation; I'll dictate a letter this afternoon to go with it. Forward the other copy to our Intelligence Section with instructions to pass it on to Customs at the border for immediate action. Some of these people are probably heading their way already."

From his hotel room Larry dialed the number Agustín had given him. It was a straight line direct to the deputy chief of the Mexican national police. Larry gave his name and said a mutual friend in Guatemala had suggested they get together.

"About a legal matter, perhaps?" Robles-Arcía asked guardedly.

"Something like that."

They agreed to meet in the restaurant of Larry's hotel at five o'clock that afternoon.

Robles-Arcía arrived at the hotel fifteen minutes early. When he walked into the restaurant, Larry was already there, seated at a table by the window, from which he had been able to watch the deputy chief drive up. The gun he had borrowed from the embassy was tucked in his belt, but he didn't expect any trouble. Robles-Arcía had come alone.

Short and stocky, with well-greased black hair and an oily mustache, he was wearing a dark suit and a heavily starched shirt that looked as if it had been worn for two or three days, the collar points standing stiffly out from his neck. He had small, deceptive eyes. The hostess brought him to Larry's table.

Over drinks—tequila for the Mexican, scotch and soda for the American—the two men spent twenty minutes in the courtly ritual of drug dealers feeling each other out, neither willing to make the first explicit statement. Robles-Arcía hinted he knew the identity of Larry's contact, the "mutual friend" Larry had mentioned on the phone; Larry hinted a confirmation, but no names were mentioned. When they were ready to talk business, it was Robles-Arcía who gave the signal. "How can I be of assistance to you?" he asked.

"I represent a small group that has been doing business with our mutual friend," Larry said, slipping into the coded language always used on such occasions. "Since he cannot meet all our needs, he has suggested that perhaps you could help us with an item he is unable to supply."

The deputy chief took a long swallow of tequila and grunted for Larry to go on.

"Brown sugar," Larry said. Unlike heroin from French or Southeast Asian labs, Mexican heroin is brown, the color and consistency of potted earth.

Robles-Arcía smiled. "Perhaps I can be of some small assistance to you," he said. "From time to time I am in a position to make such arrangements. Is your need immediate?"

"Immediate and ongoing. We are interested in establishing a permanent relationship."

Robles-Arcía nodded with satisfaction. "I see," he said pleasantly. His eyes wandered restlessly around the dining room as he spoke, rarely lighting anywhere. "What quantities are you considering?"

"That depends upon the price."

"Perhaps so. Perhaps the price depends upon the quantity." He smiled, showing gold teeth.

Larry ignored the smile and switched to a hard, businesslike tone. "We are not interested in small quantities," he said. "How much can you do?"

Robles-Arcía shrugged evasively. "I can get you several kilos. Perhaps I misunderstood. You are ready now?"

Larry realized he had gone a little too far. Robles-Arcía was not ready to talk specifics yet, and Larry had come on too strong, pushing him for a commitment. "How much time will you need?" he asked, skirting the issue.

"Three days."

"That will be fine. It will take me a few days to make the arrangements on my end. I have some other business to take care of first. I will be getting in touch with you shortly."

The deputy chief understood the meeting was over. He rose from the table and drew a printed business card from his billfold. He wrote a telephone number on it and handed it to Larry. "You can reach me in the evenings at this number. I would prefer that it be done that way."

Larry waited at the table until he saw Robles-Arcía drive off, then signed for the drinks and returned to his room, satisfied that his preliminary meeting with the deputy chief had accomplished its purpose. He still had some loose ends to tie up about the marijuana deal for GBI, so he placed a call to Gus McClellan in Atlanta. It took five minutes for the operator to make the connection.

"Gus? Larry."

"Where the fuck are you, man?"

"Mexico. Your little Indian friend sold us out, got us rousted out of the fucking jungle. It was all I could do to get my ass out of the country. But I got some contacts in Mexico now; we can do it from here."

"The hell we can," McClellan snapped back. "Everything came apart up here. I can't explain it on the phone. We got a whole new deal. Get your ass back up here, we gotta talk."

McClellan was giving Larry a difficult choice. He was tempted to stay in Mexico and work the heroin-dealing deputy police chief for the DEA. But his first loyalty was still to the agency that had sent him on his mission, and he knew that if there was any chance of salvaging the case against Dan Gordon, he wouldn't be able to work it out on the phone. So he cursed under his breath and told McClellan he would be on the first Eastern Airlines flight out of Mexico City in the morning. Then he hung up the phone and called the American Embassy. The switchboard operator there tracked Ray Basch to a restaurant and took Larry's number. Two minutes later Basch called back.

"How'd it go?"

"Perfect, but I've got a problem. Our boy is ready to go, says he'll need three days from the time we strike a deal. But I just talked to the bad guys in Atlanta. Something's come unglued up there, and I've got to go back and straighten it out."

"Can't it wait?"

"I don't think so. But whatever it is, I think I can get it back on the tracks pretty quick."

"You're the boss," Basch said, making an effort to hide his disappointment. "What do you want us to do?"

"Nothing you can do," Larry commiserated. "Just put the whole thing on hold. I'll be back as soon as I can."

"When are you leaving?"

"First thing in the morning."

"All right," Basch said. "Good luck. I'll send someone by your room to pick up the equipment. Keep us posted. And don't forget, we're counting on you."

"Yes, sir," Larry said crisply, grateful for the compliment and for Basch's tact in not trying to force the DEA's priorities on him. He placed a call to Inspector Peters at home in Atlanta and told him McClellan would be meeting his flight when it arrived in the morning. "I'll report in as soon as I get through with him."

He hung up the phone and packed his suitcase. At eight o'clock an agent knocked on his door and said he had come to pick up a package for Mr. Basch. Larry gave him the empty Walther, both clips, and the box of ammunition. Then he went down to the bar to kill the evening, hoping he would get lucky.

He didn't.

Ten

Mike Eason was waiting in the sealed-off customs area when Larry's flight landed in Atlanta. He seemed nervous.

"Your friends are waiting for you outside," he said. "They'll probably want to take you somewhere. We've got the whole airport under surveillance, and we'll be right behind you."

Larry asked if GBI wanted him to wear a wire.

"I don't think so," Eason mumbled. "A little too risky. We've been watching them since you left, and lately they've been acting kinda strange."

"Whaddya mean strange?"

"I don't know, just strange. Like a little skittish maybe. Where does the thing stand now anyway?"

Larry didn't know. All he knew was that McClellan told him the deal had fallen through and he should get back to Atlanta. "I'll know better after I've talked to them. Who's here? Gordon?"

"No. Just McClellan and Winter. They're waiting on the other side of that door. Look, don't worry. We've even got Clardy in a Highway Patrol chopper. If they take you outta the airport, he's gonna tail you in case they get any funny ideas."

"Is that what it looks like?" Larry asked.

Eason shrugged.

Larry grabbed his suitcase from the inspection counter and pushed through the windowless swinging doors to the small waiting area outside.

McClellan and Winter came up to meet him, Gus swinging in on his left, Jack on his right. Walking three abreast, they headed down the long corridor to the front of the terminal.

As they passed through the broad open foyer at the center of the terminal, two men Larry had never seen before fell into place alongside Gus and Jack. One was blond, over six feet; the other, shorter and darker. Neither said anything. McClellan and Winter walked on, keeping Larry between them, crossing quickly through the parking area to a black Oldsmobile Toronado. McClellan slid in behind the wheel, Winter took the passenger seat, and Larry found himself in the back between the two scowling strangers. The Olds slipped out onto the expressway heading north into the city.

"What the hell's going on?" Larry demanded.

For a long time no one answered. Then McClellan said, "We've been followed."

"Whaddya mean?" Larry asked. He thought McClellan had picked up the tail Eason put on him at the airport.

"Last week, when we were fixing to fly down to Guatemala, we had the airplane over at Fairburn, checking it out and installing the fuel cell," Winter answered. "We got through about two in the morning, and Gus and I flew the thing over to Peachtree to get my van and go home. We're not airborne but two minutes when approach control calls and asks my destination. Now we were way outside the terminal control area, so I knew that hadda be hokey. Someone was just keepin' tabs on us. Then we land and tie down and get some stuff outta the plane. By then it's drizzling rain, right? And Gus looks up on the hill and he thinks he sees this guy up there. I tried to tell him it's just a bush, but then it gets up and walks away. So we jump in the van and tear ass around the hill, and there's a Pontiac wheeling outta there so fucking fast there's no way we can get near him. We got the tag, though, and I gave the number to airport security. They ran it, and it came back not on file, which has gotta mean cops. The security guy gives me some line of bullshit that they've had a lot of stuff stolen around the airport and I'm supposed to think it's connected to that. But I figure they were there watching us, whaddya think?"

"I don't know, could be," Larry said evasively. He knew the Pontiac was Agent Paul Carter's car. "Is that how come you never showed up?"

"Yeah, more or less. See, the thing of it was there was this tropical depression over the whole fucking Gulf, so we were kinda holed up waiting for that to clear. And then when this thing happens, Gus and I go see

Gordon, and we lay it out for him, tell him we're being tailed and the weather's all screwed up and all that. And he blows a gasket. Says he's already out three and a half grand, what with what he gave you and all, and he's got another seven and a half grand tied up for the deal, and we just better fly down there and get his shit or he's gonna have to explain to his associates about us. Which means Harrel does a number on our heads, right?"

"See, the thing is Gordon doesn't give a damn if we get busted," McClellan cut in, whining. "He doesn't want to know anything about anything. If we make it, he gets his grass. And if we get popped, he never heard of us."

Larry nodded sympathetically. "How did you leave it with him?" he asked.

Winter smiled, the first sign of friendliness Larry had seen. "That's just what we did, we left it with him," he said. "Ray and Tony here are friends of mine, sorry I didn't introduce you, I was kinda wound up. Ray, Tony, this is Larry."

The three men in the back seat shook hands awkwardly. The menacing looks Ray and Tony had deliberately adopted in order to impress Larry dropped like masks, and their faces wore slightly sheepish expressions.

"And I knew they were kinda interested in getting into the business," Winter went on without missing a beat. "So Gus and I told them the whole story, told them, y'know, you're sittin' down in Guatemala with all the grass in the world just waitin' for somebody to fly down and pick it up. So they got up some money, and we paid Gordon back every cent he put up. We got enough left over to do the deal."

Ray, the tall, husky one with the blond hair, said, "I took out a second mortgage on my house."

Tony said, "I cosigned the note."

Larry wondered what kinds of idiots take out second mortgages in order to get into an amateur smuggling operation that was already under police surveillance. He felt sorry for the whole lot of them.

As Larry filled them in on Mexico, he realized that Eason, Clardy, and the others tailing him at that moment had no way of knowing he was in no danger from the men in the car with him. To the agents, it probably looked as if he were being taken into the woods north of town to be shot. What amused Larry was that his GBI partners must have known Winter and McClellan had spotted them that night at the Peachtree-DeKalb Airport, and they had been too embarrassed about blowing the tail to tell him about it. So if they were sweating it out now, he figured they had at least that much aggravation coming.

Winter pulled the Olds into the parking lot of a drive-in restaurant and went inside for containers of coffee. The five men talked for almost an hour, mostly about where they would go from there. Larry answered evasively, for in the back of his mind he was already toying with the possibility of dropping Winter and McClellan. They had tried their hands at drug smuggling and found it a lot more complicated than they had expected. Maybe they had learned their lessons and would go back to whatever it was they had been doing before. They were small fish, and this was his chance to throw them back into the pond. If they swam into somebody else's net, they'd have no one to blame but themselves. He told Gus and Jack he would get back in touch with them in a day or two.

"They're not smugglers," Larry said firmly, leaning forward, his elbows on the conference table. "They want to be, they're trying to be; but they've got their shit scattered over ten city blocks, and I can't see they're ever going to get their act together. No sense wasting my time and our resources to turn them into what they're not so we can bust 'em."

Inspector Peters was stroking his chin. "You never did feel right about working them, did you?" he asked insightfully, the faintest trace of grudging admiration in his voice.

"That's not the point," Larry protested. "I'll keep an eye on them. If they look like they're getting close to anything, we'll move on them. But for now they've served their purpose. They got me in with Gordon. If I play it right, I can swing it around so I go to work for him. He's the one that's worth having."

"You already are working for Gordon," George Clardy said. "What do you have in mind?"

Larry chose his words carefully. "Right now I'm on the outside. He was backing us and selling for us. I'm talking about getting inside his organization."

Phil Peters always had the last word at all strategy sessions of the Controlled Substances Section. "If you can do it, Larry," he said.

An hour later Larry was standing over the slender red-headed receptionist in Dan Gordon's insurance office. "No, I don't have an appointment," he told her firmly. "He'll see me."

The shock in Gordon's voice was clear even through the intercom. He wasn't used to seeing associates from his illegal business empire at the office. "Have him wait. I'll be with him in a minute."

Larry took a magazine from the chrome-and-glass table and sat on the chrome-and-leather couch to wait. Barely a minute passed before the door to Gordon's office opened and Gordon ushered out a client whose face showed his puzzlement at the sudden bum's rush. Not until the elevator doors closed on the client did Gordon turn to Larry, his face now a perfectly composed mask of geniality.

"Mr. Spivey, what a pleasant surprise. I'm sorry I had to keep you waiting."

He held open the office door, and Larry stepped through. "No calls, Linda," Gordon said, closing the door firmly.

He crossed to his desk and turned on Larry, his voice suddenly venomous. "What's the idea? I told you never to come here," he hissed.

"That was before you sent me into a setup," Larry shot back belligerently.

Gordon could hardly believe his ears. "I sent you into a setup? What setup? I didn't send you anywhere," he spluttered, not quite sure what line he should take.

Larry was doing a perfect imitation of controlled rage. "Look, from day one I told those two jackasses I didn't want to get mixed up in this. But when you said it was okay, I figured that was good enough for me. I figured a guy like you was supposed to know what he was doing. Maybe that was my mistake."

Gordon's curiosity sucked him in. "What happened?"

As tersely as he could, Larry ran through the situation as it had unfolded in Guatemala, leaving out all references to the DEA and portraying Jefferson Juárez as a double agent working for the Guatemalan police. He told about his escape to Mexico with Guatemalan authorities hot on his trail. "Next time you want to send anyone to do your work, you make sure you've got a pretty damn good idea where it's gonna come out."

Gordon pursed his mouth and rubbed the fingertips of his right hand over the fingertips of his left. He couldn't help being impressed with the intrepidity of a man who could walk into a setup and walk out the other side.

"I didn't know," he apologized. "I had no way of knowing. Your friends had been down there, at least McClellan had. He said the man was okay."

Larry cut him off. "Face it, you didn't give a shit. It was my ass on the line down there, not yours."

"Perhaps," Gordon shrugged urbanely. "I didn't make the world, those are the rules. I look after my own people, but that's all I can do. I could use a good man, though."

"No fucking way. I'm tired of dealing with amateurs."

Gordon bit his lip. "I assure you we are not amateurs. This may be your first introduction to the business, but it is not mine. Accidents happen. But I wouldn't be here today if I wasn't pretty good at making sure they only happen to other people. If you think about what you just told me, you'll see that's true."

"I don't doubt it. But there's no way I can go back down there. I'm hot."

"No, no, of course not," Gordon purred ingratiatingly. "I have something more interesting in mind. I think we can forget about this south-of-the-border stuff. There are better ways. Back when McClellan first came to me, he said he already had been down to Guatemala with another man, a pilot who works out of Roanoke. This pilot's pretty well connected, from the way McClellan told it, and McClellan was supposed to do the deal with his Virginia organization. But for some reason or other the thing fell through. McClellan said the pilot didn't know what he was doing, and I believed him. The way it looks now, we just backed the wrong horse. What do you think?"

"I think *you* backed the wrong horse. Kind of hard to go double or nothing when you're losing, though, isn't it?"

Gordon actually laughed, a short, unpleasant laugh that had absolutely no humor in it. "Oh, I didn't lose anything," he said. "I'm not a loser, Larry. You ought to know that by now. I think it's worth another try. I think you ought to find out that pilot's name from McClellan, get in touch with him, see what that Virginia organization is. There might be some people we can work with up there. It always pays to keep your horizons open."

Larry stood up and stretched his hand toward Gordon. "It's definitely worth looking into," he said. "If there's anything there, I think we can do business."

He took a cab from Gordon's office, stopping a few blocks away to call GBI from a pay phone. He got Mike Eason on the line.

"How about you buying me a drink somewhere?" he asked. "I just got myself a job."

Gus McClellan whined, whimpered, and complained. He couldn't understand why Larry wanted the pilot's name. "I told you, the guy was an asshole; you don't wanna get mixed up with him," Gus groaned petulantly.

They were sitting in the litter-strewn living room of the $75,000 ranch house Gus and his wife Jo had turned into an instant slum. Larry took a long sip of beer from the can McClellan handed him.

"I don't want to get mixed up with him," Larry told him. "Somebody gave me a name, I want to know if this is the same guy."

"You tell me the name, I'll tell you if it's the guy."

"Don't play games, Gus."

"You're still gonna do that deal with us, aren't you, Larry?" He sounded like a kid afraid he wasn't going to be taken to the zoo.

"Sure, Gus. The pilot?"

"Sorenson. Roger Sorenson. But you're not gonna do a deal with him, are you, Larry?"

"See you around, Gus."

"I talked to Ray and Tony; they're expecting to hear from you in a couple of days."

"Sure, Gus. See you around."

From earlier conversations with McClellan, Larry already knew that the pilot operated out of Roanoke and flew a Cessna Skymaster. At GBI headquarters he got on the WATS line and started calling all the airfields in the Roanoke area. At the sixth field he called he got a line boy at one of the fixed base operations who knew Sorenson. "Yeah, he flies out of here a lot, but he don't keep the plane here," the line boy said.

"Do you know where he keeps it?"

"Gee, y'know, like I don't really know who you are, mister. You a cop or something?"

"Nothing that interesting. I didn't know there was any reason the cops would be looking for him."

There was an embarrassed silence that told Larry something about Sorenson's reputation. If a pilot is flying to odd places, the line boys usually know.

"It's simple," Larry said. "He mentioned he was thinking of selling the Skymaster. I wasn't interested then. I am now. He gave me his card, but I lost it."

The shrug on the other end of the line was audible over the telephone. It meant the boy didn't particularly believe Larry and didn't care. "Okay, okay, no sweat off my ass. He ties down in Gainesville, that what you wanna know?"

The fixed base operator at the field in Gainesville, Florida, also knew Sorenson. "If he's tryin' to sell you that plane, mister, he's pullin' your leg. It ain't his."

"No, no, I know that," Larry said, shifting gears deftly. "He told me he was the pilot. But I don't remember his boss's name, and I remember his. Can you help me out?"

"Sure, mister. The plane is registered to a Floyd C. Farnum. Business address is a roller skating rink up to Martinsville. Want the number?"

Larry took the phone number.

Floyd Farnum answered his own phone. He sounded young, a voice that drifted all over the lot, with a gentle Virginia accent that came across as almost Yankee to a Georgian.

"My name is Larry Spivey in Atlanta, and I'm looking for your pilot Roger Sorenson. I know a guy down here who made a business trip down south with him. I understand they had some problems, and I've had more or less the same problems with the guy, so I figured Sorenson and I had something in common. It might be worth our while to get together."

"Could be. I'm a little busy right now. Give me your number. I'll call you right back."

Larry gave him the number of the "cool phone" in the GBI Controlled Substances Section. The line had two extensions, one in the squad room, the other plugged into a tape recorder in Billy Shepherd's office. Used primarily to receive calls from confidential sources, these telephones were always answered simply "Hello." The number was unlisted and untraceable through phone company records.

Ten minutes later the red phone in the squad room rang. Larry picked it up.

"Hello."

"Mr. Spivey? Floyd Farnum. I've spoken to my associate and he agrees that perhaps you and he would have some things in common. How about telling me a little bit about exactly who you are?"

For a full twenty minutes, Farnum asked questions and Larry answered them, questions ranging from Larry's schooling and career to the details of his bankruptcy. It was clear Farnum intended to check out everything Larry told him. When the interrogation was over, Farnum said, "Tell you what, why don't you come up to Charlotte tomorrow night? The man you want to talk to is over there and I've got to be there on business."

Larry hung up the phone, feeling as if he had just applied for a loan. The next night he threw copies of old newspaper clippings about himself as a real estate developer, copies of his bankruptcy documents, correspondence on real estate deals he had negotiated, and other business papers into a briefcase and boarded a seven o'clock flight for Charlotte, North Carolina.

An immaculately groomed and slightly artificial young man in a brown leather jacket was loitering by the baggage carousel when Larry went to pick up his suitcase. He was in his late twenties, with light brown hair and a tidy mustache designed to make him look older. He waited until all the other passengers had claimed their luggage, then introduced himself to Larry as Rog Sorenson. Attempting to sound as exotically sinister as possible, he said only, "Come with me. I don't like to keep the man waiting."

They drove in Sorenson's Datsun, racing along the expressway to a suburb on the far side of Charlotte. Sorenson was silent and tight-lipped the whole way. He eased into a large macadam parking lot in front of a long one-story metal building. With a gesture of his head, he motioned for Larry to follow him inside, where dozens of youngsters were squealing boisterously as they glided silently over the mirror-smooth vinyl floor on rubber-wheeled roller skates. Skirting the skating floor, Larry and Sorenson walked quickly past a bank of pinball machines and a concession counter and entered a sparsely furnished office separated from the rink by a heavy partition wall. Sorenson closed the door on the teenage roller skaters, shutting out the childish noises with surprising efficiency.

"He's not here yet," Sorenson said. "We'll talk when he gets here."

Floyd Farnum parked his silver XKE in the space marked PRIVATE and stepped out onto the macadam. The circular sign that rose high above the long one-story shed said ULTRASKATE 5—a red, white, and blue bunting motif patterned after the American flag. His first two roller skating rinks, the ones he had inherited from his grandfather, were both in Roanoke, where Floyd had been born and raised. It used to bother him as a kid that such money as the family had came from roller skating. With a somewhat grand vagueness, he would tell his friends at the tony private schools he attended that his family was in the "recreation industry." The prospect of his someday running the rinks himself appalled him and filled him with adolescent shame.

Then, one afternoon in the spring of 1970, he suddenly saw the whole picture in a completely new light. The realization came to him with such startling clarity that he would always remember exactly what he had been wearing, what booth he had been sitting in, what he had been having for lunch. A hamburger with ketchup and a pickle, french fries, and a Coke with lemon. At the time he was twenty years old and a junior at Virginia Tech, where, as he later became fond of saying, he "majored in income tax evasion."

What Floyd Farnum realized that warm sunshiny afternoon in Blacksburg, Virginia, was that a roller skating rink sells absolutely nothing. The very restaurant he was sitting in had to buy its hamburgers (premolded into patties), its potatoes (precut for frying), and its Coke from restaurant suppliers who kept records of their transactions. Jesus Christ himself couldn't grill and serve a thousand hamburgers out of ten pounds of meat. Small-time hustlers thought in terms of making more money than they had to declare, but a big-time hustler needed a business where he could declare more than he made. That was where a roller skating rink was perfect. Eight kids might show up in the afternoon or eight hundred, and there wasn't a damned way IRS or anyone else could tell which it was. It followed, therefore, that a roller skating rink was the perfect front.

A week after his graduation, Farnum offered his services to a mobster in Richmond. The mobster had no use for the roller skating rinks, but he liked the kid's style. He set Floyd up with a tennis and swimming club on Grand Cayman Island in the British West Indies. The club was a front for a money-laundering operation that gave the mobster a tax-free and legitimate source for the fortune he made in drug smuggling and distribution, gambling, prostitution, counterfeiting, contract murder, and truck hijacking. Farnum in turn laundered his 10 percent share of the money he handled through the rinks.

Within a year, the apparent popularity of roller skating in Roanoke had doubled, then tripled and quadrupled. Every kid clattering in circles on the hardwood floor had three invisible companions skating beside him. Farnum expanded. He opened UltraSkate 3 in Martinsville, then crossed over the border into North Carolina for number four in Burlington and five in Charlotte. Meanwhile, the swimming and tennis club in Grand Cayman had grown into a resort complex on the beach overlooking West Bay. At least once a week Farnum took his own Cessna Skymaster from Roanoke to Grand Cayman to oversee construction of the resort. Invariably his pilot, Roger Sorenson, accompanied him, carrying a suitcase filled with American currency in need of a cleaning.

At twenty-nine, four years older than his boss, Roger Sorenson served Floyd Farnum not only as a pilot and bagman but also, more prosaically, as manager of the UltraSkate 5 rink in Charlotte.

"Is this the guy?" Farnum asked as he strode into Sorenson's office at the back of the rink. It was perfectly in character that he didn't bother with such amenities as "Hello" or "Good-bye."

"That's what he tells me."

Farnum turned to Larry with more questions. He wanted to know where he knew McClellan from and asked for a rundown on the Guatemalan affair. Sorenson seemed to enjoy the story, for it confirmed what he had told his boss about McClellan's connection.

"It's a good thing for him I saw through him," Sorenson boasted. "If anything like that happened to me down there, that asshole blacksmith would have been melted down for the blubber by now. We don't like it too much when guys cross us."

It was the same kind of talk Larry had heard from Gordon's macho henchman Harrel the first time he had met him. Arresting Farnum was going to be his job, but right then he made up his mind that arresting Sorenson would be pure pleasure.

Farnum paid for dinner at a fancy restaurant near the rink that served the North Carolina equivalent of French cuisine. The talk was all drugs, a few hours' worth of vague representations couched in the coded argot drug smugglers use to feel each other out. Larry dropped a passing reference to an "associate" in Atlanta, Farnum talked about "doing business," "suitable arrangements," and "quality goods," while Sorenson confined himself to making threatening noises punctuated with ominous references to "the organization."

When the check came, Farnum shoved it in Sorenson's direction and stood up. "Take care of this," he said, flicking his forefinger in front of the pilot's eyes. "I'm gonna go check Spivey into the Ramada Inn. I'll give you a call tomorrow."

They left Sorenson at the table like a wallflower at a dance and drove to a nearby motel, where Farnum signed Larry into one room and himself into another, paying for them both with his gold American Express card. Farnum went to his own room just long enough to drop off his luggage, then showed up at Larry's door, having already asked room service to send up a fifth of Cutty Sark and a couple of bottles of soda.

Farnum still dressed like a college sophomore, in unpressed slacks, cotton socks, and well-scuffed Hush Puppies. He had soft, round features with a bristling black mustache that failed to give his face character or definition. Except for the cold hardness in his eyes, he was unsettlingly nondescript, and when he poured himself a drink, settled into the chair next to the bed, and kicked off his shoes, he exuded a laconic charm that made it difficult for Larry to appreciate the calculating deliberation behind his every move.

In the tone of an old friend asking what he'd been doing with himself the last couple of years, he started pumping Larry for more information about his business career, especially the causes of his bankruptcy. Larry drew the documents from his briefcase and spread them across the small writing desk, but Farnum glanced at them only perfunctorily. It was clear from his questions that he had done some checking of his own, based on the information Larry had given him over the telephone, and was now only going through the motions.

"You don't take any chances, do you?" Larry asked lightly, with just a hint of sarcasm to let Farnum know he understood what was going on.

Farnum smiled philosophically, his expression both knowing and condescending. "Of course I take chances. This is a risky business. It wouldn't be fun or profitable if it wasn't. But it never hurts to be careful. I checked you out. I'd be a fool not to. I have a friend in Atlanta in the printing business, if you know what I mean. He ran a thorough credit check on you, tells me you just about set the indoor record for going broke fast."

Larry sipped on his scotch without answering. It was clear already that Farnum was a man who liked to talk, and Larry settled himself in for listening. He would have to draw him out slowly, carefully, letting Farnum roll along at his own pace so that even a day later, when the bland young entrepreneur looked back at the evening after a good night's sleep, it would never dawn on him he had been interrogated.

He talked about his connection with what he invariably called the organization, an underworld network that reached from Virginia through North and South Carolina into Georgia and Florida.

"I don't know," Larry demurred. "All I want to do is to do some business. I don't know that I'm looking to get myself tied in with the mob."

Farnum laughed. "Pretty new at this, aren't you?"

"Not so new. I'm not Lucky Luciano, but I've done some deals."

"Then maybe this will come as a surprise, and maybe it won't. Don't sweat getting tied up with the organization. In the first place, it's not what you're thinking. I'm not talking about a bunch of Eye-talians with the pinkie rings and the white-on-white shirts. Not that there aren't some of them around, but down here they pretty much leave us alone. We're just a bunch of good ol' southern boys tryin' to hustle a buck. So that's the first thing. And the second is, our organization is all over the place.

Nothing moves that we don't move, and that's the truth. If you've done some deals, you're in with us whether you know it or not. Usually we keep it so you don't know. Most guys working the streets, working the planes, bringing the shit in, they're working for us, except they never know it. You do know it. But it makes no difference either way."

"Who's this 'us' I'm working for?" Larry asked skeptically.

"Me."

"Bullshit. I'm looking to deal with you, but that's all. I'm not working for you."

Farnum smiled like a pumpkin, round-faced and benign. "Call it what you want," he said. "I've got no ego problems. It comes to the same thing."

They talked until morning, loose talk that flowed more naturally than it should have, considering the business they were in. If Farnum had been trying to cop a plea by confessing, he couldn't have been more informative. Before the night was halfway through, Larry's head was spinning, as much from what he was hearing as from the scotch. For openers, Larry learned that the printer in Atlanta who ran the credit check for Farnum was actually the owner of a large chain of finance companies who manufactured twenty dollar bills as a sideline. Farnum grinned impishly as he described the fun he had taking Rog Sorenson with him as he drove around Roanoke, making a game of seeing how many of them he could pass in an afternoon. "It scares Rog silly," he said. "In fact, that's half the fun of it, watching him shit bricks. They'd fucking kill me if they knew."

"Who?"

"The organization. They wouldn't like it one bit. I'm their front. I'm supposed to stay clean."

As Farnum explained it, he was the conduit through which all of the organization's earnings flowed, emerging at the other end as clean as any workingman's paycheck. "It's kind of like plastic surgery," he told Larry. "They take some skin off your ass and put it on your nose or your ear or whatever. Ends up looking like a nose, and if it's done right, you and the surgeon are the only ones that know it's really your ass. That's why they don't want me fucking around with any of this stuff myself, because I know too much and they're afraid of what could happen if I ever got busted. The whole damn house could fall like it was matchsticks."

Slowly it was becoming clear why Farnum was being so loquacious. The mob was making him wealthy, but he was frustrated by the role they had assigned him on the sidelines. He had an almost adolescent compulsion to be in on the action. Personally passing counterfeit money was only a part of it. He had a fencing operation going at his roller skating rink in Charlotte, buying and selling the fruits of nickel-and-dime heists by local juvenile delinquents. That a man who made $3 million a year as his percentage of the $30 million cash flow that passed through his hands should risk arrest in order to make a $10 profit fencing a stolen car radio was so irrational Larry could hardly comprehend it. Yet this paradox was the key to Floyd Farnum's personality, and it explained why he was disclosing so much to a man he had just met.

Farnum couldn't afford to go into the drug business without a front man. He had already been called on the carpet more than once for getting himself mixed up in illegal activities and had been warned to keep himself clean.

"You don't take a hint too well, do you?" Larry asked.

Farnum shrugged. "I don't like being pushed around. That's where you come in. You do the buying for me. You sell to your people in Georgia. Nobody up here has to know I'm in it. We split fifty-fifty."

"Fine for you, but what's in it for me?"

"Contacts. I can get you in to people no one gets to see without printed invitations. You'll need them unless all you want to handle is chickenshit amounts."

Larry considered a moment, then nodded crisply. "You've got yourself a partner," he announced.

Eleven

Larry flew back to Atlanta late that afternoon and reported immediately to GBI headquarters. He knew he could have gone a lot farther with Farnum at their first meeting, but he was reluctant to get in too deep before clearing it with GBI. He was working in another state, where he had no authority to act as a narcotics agent, and he didn't know whether GBI could be sold on a case against Farnum. There was no question in his mind that Farnum was an infinitely bigger objective than Dan Gordon, even though he was only a neophyte at drug trafficking. If even half of what he said about himself was true, his value as a source of information was potentially limitless, reaching far beyond narcotics trafficking into virtually every area of organized criminal activity.

Inspector Peters was delighted with the turn Larry's undercover operation had taken. "Sounds to me like you've gotten us way out of Gordon's league, Spivey. Good work," he said. "Seems to me we don't have much call to bother ourselves with Mr. Gordon much longer. We ought to consider taking him down now."

The agents gathered around the conference table all saw it the same way and turned to Larry for suggestions. When Gordon sent Larry to make contact with Farnum's pilot, his purpose was to secure a supply of top-grade marijuana. He said at the time, "I can get all the cheap Mexican shit I can handle, but the good stuff is getting hard to find." There was no reason to think he was lying about his access to Mexican grass, and Larry figured that was as good a basis for arresting him as any.

"I'll tell him they're even hungrier up there than he is," Larry suggested. "I'll tell him I couldn't find any sellers, but I found plenty of cats looking to buy. Which one of you guys wants to be the grass buyer from Virginia?"

"Don't look at me," Mike Eason said quickly. There were chuckles all around the table.

"Mike doesn't work undercover," Clardy explained. "He can't keep a straight face. Last time we sent him in to do a buy-bust, he broke up, giggling like a fucking girl."

"I don't know what it is," Eason confessed sheepishly. "I just can't help it. I'm supposed to be doing a buy. The guy's showing me the stuff, and I just start in laughing. I'm trying like hell to hold it back, but it's getting out of control. 'What's so funny?' the guy asks. 'Nothing, nothing.' But it just gets worse and worse. The guy's starting to get edgy. Finally, he says, 'What the hell's going on here?' And I just hadda tell him, 'Fuck it, man, you're under arrest.' Guy couldn't believe it. Even after we had the cuffs on him, he thought it was some kind of a gag. I guess he's figured it out by now."

Larry shook his head, amused and slightly perplexed, wondering in spite of himself what kind of outfit he had gotten himself mixed up with.

Peters broke through the laughter and said, "We don't have to decide who's gonna do the buy yet. Let's just wait and see who's available when the time comes. You set it up with Gordon, but make sure you're in solid with those people in Virginia first. Nothing makes a doper more nervous than knowing he's dealing with somebody mixed up in a recent bust."

Peters went on to suggest that Larry return to Roanoke in a day or two and simply play it by ear, getting as close to Farnum as possible. Eason meanwhile would contact some friends in the Virginia State Police's intelligence unit, fill them in on what was going on, and set up a liaison for handling the investigation.

"Specifically," Peters said, lapsing into law enforcement jargon, "your mission for the time being will be in an intelligence capacity. Find out all you can. When we have the intelligence and can assess it, that'll be time enough to plan enforcement strategy."

Dan Gordon bought Larry dinner the next night. They met at the Moorings, a fashionable restaurant in Smyrna, an Atlanta suburb. Seated at a window table from which they could watch the muddy waters of the Chattahoochee River churn by, they were able to conclude their business by the time their soup bowls were taken away. Gordon was definitely interested in unloading his supplies of Mexican. "Line up the buyers," he told Larry as they helped themselves from the salad bar. "I'll have Harrel get in touch with you to work up the details."

That was as much as he would say, but it was enough. He drove Larry back to Marietta and dropped him at his motel. The phone was ringing as Larry unlocked the door.

It was Charlene. "Where in God's name have you been?" she demanded, her voice icy and sharp.

Larry didn't think that was any of her business.

"Maybe not," she said, not conceding anything. "But I think you should know what you missed. Our divorce is final. I was wondering what you're going to do about the money."

Larry felt like someone who picks up a party line and finds himself in the middle of someone else's conversation. "What money?"

"The five thousand dollars you owe me."

"I owe you five thousand dollars?"

"You sure do. That's what the judge awarded me. You got off lucky, sweetie. This way you don't have to pay me alimony."

"Back up a minute, you lost me somewhere along there. It couldn't be final unless I was notified."

"You were notified. Three weeks ago. But you didn't show up in court."

Three weeks ago Larry had been in Guatemala overseeing fifty drunk Indians.

"Of course not, I was out of the country," he shot back, momentarily triumphant. "I think you outfoxed yourself this time, Charlene. It's not legal unless I'm served with a summons."

"You were."

"Like hell. Where was it served?"

"Here. You didn't leave a forwarding address."

"Who acknowledged service?"

"I did."

He had expected that answer. She had known he would be away—he hadn't told her where—and had picked a time when he wouldn't be able to contest her claims. There was a silence on the line. Then Charlene said, "Well?"

"Well what?"

"When do I get my money?"

Larry laughed. Her money? They had been married only four months. "You must have done a hell of a number on the judge to convince him a man ought to pay twelve-fifty a month for being married to you."

"I don't have to listen to that kind of talk."

"No, you don't. Good-bye, Charlene."

"What about my money?"

He made his voice as earnest as he could, trying to match the coldness in hers. "Charlene, I don't have five thousand dollars or anything like it. I couldn't get my hands on five hundred. I get paid next week. Four hundred and thirty dollars. If you want some of it, I could give you fifty."

"You're not going to get away with this, you son of a bitch," she hissed.

Larry didn't answer. In the silence that followed, he could tell she was trying to think of something to say but was having trouble. The fact was she knew Larry was broke. "You'll hear from me, Larry," she said at last, giving up. "I promise you that. If you can't get the money, maybe those people you work for can. You're so goddamned important to them, maybe it'll be worth it to them. If not, I'm going to tell Gus what you're up to."

Larry knew she was just talking wildly, spitefully, not giving it any thought. But he also knew she was capable of anything. When she had had time to mull it over, the conclusion she would come to would be precisely that blackmail was the only way to get what she wanted. For the moment she hadn't realized how dangerous her threat was, but as soon as she did, she wouldn't hesitate to carry through on it. He put her off with a promise to see what he could do. Mollified, she let it go at that—for the time being.

Floyd Farnum lived in an ultramodern twelve-room house on eight acres of cleared land in the woods just outside the tiny hamlet of Bassett Forks, Virginia. The entire back wall, looking out over the flagstoned patio and the pool, was glass, and on the first floor even the interior walls were glass. All the furniture was built low, close to the carpet, giving unbroken sight lines from the stone fireplace in the living room to the ceiling-high bank of high-fidelity equipment in Floyd's study, from the front foyer to the back of the kitchen.

Larry and Floyd were met at the door by a flawlessly beautiful brunette in her mid-twenties. She had large brown eyes and the professionally perky look of a model in a soap ad. Her name was Tracy, and Farnum introduced her as his ex-wife. He accepted a kiss on the cheek and sent her upstairs.

"Was that some kind of a joke?" Larry asked.

"Nope. Married her about five years ago, love at first sight. She's a helluva little lady. A couple years ago we had this real killer of a fight. She was giving me backtalk like I hadn't heard since the day I met her, and I'm laying a ton of stuff on her. You've been married, you know the scene. All of a sudden she starts telling me I can't afford to fuck her over on account of how she could soak me for a fortune if she ever made up her mind to divorce me.

"Well, it all blew over, right? Except that nothing ever blows over with me. It's the kind of guy I am, you'll see. And anyway, talk like that scares a man, losing everything he's worked for. So I get together with my accountant, my lawyer, and we work it out. Before she knows what hit her, I divest myself of everything, and I mean everything. I'm not worth two bits on paper. Then I divorce her. Her lawyers are looking everywhere for the money, and they can't find it. We go into court for a settlement, and the judge awards her three dimes and a nickel. What can he do? I'm not a rich man. So now we're a couple again; only we're not married, and she's got no hold over me. I haven't had a problem with her since."

Larry laughed. "For some guys everything works," he said. "My ex-wife is still coming after me. And I really am broke."

Farnum's gesture indicated financial worries would soon be a thing of the past. "How'd it go in Atlanta?" he asked.

Larry ran down the list of known drug dealers in Atlanta supplied to him by the intelligence unit at GBI. He quoted the top prices they would pay. "I've got more buyers than you can handle," he said.

Farnum was impressed. "You've sold to all those cats?" he asked.

"I get around," Larry answered evasively, just in case Farnum checked with any of them. "Right about now the heaviest dude I know is a guy named George. White guy, sells mostly to the spades. He'll take any kind of shit that burns. He's just got to see some samples. I figure between him and the others we can move a couple thousand pounds a week, maybe some coke on the side."

"Couldn't be sweeter," Farnum said. "Let's get moving."

He led Larry into his study. With a long-shafted old-fashioned key he took from a desk drawer, he unlocked the door to a large walk-in closet and pulled the light chain, turning on a naked hundred-watt bulb in the ceiling. Standing all along the wall like a row of sentries, their stocks on the floor, their barrels aimed toward the ceiling, were at least a dozen gleaming automatic weapons.

Larry let out a whistle of surprise. There were a couple of nine-millimeter Schmeissers with their folding wire stocks, a pair of military Thompson submachine guns, a few old M-3 grease guns, an M-2 carbine, a .30-caliber air-cooled light machine gun, and maybe six, maybe more, M-16s, each with a clip in it, a box of extra clips on the floor next to them. Ammunition was stored in boxes on reinforced shelves at the far end of the closet. Vertical partitions divided the shelves neatly into pigeonholes.

"You're going to need some equipment to work with," Farnum said blandly. "Something that'll fit in a briefcase."

He grabbed both Schmeissers by the barrels, one in each hand, and offered them to Larry, who stepped out of the closet to examine them.

"Nearest neighbor's eight miles away," Farnum said. "C'mon."

He scooped several boxes of ammunition from the shelves and led the way through the kitchen to the patio out back. Larry carried the two eleven-pound weapons, one in each hand. Farnum set the ammo boxes on the long redwood picnic table. "Here's good enough," he said.

Larry snapped out the straight thirty-round clips and loaded them, slid them back into the weapons, and slapped them into place with the palm of his hand while Floyd rummaged through a trash bin and came up with about a dozen empty beer cans. Having set them in a line halfway back on the gently sloping lawn, about seventy-five yards away, he walked back to the table and nodded for Larry to fire.

Larry raised the first gun to his shoulder, stepped forward on his left foot, and leaned toward the target, deliberately bringing the barrel of the weapon down toward the cans. He squeezed on the trigger, sending a quick burst of eight or ten rounds dancing into the tin cans. He released the trigger, and the sharp noise of the gunfire died away, followed by the tinkling of the ejected shells falling against the flagstones. He squeezed off another round or two, followed it with a long burst, a short one, and another long. The action felt sharp, mechanical, crisp, like knuckle joints about to crack.

He repeated the process with the second gun and turned to Farnum. "I'll take this one," he said, offering no explanation.

Farnum handed him an unopened box of ammunition and led the way back to his study, where he got a can of gun-cleaning solvent, some oil, and rags from the closet. Then they sat in the living room cleaning both guns, while Tracy came downstairs and started preparing lasagne in the kitchen.

As they worked on the guns, Farnum began explaining the mechanics of drug dealing, Virginia style. The organization bought marijuana in tonnage quantities, bringing it in either on coast-plying vessels or by air. The shipments were then broken up and divided among the various stashes hidden throughout the Virginia-North Carolina-Tennessee tristate area. Each stash came under the control of its own "coordinator," who employed a "runner" and a "baby-sitter." The baby-sitter actually lived with the stash, guarded it with his life, and made sure that no one other than the runner got anywhere near it. Buyers and prospective buyers never got close to the drug supply. They dealt with the runner, who conducted his business far from his goods, taking with him only the samples he needed or the quantity actually purchased. In the entire organization, no one other than the coordinator, the runner, and the baby-sitter knew the locations of the individual stashes, thus ruling out the possibility of a massive raid involving more than one local cache.

"About those samples," Farnum said. "My cousin Tommie can round them up. He's in tight with three or four runners, buys from them fairly regular. I'll give him a call; he'll be able to have them for us tonight."

"Here?"

"Are you fuckin' nuts? No, man, I'm not in this, got nothing to do with it, remember? We've got to get back to Roanoke."

When the guns were clean, Larry folded back the stock of the one he had selected, and Floyd stowed it in the trunk of his car. The other Schmeisser was returned to the study closet. The two men killed an hour or so over a few scotch and sodas in the backyard, then ate in the dining room, Tracy disappearing discreetly after the food was on the table. It was December 1 and already dark when they set off for Roanoke. On the outskirts of town, Farnum pulled into the parking lot of a gun shop and climbed from the car. "You're gonna need something you can walk around with," he said.

Larry picked out a square-handled model 36 Smith & Wesson .38 Special with a two-inch barrel, a Bucheimer upside-down shoulder holster, and a small leather ammunition pouch that attached to the strap of the holster. Adding a box of 158-grain hollow-point ammunition for the .38, Farnum paid for the purchases in cash, and they returned to the car. The next stop was a K-Mart discount store, where Farnum bought a footlocker for transporting the marijuana samples. In the K-Mart parking lot, Larry transferred the Schmeisser to the footlocker, and they drove to the Holiday Inn near the airport, where Farnum checked them into a single room.

He left Larry in the room while he went off to get the samples from his cousin. An hour and a half later he returned, quietly letting himself in with a key. Larry was watching television.

Farnum glanced around the room quickly. "The stuff's in the car," he said. "C'mon."

He took a large green plastic garbage bag from the trunk of his Jaguar, slung it over his shoulder, and went back up to the room. Larry put the chain lock on the door while Floyd untied the knot at the neck of the bag. Inside were eleven pounds of marijuana compressed in five one-kilo bricks, each wrapped in slick white butcher paper. "Couldn't get any coke right now," Farnum said, setting the foot-long bricks in a row at the foot of the bed. "Supposed to be a shipment from North Carolina in a few days. I'll have Sorenson bring you down a sample."

Larry unwrapped the bricks and examined each one in turn. There were clear differences in texture and color, but he avoided comment, simply nodding noncommittally as he studied each brick before rewrapping it and setting it carefully in the footlocker. For each brick Farnum quoted a price, which Larry wrote on the butcher paper. Already penciled on each brick was its exact weight in grams. The prices ranged from $140 to $200 a pound. When all five bricks were in the locker, Larry set the Schmeisser on top of them and filled in the empty space with hotel towels, then snapped the locker shut.

It was already too late to catch the last flight to Atlanta, so Farnum called the airport and made a reservation for Larry on the first flight in the morning. Larry said he would be seeing his buyers as soon as he got to Georgia.

"Sorenson's gonna be with you," Farnum said. "He'll meet your plane when it lands."

Larry shrugged indifferently, indicating both that he saw no call for this kind of baby-sitting and that he wasn't about to object. In reality, Farnum was playing into his hands by not trusting him. Sorenson's involvement in the sale of the samples would make both him and Farnum indictable in Georgia.

Farnum left, promising to return in the morning to give Larry a lift to the airport. Larry waited until he had been gone fifteen minutes, then went down to the bar for a few drinks. When he was satisfied that he wasn't being watched, he went to a pay phone in the hotel lobby and put in a call to GBI headquarters in Atlanta. The dispatcher patched him through to Mike Eason at home.

"Hey, buddy, howya doin'?" Eason began, the only greeting he knew.

"I'm due in on the eight-oh-five from Roanoke in the morning. I'm checking a green footlocker onto the plane. The stuff is going to be in it. There's eleven pounds of grass and a German submachine gun the bad guys issued me. Oh, yeah, and a two-inch thirty-eight Smith. You want the good news or the bad?"

"Start with the bad."

"Tell you the truth, they're both the same. The pilot I told you about, Sorenson, is supposed to meet me at the airport. He'll stay with me till the deal goes down. That gives us a Georgia case, but it means we've got to put on a show for them."

"We'll need pictures of the contents of that locker for evidence."

"No sweat. Just pull it off the plane before it gets to the baggage claim. There's a men's room on the main concourse. Meet me there. I've got an extra key to the footlocker. You can take your pictures and whatever. Just make damned sure that locker shows up at the baggage claim area with the rest of the luggage. I don't want Sorenson wondering why it's getting special attention."

"Will do. What else?"

"I'm going to need a dope buyer. I told him I got a guy named George."

"So we'll send Clardy. What's the problem?"

"No problem. Perfect. I told him that George dealt mostly with spooks. Let him know, so he'll know how to play it. I'll give him a call on the cool phone as soon as I get set up with Sorenson."

Eason signed off, and Larry went back to the bar for a couple more scotch and sodas.

In the morning Floyd Farnum was knocking on his door by seven-thirty. He had already paid the tab and checked Larry out of the hotel. They drove to the airport, checked the luggage, and had a quick breakfast in the airport cafeteria. The flight took only an hour. As Larry walked through the boarding telescope at Hartsfield International Airport on the outskirts of Atlanta, he scanned the lounge area at the gate and saw no sign of Sorenson, who was probably waiting for him at the baggage claim area.

This told him two things about Rog Sorenson. First, he was stupid. He had put himself out of position to see if Larry was meeting anyone or making any calls Floyd Farnum might want to know about. Secondly, he was armed. The only reason for his not meeting Larry at the gate was that he couldn't make it past the metal detector.

Stupid and armed were a bad combination that could lead to a lot of problems later, but for the time being all it meant was Larry would have no trouble making his planned meeting with Eason. He hurried down the long glass-walled corridor from the gate area to the main concourse, where he turned to the left and headed for the men's room just beyond the newsstand.

Eason was waiting for him inside, combing his hair by the mirror over the sink. There was a middle-aged black man at one of the urinals. Larry moved up alongside him. When the stranger zipped himself up and left, Eason reached out his hand for the key, which Larry quickly handed him. They exchanged no words. Larry waited a minute after Eason was gone and returned to the concourse, where he took the escalator down to the baggage claim area.

Below him, as he rode down, he could see Rog Sorenson waiting by the baggage carousel, his back to the escalator, lounging against a baggage wagon with macho indolence. He turned as Larry came up behind him, and they shook hands. Sorenson was in a surly mood. As they waited for the carousel to start turning, he grumbled bitterly that he had driven all night in order to make it down from Charlotte after Farnum had called him and told him to be in Atlanta by the time Spivey's flight got in. Apparently he didn't understand Farnum's purpose in sending him. "Shit, mister," he snarled, "if you don't know how to do one of these deals yourself, I don't know what the hell he's bothering with you for."

Larry smiled amiably. "It's not that, Rog. He thinks the world of you, that's all."

Sorenson blinked a couple of times and cocked his head slightly, trying to figure out if he was being ragged. In the end he decided to take it as a compliment. "Yeah, I guess so," he said.

Larry told him he would contact his buyer as soon as they got set up somewhere and asked Sorenson if he had any place in mind.

"Shit, no. This is your town, not mine."

Larry mentioned a Howard Johnson motel at the north end of Atlanta, not far from where he was staying.

"Fine with me," Sorenson snarled. "What the fuck's taking so long with this fucking baggage?"

His voice was loud, the profanity as startling among the silently waiting passengers as the sound of someone breaking wind at a concert. A few strangers eyed him coldly, then looked away, while a young mother with a child in her arms shook her head. Ten minutes passed before the carousel started to turn.

Larry reached for the footlocker as soon as it came off the conveyor, grabbed it by the handle on the hasp side, and followed Sorenson to the parking lot. As they picked their way through the ranks of cars in the unattended lot, Larry noticed George Clardy's brown Chevelle, Clardy at the wheel. When they walked behind it, the engine kicked over, and the car started to back out. Larry knew it would be on Sorenson's tail the rest of the way.

He threw the footlocker into the trunk of Sorenson's Datsun, climbed into the passenger seat, and gave directions for the thirty-five-minute ride to the motel, where Sorenson checked him into the cheapest room they had and accompanied him upstairs. Larry went straight to the telephone and called the cool phone in the squad room at GBI headquarters. It was picked up on the second ring.

"Hello."

"George there?"

"Stepped out a few minutes. Who wants him?"

"Tell him Larry; have him give me a call." He gave the number. "When's he supposed to be back?"

"Few minutes, I don't know."

Larry hung up the phone and turned to Sorenson, who was rocking impatiently on the balls of his feet. "The guy's out. He'll get back to me."

"Sure, sure. Look," Sorenson said, "I know a chick who lives right around here. I'll give you her number; call me there when you get the guy."

"Stick around, man. He's supposed to be back pretty soon."

Sorenson shook his head. "Who needs that? Got some time, no use wasting it. I think I'll rip off a piece."

"At ten o'clock in the morning?"

"Best time, believe me."

Even before Sorenson was out of Larry's motel room, the dispatcher at GBI had raised George Clardy on the radio and requested him to call in by telephone.

Clardy was at the far end of the Howard Johnson's parking lot, a good fifty yards from where Sorenson had parked. He saw Sorenson pushing through the glass doors from the lobby. "Seventy-one, GBI. I'll give you that call in a minute."

He watched Sorenson drive off and swung in well behind him, raising Mike Eason and Billy Shepherd on the radio as he drove. Along with Clardy, they made up the three units tailing Sorenson. When the Datsun was safely on the expressway, Clardy let his partners know he was dropping out and drove to a pay phone, where he placed a call to GBI.

"What's the story?"

"Spivey called, gave me a number where you're supposed to call him back. We ran the number. It's the Howard Johnson Motor Lodge on Boswell Road, Sandy Springs."

"I know that. I tailed him."

"Room two-fourteen."

"I'll give him a honk."

He put in a dime and dialed the number. "Larry?"

"Yeah. He split. Did you pick him up?"

"Billy and Mike are on him. Where's he going?"

"To get laid."

"At ten o'clock in the morning?"

"Says it's the best time."

"Well, he oughta know. What's happening?"

"I got the stuff here. The room's in his name, the dumb schmuck. Come by in an hour. I'm supposed to call him when I hear from you. I'll give him a chance to get rid of his headache first."

"I'll come by now," Clardy said.

He hung up the phone and called GBI to instruct Paul Carter to report to the hotel with the monitoring equipment. Eason and Shepherd were to remain on the surveillance. If Sorenson's girl friend kicked him out and he headed back for the motel, Larry was to be notified immediately by telephone.

Five minutes later Clardy knocked on the door to Larry's room. "What can you tell me?" he asked.

"He's armed."

"Where's he carry it?"

"I don't know, I didn't see it. But he didn't want to come to the gate at the airport."

"Anything else?"

Larry unlocked the footlocker and flipped back the top, like a kid showing off his Christmas presents to the kids down the block. He had been an undercover agent two months, and this was the first drug shipment he had been able to turn over.

Clardy's phlegmatic reaction cooled him off instantly. "I know," the veteran narcotics agent said tonelessly. "We saw it at the airport, took a bunch of pictures for when these bastards go to trial. Do you think the hotel's cool?"

"Sure, I guess so. I picked it, he didn't," Larry answered confidently. The thought flashed through his mind that he still had a lot to learn. He had almost let Sorenson pick the place for the buy.

Clardy reached for the phone and called headquarters again. "Tell Shepherd it's okay to come in and set up. And tell Carter to bring a grand."

133

When he hung up, Larry reminded him that $1,000 wasn't going to do it. The prices ranged from $140 to $200 a pound, and there were eleven pounds.

Clardy shook his head. "No, no," he said. "I'm gonna hit on him twice. I'll take two or three keys for distribution now, get back to him in a day or so after my people check it out. Then I take the other sample and make arrangements to do some more business. That way we get two counts against him. It kills the I-don't-know-what-I-was-thinking-I-made-a-fool-ish-mistake-but-please-don't-put-me-in-jail-for-it-your-honor defense. And there's another reason, too. It keeps him in town overnight. Maybe we'll get a chance to find out something about who his friends are, who he sees, stuff like that. Two meetings are always better than one. You can learn twice as much about him."

There was a knock on the door. Larry tensed reflexively, but Clardy just turned and opened the door. Paul Carter, the blond agent who had recruited Larry for undercover work, stepped into the room and closed the door behind him. He handed Clardy an envelope containing $1,000 in old bills—mostly hundreds, with a few fifties, twenties, and tens thrown in. Folded in with the bills was a receipt form listing the serial numbers of each bill.

"I'll take your word for it this is right," Clardy said, signing the receipt and returning it to Carter. "Are they all set upstairs?"

Carter slid the receipt in his jacket pocket. "Couple of minutes," he said.

Billy Shepherd had rented the room directly above Larry's and was at that moment busily installing the monitoring equipment for the transmitter Clardy would wear during the buy. Shepherd and Carter would remain with the recorder throughout the deal because federal law requires two witnesses if the fruits of any electronic surveillance are to be admissible in federal court. To be on the safe side, GBI made it a matter of policy to prepare all drug cases according to federal standards in case there were reasons later for going that way. This was especially important in a case such as this, with its obvious interstate ramifications.

While Clardy was upstairs being outfitted, Larry placed a call to the number Sorenson had given him. "I talked to the guy. He says he's gonna be here in fifteen, twenty minutes," he told Sorenson.

Sorenson said it would take him about a half hour to get there.

Alone in the coldly impersonal room, like thousands of identical motel rooms everywhere, Larry felt a sharp escalation of tension like an increasingly heavy weight pushing at the back of his neck. For the first few minutes everything in the room looked strange to him, as though he might look out the window and find he had been magically transported to New Guinea or Marrakesh. It took him a moment to realize it was his own disorientation he was feeling, and he wondered if he would ever be able to reconcile the strange and foreign role he was playing with the utter banality, the utter normality of the settings. He consciously asked himself if he was scared and told himself he wasn't. But to be on the safe side, he got the Smith & Wesson .38 Farnum had bought him from the footlocker, loaded it, and tucked it in his belt on his right side toward the back. He pulled his shirt out from his pants just enough to let the material drape over the handle of the gun.

With the gun within reach he knew he wasn't afraid; but the tension wouldn't go away, and he realized it was nothing more than a kind of stagefright that would leave him the moment the curtain went up.

In fifteen minutes Clardy came back. "Get over on the other side of the room," he told Larry.

Larry crossed toward the bathroom door.

In a low, conversational voice, Clardy said, "Are you reading me?"

There was a knock on the ceiling.

He told Larry to say something and then asked, "Did you get that too?"

There was another knock.

"Awright. Lemme know when you spot Sorenson."

The next knock didn't come for almost half an hour. Clardy scooted from the room, and Larry locked the door behind him. Five minutes later Sorenson was pounding at the door.

"Is he here?" Sorenson asked, scanning the room as he stepped through the door.

"Not yet."

"You said he was gonna be here. Where the fuck is he?"

"He'll be here."

Sorenson tossed his head scornfully and crossed to the desk in the corner of the room. With his back to Larry, he reached under his fawn-colored leather jacket, pulled a long-barreled revolver from his waistband, and flipped out the cylinder with an ostentatious click. He spun it once, snapped it back into place, and repositioned the gun in the waistband of his beltless slacks before turning to face Larry.

Larry figured that if that act was supposed to get a rise out of him, he wasn't about to give Sorenson the satisfaction.

"George and I go back a long way," he said.

"That's interesting."

Larry pretended not to notice the way he said it. "Yeah, he's been dealing for years. I remember him when he was just, like, buying for friends."

Sorenson didn't say anything. He paced the floor with a show of impatience. When Clardy knocked, he gestured with his head for Larry to get it.

The two undercover agents greeted each other effusively, like long-lost buddies. Then Larry introduced Sorenson and Clardy, using only first names. "I was just telling Rog about the old days," he said. "I can remember when you used to think five pounds of grass was a big score."

Clardy acted embarrassed, and Larry went on for a few more minutes of reminiscing. Finally, Clardy said, "So what's the point, Spivey? We all gotta be kids sometime. I suppose you was born dealing heavy?"

Larry said, "Aw, fuck it, I didn't mean anything."

Sorenson ate it all up, the pettiness of his two new associates working on him like an aphrodisiac, bringing out the arrogance that was never far from the surface with him. "As soon as you guys are ready to stop playing with each other, maybe we can do some business," he cut in. "I got better stuff to do than fuck around here."

Clardy shrugged elaborately.

"You got the key to that thing, Spivey?" Sorenson asked.

Larry flipped him the key, and he unlocked the trunk, threw back the lid, and tossed the towels across the room. Clardy's eyebrows went up a notch when he saw the machine gun on top of the marijuana bricks.

"Jesus, what business did you say you were in?" he asked admiringly.

"We try to stay diversified," Sorenson answered coyly.

"That wouldn't be for sale, would it?"

Larry said, "No, that's mine."

"There's more where that one came from," Sorenson chimed in quickly, an overanxious salesman.

Clardy looked at the submachine gun for a long time. "I reckon there must be," he said finally. "What the fuck is it anyway?"

"It's a Schmeisser," Larry told him. "German gun, Second World War."

"No shit."

Sorenson stooped to the footlocker and picked up the gun and the clip that lay next to it. He snapped the clip in and held the weapon out toward Clardy. "Interested?"

Clardy hefted the gun judiciously. He handed it back to Sorenson. "Could be. I'm in with some pretty mean spades. Lemme run it past 'em, see if they're still into black power. These Shmeezers all you got?"

"Shit no. We got anything you want. Get you enough M-sixteens to liberate fucking Cuba if you want, get 'em by the truckload. New stuff, never been fired."

Clardy said, "Well, awright, we'll see what we'll see. Let's do some business."

Sorenson handed him one of the bricks, and he examined it closely. One by one, Sorenson passed him all five. Clardy inspected each in turn, sitting at the foot of the bed and laying the samples within reach. "How much you want for these pressed Mexican turds?" he asked when he was finished studying them.

Sorenson gave him the prices. They dickered over money for a few minutes; but Sorenson refused to budge, and Clardy seemed only half-hearted.

"Tell you what," he said. "Gimme these three, I'll run 'em by my people and get back to you tomorrow if it's all copacetic. These cats will smoke anything."

Sorenson did the math on a piece of hotel stationery, converting the gram figures on the butcher paper to pounds. Clardy had picked the three palest-looking bundles, and the total bill came to $940. He fished into his pocket, pulled out the roll of bills, and counted it. Sorenson watched him closely and then stuck the money in his pocket without re-counting it.

"You be here tomorrow?" Clardy asked.

"Spivey'll know how to reach me."

"Right on. You got something I can tote this shit in?"

There were a few minutes of low comedy while everyone searched around for something big enough to hold the three foot-long bricks. Finally, Sorenson offered to go down to his car for a shopping bag he thought he had in the trunk.

It was all Larry could do to keep from bursting out laughing the moment Sorenson left the room. But Clardy was a study in nonchalance, giving Larry the same silent treatment veteran ballplayers use to greet a rookie's first home run. "Interesting line of work, wouldn't you say?" he asked at last.

"Jesus," Larry said. "Is it always like this?"

"Not really. This guy's a special turkey. Cool it, I think he's coming back."

Sorenson returned with the shopping bag and personally packed the three bricks. He had brought a couple of rags with him from the car and laid them over the marijuana, tucking them in around the sides so they wouldn't slip off. "All right, man," he said coldly, handing the bag to Clardy. "You just better not be jerking me around. I'll see you tomorrow, right? I didn't drag my ass all the way down here to deal three keys, y'know."

Clardy picked up the bag and headed for the door. "Fuck off," he said. "If the stuff's any good, we'll deal. If not, not."

Sorenson stood stunned but recovered just as Clardy stepped through the door. "Hey, George," he called after him, "tell me something."

"Yeah?"

"How come you deal mostly with niggers?"

Clardy grinned from ear to ear. "They got the need, I got the weed and the greed. Don't ask so many questions, asshole."

The door closed with a firm click.

Twelve

eorge Clardy arrived at the motel for the second meeting the next day straight from delivering a crime prevention talk to a women's club. He was wearing a three-piece suit. Because he had known he would be cutting his schedule pretty close and wouldn't have time to check in at the upstairs room to get wired, Larry wore the transmitter. He kept the toggle switch under his belt in the off position until Sorenson knocked on his door a few minutes before George was supposed to show up.

Clardy was right on time, offering a facetious explanation for his attire. Sorenson was in an expansive mood, launching into a full-tilt sales pitch for his organization the moment George paid him for the second half of the grass sample. Bragging about counterfeit money and cocaine, about machine guns and mysterious accidents that had befallen those who crossed the mob, he left nothing to the imagination of his potential prosecutors. At the end of the meeting Clardy committed himself to a bigger deal as soon as Sorenson could get his hands on five or six hundred pounds of good weed, for which he was willing to go as high as $270 a pound.

Clardy left with the drugs in a small canvas satchel he had had the foresight to bring with him this time. The door had no sooner closed on him than Sorenson put in a call to Floyd Farnum in Bassett Forks. Although there was no phone tap in the room, the bug taped to Larry's chest was able to pick up Sorenson's end of the conversation, in which Farnum was addressed by name a couple of times.

Farnum hung up to make a quick call to his cousin, then called back with a confirmation. A runner with a stash outside Roanoke had gotten in an argument at a local bar and shot a man. The mob got him out on bail but didn't trust him to stand up under the charge, which could go up to manslaughter or murder two if the guy died but down to felonious assault if the runner cooperated with the cops. They wanted to close down his stash as quickly as possible, which meant dealing the 640 pounds it contained to anyone who could handle that kind of traffic in a hurry.

"Tell your man he can have the stuff tomorrow or as soon as he can get the bread up," Farnum said. "But no later than Monday or Tuesday, or it'll be off the market. They'll dump it in the fucking reservoir sooner than sit on it more than a day or two."

Larry agreed to contact Clardy as soon as possible and then get back to Sorenson with Clardy's go or no go decision.

Late that night Larry met with Inspector Phil Peters and the other agents on his team at GBI headquarters. Peters listened to the tapes and read the investigative summaries Larry, Eason, and Clardy had dashed off in the office that evening. As Peters evaluated the case, Sorenson already could be indicted for two counts of trafficking in marijuana. "But this was just samples," he concluded. "We want the big buy, and we want Farnum in it up to his Adam's apple."

Larry was instructed to arrange the 640-pound deal in such a way that Farnum came out in the open. "So far we don't have him on tape, and we have only one witness to put him in possession of the grass," Peters said.

The one witness was, of course, Larry, and Peters was unwilling to go into court with no more than circumstantial evidence and the testimony of one fledgling agent. "When you set it up this time, make sure he's in the middle of it," Peters told Larry. "I want you to fix it so he meets George."

Larry nodded glumly, not unaware that behind these instructions lay the implication that he hadn't yet proved himself to Peters and the professional narcotics agents with whom he was working. "There's one problem," he said. "I don't know that Farnum will be willing to come down here to do the deal. Sorenson said something about flying the load down, but Farnum would stay up in Virginia. We'll have to deal with him up there."

That meant liaison with Virginia authorities. It was one thing to send a single undercover man into another state, but now they were going to need at least two men to do the deal from the inside and more men on the outside, monitoring the recorders and working as backup. They would need Virginia men for the monitoring to make sure the tapes would stand up in court.

"I can set it up with my man up there," Eason said. "But I think it's got to take a little time. I don't reckon as I can get them all moving by tomorrow. What's the chances of stalling this thing out a little?"

Larry guessed he could have a few days but not much more.

In the morning Larry called Farnum in Basset Forks. "Look, Floyd, I got in touch with my guy, and he's ready to go, but we've got a problem," he reported.

Farnum said, "I don't wanna hear about it. You got a problem, you tell Sorenson."

"Sorenson's the problem. George doesn't want to deal with him, says he's got too big a mouth."

"That's bullshit."

"It is, huh? I've got him right here, I'll put him on the line. Ask him who's Peter Walzer."

Peter Walzer used to be a crooked lawyer in Lynchburg until the organization had had him hit. He was one of the examples Sorenson had cited to Clardy, who now took the phone and recited the facts as Sorenson had given them.

"See what I mean?" he asked. "I can use the weed right about now, but that asshole's fixin' to get us all popped. I know a shitload about your business already, mister, and I ain't even met you. No way I want that myna bird knowing what I'm into."

Larry had known beforehand that the ploy would work. Unless he was completely wrong about Farnum, it wouldn't take much to get him to do his own dealing. That was really what he wanted in the first place, and he was using Sorenson only because he felt obligated to exercise a certain amount of caution for form's sake. But it was recklessness and recklessness alone that appealed to him, and sooner or later he would come out front without prompting. The prompting made sure it was sooner.

"Get up here, we'll talk," he said. "You and Spivey both."

At dawn the next morning, December 8, Larry, Mike Eason, and George Clardy set off for Roanoke in a Volkswagen minibus owned by GBI and registered to a nonexistent owner. Early in the afternoon they pulled to a stop at a pay phone on Williamson Road in Roanoke. Eason called the state police barracks and had the dispatcher raise Trooper Barry Keessee, who radioed back instructions that they stay right where they were.

Ten minutes later a light tan Pontiac LeMans pulled up beside the VW, and the muscular driver motioned for Eason to follow. They wound through a modest residential district of crisply painted homes set smack in the middle of their precise little lawns. The Pontiac swung into a driveway, and Eason slid the VW in behind it.

A blond giant of a man unfolded himself from behind the wheel of the Pontiac. Barry Keessee stood six feet six inches tall and weighed a good 270 pounds, every one of them seriously muscled. His hair, thinning slightly and starting well back on his forehead, was cut short and lay limply across his skull, making his head look that much more immense. Like his father before him, being a cop was the only job he'd ever known. He hated all criminals and went after them with a fierce intensity that would have been downright grim if it wasn't tempered by his boisterous, Rabelaisian wit. He shook hands with Eason, who introduced him to Clardy and Spivey. The four men went into the house through the kitchen door at the side.

There was another round of introductions to Keessee's wife Peggy, a tall, well-shaped young woman with long jet black hair falling far down her back. Keessee scooped two six-packs of beer from the refrigerator and led the way down the basement stairs. State Troopers Carl Beavers and Wayne Oyler were already waiting in the den. Beavers clicked off the television as Keessee ushered in the Georgians.

The oldest of the trio at thirty-eight, Beavers was attached to the State Police Intelligence Section. Oyler, ten years his junior, was with the Organized Crime Narcotics Section. They ripped the tabs off the beers Keessee tossed their way and settled onto the couch, ready to listen.

Eason led off with a full outline of the case, which sounded all too familiar to the Virginians. None of them had ever heard of Floyd Farnum, but they were sure they knew the organization he worked for. Keessee had spent virtually all of the last two years undercover, trying to learn something about the intricate finances of some of Virginia's leading known racketeers. He confessed he hadn't been able to get to first base. "Whoever does their bookkeeping has gotta be some kind of a genius," he confessed grudgingly.

"That's Farnum," Larry said. "He is."

Beavers explained that Virginia intelligence had documented several large drug deals involving the organization Farnum apparently worked for, the largest of which was an eighteen-ton load handled by three Mexican brothers operating out of Texas.

Eason and Clardy exchanged glances. "The Vázquez brothers, right?" Clardy asked. "Son of a bitch, I think just about everything's coming in from Mexico right about now, and a good half of it's going through them. We almost had a line into the whole outfit. Last spring this guy named Andy Plott flew in eleven thousand pounds of grass, put it down just outside Winder. We never would have known about it, except his navigator flipped on him. Seems he just signed on to make a regular cargo run, picking up a load of carpet or something like that. When they get him up in the air, they hand him a new set of charts and tell him to plot a course for somewhere a half a day from nowhere in the middle of the fucking Colombian jungle. The next thing he knows he's on this dirt runway and there's Indians loading bales into the plane. Don't look like no kind of carpet he ever saw. So I asked him what he did then.

"And he says, 'Hell, I went back and helped. What would you have done?'

"Anyway, when they get back to Georgia, this Plott guy pays him ten grand, and he makes a beeline to our office, lays out the whole story for us. We had an indictment all set on Plott, who was a nervous kind of guy. Figured if we squeezed him good, he might hand up the whole fucking show. But the son of a bitch makes another run and ends up all over the side of a mountain in Dawson County. Till Larry here comes on the scene, that's the closest we ever got to sinking our hooks into anybody that knows the score."

Eason said, "We figure that group's been good for bringing in seventeen million bucks' worth of shit that we know about. Christ knows how much we never heard of. Even the ones we know about, maybe twelve million of it hit the streets. They're making us look like a bunch of assholes."

Keessee stood up and stretched, his knuckles against the ceiling. "No sense bellyachin' about it," he drawled. "We got our chance now. This time we do it the right way."

It was clear that Floyd Farnum had no knowledge of the regular smuggling channels used by his organization and no connection with them. But that didn't matter. He knew the men who did, and he had enough information on them to put all of them away forever. The trick was to work him into a good case, do a buy-bust that would leave him standing all by himself on this end of a thirty-year lease on a prison cell, and then turn him around. "If a guy like that sings," Oyler gloated, "you can bet your ass it's gonna make the hit parade."

Larry looked around uncomfortably. It sounded too easy, and he doubted that Farnum could be turned. What he wanted to do was work Farnum and use him to gain access to the men he worked for. "You know, it could be we'd be better off trying to take the guy as far as we can instead of busting him now," he suggested tentatively.

Clardy eyed him coldly. "And it could be we know what we're doing," he answered.

For a few minutes no one said anything. Then they went ahead planning how to take down Floyd Farnum.

When the meeting broke up, Eason drove to Roanoke with the three Virginia troopers. Larry and George took the VW and got to the Holiday Inn near the Roanoke Airport about a quarter to six. They had told Farnum to expect them at six. Roger Sorenson was waiting for them in the lobby when they came in with their luggage. He wore his usual mask of petulant indifference, making it impossible to tell whether he knew they had complained to Farnum about him.

"We're just going to put our stuff upstairs and clean up," Larry said. "We'll see you in a couple minutes."

Sorenson nodded but said nothing.

On the way to the room Larry stopped George in the corridor. "Farnum's into electronics," he said. "When I was at his house, he showed me some bugging equipment that's better than the stuff we've got. We'd better not talk in the room."

As they unpacked some clothes and washed up, the two agents played their roles as diligently as method actors keeping in character offstage. Crossing through the lobby on their way to meet Sorenson, they spotted Eason, Keessee, Beavers, and Oyler checking in at the registration desk. Sorenson was in the lounge, drinking a Rob Roy.

"You know what," he began awkwardly when they joined him. The loose phrases of casual conversation never came easily to him, and whenever he tried to sound friendly, there was always something in his speech that came off as unnatural, as though he hadn't learned English until he was a grown man. This time he hesitated after "You know what," as though it were a real question. "Floyd asked me to meet you, said he'd be a little late," he went on. "As soon as he shows up, I'm splitting. Got a little action going. Give me your key a minute, I think I'll spruce up."

Larry handed him the key, and Sorenson downed the rest of his drink and left.

"I guess I was wrong about the room being bugged already," Larry whispered to Clardy. "He's going to do it now."

Sorenson returned a few minutes later and had just ordered another drink when Farnum walked in, signaling Sorenson to join him in the lobby for a brief private conversation—probably to confirm that the hidden microphone was in place, Larry figured. When Farnum came back into the lounge, he was alone.

Larry introduced him to George, and they immediately got down to business. Clardy said he could handle four hundred pounds, and Farnum gave him a price of $56,000, figuring $140 a pound, which was cheap for the quality grass Clardy wanted.

"This isn't some horseshit Mexican stuff, is it?" Clardy asked.

"No. I told Larry, I thought he told you. We've got ourselves in a kind of a bind, and we have to unload fast. So we're having a special. Are you sure four hundred's all you can handle?"

Clardy nodded.

"No sweat. Then here's what you do. When the deal's set, I'll give you a call in Atlanta. Have the bread ready. Larry will be with you. He checks the bread, gives it a count, and lets me know. Then you guys fly up here and check in. I'll have rooms reserved. Have the money with you. As soon as you're here, I'll call Sorenson and have him load the four hundred pounds. He flies down to Newnan—that's just south of Atlanta. Know where it is?"

Clardy said he did.

"Okay. We've got the airfield secure. Have your own man there to take delivery. When he gets the stuff, he calls you from the pay phone on the field and you turn the bread over to me. Got any problems with that?"

"I got no problems with it," Clardy answered crisply. "But I'll pick the hotel, and I'm gonna have a guy with me. My mammy didn't raise up any fools."

"Have all the guys you want," Farnum agreed. "But after that phone call comes through from Newnan, nobody leaves the fucking hotel till I'm out of there with the bread."

Larry asked what he was supposed to do after he delivered Clardy and the $56,000 to the hotel.

"You stay with him," Farnum said flatly. "Make sure nobody gets any strange ideas."

The three men shook hands around the table, then adjourned to the dining room for dinner. Farnum paid.

Late that night Larry and George checked out of the hotel and returned to Keessee's house, where they picked up Eason and drove to Atlanta.

Eason had managed not only to observe the meeting in the cocktail lounge but also to photograph it. On the negative side, the tape from the transmitter Larry had been wearing turned out almost totally inaudible, the voices drowned out by the lounge band.

Nevertheless, Eason was jubilant. "Fuck it, we don't need that," he chuckled. "We've got that poor fucker every way there is. By this time next week we'll have Farnum, his pilot, his grass, and his plane. Looks like GBI's gonna have itself an air wing. What kind of plane's he got?"

"Cessna Skymaster."

Eason nodded knowingly, although he knew next to nothing about aircraft. For a few minutes they drove in silence. "That's a good plane, isn't it?" Eason asked.

"Good enough."

"It's not a jet, is it?"

"Shit, no."

There was silence again. Then Eason wondered out loud who he would have to bust to get a jet.

Farnum and Sorenson would be Larry's first arrests, but he wasn't looking forward to it. At a headquarters strategy meeting he tried again to argue that his connection with Farnum should be exploited further instead of terminated with an arrest. But Phil Peters had the last word, backing up Eason's and Clardy's decision to do a buy-bust. To Larry, Peters's contention that he couldn't justify the continued expenditure of Georgia funds on an out-of-state case sounded depressingly parochial, but there wasn't a thing he could do about it.

The next few days passed slowly, as Larry waited for the phone call from Farnum that would tell him the deal was set. When it came, Larry, George, and GBI Agent Wally Brooks hurried to the airport and climbed aboard a state plane piloted by a member of the Georgia Highway Patrol. Heading north into Virginia, they flew over the Martinsville airport, where they spotted Farnum's twin-engine Skymaster parked on the ramp. Virginia troopers had the airport staked out and would report the moment Sorenson took off with the load. The Georgia plane would then tail it so that the drugs wouldn't get lost in case of accident, engine trouble, or any other contingency that aborted the delivery.

Landing in Lynchburg, the Georgians were met by Keessee, Beavers, and Oyler, who drove them to the state police barracks in Salem. There Keessee introduced them to twenty handpicked men, who had been pulled in from all over the state to handle the case. Oyler would accompany Clardy as the bodyguard Clardy had promised to bring. Other teams would be in nearby rooms as backup in case any of it started to go the wrong way. Surveillance and photography would be done from an upstairs room on the other side of the swimming pool.

Virginia also was providing a small airplane, a chopper, and a number of cruising vehicles that would attempt to locate the stash. The Virginians had reason to believe the drugs were stored within twenty minutes of Roanoke. It was a long shot, but if they saturated the area with reconnaissance teams and took enough air surveillance photos, they might be able to run their film backward when they found out how the delivery was being made to the airport and thus learn where the drugs had come from.

Larry, George, and Oyler waited at the barracks to give the troopers who would be covering the hotel a head start. When it was time to go, they were driven to the Roanoke Airport, where they got a cab to the Holiday Inn.

As soon as they were checked into the room the Virginia troopers had prearranged with the hotel management, Larry put in a call to Floyd Farnum.

"Where are you staying?" Farnum asked.

"Holiday Inn. Same place you told us to stay."

Farnum had guessed they would do that. "I'll be right over," he said. "Gimme twenty minutes."

Larry paced the floor as he waited. Clardy seemed relaxed, almost bored, but his mind was sorting through the contingencies, running a last-second check on all the things that could go wrong. It dawned on him that Farnum hadn't known Larry long enough to trust him completely, especially since Larry and George were supposedly old friends. He would have to take precautions against a rip-off. Probably he'd bring a couple of goons with him to make sure George didn't try to split with the money after the drugs changed hands in Georgia.

Clardy explained his thinking to Larry. "I want you to find out if he's got anybody here," Clardy instructed. "If he does, you're going to have to get with them and neutralize them."

Larry reminded Clardy that Farnum's orders were for him to stay with the money.

"Don't worry, I'll take care of that," Clardy said.

Farnum was running late. A half hour passed, then forty-five minutes.

There was a knock on the door, and Larry ran to get it, swinging the door back a few inches with the chain lock on. It was Floyd Farnum, alone. Larry let him in.

Farnum nodded in Clardy's direction and studied Oyler without saying anything. It was his first big drug deal, too, and he was as tight as an overwound watch. "Where is it?" he asked.

Oyler shifted in his seat, ready to go for his gun, while Clardy pulled a valise from under the bed and flipped the locks open. He lifted the lid and took out a gray steel cashbox, which he set on the bed in front of Farnum.

It took Farnum about ten minutes to count it. The money was in old bills, twenties, fifties, and hundreds, bundled into $10,000 and $20,000 packets. Satisfied, Farnum took a Polaroid snapshot of the money in order to prove to his cousin he had it. Then he closed the cashbox and handed it back to Clardy. "I'll be back as soon as we're loaded up," he said, moving for the door.

"Take this guy with you," Clardy said abruptly, gesturing toward Larry.

Farnum turned, challenged.

"You heard me," Clardy growled. "Spivey goes with you. He's your man, and he makes me nervous."

Farnum's eyes went from Clardy to Oyler, who shifted again and then stood up, unbuttoning his jacket. For a moment Farnum held his ground, staring at them coldly while he did a few quick calculations. Then he turned to the door again and opened it. "C'mon," he said softly, signaling Larry to follow.

When they had gone about a dozen yards down the corridor, Farnum stopped at a door and knocked sharply, one quick rap followed by two more. The door swung open, and Farnum stepped in, Larry right behind.

"Son of a bitch thinks he's smart," Farnum snapped with a slightly malicious chuckle. "It's okay, though, I've got him covered."

The man who opened the door held a shotgun cradled in the crook of his arm. A second man stood at the far side of the room next to a night table by the bed. He also held a shotgun, which he had lowered to his side when his boss stepped in. There was an FM radio receiver on the table, plugged into a wall socket.

"When it was just gonna be you and him, I figured we'd be okay," Farnum explained. "But with him bringing artillery, the two of them would have had you outnumbered. He escalates, I escalate, right?"

"Can't hurt," Larry agreed. He nodded toward the radio. "What's that about?"

Floyd Farnum was his own best audience, delighting in his cleverness. He unbuttoned his shirt and opened it, exposing a slender silvery antenna wire taped to his chest. "When you go into a cave, you tie a string to the outside," he said. "You wait here with Frank and Rupert. I'll go check in with my cousin."

He turned on his heel and opened the door, leaning his head out to peek down the corridor toward Clardy's room. Then he disappeared, pulling the door quietly closed behind him.

Frank and Rupert were pure types, Central Casting's version of the standard bodyguard. Taciturn to the point of moroseness, they wore studiously fierce scowls even when they looked at each other. Larry felt no inclination to talk to them, mostly because he knew it would have been impossible. If he had so much as asked, "How are you?" one of them undoubtedly would have come back with: "Who wants to know?" So he clicked on the television and settled back to await Farnum's return.

It was late in the afternoon and already dark when Farnum rapped on the door with his coded knock. One of the goons grabbed his shotgun and opened the door gingerly. Farnum motioned for Larry to come out.

"Jesus, Floyd," Larry complained as soon as they were alone in the corridor. "If I make George nervous, you've got no idea how nervous Godzilla and Rodan in there make me. Where the hell did you find them?"

Farnum laughed. "Just drive careful when you go through Roanoke," he said cryptically.

"I don't get it."

"They're cops, Roanoke city cops."

Larry was aghast. "Can you trust them?" he asked, to have something to say to account for the expression on his face.

"Don't sweat it, they're more crooked than we are," Farnum said offhandedly. They had reached Clardy's door, and he knocked sharply.

Clardy let them in. "We in business?" he asked.

"Not yet, but it's moving." Farnum explained that the pictures had satisfied his cousin to go ahead with the deal. Although Floyd didn't say so, apparently his cousin didn't trust him very much and was going out on a limb ordering such a large load. But everything had gone according to plan, and the cousin had sent word to the runner to begin loading the four hundred pounds for transfer to the airport. Farnum expected a confirmation from the runner to reach his cousin within a few hours.

"A few hours?" Clardy gasped. "What takes so fucking long?"

"They're careful," Farnum said. "Let's get some eats."

They ordered dinner from room service. When they had eaten, Farnum went back to his cousin's after first redepositing Larry with Frank and Rupert.

At ten o'clock Farnum was back. His pudgy, shapeless body looked slightly saggy from the strain he had been under all day, and he seemed a bit irritable as he reported on the progress.

Through the night he shuttled back and forth between his cousin's house and the motel, bringing meaningless updates on the situation. His moods swung all the way from bitchy to silly, and if he had been a three-year-old child, he would have been described as overtired. For the most part, though, he kept his usual cockiness intact, at one point showing up at the room with a Monopoly board in a paper bag. He insisted on unpacking the cash in the money box and dealing it out. For an hour and a half Larry, Clardy, Oyler, and Farnum played Monopoly with real money. Farnum said that had been one of his fantasies ever since he had been a kid.

The sky was already turning yellow when he left the motel for what he hoped would be the last time until he returned for the money. Larry waited in Clardy's room this time, simply pretending he was too lethargic to get up when his boss left. It was the first chance he had had to inform Clardy and Oyler about the two gunmen down the hall. He also told them that Farnum had himself wired, which meant his bodyguards would know the moment the arrest was made.

Clardy assessed the information and didn't seem particularly worried.

"I don't know," Larry cautioned. "It could get pretty hairy. When we try to take him out of here, those cats with the shotguns are going to think it's a rip-off. They'll probably come out shooting."

"Not if the bug's working," Clardy countered. "When I badge him, I'm gonna say it real loud and just pray they're listening. Twenty to one they just climb into bed and make like two faggots minding their own business. They're not gonna wanna even know from Floyd Farnum."

Three more hours passed before Farnum returned. His face was the color of the off-white motel room walls, and he threw himself into a chair without speaking. Finally, Clardy asked, "What the fuck's up, man?"

Farnum looked up with sorrowful eyes, like a kid whose best Christmas toy ends up broken before breakfast Christmas morning. "It's off," he said so softly his words were almost inaudible. This was to have been his first big drug deal, and he had thrown himself into it with abandon. He gave the impression he liked playing around, but Larry knew how much his games meant to him. For a minute Larry thought Farnum was going to cry.

Clardy was thinking the same thing. "What happened?" he demanded, to get the situation under control.

Farnum took a minute to get a grip on himself, then explained. Around midnight the Virginia State Police had raided a pot party in Blacksburg, about thirty miles away. They had netted nineteen people, one of whom was the runner for the Blacksburg stash.

"What's that got to do with this?" Clardy asked.

"Maybe plenty. Maybe it wasn't just luck. Could be they weren't just busting up a party. Could be they were tipped off the runner would be there, so they hit the party to make it look like an accident they got him. I told you, the runner at the stash we're dealing from is facing an attempted murder. So maybe he got turned around."

"Sounds like a reach to me," Clardy said, unconvinced.

"Yeah?" Farnum challenged. "When's the last time the fuzz busted a party? Anyway, the organization shut down everything just to be sure. Nothing moves until they can assess the damage."

"What about the runner?"

"Which one? The one in Blacksburg? They'll post bond for him in the morning, find out what he's been saying."

"And the one here?"

"He'll be taken care of. If he talked, he's got it coming. And if he didn't, then at least we'll be sure he won't."

On the flight back to Atlanta, George Clardy was livid with rage. Their own security precautions had undone them. The twenty Virginia troopers assigned to work the case had been borrowed with such secrecy that no one other than themselves and a few high-ranking headquarters types knew about the operation. If knowledge of it had been more widely disseminated, the pot party raid never would have been allowed to come off for fear it would have precisely the effect Clardy had just witnessed. Despite his frustration, Clardy knew no one was to blame. He couldn't even fault the Virginians for lack of coordination, for it was he and Eason who had insisted on total secrecy.

Larry sat next to him on the plane and looked at the matter from an entirely different perspective. He couldn't have been more delighted. For just a moment, when Farnum first broke the news, he was as disappointed as Clardy. After all his work in Guatemala, Mexico, and Atlanta, he was still a virgin, and he had himself mentally geared up for his first arrest. But it took him only a minute to realize that fate had worked the case out exactly the way he had vainly urged Inspector Peters to handle it. The deal had fallen through; but it wasn't his fault, and it wasn't Clardy's. He had set it up, and Clardy had come through with the money, which Farnum had actually held in his hands. As soon as Farnum had a chance to recover from his disappointment, he'd be back—hungrier than ever.

At the GBI debriefing meeting that afternoon, Larry had a hard time masking his satisfaction. Both Clardy and Eason had been rubbed the wrong way and were in no mood for hearing anything about the bright side of the picture. Peters didn't help things any when he said, "Well, it looks like you got what you wanted, Larry. You damn well better prove to us you were right."

Larry left the meeting with a queasy sense of elation, like the sheepish pleasure a man feels when he hears his best friend has been turned down for a job for which he is also applying. When he got to his motel room, the phone was already ringing. It was Clardy, who had remained behind at headquarters.

"Nice bunch of friends you got up there," Clardy began. "I just talked to Virginia, and they say the runner from Roanoke had nothing to do with the Blacksburg raid. He wasn't talking at all, hadn't told them a thing. And he's not going to either. Turned up dead this afternoon."

"What from?"

"Cerebral hemorrhage," Clardy said. "Three bullets in the back of his brain."

Thirteen

"Floyd, you've got the resiliency of a silicone tit," Larry said when Farnum woke him up the next morning with an urgent call for him to fly up to Roanoke. He checked in with GBI and caught the noon flight, arriving at Farnum's Bassett Forks home for lunch. Roger Sorenson was there.

"Look," Farnum said breathlessly, "I can't see dealing with this horse-shit outfit anymore. Fuck 'em. Who needs 'em? Eliminate the middleman, right?"

"What are you talking about?" Larry asked, trying to slow him down.

"I'm talking about doing a deal with George. Only this time we do our own smuggling. You said you knew some cats in Mexico, right?"

It was more than Larry had dared hope for. He still had some unfinished business to take care of with Dick Foiles and Bradley in the trailer park outside Oaxaca and with Deputy Chief Robles-Arcía in Mexico City. "Sure," he said. "If they're still there."

Farnum outlined his plan. He wanted Larry to get in touch with George to see if he could raise another hundred thousand or so on top of the fifty-six thousand he already had. Then Larry was to get in touch with his contacts in Mexico and line up a thousand pounds of the highest-grade Oaxacan tops he could find. The way Farnum was figuring it, he wouldn't have to pay more than $50 a pound if Larry's contacts were still willing to live up to the price they had quoted when he was there. Add $10,000 for expenses. George would probably go as high as $160 a pound for *primo*

Oaxacan, so the profit would come to a cool and tidy $100,000. Sorenson would fly down in the Cessna Skymaster to pick up the load.

"You reckon George can handle that much about every week or so?" he asked.

"Shit, I don't know if he can do it now," Larry answered cautiously. "Right now he's pissed at you, and his people are pissed at him."

Nothing dampened Farnum's enthusiasm. Even before Larry could get through to George, Floyd sent Sorenson down to Gainesville, Florida, to have the Skymaster serviced so it would be ready for the run. He had a mechanic there he trusted to ask no questions when he was requested to rip out the passenger seats to make room for the load, remove the copilot's seat, and replace it with a fuel drum to extend the aircraft's range beyond its normal twelve hundred miles. He ordered Sorenson to call him as soon as the mechanic could give an estimate on when the work would be done.

Larry got through to Clardy on the cool phone at GBI headquarters late in the afternoon. He began to explain what Farnum had in mind, but Clardy cut him off. "Let me talk to him," he said.

"Awright, weasel, what are you shaking my tree for?" Clardy began as soon as Farnum was on the line.

"I want to do some business."

"I already did business with you, you know that. Kinda like fucking an empty bed."

"Look, man, that wasn't my fault and you know it. It was those other assholes. This time we don't have to go through them."

"Awright, lay it out for me and I'll listen. But I'm not making any promises."

Farnum told him what he had in mind. Clardy hemmed and hawed and finally conceded he was hurting for lack of goods to sell. "Count me in," he said. "Only this time it better move in the right direction or I'm coming up there personally and shredding your hide. I got some niggers here'll smoke you if they can't get nothin' better."

They talked a few minutes more. Clardy said it would take him a few days to line up the money, which was acceptable to Farnum since it would take him that long to make the arrangements on his end. As soon as Farnum hung up the phone, Larry placed a call to the trailer park outside Oaxaca, where he left word for Bradley to call him back. An hour later Bradley returned his call.

"Shit, man, we was wondering what happened to you," the young smuggler began.

"Keeping busy. Look, those shirts I talked to you about importing, are they still available?"

The code term *shirts* had been selected because Bradley did a small legitimate business exporting *típicos*—handmade Indian shirts.

"Sure. You interested in placing an order?"

"Wouldn't have called otherwise. The only thing is the quantity. We talked about two hundred, but my buyers here think they can move a thousand if the quality is as good as the merchandise I saw."

"No shit. Yeah, I can handle it. How soon?"

"I can be there day after tomorrow, arrange for delivery."

"Cool. I'll need two and a half bills to cover my expenses. Wire it down. We'll straighten out the rest when you get here. Same price, fifty, right?"

"Right."

Farnum gave Larry $1,250, $250 for Bradley and $1,000 to cover his own expenses on the trip. Returning to Atlanta that evening, Larry met with the GBI team at headquarters and briefed them on his plans. In order to pick up the dropped stitches of the case he was weaving against Robles-Arcía, he called the Atlanta office of the Drug Enforcement Administration and asked it to send a coded telex to Ray Basch in Mexico City, informing Basch that "Allen Carter" would be arriving late Wednesday and would be at his disposal. Shortly before Larry left for Mexico, Farnum called him at his motel to say the Skymaster was ready and Sorenson would be flying it down, stopping first at Veracruz in order to enter Mexico legally. Sorenson would meet him in Oaxaca on Friday.

Larry caught a late-afternoon flight from Atlanta on Wednesday, December 17. He was met at the Mexico City airport by two DEA agents, who checked him into a suite of rooms in a stately Spanish-style hotel on the Paseo de la Reforma not far from the American Embassy. The DEA had a permanent lease on the rooms, which it maintained as a safe house for undercover operatives.

In the bar set in a corner of the lobby, the agents introduced Larry to the DEA's chief of intelligence for Latin America as well as the senior agent in charge for Guatemala. The intelligence chief was a tall, slender man in his mid-forties, with impeccable manners and slightly clipped speech that suggested the Midwest. He looked more CIA than narc, and in fact he was carried on the books as an embassy employee rather than a DEA agent. The agent from Guatemala was younger, shorter, and darker, of indeterminate Latin origin. He opened the discussion by apologizing for Taveras's blunders in Guatemala on Larry's last trip. Then he asked for Larry's assessment of the situation in both Guatemala and Mexico.

Speaking quickly and keeping to the essentials, Larry outlined three cases. The first was Quintana in Guatemala. Larry would test the waters with Jefferson Juárez but wouldn't return to Guatemala himself because of the danger that Juárez and Quintana knew his true identity. If it seemed they didn't, and if Juárez was still interested in dealing the cocaine, Larry would arrange an introduction to an undercover DEA agent, who would take it from there. The second case was Robles-Arcía, whom Larry would handle himself. The third was Bradley and his friend Dick Foiles. On Larry's last trip to Oaxaca, Foiles had mentioned a cocaine factory in Peru. He had said he was trying to get something set up. "I think if we work it right, we can close them down," Larry suggested.

At nine o'clock the next morning Larry reported to the American Embassy, where the code name Allen Carter magically opened the series of combination-locked doors leading to Deputy Director Basch's office. Basch crossed an acre of carpet to greet him, smiling warmly with his hand extended as though he were steering himself through a crowd. After a few pleasantries, he turned Larry around and led him to the lounge area, where the two men Larry had met already and two others he had never seen before rose from the upholstered chairs. Basch made introductions.

Raúl Moncado was chief of Mexico City field operations. A balding, overweight man in his mid-fifties, he was a second-generation American of Bolivian descent who had come over to the DEA after resigning with the rank of captain from the San Francisco Police Department. Sante Barrio, who called himself Sandy, was a scowling Italian with the dark good looks of a movie actor and the constantly moving eyes of a practiced undercover agent. "Sandy will be going to Guatemala to have a crack at Quintana," Basch said. "If he can't set up anything with them, no one could. He's the best undercover man we've got. But before he goes down there, he's going to stick around here awhile and give you all the help you need."

Basch tried to lead the ensuing discussion, but Larry took the ball away from him, insisting there would be no basis for cooperation unless the DEA was willing to accept his priorities. No move would be made that jeopardized his Georgia case. Larry agreed to contact Robles-Arcía immediately and arrange to introduce him to Barrio, who would work out a heroin deal. As soon as the undercover agent and the corrupt deputy chief had been put together, Larry would leave for Oaxaca, where he would remain in contact with Bradley and Foiles until Roger Sorenson was safely on his return flight to Georgia with a thousand pounds of Mexican marijuana stowed in the belly pod and the stripped-down passenger section of Floyd Farnum's Skymaster.

Larry insisted on and got Basch's personal assurance that no move would be made against Robles-Arcía until Sorenson was airborne out of Oaxaca. He didn't want a premature arrest in the Mexican case blowing his cover and aborting the deal with Farnum, which had fallen through once already.

"I'll send Bradley and Foiles back up here when I'm finished with them in Oaxaca," he said, addressing himself directly to Barrio. "I'll get them together with you for a load of coke. You've got to come on heavy because I think they can handle small quantities themselves. But for a big enough order, they'll cut out whoever they're buying from and head straight for the lab in Peru. Then it's yours."

The corners of Barrio's mouth pulled back in a tight-lipped acknowledgment, but he said nothing.

The meeting broke up late in the afternoon, leaving everyone satisfied with the scenario that had been worked out for the cases in Mexico, Guatemala, and Peru. As Larry left the office, Basch took him aside and thanked him again for the information he had given on his last trip about the smugglers working out of La Higuera trailer park. Larry's report had been passed on to Customs, and it had resulted in forty arrests at various points along the border in California, Arizona, New Mexico, and Texas.

Larry and Barrio left the embassy together, knowing they would have no further contact with any law enforcement agency in Mexico until their missions were completed. From the moment Larry got in touch with Robles-Arcía, he would be subject to wiretaps and surveillance by corrupt police officers working under the drug-dealing deputy chief. Barrio would fall under the same scrutiny the instant Larry introduced him to Robles-Arcía. So they were on their own, with no tie line back to the agencies they worked for, no access to the straight world except through each other. For however long it took, they would be actors trapped onstage, forced to keep in character even in their sleep. Larry remembered that when he was a kid his family had taken him to New York, where he fed a hippopotamus named Rosa in the Central Park Zoo, went to the top of the Empire State Building, and then went to Radio City Musical Hall. The picture was *The Greatest Show on Earth,* and there was a clown in it who never took off his makeup.

He had dinner with Barrio at a small restaurant near Barrio's hotel. When they finished their meal, Larry called Robles-Arcía at home. The Mexican agreed to meet them for drinks later that evening.

He arrived alone, as he had done the first time he met Larry. This time there was no small talk. Larry introduced Barrio as the man who would be handling the arrangements for the American syndicate they both worked for.

"You are considering what quantity?" Robles-Arcía asked crisply.

"We are ready to start with twelve kilos," Barrio answered before Larry could say anything. "We will need the usual assurances."

"Inevitably." Robles-Arcía smiled, his gold teeth gleaming phosphorescently in the dark gold glow of the candlelit bar.

Larry stood up. "I'm sure you'll work out what needs to be worked out," he said. "There is no reason we shouldn't have a mutually beneficial association."

Robles-Arcía stood and reached out his hand for Larry's, gratified by the cold courtliness of Larry's manner, which perfectly mirrored his own style. The three men shook hands all around. Then Larry downed the rest of his scotch to seal the understanding and left the bar. Robles-Arcía belonged to Barrio now, and there was nothing further for Larry to do.

At his own hotel he drank alone in the bar until midnight, stopped at the front desk to leave a wake-up call for seven o'clock, and went to bed. In the morning he caught an Aeromexico flight for Oaxaca and arrived a few hours before noon. Foiles met him at the airport and checked him into a hotel. The young smuggler followed him upstairs to his room, grinning like a kid bringing a good report card home from school. He closed the door and locked it, looked around for spies lurking in the corners, and then announced, "We can talk here."

"We could have talked in the van," Larry reminded him. Foiles was blessed with an incapacity for perceiving when he was being put down.

"We got it all lined up," he bubbled. "Half a fucking ton, and it's gonna go like we was selling potatoes. No sweat. We're having dinner tonight with the biggest fucking grower in Mexico." He pronounced it in Spanish, *Mejico.*

"He'd better be," Larry said coldly. "My man's flying in tomorrow, and he expects to be looking at a thousand pounds."

Bradley was waiting for them downstairs under the umbrella that rose from the middle of a table in front of the hotel. They spent an hour

158

drinking beer from half-gallon pitchers as they watched the languorous comings and goings of Mexicans through the large, sun-soaked square. In the center of the square stood a wedding-cake gazebo, its intricate rococo lines challenging the adobe flatness of the buildings sprawled at its flanks. Larry noticed that a large dark-haired American seated with a brunette at a café down the street seemed to be studying him. Not wanting to spook Bradley and Foiles, he watched the man out of the corner of his eye, careful not to call their attention to him.

The man was still there when Bradley said it was time to go. They walked to Foiles's van, which was parked just beyond the square, and drove to the airport on the outskirts of town. There they were met by a taciturn Mexican sitting behind the wheel of a Dodge four-door pickup truck. Larry and the two drug dealers climbed into the back seat, and the Mexican drove off, heading to the southwest. "The farm's about a half hour from here," Bradley explained.

As they drove through the flat, featureless valley, the mountains rising around them like the sides of a clay bowl still imperfectly shaped on a potter's wheel, Larry memorized the few turns they made. The pickup wound from the main highway onto a series of badly paved and unpaved side roads, leading finally to a straight road overarched by a canopy of regularly spaced trees. The driver pulled onto the shoulder and executed a U-turn, driving back up the road about two miles before U-turning again. He pulled to a stop, and a tall, almost gaunt Mexican stepped from behind a tree. Larry noticed that his left arm hung limply by his side.

The tall Mexican climbed into the cab. "We were not followed?" the driver asked in Spanish.

"*No. Vamos,*" the tall Mexican growled. From his armpit he removed a sinister-looking Ruger .44 caliber revolver with a long seven-and-a-half-inch barrel. He laid the weapon on his lap.

"This is Mako," Bradley said. "The operation is his."

The Mexican grunted a greeting but kept a hand on the gun in his lap.

The pickup turned onto a rutted access road that ended at a small shed in the middle of a thickly growing field. This time Larry knew enough to recognize the vegetation around him as marijuana. There were perhaps seven or eight acres of the weed in the field in front of the shed. The field behind lay fallow. A middle-aged Mexican with a badly pockmarked face was waiting for them by the shed. He worked the field for Mako.

"Is it ready?" Bradley asked, after Mako had conferred with the farmer.

"Come, I will show you," Mako growled.

The tin-roofed shed measured no more than twelve by twenty feet. Its walls were wooden slats, and there was one door, closed with a heavy padlock. Mako dragged a key from deep in the pockets of his baggy trousers and swung the door open. Larry followed Bradley and Foiles inside.

Along the back wall, piled to the ceiling, were dried marijuana plants. A hydraulic press powered by a hand pump stood in the middle of the dirt floor. Mako walked past the three Americans to a jumble of well-stuffed burlap sacks clustered in a corner. He folded back the mouth of one of the sacks and stepped back, displaying his wares—about forty tightly compacted kilo bricks of rich brown marijuana.

"It's dynamite shit," Dick Foiles volunteered. "We came out the other day and smoked some."

Larry pried a few leaves loose and examined them, massaging them between his thumb and his fingers. "The color's good," he said laconically, dropping the loose fibers into the sack and folding the burlap closed. He turned to walk out of the dark shed, but Mako stopped him.

"You would like to see, perhaps, the *tecata*?"

Larry looked at him questioningly.

"Heroin," Bradley said.

"*Sí, heroína. Heroína morena.* Brown heroin."

From a low shelf tacked to one wall of the shed Mako removed a square cardboard box. Another identical to it remained on the shelf. The Mexican opened the box and handed it to Larry.

The coarse powder was the color and texture of potted earth, and Larry estimated there was as much as two kilos of it in a single sealed plastic bag. He handed the box back to Mako.

Outside, under the glaring sun, Larry said, "My people have a definite interest in the heroin. If everything is satisfactory with this first load, we will talk."

Mako's bony arm was draped over Larry's shoulder as they walked back to the pickup truck. "Yes, yes," he said, smiling ingratiatingly as he leaned around so far he was practically looking straight into Larry's eyes, even though they were walking side by side. "We will talk tonight about the marijuana, *señor*. My man will drive you back to your car. You will honor me by dining with me in Oaxaca tonight?"

It was a question.

"Yes, it must be tonight," Larry said. "Delivery will be tomorrow."

"Then there is much we must talk about. It is more pleasant over good food, a glass of whiskey, no?"

160

Larry climbed into the back seat of the pickup, between Bradley and Foiles. As they retraced their path through the fields, they saw the farmer they had met at the shed. He was squatting in a parched field in front of a small house Larry hadn't noticed on the way in. With him was a little girl, perhaps eight or ten years old, her face a mask of concentrated attention as she listened to something the man was telling her. She was a pretty child, with dark, innocent eyes.

"His daughter?" Larry asked.

"*Sí,*" the driver said, turning over his shoulder to look at Larry, as though he were surprised by the question. In the field, the man didn't look up as the pickup drove by.

At the airport the three Americans transferred back to Foiles's van and returned to their table at the café. They ordered another pitcher of beer. Larry noticed that the dark-haired man who seemed to have been watching him earlier in the afternoon was no longer around, but a half hour later he was back again at the same table at the same café down the street. He still had the pretty brunette with him.

More than an hour passed, and then the stranger rose from his chair and stooped to whisper something to the brunette. He stood well over six feet tall, was wearing an open shirt, blue jeans, and leather sandals. He patted the girl on the top of her head as one pats a dog, then turned in Larry's direction, walking slowly with long strides, as though the dusty sidewalk were his property.

Dick Foiles saw him coming when he was still fifty feet away. "Drake," he whispered urgently to Bradley, who turned to look.

Bradley turned back to his beer and kept his eyes there as Drake came up and stood over his shoulder, his shadow falling across the table as though he had arranged the lighting on purpose. "Beat it, Shel, we're talking business," Bradley said, his eyes still on the glass he held in both hands.

"Who's your friend?" Drake asked. His voice was a surprising tenor, a whole octave higher than it should have been. Larry picked the accent as Deep South, probably Mississippi.

"It's none of your business, Shel," Bradley said, holding his ground well. "Beat it."

The tall man stepped around from behind Bradley and stood directly over Larry. "The name's Shelton Drake, mister. I'm at the Río, just back of the square. Ask anybody, they'll know how to find me. If you're doing business in town, it don't make no sense doing it with these turkeys. Not smart either, right? Take care, Bradley. Dick."

He turned and swaggered across the sunlit square like the bad guy in a cheap Western. Instead of disappearing behind locked doors and sealed shutters, however, the locals in Oaxaca made nothing of him either way, and for an instant Larry wondered if he was the town joke. But the blatant bulge under his tight-fitting shirt was a real enough gun, and Bradley and Dick didn't seem to think there was anything funny in what had just happened.

"What the hell was that?" Larry asked when Shelton Drake had vanished beyond the far side of the sun-washed plaza.

Bradley sucked on his lip before answering. "Shelton Harrison Drake the Third, crazy as a fucking bedbug. But he's heavy, don't kid yourself."

"What's he got, a lease on the territory or something?"

"No way. Half the time he's laid back, coolest son of a bitch you ever saw. You can talk to him, know what I mean? And the other half he's something between Hitler and Al Capone. Coked up higher than a blimp and thinks he runs the world. But he's got that forty-five, and I know he's used it. I mean I know it, man. Wasted a couple cats for dealing with somebody else. He's been here like nine years, never been busted, and a thousand percent convinced he never will be. Could be we've got some trouble, I don't know. And it could be we won't see him again."

Larry said, "Well, I'll tell you one thing. I don't want a tiger like that coming up in back of me. Can he be talked to?"

"Like what?"

"Like if I tell him we already got the deal set, but I make him some promises for next time. Is that going to do any good?"

Bradley thought it might, but he wanted assurances Larry wouldn't take his business to Drake. Larry gave them, but already a plan was forming in the back of his mind to take the man down. Drake had nothing to do with the case he was working on, but Larry didn't care. He was on his own now, and he felt a sudden and inexplicable revulsion for the tactical intricacies of carefully plotted moves and countermoves. Drake dealt drugs, and busting drug dealers was the name of the game. There was no reason it had to be more complicated than that.

Mako didn't arrive until dusk was well along toward night. He joined Larry, Bradley, and Dick at their table, where he immediately summoned a waiter and ordered massive servings of practically everything on the café's menu. He ate little himself. The moment dinner was over and the coffee served, he got down to business, promising to deliver a thousand pounds of the marijuana Larry had seen that afternoon to a location to be designated by Bradley the following day.

When Mako had paid for dinner and left, Larry informed his suppliers that he was going to try to make peace with Shelton Drake. "Just don't make any deals with him, that's all," Bradley repeated. "We'll match his price on any quantity, and we'll get you better shit."

Larry promised to meet them at the café in the morning. He crossed the square in the direction Drake had gone and had no difficulty finding the Hotel Río, a square three-story wood building from which all the paint had long since peeled. A balcony supported by slender poles ran along the front. The desk clerk directed Larry to a room on the second floor.

The brunette opened the door, inching it back only enough to see who was on the other side. Behind her Larry could see Drake standing by the far wall, his hand on his flank where he kept the .45. Pushing against the door firmly enough to move the girl back, Larry stepped into the room. "You wanted to see me?" he demanded.

Drake tensed momentarily, then grinned. "You bet your ass, ace," he said. "C'mon in."

The girl closed the door behind Larry and locked it with the sliding bolt.

Larry tossed his head in her direction. "Does she have to be here?"

"Jackie's okay. She's in the business."

"I don't give a shit what business she's in. She's not in my business."

"Hey, no call to come on like that, ace," Drake said, his hands in front of him, palms down. "If y'all wanna do some dealin', le's get this thing started on the right foot, huh?"

Larry knew he was expected to be angry. His role as a dealer called upon him to protest when an outsider tried to muscle him, and he had to play out the part. When it had gone on long enough, he would let Drake calm him down.

"I didn't come here to do any dealing," he said. "I did my dealing with my friends downstairs. I just thought we had to get something straightened away, like about what happens to guys who come up in back of me when I'm busy."

Drake grinned again but said nothing. Threats meant nothing to him.

Larry said, "Thanks for setting my mind at ease. Now that I know there won't be any more mistakes like that, I can rejoin my friends."

He turned for the door, but Jackie was standing squarely in front of it. "Pleasure meeting you, ma'am," he drawled, exaggerating his accent. He put his hand on her shoulder and moved her out of his way.

"I didn't even get the name, ace," Drake said coolly.

"Spivey."

"Well, don't be in such a hurry, Spivey. I'm just tryin' to do you some good."

"Like what?" Larry's hand had moved to the door lock.

"Like those guys are turkeys, ace. I wouldn't shit you. Ask around."

"I'm satisfied."

"Could be. There's a first time for everything, ace. Only they ain't done nothin' right since they been in this fuckin' armpit of a town. Have they made a load for you yet?"

"Is that any of your business?"

"Stay cool, tiger. I just don't like no one leavin' Oaxaca 'cept satisfied customers. Gives the town a bad name. Guaranteed if they make a load for you, it's a miracle. No way they'll make two. If you don't mind my sayin' it, ace, you don't look like the kinda cat that's jes' buyin' himself smokes. I reckon you're lookin' for something kinda steadylike."

"And that's you?"

"Better believe it," Drake said. "Do yourself a favor, man, and take a look here."

Drake crossed to an unpainted pine dresser and yanked open a drawer. It was packed with dried marijuana tightly bundled with twine. He opened a second drawer and a third, threw open a closet door, and stepped back to gauge the effect of the display.

Even from where he stood, Larry could see that no two of the bundles were the same. There must have been samples of thirty different strains of marijuana, some of it almost lime green, some the same rich brown as Jackie's hair, some a deep burnished gold. Jesus, Larry thought. His eyes showed that was what he was thinking.

"C'mere," Drake said, leading the way to the bathroom. From a wicker hamper he extracted a gallon jar filled to the neck with small white tablets the size of aspirin. Larry examined them closely. They were scored across the diameter, the letters *ROR* stamped above the scoring, the number 714 below. Quaaludes.

"Got smack, white and brown, got coke, pink coke, got syringes, any fuckin' thing you want. C'mon, ace, let's have a smoke."

He went back to the dresser, rummaged around until he found the sample he wanted, and held it up for Larry's inspection. It was a beautiful gold, lighter than any grass Larry had ever seen, the color of toast. Clearing a space in one of the drawers, Drake cleaned the leaves, letting the stems and fibers drop into the drawer. He rolled a joint, lit it, and passed it to Larry before rolling two more for himself and Jackie.

Larry sucked the hot, pungent smoke into his lungs and held it there, then exhaled slowly. He paused and took a second drag, peering into the smoke that curled through his fingers, weaving them like a cat's cradle. Beyond the filaments of smoke he could see Shelton Drake drifting backward in the room, floating in space, his feet barely making contact with the undulating floor. Jackie was by his side, bobbing like a marker buoy in a gently swelling sea. Larry stared at her hard, trying to get his bearings. He could see through her clothes, could see her full, rounded breasts only so slightly flattened against her suddenly transparent shirt.

Then she was moving toward him, borne on the air, just her face framed in brown hair, her breasts, and her nipples like the malevolent red eyes of a wild pig coming on him in the dark. He looked around for Drake and couldn't find him, and at that moment he realized he was going to be sick.

He took a lurching step toward the bathroom, stumbling, then falling, as the floor and ceiling switched places. Holding firmly on the doorjamb, he managed to pull himself into the bathroom and got the toilet seat up before puking everything inside him into the bowl. He crashed to the floor, yanking the toilet handle as he fell. For a long time he lay motionless, his left temple pressed to the cool tile while the sound of rushing water went on and on, carrying everything away. With his eyes closed he could see in the torrent pink lungs and long bilious yellow intestines the color of banana peels hurtling downward through a gleaming chrome pipe. There were particles of food, a heart the color of raw meat, and a thousand other garish things he didn't want to recognize. The water from the toilet churned itself to a phosphorescent froth before it finally stopped. The pipes drained dry, and then he couldn't see into them anymore.

He opened his eyes and reached for the bathtub to pull himself to a sitting position. The motion of the walls was milder now, and he made it to his feet. He blinked twice, twice more, hoping it would help him think.

Jesus Christ. He had smoked grass before, barely getting high, even when it was supposed to be good stuff. Not quite true. He had been high, but not anything you could call stoned, not even, really, well buzzed. He used to think it was because he was too uptight, like the type of personality they say can't be hypnotized. Either that or marijuana was overrated. But this was like nothing he had ever known before, and if he had been asked, he wouldn't have thought it possible. There must have been something in that grass, something Drake had treated it with.

He took a deep breath with his eyes closed and then got a firm grip on the towel rack before exhaling and opening his eyes. Still holding on, he took a tentative step forward with his left foot, planting it firmly while he paused to gauge his balance. It felt as if control were returning.

Of his feet, yes. But he was oddly disembodied, as though the wobbly, bearded man in the middle of the bathroom floor were an unpredictable stranger for whose actions he would be held responsible. He thought of Shelton Drake's .45 and of what Bradley had said. *I know he's used it. I mean I know it, man.* He felt like he imagined a man must feel under sodium pentothal and wondered if the marijuana could have been treated with it. Over and over he reminded himself that when he came out of the bathroom, he couldn't let on who he was, but he realized he had no way of knowing what he would say and no way to control it.

He felt the blood draining from his face and knew with absolute clarity that he had never been so frightened in his life, not in Laos, not in his worst nightmares.

For an instant he thought he would be sick again, but the feeling passed. He stepped through the bathroom door and scanned the room. At first there was no one there, but he heard grunting sounds and looked harder until finally he found the two of them in bed. Jackie was on top of Drake, naked, her legs and back coppery tan, her buttocks almost luminous white, gleaming in the pale light of the lamp on the table beside the bed.

He moved closer, pulled by a strangely detached fascination until he was standing over them. Without realizing he was doing it, he put his hand on her ass and held it there, feeling her move, hearing her moan. Then he took his hand away.

"Catch up with you later, man," he said.

He turned and staggered from the room.

Fourteen

Waking up was like swimming to air out of deep water. At first the room shimmered before his eyes, like sunlight on the surface, gradually coming to clarity. He was amazed to find he was still high, but it was only a residual effect that wore off by the time he had trimmed his beard, showered, and dressed. Only then did he check his watch. It was almost noon.

At the front desk he left word for Roger Sorenson that he was having breakfast in the café and would be back within an hour. Bradley and Foiles came by while he was eating to ask if the pilot had arrived.

"He was supposed to get to Veracruz yesterday, then fly over here this morning," Larry said. "He should be here soon." He didn't tell them about his experience with Shelton Drake, and they didn't ask. They told him where he could find them when the pilot hit town, then left him alone with his half-eaten breakfast.

He checked back in at the desk around one. There was no word from Sorenson, so he went up to his room for an hour, figuring a nap might do him some good. But he was too restless to sleep, his nerves as charged up as his mind was lethargic. He left another note for Sorenson and returned to the café for more coffee. Later in the afternoon he switched to scotch.

"Mind if I join you?" a woman's voice asked from just over his shoulder.

He swung his head around, expecting to see Jackie. Instead, it was a girl he had never seen before. His eyes moved slowly up her body, in a way he hadn't looked at a woman since he had first got himself caught up in his double life. Last night in Drake's room a switch had been turned on that he hadn't realized had been turned off, and now he found himself scanning slowly from the fullness of her hips to her slender waist cinched with a double strand of black lanyard securing a large silver-mounted turquoise. Her breasts were full and obviously free under a Mexican peasant blouse. She had powder-white skin so fair he could see the light blue tracings of blood vessels in her neck and cheeks, like the delicate hatchings of an engraver's awl on a fine old etching. Her hair was shorter than he would have expected, jet black, and tightly curled, as though she had consciously opted for some signal of strength to counterpoise her overwhelming femininity.

"I'm Julie," she said, pulling out a chair and slipping into it, a gliding motion so self-conscious it reminded him of the mannered movements of an actress onstage. He wondered if there were still finishing schools where they taught girls to sit that way.

"Larry," he nodded. "What'll you have?"

"A margarita."

He signaled for a waiter, ordered another scotch and a margarita. "Larry what?" she asked.

"Julie what?"

"Cooper."

"Spivey."

It wasn't a good start, very cold, edged with a hostility he couldn't account for, couldn't even tell whether it was coming from her or from himself. But when the drinks arrived, they both loosened up. She said she was from San Francisco, a secretary between jobs. She had come to Oaxaca in September, just for a vacation, and had stayed on without really understanding why. She said she had enough money to last past New Year's, and then she would have to go back and look for a job.

"My friends probably think I'm dead," she said, laughing deliberately, her laugh like the pleasant, mechanical sound of a music box.

Larry didn't believe her but didn't care, since he had reasons of his own for lying. He told her he was a real estate developer from Atlanta. He said he had only a week's vacation, had been to Mexico City already, was allowing himself only a couple of days in Oaxaca.

They drank through the afternoon, the conversation pleasant and impersonal, about their travels more than about themselves, as though by some tacit agreement not to probe too deeply into each other's bad faith. As the hours passed, the dust-clogged sunlight withdrew from the square and shadows crept in. Sorenson didn't arrive, and Larry found himself listening absently to the girl while he tried to figure out what had gone wrong.

By five o'clock he knew Sorenson wasn't coming. With the sun already down, Sorenson would have had to fly from Veracruz on instrument regulations, which required filing a flight plan, and there was no way he would make the run if it meant leaving a record of his destination.

Larry waited until six, when a small army band began tuning up in the gazebo in the center of the square. He invited Julie to join him for dinner, and when she consented, he suggested that they meet right where they were in an hour and a half. He went back to his hotel and used the phone booth in the lobby to place a call to Floyd Farnum in Bassett Forks. It took almost five minutes for the call to go through. Farnum took his number and said he would call back.

It took Farnum no more than ten minutes to find a safe phone.

"Where's Roger? He didn't show," Larry demanded.

"I know, I know, we had some problems. He's still here."

"Jesus Christ. When the hell's he gonna get here? I can't keep these people waiting."

"Looks like you're gonna have to. I'll tell you what happened. He got the Skymaster all fitted out, and when he went down to Gainesville to pick it up, the mechanic said there were some people nosing around the plane, asking questions. They even took some pictures. The mechanic thought they were feds. I don't know how the fuck they got onto us. You didn't tell anybody about it, did you?"

"C'mon, Floyd."

"Like maybe a broad or something. You never can tell, y'know."

"Fuck off."

"Awright, awright. Well, anyway, maybe the mechanic's a little paranoid, but I think Rog did the right thing. Get your ass back up here; we'll figure something out."

Larry hung up the phone and cursed to himself. He had told the DEA a thousand times he wanted them to stay out of his Georgia case. That was the price he demanded for helping them in Mexico. But they must have put a tail on Sorenson, and they had blown it. He dialed Sandy Barrio at his hotel in Mexico City. When the undercover agent called back a few minutes later, Larry told him the marijuana deal had fallen through, and there was no longer any reason to hold back on making a buy from Robles-Arcía and arresting him. "I'm sending two men to see you. Bradley and Foiles. They've got a thousand pounds all lined up, so they'll be ready to roll on that. Feel them out on the coke thing, too. I'm sure they'll bite."

Barrio asked him what his plans were, and Larry said he wanted to stay in Oaxaca another day or so to see if anything could be salvaged. "Call the locals down here and have them get in touch with me. I've got some stuff they'll be interested in. But for Christ's sake, tell them to be a little discreet. I don't want a bunch of Mexes with badges on their shirts marching into my hotel."

He checked his watch and saw that he still had more than an hour until he was to meet Julie for dinner. He placed a call to Bradley at the trailer park outside town.

"Look, man, we got a problem. My man didn't show. I called up to the States, and the deal's off. They got troubles."

"Cocksucker! I had the whole thing set. I got commitments to that cat for a thousand pounds. What the fuck am I supposed to do with it, tell him to smoke it himself?"

"Hey, stay cool. I'll take care of you, don't sweat it. I already made a couple of calls. I got a friend in Mexico City, he says he can handle it. All you gotta do is stall off Mako for a day or two, get your ass up there and see the man."

"You're sure he's good for it? I ain't dragging up there just to get jerked off again."

"He's good for it. Said he was looking for some coke, I told him maybe you could take care of him."

"Jesus, man, you're beautiful," Bradley purred, suddenly happy again.

Larry gave him Barrio's name and a number where he could be reached. Then he went back to the front desk, where the room clerk handed him a sealed envelope. He expected it to be a brush-off from Julie but was surprised to see an unsigned note consisting of two scrawled sentences: "You want to see us. We are in the markit squar and awate you."

He was impressed. Not with the spelling, but with Barrio, who certainly worked fast. And with the local *federales,* who didn't seem to be wasting any time either. It was barely twenty minutes since he had asked Barrio to contact them.

Folding the note in his pocket, he hurried from the lobby and turned in the direction of the marketplace. Julie wasn't at the café. He walked the four blocks to the market at double time and surveyed the scene. Most of the stalls were closed already, although a few desultory Mexicans remained at their posts sullenly guarding small stocks of wilted vegetables. Three or four Indians, sinister under their flop-brimmed hats, were sweeping the plaza with limp straw *escobas.* Across the square sat a four-door Chevy with three men in the front seat. Larry waited for a sign of recognition, and when the man at the wheel gestured with a sideways nod in his direction, he crossed the damp cobbled plaza and climbed into the back seat.

"Señor Spivey, I have the pleasure to be Detective Escalera of the *policía nacional,"* the driver said, taking obvious pride in his English. "Your people in the embassy inform us you have information of some matter. You are perhaps in a ... you are perhaps pressing for time?"

"I don't think I can afford to be seen with you. I'd like to get out of here as quickly as possible."

"Of course."

Larry made no mention of Bradley or Foiles since the DEA was going to take care of them in Mexico City, but he quickly told about Shelton Drake and the narcotics showroom he maintained at the Hotel Río, being careful to point out that Drake was heavily armed and possibly unstable. He told about Mako's farm, which he said he could lead them to.

"Bueno, bueno," Escalera growled. "We will take the farm tomorrow, Señor Spivey. These animals must be made to know that we do not play games with them. They will know it *mañana."*

Larry's eyebrows went up, a gesture they could take to mean what they would. He was once again impressed, but as brief as his career was, he still had seen enough to be skeptical. If the Oaxaca police weren't playing games, it was difficult to understand how the drug industry managed to thrive so openly. On the other hand, Escalera sounded serious, even grim. "We'll see," Larry said. "What time do we meet?"

"Seven o'clock. Here in the market. *Hasta mañana, señor."*

Larry crossed the plaza quickly, to put as much space between himself and the unmarked police car as possible. He hurried back to the café, where Julie was now waiting for him, her head bowed to the margarita she held in both hands. She had changed to a simple and provocative orange-and-yellow sundress with a deeply scooped neck, the material hugging her breasts as though it clung to them simply out of desire. He brushed his hand over her cheek as he moved around to sit next to her, and she looked up, her eyes bright but inexpressive, neither cold nor inviting. The band was playing a quick march in the gazebo.

In his room after dinner she asked him to unzip her dress. She let it fall before turning to him, and he took her in his arms, pressing her to him as he kissed the crook of her neck. Her hands played over his back, working down below his belt, gripping his buttocks the way a man might hold a woman and pressing him to her. Her hips moved rhythmically, calculatingly, gauging him.

"You're a real bullshit artist, aren't you, Larry?" she said. Her voice was soft, as though she had said something endearing.

He pulled back, only enough to express his bewilderment without breaking contact. "Not especially," he said. "Why?"

"Because I know who you are."

He laughed, figuring she was going to tell him he was a married man. "All right, I give up," he said. "Who am I?"

"You're a narc."

Her words took his breath away, and this time he did step back enough to be free of her. "A what?" he asked incredulously, to gain time.

"A narc."

"You're crazy."

She turned away from him and took a cigarette from the pack he had thrown on the night table beside the bed. She lit it with his lighter, the brightness of the flame in the dark room reflecting palely off her creamy skin. Her nakedness came as a shock to him as he realized almost with alarm how white she was, her shoulders and face not even the faintest shade darker than her breasts.

She faced him squarely and let the smoke drift away before speaking. "I'm not in the least crazy," she said flatly. "I've been around, I can tell a cop when I see one. Let's not bullshit each other, okay?"

"Whatever you say," he answered indifferently, taking a step toward her. His tone was mocking, as though he couldn't be bothered proving her wrong.

She held him off with her eyes. "No, Larry, it's got to be honest. I'm a hooker, and you're a narc. I can handle what I am. Why can't you?"

Off-balance, he grabbed for something to say. He remembered that she had approached him out of nowhere in the square and wondered if it could be a setup. Bradley? Drake? "Does this mean this is going to cost me money?" he asked with mocking sweetness.

She stabbed out her cigarette in the ashtray and lay back on the bed, consciously displaying herself. "No," she sighed. "It's on the house. I don't charge, and you don't bust me if you find anything in my pocketbook."

She laughed.

"Is it a deal?" she asked, her arms rising in invitation.

Larry rolled over and made arching, fumbling motions with his left hand, trying to still the clatter of the cheap alarm clock he had borrowed from the desk clerk. He glanced to his right and saw the sun just climbing to the level of the curtains, then took a deep breath, as though the damp air held some stimulant that would convince him to get up. Rolling over to his left side, he groped in the half-light for his cigarettes and lighter on the bedside table. Julie lay next to him, asleep on her side, facing away, but she stirred in response to his movement and pushed herself unconsciously toward him, lightly pressing herself to his hips.

He glanced at the clock. It said six-thirty. Then he checked his watch. Six forty-five. Damned Mexican alarm clock had lost fifteen minutes in eight hours. He had fifteen minutes until he was to meet Escalera in the market.

Climbing from bed, he took two or three drags off his cigarette and threw the butt in the toilet, where it hissed before dying. He turned on the shower and stepped in, washed quickly, brushed his teeth, toweled his hair and ran a comb through it, then returned to the bedroom, where he stepped into khaki pants and boots, slipped on an old sport shirt, and lit another cigarette. By his watch he still had five minutes.

Sitting on the edge of the bed, he leaned over and nuzzled Julie where her ear met her jawbone. "Wake up, sugar," he said, deliberately emphasizing his accent.

She rolled over and arched her back, stretching. Her arms reached up over her head and came together behind his neck. Smiling, she pulled him to her and they kissed. He didn't know when he'd be back but told her to wait for him there.

The sidewalk outside the hotel was almost deserted, but the market was raucous with haggling peasants when he got there. Parked exactly where he had parked the night before, Escalera sat behind the wheel of a purple van with a garish mural of the Last Supper painted all the way down the right side. Three weeks earlier, on his first trip to Oaxaca, one of the smugglers at La Higuera had warned him that the van with the Last Supper was driven by *federales*. The fact that they were still driving it explained a lot about Mexican law enforcement, and he didn't exactly feel comfortable about advertising his identity by getting in. But he didn't have much choice, so he took a deep breath and scooted in, disappearing immediately behind the side panels.

When they had driven a few miles out of town in the direction of the airport, one of the Mexicans climbed over the front seat and joined Larry in back. He introduced himself only as José. He pulled back a tarpaulin near the tire well to reveal an impressive assortment of archaic automatic weapons. Rummaging among them, he drew out a well-used Thompson with a clip in it, then went back and pulled out two extra clips taped together, facing in opposite directions.

"Eh, *americano,* you know how to use thees?" he asked, handing the Thompson and the two clips to Larry.

"I reckon I've seen one before," Larry answered without much enthusiasm. "You think there's gonna be any shooting?"

"Quién sabe?" José grunted. He had selected a relatively new-looking Israeli Uzi for himself, and he eased the bolt back halfway to check the action.

"Hey, look," Larry said, "any chance we can make it back to my hotel? I forgot something."

Escalera craned his neck to look over his shoulder at the two men in the back. "What?" he asked.

"I forgot to stay there."

The two Mexicans in front exchanged glances, unsure whether he was joking. Then they decided he was and grinned broadly. Escalera looked over his shoulder again and said, "Don' worry, Spivey. We take good care of you. We never lost a *gringo* yet."

The three Mexicans laughed loudly for a self-consciously long time. Finally, Larry joined them, and the laughter stopped.

After a few minutes he felt the van lurch to a halt. José threw open the rear door, and Larry followed him out. They were at the airport, on the helicopter ramp behind the main terminal. Hector, the Mexican in the front seat next to Escalera, darted around to the back and began handing out weapons to a uniformed soldier who came up to receive them. Two bulky army helicopters, their sliding doors open, their rotors revolving listlessly, idled on the pavement a few yards away, while another sixteen or seventeen soldiers loitered nearby, smoking sullenly, their guns slung defiantly from their shoulders, expressing their sheer insolence. In a country that hadn't been to war for decades, the only place these jaded warriors could have learned such cynicism was over the bodies of dead bandits.

Escalera spoke in Spanish to the lieutenant with the soldiers. The lieutenant said nothing. When the briefing was over, he ordered his men into the choppers, dividing them between the two aircraft. By this time Escalera had armed himself with an Uzi and a .45 automatic he wore in a canted holster on his belt. Two extra clips were stitched to the holster. He motioned for Larry to come up.

"Please, *señor,* you are to go in the lead helicopter. You will direct the pilot, no?"

"I will direct the pilot."

Escalera put a hand on Larry's shoulder, a gesture more ominous than all the heavy artillery being stowed aboard. "Do not worry, *gringo,*" he said. "We have done this before. Just be certain you are the last man out of the helicopter when we land."

"Yes," Larry assured him. "I wouldn't want it any other way."

They climbed into the chopper, Larry preceding Escalera and taking a seat just forward of the door and immediately behind the pilot. One of the soldiers slid the door closed until it sealed with the decisive thunk of a vault door. The whine of the rotors went up a whole octave, spewing dust like a desert sandstorm. The chopper rocked slightly, like the trembling of strained muscles, and then lurched from the pavement, swinging around about thirty degrees as it raced over the ground at less than a man's height. Crossing perpendicular to the airport runway, the pilot eased back on the stick to let his bird fly. It soared quickly, as though it had been eager to break contact with the earth, and within a few minutes had left the airport a couple of miles behind.

The pilot obviously had been briefed. He headed to the southwest, following a three-lane blacktop road that snaked into the mountains a thousand feet below him. Flicking his hinged microphone away from his mouth, he turned to Larry. "How far do we follow this road?" he asked in English.

"About forty kilometers."

As the helicopter cruised up the untraveled road, Larry took advantage of the dead time to inspect the weapon he had been issued. The Thompson was old, with a badly scarred stock. The bluing of the barrel had been worn completely off, exposing bare metal. Larry mashed the clip release and withdrew the clip, laying it on his lap with the two extra clips José had given him. He pulled back the slide to look at the breech, observing with some satisfaction that the slide moved freely. It was possible the weapon might actually shoot.

He inserted his thumb into the breech in such a way that his thumbnail reflected the light streaming in through the window just over his left shoulder. Peering down the faintly illuminated barrel, he saw that it was spotlessly clean, and he could even detect a trace or two of riflings. He felt better now, secure with the knowledge he was at least armed, although how well was a question that wouldn't be answered until it had to be. He turned his attention to the clip he had just withdrawn.

He extracted one round and saw that it looked fresh. The brass was shiny, and the waterproofing compound was up to military standards. He slid it back into the clip and pulled the trigger of the gun with his right hand, easing the bolt forward with his left. Holding the trigger down, he worked the bolt backward and forward a few times. It was smooth, so he slammed the clip into the gun and looked around to get his bearings.

The young officer sitting beside him had been watching his activities with amusement. *"Bueno?"* he shouted, pointing to the Thompson.

"Sí, bueno," Larry shrugged, his voice conveying no enthusiasm. The officer looked away.

The chopper had been holding a steady thousand feet above the rising terrain. Below it, the narrow blacktop road had lost two of its lanes and was now a tenuous strand slithering along the barren land like a hair on a bed sheet. As they neared the crest of a hill, the pilot banked the chopper to a point slightly to the side of the roadbed in order to give Larry a better view. Flicking his mike away again, he turned to Larry. "We are almost there, *señor?* There is another road, yes?"

Larry leaned forward to speak almost in his ear. "There will be another road to the right, just as we come over the hill."

Seconds later they topped the rise, and Larry could make out the dirt road, a tawny glint in the sunlight. He tapped the pilot on the shoulder and pointed to the right. As the big Huey swung around to follow the road, Larry saw the sister ship only a few hundred yards behind. For about eighteen kilometers the dirt road rolled on, surprisingly straight, as though drawn with a knife on the swelling, brush-covered foothills. At an Indian shack opposite an intersection with a narrow trail, Larry tapped the pilot again and signaled for another turn.

"Señor," the pilot called, "I desire to come in low to give them no warning. You will tell me when we are close?"

The chopper bounded over a series of hills. Larry leaned to the pilot, his head just behind the other man's shoulder. "Not this hill but the next," he shouted.

The pilot turned to the young officer seated next to Larry and barked a string of orders in Spanish, which the officer relayed back to his men. Cigarettes were thrown to the floor and snuffed out under heavy boots.

The cabin crackled with the muted sound of machine-gun bolts being drawn, a low, clicking noise clearly audible above the steady drone of the engine. There was another series of clicks as seat belt buckles jangled to the floor. All conversation had ceased.

Larry felt his stomach muscles tighten as he snapped off his own seat belt. Leaning to look out the pilot's window, he was almost knocked from his seat as the chopper dived like a hawk, leveling out barely fifty feet from the ground.

The first hill sped by in a blur. The ground seemed to drop out from under them as they sailed over a shallow valley and headed for the next hill. The marijuana shed would be less than fifty yards ahead when they came over the second hill. Reluctantly Larry moved back to join the soldiers, feeling no eagerness for what was coming.

A soldier swung the door release level and forced the heavy door back. Suddenly the roar of the churning rotors was deafening. Below him, looking slightly backward from his vantage point forward of the door, Larry could see the crest of the last hill and knew they were already over the top. The chopper swung around hard, hung motionless for a moment before beginning to descend. Out of the corner of his eye Larry saw a figure running through the brush, then what might have been another. Soldiers crowded to the doorway, blocking his view, and he moved to the window just forward of the door.

The second helicopter hovered barely a hundred feet away, and through the window it almost seemed he was watching his own descent in a mirror. The broad opening in its flank was jammed with grim-faced soldiers, their glinting weapons like diagonal gashes in the square doorway. He half expected that if he looked closely enough, he would see his own bearded face peering back at himself from the window. Suddenly, with no sound to announce it, a small hole appeared in the Plexiglas he was staring through. A perfect aura of finely etched cracks radiated out from it about a half inch in every direction.

Even before his mind had a chance to process this new information, he felt a jolt as the undercarriage made crisp contact with the ground. Half the men already had gone through the door, and now those who were still inside stumbled for the exit, moving fast but not fast enough for Larry. He could hear the sharp, tearing sounds of bullets against metal, a steady, heavy rain of fire, and he knew he would be better off exposed to the combat than sitting in a gasoline-laden machine that might go off like a time bomb any second.

He dived out on the heels of the last man in front of him, landed on the balls of his feet, rolled over, and came up running in a low crouch toward a shallow depression about thirty yards to his left. His eyes seemed to be taking in everything as he ran, alert to danger from all quarters. But when he finally found himself flat on his back at the bottom of what turned out to be a narrow gully, he realized he had no idea about the deployments he was facing. He could hear automatic weapons fire coming from every direction, but which was from the dopers and which from the narcs was still a mystery. As near as he could tell, nobody was shooting at him yet.

He rolled over onto his stomach and tried to get some bearings, but for what seemed a long while it was impossible to locate any of the sources of fire. The helicopter, behind him and to his left, swung around to present its armored back end to the enemy. The other chopper stood maybe seventy-five yards beyond it. To the right, no more than a hundred feet in front of him, stood the shed. There was a small house a few yards to its left. He hadn't realized he had come so far, and when it came home to him that he was closer to the shed than to the chopper, he began to entertain a queasy suspicion that he had inadvertently ended up in the most advanced position. It would be a hell of a joke on someone if it turned out he was leading this raid.

Logically, the shed should have been the center of resistance, and he studied it carefully until he satisfied himself there was no gunfire coming from behind it. By this time his hearing seemed to be coming into focus and he was able to pinpoint the source of some of the gunfire. From movements of the brush he guessed there were two or three soldiers in some thick bushes to his right. They were firing in short bursts. He saw a flash of fatigue green and knew he was right.

The dopers must have seen it, too. Like a sleepwalker, one of the soldiers rose from behind his cover, swayed momentarily, and toppled forward. Larry thought they only died like that in the movies, pitching from behind rocks for the convenience of the audience, a mocking reflection that only deepened his sense of disorientation.

Suddenly an explosion ripped the air, as startling as if the gunfire had been silence, jerking his attention to a point beyond the shed. He remembered the grenades, strung like ornaments on the belts of the soldiers. There was a scream from beyond the shed that stopped quickly, and then a second explosion. The firing seemed more sporadic now and perhaps more distant, but he couldn't be sure. A soldier materialized out of nowhere, knelt, and peeled off a long, incredibly long, burst of fire, scanning back and forth in the direction of the house, the bullets sweeping the air with insane meticulousness. The soldier raised the barrel of his gun and rose to his feet, satisfied.

The firing on Larry's left had ceased, and the firing on his right had diminished to very short bursts and single rounds every eight or ten seconds. He heard two shots to his right, followed by two or three single shots to his left, followed by ten or fifteen seconds of heavy, fully automatic fire to his left. Then there was silence that lasted the better part of a minute and still seemed to be going on even when the air came alive with excited shouts in Spanish. Larry recognized one of the voices as Escalera's.

"Hey, *gringo,* you okay?" the voice called from somewhere.

"Yeah."

"Stay where you are, *gringo.*"

Three soldiers cautiously approached the shed. Its door hung loosely from its hinges, and the first soldier to get to it probed at it tentatively with the barrel of his gun, like a hunter looking for life in a dead animal. The door fell into the shed, landing on the dirt floor with a sudden thwack. There was nothing alive in there.

Larry turned away and saw five or six men in fatigues emerge from behind as many rocks and begin to close in slowly on the house, crouched low to the ground, spreading out as they approached, their guns at the ready. Maybe it was sadism, maybe the jitters, but one of them let out a burst of unprovoked fire aimed at an open window. Startled, the Mexicans with him threw themselves to the ground. The soldier who fired was on the ground, too, probably praying he wouldn't be shot from behind by his own men. He rolled over on his side and held up his right arm, waving it like a semaphore to signal the troops behind him to hold their fire. Then he began crawling toward the half-open doorway of the house while his companions waited where they lay.

Holding his weapon at arm's length so as not to expose himself, he pushed at the door with the barrel of the gun. It pivoted away from him on its leather hinges until he had a clear sight line in. He rose to a crouch, moved forward, and peered in. Whatever he saw apparently satisfied him, and he rose from his crouch, motioning the others to join him.

Soldiers were everywhere, talking in Spanish, lighting cigarettes. Larry rose to his feet, withdrew the still-full clip from his Thompson, and uncocked the gun, making sure there wasn't a live round in the chamber. With the weapon at his side, he headed for the crowd in front of the house, where he found Escalera.

"Anyone hurt?" he asked.

Escalera shrugged. "How many I do not know," he growled sullenly. "It could not be otherwise."

Four soldiers emerged from the thick brush that had been to Larry's right during the gunfight. They carried two bodies, holding them by the ankles and wrists. From the way they carried them, sagging like hammocks, there was no question they were dead. One seemed to have caught a grenade in the face, for there was little left of him above the neck. The other had been shot in the chest and arm. Their bodies were laid on the cleared ground, their weapons set beside them. Only the long-barreled Ruger lying next to the faceless man told Larry this was Mako.

A soldier went to the side of the shed to relieve himself. Others were moving into and out of the house, as though it held some interest for them. Already there was a stench of smoke in the air as a detachment of soldiers began methodically torching the marijuana fields beyond the shed. Larry watched them absently for a few minutes and then wandered into the house, a vague and nameless fear growing at the back of his mind, a fear that started with a suspicion that something must have drawn the fire of the soldier who shot through the window.

Two soldiers leaned indolently against the round table in the center of the small one-room house. Larry stepped past them and looked around, his eyes almost passing what he didn't want to see, then returning to it. In a corner lay the little girl he had seen in the yard talking earnestly with her father. For an instant he saw her dark, serious face the way it had looked then, as she listened to what her father was telling her. Now she was piled in a corner like a rag doll thrown against the wall. Blood spotted her tan frock in a mockingly neat pattern, like bright stitchwork. One hand rested palm up on the floor, and she was slumped slightly to that side, her elbow rigid. For an instant Larry wanted to move her, to make her more comfortable. But she was dead. He turned woodenly from the sight and walked out into the air, unconscious of where he was going. The smoke hung on the fields now in dense clots. The reek of burning marijuana was everywhere.

Larry paused long enough to study the smoke, like a soothsayer reading it for meaning. He asked himself if it had been worth it, but the question was its own terrible answer. He walked on, until he stood alone by the empty helicopter, where he waited until it was time to go back. Confusedly he tried to sort out his feelings and realized with horror that at that moment he had none. And the moment he saw the dead girl he had had none. He wanted to give himself credit for the numbness he felt but recognized it as no more than the spontaneous short-circuiting of his overloaded nerves. He wanted to find feelings in himself because that was the only way he knew to make himself human. But there was no horror, except for himself. No outrage. Nothing.

The dead were counted, five of them, bundled into bags, and stowed on the choppers. Larry was the last man on.

While Larry was participating in the carnage outside Oaxaca, drug authorities in Mexico City were no less active. Exploiting the introduction Larry had given him, DEA Agent Sante Barrio set up a heroin buy with Deputy Police Chief Robles-Arcía.

Because the case concerned a prominent member of the government, DEA Regional Director Ray Basch called on the president of Mexico in his office, bringing Barrio with him. The president mouthed a few appropriate pieties about eliminating corruption from his government and pledged the cooperation of the national police.

Basch and Barrio knew they had to move fast. Robles-Arcía's career as a narcotics merchant probably was an open secret in high government circles, where one gentleman would never dream of questioning another gentleman's right to be corrupt. Anything was permissible, so long as it was kept in the family. But in allowing himself to get caught by outsiders, Robles-Arcía had committed an unforgivable breach of etiquette. There would be a scandal, and the Mexican government had an efficient way of dealing with scandal. Not given to subtleties, it wouldn't bungle around with denials, denunciations, or explanations. Instead, orders would go out that Robles-Arcía was not to be taken alive. Basch and Barrio knew they would have to get the deputy chief before his countrymen did.

Barrio contacted Robles-Arcía, told him he had the money and was ready to move. Arrangements were made for a buy at Robles-Arcía's home that evening. In all his years as an agent, Barrio had never heard of a drug dealer operating out of his own home, but then he had never before made a case against a man who had every reason to believe he was above the law.

Barrio went in to make the buy. At the very last minute Basch, who was technically serving as an adviser to Mexican authorities, dragooned a small squad of Mexico City policemen into blockading both ends of the street where Robles-Arcía lived. The blockade had no sooner been established than a dozen national police arrived on the scene, insisting they had been sent to help out. Basch guessed their real purpose and deployed them at the end-of-the-block barricades, where there was the least likelihood of trouble.

Barrio remained in the house almost an hour, accompanied by three DEA agents, one posing as a chemist, the other two as bodyguards. The buy went like clockwork. At the conclusion of the transaction Robles-Arcía, flanked by his own bodyguards, walked the four Americans to the front door. At just that moment, by the purest bad luck, a civilian who lived on the block pulled to a stop at the sawhorses set up at the end of the street. He looked around and saw no one, for the *federales* had concealed themselves. Seeing no reason not to go home, he hopped his car onto the sidewalk and drove around the barricade.

From behind the stonework fences enclosing the yards on both sides of the street, the *federales* opened up on him with automatic weapons fire. He was virtually ripped from behind the wheel, killed instantly. His car continued gently rolling down the street long after the firing stopped, finally coming to rest against a tree by the curb.

Inside the house, Robles-Arcía heard the firing and leaped backward in alarm. Barrio and the other agents had no idea what had gone wrong but had to act quickly. They wheeled around, drawing their guns and identifying themselves as drug agents. Robles-Arcía's hands went up in surrender, but his two bodyguards attempted to flee. Barrio sent a pair of agents after them and immediately shoved Robles-Arcía away from the door, where he would be an easy mark for Mexican troops charging into the house.

The deputy chief's two bodyguards made it all the way to the kitchen door with two DEA agents on their heels. Ignoring an order to halt, they yanked open the door and tumbled into the yard, where they were instantly gunned down by *federales* staked out in back. Basch and Barrio whisked Robles-Arcía to safety and had him booked at the federal jailhouse.

Barrio recounted all these events to Larry over tacos in a dingy restaurant where they met just an hour after Larry's return from Oaxaca. His voice was flat, and he gave as few details as possible, as though he were merely passing on a perfunctory report.

"Oh," he added, almost as an afterthought. "We got that other thing going, too. Those two guys you sent up here are all set to deal. Bradley and Foiles. I got them hot for a coke deal. They're gonna pull the strings in Peru for me, leaving tomorrow. I think that one's gonna turn out to be all you said it was."

Larry didn't know whether to be pleased or not. He had been in Mexico only five days, and so far just about everyone he had dealt with was dead. He couldn't feel the same way about setting up a case down here now that he knew how heavily the odds were stacked against the subject's coming out of it alive.

"Well, for Christ's sake, go easy on them, will you?" he pleaded. "These guys ought to be locked up, but I'd hate to see them wind up dead. I've got enough to think about the way it is already. There's five dead in Oaxaca and now three more up here."

"Four," Barrio corrected.

"Four?"

Barrio nodded. "Robles-Arcía. We got him into the joint, but that was all we could do for him. He hanged himself in his cell last night. Case closed."

Larry was aghast. Nothing he had seen in his meetings with Robles-Arcía testified to such a highly developed sense of honor. "How did he do that?" he asked.

"A rope."

"How the hell can a man in jail get himself a rope?"

"I don't imagine he can," Barrio said. He turned in his chair and signaled for the waitress.

Fifteen

F loyd Farnum hadn't been idle while Larry was in Mexico. He was moving fast, desperate to get into the drug business. The moment Roger Sorenson informed him that the Skymaster was under surveillance, Farnum began leaning on his cousin to set up a buy to replace the one aborted two weeks earlier. Reluctantly his cousin informed him that the organization was expecting a shipment to arrive by DC-3 within a few days. "Put me down for a thousand pounds," Farnum ordered.

That was on Thursday, December 18. On Sunday, the twenty-first, when Larry got back to Atlanta, the front desk at the motel where he was living was loaded down with urgent messages for him to call a number he recognized as Farnum's.

"Have you talked to George yet?" Farnum asked breathlessly.

"I just got in."

"You haven't told him it fell through?"

"I haven't told him anything."

"Well, don't. I mean don't tell him it fell through. I think I got a way to bail us out."

"Like?"

"Like there's a shipment coming in. I got us lined up for a thousand pounds, due in tomorrow, Tuesday at the latest. Mexican shit, coming up from Texas or Tucson or something like that. A big DC-Three, gonna land

184

in Georgia, probably take a day or two to get up here. Call him, tell him sit tight, and we'll have his shit for him, say, Wednesday."

Larry hung up the phone and called GBI headquarters. An hour later he was in the conference room getting the go-ahead from Phil Peters. Clardy would do the buy just as he would have if Sorenson had brought in the load from Oaxaca. Larry called Farnum back on the cool phone and told him George was in.

Once again, though, the fates had worked it out to prevent George Clardy from playing out his role as a drug buyer. This time the fates took the form of the Drug Enforcement Administration, which traveled the road of interagency cooperation as though it were a one-way street. While Larry was keeping DEA agents posted on the progress of his GBI case in Mexico, it would never have occurred to them to return the favor. They never let on that they were aware of the DC-3 shipment Farnum was counting on. In fact, they knew more about the load than Farnum did. They had succeeded in planting an undercover agent inside the Texas organization that was bringing the marijuana in from Mexico. He in turn had hired another undercover agent to fly as copilot on the flight into Georgia. The DEA game plan called for agents to stake out the airport where the load was scheduled to land, follow the shipment overland to Virginia, and then round up the buyers. If everything had gone according to plan, George Clardy would have ended up under arrest.

When the DC-3 touched down early Monday evening at an airport in Berry Hill, just south of Atlanta, about a dozen DEA agents were carefully deployed in the area, observing the field from concealed locations. With them was a twenty-eight-year-old black man named George Singleton. An experienced customs agent, Singleton had been invited in on the raid by the DEA because his presence would simplify the DEA's task. Under law, U.S. Customs is the only enforcement agency in the country empowered to make a warrantless search. With a customs agent in attendance, the DEA wouldn't have to worry that the smugglers might raise the issue of illegal search and seizure as their defense.

For an hour and a half, six smugglers worked in near darkness, unloading bales of marijuana into two vehicles, a Winnebago camper and a Dodge pickup. Two DEA agents, using cameras loaded with infrared film, photographed the operation. The total load looked to be well over a ton, almost two-thirds of it going into the Winnebago. Shortly before seven o'clock the undercover agent who had flown in as copilot on the DC-3 left the scene in a Ford Pinto, accompanied by two of his fellow smugglers.

The three men left behind killed ten minutes relaxing against the camper, smoking cigarettes. Then one climbed behind the wheel of the Winnebago, the second disappeared into the back, closing the door behind him, while the third took the pickup. Five carloads of narcotics agents moved into position to tail them.

The two marijuana-laden vehicles made for the nearest entrance to Interstate 85, driving cautiously. They cruised through Atlanta on the expressway and came out the other side still on I-85, slanting to the northeast toward the South Carolina border. For the first hour they stayed in convoy, keeping well under the speed limit. Gradually the Winnebago opened space, riding the gently rolling highway at a shade over sixty. The DEA cars laid back to keep the pickup in sight, while the other three stayed with the lumbering mobile home, leapfrogging almost playfully to conceal their presence.

Somewhere around Homer, in rural Banks County, the DEA agents started to get edgy. Suddenly it seemed there were too few of them for a moving surveillance that still had a long night's drive ahead. There were only so many positions they could take before the drug smugglers started noticing the same vehicles in their rearview mirrors. They would get burned. They called the Georgia Highway Patrol for a backup of unmarked units. They called ahead to the Franklin County sheriff's office for help. By a quarter to nine, twenty cars were involved in the operation, melting into the midevening traffic to form an invisible web around the Winnebago and the truck, their taillights like random stars in a constellation, meaningful only if one knew where to draw the connecting lines.

But the reinforcements didn't help. With so much manpower concentrated on so small a target, the edgy possibility of being burned quickly grew to a certainty. At nine o'clock one of the agents tailing the pickup thought he detected something. "They may have made us," he radioed. "Let's take them down."

Most of the agents had been on the job since early that morning, tensely staking out the Berry Hill airport since first light. They had had enough and didn't put up an argument. "If that's what you gotta do," the transmission came back. "We're gonna sit on this other vehicle a little more."

Just inside the Franklin County border, five carloads of law officers eased into position behind the Dodge pickup. One of the DEA cars moved up to overtake, then slid in from the passing lane so the Dodge's taillight was right on his bumper. The second federal car pulled out to pass, eased back on the accelerator, and matched its speed to the pickup's, riding abreast of it. The agent in the passenger seat rolled down his window and signaled the pickup to the side. He had his gun in his hand.

In the cab of the pickup, the driver's head swiveled as if it were on springs. He was alone in the truck, a twenty-nine-year-old Virginian. A kid might have done something crazy, but he was old enough to know there was no way out. He simply lifted his hands from the wheel long enough to offer a gesture of surrender, then steered for the shoulder. Even before the truck was fully stopped, he was surrounded by narcotics agents and troopers, their guns drawn. The DEA agents were carrying shotguns.

"Piece a' cake, piece a' cake," one of the agents radioed ahead. "One down, one to go."

The agents trailing the Winnebago took it as a signal to move in. Red Herndon, who had been with the DEA two years, on loan from the Clayton County Sheriff's Department, maneuvered himself in front of the larger camper. Customs agent George Singleton sat in the passenger seat beside him, his gun already drawn. In his mirror, Herndon saw a Franklin County car and a DEA car moving up fast in the passing lane. They sailed on ahead, and Herndon glanced over to Singleton and nodded his readiness.

A third vehicle moved into the passing lane and hung for what seemed a long while just by the camper's door. Herndon couldn't see the signal to pull over, but he could see that the Winnebago had slowed, for there were suddenly thirty yards of space behind him. He shifted his foot off the accelerator and brushed gently at the brake, slowing enough to close the space, leaving the camper no room to maneuver. The needle on his speedometer dropped like the countdown clock of a missile launch, fifty, forty, thirty. At twenty the Winnebago slipped from the pavement to the asphalt shoulder at its left, and Herndon matched the maneuver. He braked quickly now, threw the transmission in park, and bolted from the car.

Singleton was already coming around from the passenger side, his gun in his right hand, his leather badge case in his left. There was only one man behind the windshield, and Herndon had no reason to expect trouble, but his nerves tingled because no bust is easy until it's over. Out of the corner of his eye he could see agents, deputies, and troopers charging up the highway from behind the camper. He heard wheels churning the loose shoulder and footsteps behind him. He heard Singleton shout, "Hey, what the fuck!" and at that instant he noticed the same thing the black customs agent had seen.

The Winnebago was rolling straight for them. Herndon raised his shotgun and got off one blast at the tires of the fast-closing camper, almost exactly at the same instant Singleton fired his revolver, the two explosions indistinguishable from each other.

Instantly the sound of their guns was answered by more firing than he would have thought possible outside war. Herndon dived for cover, noticing as he flew through the air that there was no one behind the wheel of the Winnebago. He felt a sharp pain in his leg and thought for a moment he had sprained it falling, but when he looked down, he saw the blood and knew he was hit.

George Singleton never had a chance to get away from the front of the camper. Waves of shotgun pellets slammed into him, lifting him from the ground, spinning him around like a second baseman making the double play. He came down in a heap, motionless before the grille of the now-motionless camper.

The firing went on and on, the frenzied drumroll of explosions punctuated by the screeching rending of metal, the pounding so intense that the Winnebago seemed almost to rock on its axles like a hippo wallowing in mud. Slowly the gunfire wound down, dying the way a rainstorm dies. When it stopped, half a dozen agents rushed to where Singleton lay. He had been hit in the head and chest, in the chest at least twice, maybe three times. There was so much blood on his face and in his hair it was impossible to tell where he had been hit or how often. But he was still alive. Two men picked him up and raced with him to a Dawson County car, which sped off for the hospital in Carnesville.

The rest of the men converged on the Winnebago, their footsteps counterpointed by the click of weapons being reloaded, even though it didn't seem possible anything was alive inside. A DEA agent threw open the door and let his shotgun barrel scan the interior while his partner's flashlight played along the surfaces, illuminating the huge pockmarked bales of marijuana that seemed to fill all the available floor space. The walls of the camper were riddled with jagged tears, like a jar lid punched out for air holes. In the tense, eerie stillness, a soft voice said, "Don't shoot. We're coming out."

The palms of four hands appeared from behind one of the bales, then four wrists, two heads, rising so steadily it almost seemed the bales in front of them were melting down. Not for their lives would the two terrified smugglers make anything like a sudden movement.

George Singleton died in the Carnesville hospital before morning. It took days for the incidents on Route I-85 to be pieced together, and when they were, the investigators filed reports that made very unpleasant reading. In all, the DEA confiscated three thousand pounds of marijuana, a ton in the Winnebago, half a ton in the pickup. Five men were arraigned, including the two who had left the Berry Hill airport with the undercover DEA agent. More than fourteen hundred bullet holes were counted in the sides of the Winnebago, and there was no way to number the shots that went wild.

But it is known there were at least six—the one that broke Red Herndon's ankle and the five that killed George Singleton. They hadn't come from the smugglers, for when the inside of the camper was searched, no weapons were found.

"If it's not one fucking thing, it's another," Floyd Farnum groaned into the telephone. "Tell George to sit tight. That load we were setting up for him just got popped. I'll get back to you as soon as I get something else lined up."

Larry mumbled a few obscenities. "I'll tell George where it's at, but I guarantee you he's not gonna be sitting around playing with himself till you get your act together."

At the GBI strategy session later that afternoon, Mike Eason was in a sour mood, his wit acerbic. "I feel for that guy," he growled sarcastically. "There's a good man dead, and he's bitching he can't get the fucking grass. I'd like to take that grass—"

Inspector Peters cut him off. "If you do, it'll be the only thing we've accomplished. We're chasing our tails. What are we going to do about it?"

The question hadn't been addressed to anyone in particular. As the least senior man at the table, Larry thought he had every right in the world not to be the one to answer it. No one else said anything either.

"Larry?" Peters said.

With a who-me look on his face, Larry started talking before he knew what he was going to say. He wanted to keep up the contact with Farnum, confident that the manic little entrepreneur would come up with something. With the death of the customs agent, the stakes seemed to have gone up, making it all the more important to get something on the Virginia organization.

"Yeah, sure, Farnum," Clardy cut in. "That's great, but we can't cool our heels till he does something. Whaddya say we take down Gordon, at least get something to show for all this?"

Eason jumped at the idea. If he didn't get an arrest soon, he wasn't going to be fit to live with. "Set up a buy with him right now," he suggested to

Larry. "Make it so it goes down New Year's Day, start the year off with a bang."

Peters endorsed the suggestion, and Larry had no quarrel with it. As far as he was concerned, Gordon had outlasted his usefulness. He could be reeled in at any time, and now was as good as later. The squad needed it for morale reasons, if nothing else.

Larry met with Gordon that evening in a Marietta restaurant. "Can you still get that cheap Mexican shit?" he asked.

"I can get it. I can't sell it. How did it go with you and that guy in Virginia?"

"It's going; it didn't go yet. But I got a guy looking for whatever burns, says he's ready to start shredding White Owls and selling it for pot. Can you fix him up?"

"I'll get samples over to your place tonight," Gordon promised. He paid for dinner.

He stopped by Larry's motel around eight o'clock, staying outside in his Mercedes while Johnny Harrel brought in the sample. It was an ounce or two of dull green marijuana in a plastic bag. Larry said he would get it to his buyer in the morning.

He closed the door on Harrel and flipped the bag onto the small writing desk in the corner of the room. It slid along the polished wood surface until it went over the edge, plopping softly to the carpet. As Larry crossed to pick it up, he suddenly realized how depressed he was. It was a feeling of almost disabling lethargy, and he found himself standing in the middle of the room unable to make up his mind whether to pick up the plastic packet or just stretch out on the bed for a while.

He sat on the edge of the bed, then lay back and pulled his legs up while he tried to figure out how long he had been feeling like this. It was vaguely possible it had been going on since Mexico without his noticing. Harrel had triggered it, for there was no one he had met in the drug underworld he despised as intensely as the little red-haired thug who had first dragged him into this sordid business.

But Harrel wasn't the worst of it. The worst was the little Mexican girl lying dead in the corner of a shack so that seven acres of marijuana could be torched. When he closed his eyes, he saw her, and when he opened them, she wouldn't go away. Her eyes were open, her head sagging limply to the side. She looked sad and crumpled, and the only way Larry could stop himself from thinking about her was to think about nothing at all.

He pulled himself from the bed and clicked on the television, hoping it would bring oblivion. There was a Christmas special on, a big production number with a dozen dancers and a garish set, and it suddenly hit Larry that the next day was Christmas Eve. He reached for the phone and for some reason dialed an old hunting buddy he hadn't seen for three years. Chuck said he was delighted to hear from him, but they had little to say. Yet he sensed Larry's loneliness and invited him to Christmas Eve dinner. Larry accepted.

He hung up the phone and called Charlene. She sounded as bad as he felt, and they talked for almost two hours, a rambling, intimate conversation that didn't make the slightest dent in the almost palpable distance between them. But the talk did him some good, and when he hung up, he felt he was somehow more in touch with reality. The last thing she said was that she hadn't forgotten he owed her $5,000.

When he woke up around noon, the television was still on. He went for breakfast in the motel coffee shop, then went back to his room to shower and change his clothes. He killed the afternoon doing nothing. Around seven o'clock he drove to Chuck's apartment in Red Oak, a suburb on the southwest edge of Atlanta. A six-year-old boy in a plaid bathrobe opened the door for him and then went into a shy act, racing back to the kitchen.

"Gee, I hope I don't have that effect on your whole family," Larry joked when Chuck came up to greet him. Chuck said it was probably the beard. They had drinks in the living room while MaryAnn served dinner to the kids in the kitchen. Then Chuck put them to bed in shifts, first the baby, then the twins, then the little boy in the bathrobe and his eight-year-old sister. While Chuck was busy with the children, MaryAnn commiserated with Larry about his bankruptcy and divorce.

"I don't know why I'm saying all this," she laughed. "I never even knew you were married until I heard about the divorce."

"Yeah," Larry agreed. "That's more or less the way it happened."

Their apartment was warm, with a real feeling of family even after the children were asleep, as though their presence permeated the furniture and hung in the air like perfume. MaryAnn served a beautiful stuffed turkey, and after dinner the three of them sat in the living room, filling each other in on their lives. Larry, of course, was forced to lie, and it put a distance between them that threatened to bring the loneliness back.

"I hope you don't mind, Larry," MaryAnn said, "but I invited a neighbor to join us. I don't want you to get the idea we're fixing you up; but she's divorced, and it can get pretty bad around this time of year."

Larry had no objections. Even if he had had any, they would have evaporated the moment Jerri let herself into the apartment through the kitchen door.

She was one of the most beautiful women he had ever seen. Tall, in her early thirties, she had long sun-blond hair and the kind of figure that makes traffic jam up for miles around. She carried herself confidently, with great self-assurance, as though she were on display, yet he couldn't detect in her the slightest trace of self-consciousness. He had known few beautiful women for whom beauty was not at least as much of a burden as it was an asset, but Jerri struck him from the very moment he was introduced to her as a woman totally comfortable with herself. He knew then that he trusted her.

The evening passed pleasantly, the conversation easy and natural. Jerri talked about Mark, her twelve-year-old son, and the problems he was having adjusting to living without his father. He was, she said, reaching an age where it was important for a boy to have a man around as a model. When she excused herself around midnight because she had to go home and assemble the bicycle Mark was going to find under the tree in the morning, Larry volunteered to help. Chuck and MaryAnn saw them to the door, smiling with smug satisfaction.

"They're pretty proud of themselves," Larry said as they strolled down the walkway to her apartment.

Jerri laughed. "I know. We're their good deed for the day. I hope you're in the mood for an affair. I'd hate to let them down."

"Yes," Larry agreed. "That would be a shame after they've been so nice."

Jerri's apartment was in another building in the complex. She looked in on her son and returned with the disassembled bike and an assortment of tools. She made two cups of powerful eggnog and sat on the floor next to Larry, her legs curled under her, peering over his shoulder at the illustrated assembly instructions.

With tools in his hands, Larry was always single-mindedly grim and purposeful, the feel of a wrench and a piece of painted metal tubing drawing him off into a private manly world in which the fragrance of her hair was no more a part of his consciousness than soft music in a restaurant. Yet as the jumble of parts more and more came to resemble a bicycle, the nutmeg, rum, and perfume, the softness of her voice worked on him, and he knew he would be staying the night.

He cleared a narrow aisle in the stack of brightly wrapped presents under the tree and backed the bike into it, then stepped back to contemplate his work, seeing it through the eyes of a twelve-year-old. It was a beautiful bike, shiny and perfect, and for an instant he thought about his own children, whom he hardly knew. He hadn't seen them in years, so the only way he could imagine them was as little, childish faces on impossibly large bodies. He felt closer to the boy sleeping in the bedroom than he did to them.

Jerri guessed what he was thinking and said, "I'm sorry there isn't a present for you. I wasn't planning on this."

"I think I was," he said, taking her in his arms.

Sixteen

The day after Christmas Larry packed up everything in his motel room and moved in with Jerri. He made contact with both Gordon and Farnum, telling Gordon that the buyer wanted a thousand pounds for delivery New Year's Day. "Arrange it however he wants," Gordon said. "Just make sure we're protected."

The call to Farnum was less productive, for the Virginian still hadn't come up with a source of marijuana. "I don't know what it is. Everything's going to hell. Fucking Christmas I guess. Can't even find the right people to talk to."

"That's too bad," Larry commiserated, making Farnum promise to get in touch the instant he got a line on any grass. "George is going crazy down here," Larry said.

At the staff meeting that afternoon Larry reported on his progress with Gordon. Mike Eason groaned. "Jesus, Larry, I didn't think you'd take me that serious," he complained.

"Do you mean to tell me you don't want him?" Larry bristled. "I went to a lot of trouble to set it up."

"Sure, we want him. But not New Year's. Who the fuck wants to work New Year's Day?"

Larry laughed. "I don't know. But I sure as hell know a couple guys that are going to."

For the next few days Larry, Eason, and Clardy went ahead laying the groundwork for the arrest of Dan Gordon. On Monday, the twenty-ninth, Floyd Farnum called.

"Don't say anything, just listen up a minute. I've got a great idea. Remember that pilot that landed a big fucking DC-Four on top of a little mountain somewhere down there in your neck of the woods?"

The famous Polk County pot plane landing had taken place before Larry came into GBI. All he knew about the case was what he had read in the newspapers and what he had been told by other agents.

"Yeah, he was from Florida or something, right?"

"I guess so. His name's Ron Agee. Whaddya say we get in touch with him, get him to fly us up a load?"

"Wasn't he busted?"

"Well, yeah, that's what I thought. I mean he was, and I figured they put him away. But I just heard he beat the case. Some horseshit thing about a warrant."

"Sounds like a lucky son of a bitch to me."

"Yeah," Farnum agreed. "He's lucky. But he's good, too. Find out what you can about him, and let me know."

The moment Farnum got off the line, George Clardy threw down the headset on which he had been monitoring the call and let out a triumphant rebel yell. "You made my day, man," he said, pounding Larry on the back. "Nothing I'd like better than another shot at that bastard."

"I didn't know that was your case," Larry said.

"Wasn't nobody's case. It was over as soon as it started. They blew it from the get-go. What happened was some hick deputies tumbled to it by accident, saw this truck tooling around, and stopped it, figured they were moonshiners. And that's what the warrants said. Imagine their surprise. So the whole fucking case gets thrown out of court. There's no hootch, so everything else is inadmissible. That fucker Agee made every damn one of us look like assholes. You set it up. We'll take him down."

Larry made a few phone calls, tracing down pot plane pilot Ronald Granger Agee through the Polk County district attorney's office and the sheriff's office in Broward County, Florida. Agee lived in Fort Lauderdale and had an unlisted phone number, which the sheriff was able to provide. Unwilling to give the number to Farnum, who might wonder how he had got it, Larry called back up to Bassett Forks and reported only that he had learned Agee's address. "Don't sweat it," Farnum said. "I got connections. I'll get back to you in a half hour."

Farnum's connections were as good as he said. In barely fifteen minutes he called back with the same number the Broward County sheriff had given.

Larry dialed it. A man with a deep voice and an accent from somewhere up North answered on the second ring.

"Ron Agee?"

"Could be. Who's this?"

"Larry Spivey."

"Do I know you?"

"No, but we've got some mutual friends. I'd like to talk with you."

"About what?"

"Business."

"It's your dime."

"Not on the phone."

"Sure. Where are you calling from?"

"I'm not in Florida."

"How soon can you get here?"

"This afternoon."

"Come on down, as they say. Get yourself checked in somewhere, and then give me a call. I hope you can get a room."

Ten minutes after he hung up the phone, Larry was on his way to the airport with a few hundred dollars in expense money in his pocket. Two hours later he was in a pay phone at the Fort Lauderdale airport, feeding in dimes until he finally found a hotel with a vacancy. The town was swarming with college kids like a carcass with flies.

The room he got was in a motel so far out toward the Everglades he half expected to be sharing it with an alligator. Even so, the parking lot had been taken over by partying teenagers, who had installed a pair of immense loudspeakers hooked up to an amplifier in one of the rooms. Virtually every garbage can the municipality owned had been filled with ice and beer cans, and cases of beer were stacked six feet high at strategic locations.

Larry closed all the windows and stretched the phone cord into the bathroom to give himself an outside shot at hearing what Agee had to say. The pilot sounded like he had forgotten inviting him down.

"Yeah, well look, I'm kind of tied up right now," he said, not particularly apologetic. "Why don't you go find yourself something to play with and get back to me in the morning? Give me a honk around eight; we'll grab some breakfast somewhere."

Larry entertained himself that evening with one of the minor bowl games on television, then went downstairs for a few drinks in the bar to get away from the collegiate rites of winter being enacted outside his window. He finally managed to fall asleep with the booming sound of heavy metal rock vibrating the bed, the room, and the inside of his head.

At eight o'clock his phone rang. He reached for it, surprised at the silence from outside.

"Spivey?"

"Who's this?"

"Ron Agee. I'm here at your motel. Get your ass over here to the lobby if you want to do some business."

Larry pulled on his clothes, pushed a comb through his hair, ran some toothpaste around his teeth, and headed for the front desk. An unnervingly large man, 240 pounds, six feet four at the least, was waiting for him. He had a curving brown mustache that looked like it must have been hooked into his nose with clips. Square-jawed with weathered skin, he looked a good eight or ten years older than his twenty-eight years.

"Spivey," he called. "Let's get some chow."

In the motel coffee shop Agee ordered a breakfast steak and a couple of eggs; Larry, just coffee. They talked about drugs as though neither was in the business, a conversation filled with vague references to things other people had done. By the time they had finished eating, Agee apparently had satisfied himself that Larry was straight. A few things he said suggested he had done some checking before coming to the motel.

When the plates were cleared away, Larry dropped a few admiring references to the now-legendary landing on top of Treat Mountain. He said it was the most amazing piece of flying he had ever heard of. Agee concurred, nodding his appreciation of Larry's judgment without explicitly acknowledging he was the pilot. "I'll bet you didn't know that DC-Four's still sitting just where it landed," he said.

"What are they waiting for?" Larry asked, purposefully naïve, playing into him.

"They're not waiting for anything. They've had maybe three dozen engineers up there trying to figure out how much it's going to cost to dismantle that fucker and truck it down the mountain. They finally came to the brilliant conclusion it isn't going to pay anyone to do it. For a while they toyed with idea of just cutting it up and selling it for parts. Now the sovereign state of Georgia in its infinite wisdom has decided to just auction it off and let the poor bastard that buys it figure out what to do with it.

Which is beautiful for me, because nobody is going to bid more than a buck and a quarter for it, on account of what they figure it's going to cost to get it off there. I got a guy that's gonna buy it, pay me a grand, and I get it down for him. It's the bargain of the century."

He grinned like a kid with a secret, inviting Larry to ask him how he planned to do it. Larry did.

"Same way as she got there," he said eagerly, his eyes sparkling with excitement. Just talking about flying turned him on. "She flew in, and she's going to fly out. She'll be light as a feather, no cargo, no more fuel than I absolutely need. All I have to do is taxi her to the upwind end of the strip, then back her all the way up till I got her tail feathers sticking in the bushes. I clamp on the brakes and rev her up as high as she'll go. Man, when you get one of those big babies all charged out, she'll be flying in place. But you've got to know what you're doing. The trick is to get her off the ground just as damn quick as you can, and the way to do that is same as how you teach a kid to ride a bike. You just put him up there, right? So when she's all revved up, I yank on the landing gear lever and drop off the brakes. She's light already, damn near flying, but the gear stays down until the struts are fully extended. Which isn't going to take more than a couple hundred feet. When the struts are all the way out, the gear snaps up, and I'm gone. That's all there is to it."

Larry knew enough about flying to know it could be done. He also knew it was crazy. "Lotsa luck," he said. "I don't figure I'd want to be on that plane when you try it."

To Ron Agee, that was the highest form of flattery. He drew a cigar from his shirt pocket, clipped the end, and lit up, instantly filling the small coffee shop with smoke.

"Tell you what, Larry," he said crisply, abruptly returning from his ego trip. "I've got an associate you might want to meet. We'll catch you around one-thirty, have some lunch, and get down to cases."

Larry agreed, and Agee disappeared in a matter of seconds, sticking Larry with the breakfast check. Four hours later he was back. He met Larry in the lobby, and they returned to the coffee shop, where a man was waiting for them. He seemed to be in his late twenties, was thickly built and impressively solid. A yachtsman type, he wore a blue blazer over a yellow turtleneck. His name was Gene Ehrlichman, and six months earlier he had almost gone crazy in the copilot's seat when Agee had made the Treat Mountain landing.

The three men ordered sandwiches. When the waitress left them alone, Ehrlichman launched into a monologue that was nothing less than a sales pitch for a full panoply of smuggling services. He claimed to have a connection in Colombia with access to limitless supplies of Colombian grass, the most sought-after strain of marijuana in the southeastern market. He claimed to have a deal worked out with corrupt officers from the Colombian air force that allowed him to fly into remote air bases to pick up shipments of marijuana. Security for the loading operation was supplied by armed Colombian soldiers. He bought ten tons at a time, paying fifty dollars a pound. The terms of the deal specified ten dollars per pound to be paid ten days before the flight, the remainder not to be paid until the marijuana was sold in America and the smugglers returned for another load. In effect, someone in the Colombian government was fronting the drug merchants for 80 percent of the cost of the marijuana.

Larry asked if they had the aircraft for such an operation.

Agee laughed a short, humorless giggle. "Man, I could name a couple dozen countries and a couple hundred airlines with less airplanes than we've got."

Ehrlichman shook his head, as though the boastfulness of his partner embarrassed him. "I own a business in Tucson, Mr. Spivey," he said crisply. "We buy surplus commercial and government aircraft and then refurbish it for sale. We have an eighty-man shop in the desert and a considerable inventory at present. Right now we have twenty DC-Fours, eleven DC-Sevens, three C-One-nineteen flying boxcars, a C-One-thirty Hercules, and two Seven-oh-seven jets. That should be adequate for our purposes."

He went on to explain that whenever a smuggling run was contemplated, Agee selected an appropriate aircraft, ownership of which was then transferred to an offshore corporation specially set up for that purpose in the Cayman Islands.

He paused and smiled smugly. "I trust you remember that incident in Polk County. The DC-Four involved in that one was registered to Mr. Agee, and it caused him a great deal of embarrassment. With the arrangements we have now, we have eliminated the possibility that such an incident would repeat itself."

Larry had to restrain himself from asking where the hell he had gone to college. Instead, he asked him to spell out what it would cost his people in Virginia to do business with the Ehrlichman smuggling enterprise.

"Not much at all, I assure you," Ehrlichman answered in the tone of an insurance salesman. "We can offer you a very attractive arrangement. You and your associates put up the front money. You also buy an airplane, either from us or locally, whichever is more convenient. We'll help with the arrangements either way. If we are indeed talking about ten tons, your total cost for the goods comes to one million dollars even, out of which you have to advance only two hundred thousand plus the cost of your personnel. Depending on what kind of arrangements you have for selling at your end, you can figure around two hundred dollars a pound. The transaction will gross, say, four million. You take your expenses off the top, and we split the profits fifty-fifty. I suggest you take that back to Virginia and see if it floats. If you're interested, we'll want to move fast."

As far as Larry was concerned, he was moving fast already. He had long since passed the stage at which he could be shocked by anything, but the sheer professionalism of the operation Ehrlichman was running beat anything he had ever heard of.

After lunch, Agee drove Larry to the airport for a flight back to Atlanta, where Larry immediately reported in at GBI headquarters. "This Ehrlichman character claims to have a fleet of thirty-seven aircraft and an ongoing hookup with the Colombian air force. I didn't know whether to laugh or cry," he told Eason, Clardy, and Peters.

"No, don't laugh," Inspector Peters cautioned. "We've suspected for a long time that there were operations like that around. We've just never known where to find them. Set it up with your Virginia friend, and when you've got something going, we'll be able to assess it better."

Larry was jubilant, for he had half expected to hear the same song and dance about wandering too far beyond Georgia's borders. He promised to get in touch with Farnum right away.

"Fine. That takes care of the big fish," Peters said. "Perhaps you'd be interested in hearing what we've been doing about the little fish. Mike, please brief the man."

Eason quickly explained that everything had been geared up for the arrest of Dan Gordon. GBI had rented three rooms in the Holiday Inn on I-85 in Doraville, one of Atlanta's numberless suburbs. The rooms were carefully selected to minimize the danger, for all of the agents under Phil Peters prided themselves on the meticulousness of their planning. It was their boast that a tragic fiasco like the Winnebago shoot-out never would have happened if GBI had been running the show, and they had the statistics to back it up. The Georgia Bureau of Investigation had never had a subject seriously injured in the process of arrest and had never lost a man.

The buy would take place in a corner room on the second floor of the motel, and the room adjacent to it would be rented to eliminate the possibility of accidentally involving innocent bystanders. Backup agents would be deployed at key locations to prevent anyone from wandering into a potential line of fire.

The Holiday Inn had been chosen for the buy because its architecture lent itself perfectly to their purposes. The rooms faced an open parking lot, with access via an exposed walkway, at the end of which the building doglegged to the back. The agents rented a third room just around the bend, where they would establish their command post. To make the arrests, agents would move in on the subjects from the command post and from the foot of the stairway just beyond the room where the deal was taking place. The GBI philosophy invariably called for a major show of force in order to minimize the likelihood of resistance.

"It's goin' down January first, Spivey. Just the way you wanted it," Eason chided morosely. "This damn well better turn out more interesting than the fucking Rose Bowl, or you're gonna wind up in the joint with that guy."

Fortunately for Larry, GBI's New Year's party for Dan Gordon proved to be interesting. Everything went exactly as expected, which meant that very little happened according to plan. For if there is a Newtonian first law of motion for drug dealers, it is that nothing will ever happen the way anybody says it will. The simplest transaction involves dozens of ritualized security steps, a good half of them utterly useless. The buyers and the sellers never get down to work until they have eyeballed each other like a cobra and a mongoose. The money turns out to be in one place and the drugs in another, and neither can move until the other is there. Eight to ten hours are not abnormally long for a deal that could have been done in fifteen or twenty minutes, and during those hours most of the things that can go wrong will.

GBI had the motel staked out by early New Year's morning, using DeKalb County sheriff's personnel as backup. A county helicopter was on alert nearby, ready to take to the air if there was any need for it. Like actors positioning themselves onstage before the curtain goes up, Larry and Agent Gary Newman arrived at the command post motel room an hour before their scheduled noon meeting with Gordon. As the buyers in the deal, their roles demanded that they let Gordon get there first, for if there is one thing that alarms a drug seller, it is a buyer too eager to make a deal. Also, by letting the subject of the investigation get to the scene before they do, the narcotics agents gain a subtle psychological edge. A dealer feels uncomfortable walking into a room where the buyers are waiting for him, for he is then in their territory. But if he has established the space as his own before they get there, he is likely to be a bit more communicative. Putting the subject at ease is the name of the game, both because it diminishes the chances of resistance and because it increases the possibility that valuable information will find its way into the microphones worn by the agents.

Newman, a slender twenty-six-year-old with black wavy hair and dark eyes set off by porcelain-white skin, appeared nervous as the GBI technicians fitted him with a wire. Larry kept up a running stream of patter to calm him down, but one of the other agents in the room took Larry aside and assured him he had nothing to worry about. "He always acts like this, sweats it out like it's the first time he's made a buy. But it's just stage-fright. Once he gets in there, he's the coolest son of a bitch you'll ever work with."

Gordon was late. At twelve-thirty the radio in the command post crackled with word the subject had entered the lobby and was approaching the restaurant. "There's another man with him. Male Cauc. Five-five or -six, red hair."

"Harrel," Larry said. His presence was a good sign; it meant Gordon was feeling cocky. It also gave Larry an idea he didn't want to tell anyone about until he had a chance to see whether he could swing it. He and Newman gave the two drug merchants about fifteen minutes to get settled in before they left the command post for the meeting.

Larry feigned annoyance at seeing Harrel but let it drop quickly. Just getting it on the record served his purpose. Drinks were accompanied by totally inconsequential small talk. Gordon, who had been told Newman was from Virginia, asked if he had had a pleasant trip down, how long he had been in Georgia, what part of Virginia he was from. Newman was superb, his performance finely etched down to the smallest detail. Larry noticed he even smoothed out his north Georgia accent slightly, giving it a light Virginia roll.

As soon as lunch was served, Gordon began to get down to business. "You saw the samples?"

"Larry brought it around, sure," Newman said.

"Good stuff, right?"

"It'll do."

"It's good, believe me. Oaxacan. We want one-sixty a pound. I assume that's agreeable with you?"

Larry and Newman exchanged glances. The price Gordon had quoted to Larry was one-forty, and they couldn't afford to look so hungry they'd put up with a last-minute change in the terms of the sale. "Don't run a number on me, mister," Newman said sharply. "Larry told me one-forty. Now are you good for that or aren't you? Besides, that shit we saw ain't Oaxacan."

Gordon's eyes narrowed darkly and, next to him, Harrel made a preliminary gesture at reaching for his gun, the only negative reaction he knew. But Gordon had enough sense to back down when his bluff was called. He laid a hand on Harrel's sleeve to restrain him and tried to lie his way out. "No, no, I know the samples weren't Oaxacan, I didn't mean to say that. But the stuff you saw is gone. Shit, at one-forty a pound we unloaded it like prune juice at an old folks' home. Sold the hell out of it. What I've got now *is* Oaxacan, you can take my word for it."

"Offhand, you don't happen to have a reason I ought to do that, do you?" Newman purred sarcastically.

Gordon made a pacifying gesture, his hands, palms down, describing small circles over the tablecloth. "I know how you feel, but I'm not trying to pull anything on you. I've been in the business seven years, and I've never had any problems. Not from the buyers and not from the fuzz. Larry can tell you that."

Newman looked to Larry, who said softly, "He's all right."

"That's right. Now this stuff I've got now is costing me more, so I have to charge you more. I'm in this for the money, remember? I can get you another sample if you want. I'll send Johnny right over; he'll be back in half an hour. But I don't think we've got to mess around with that. I wouldn't con you."

Newman smiled, showing even white teeth a male model would have envied. "I know," he said coolly. "You wouldn't be that dumb."

Gordon reacted to the pressure Newman was putting on exactly the way he had reacted when Larry had pushed his way into his office after the Guatemalan buy with McClellan had fallen through. He saw himself as much tougher than he was and always ended up admiring any man who would stand up to him. "There's one other thing," he said tentatively. "I know we talked about six hundred pounds, but we're a little light on this Oaxacan. About all I can make is four hundred. That's not a problem, is it?"

Newman seemed to be barely tolerating him by this point. "I don't give a damn. Let's just get this Mickey Mouse shit over with."

With the green light flashing in front of his eyes, Gordon was suddenly all salesman again, his confidence restored. "The thing is, that puts me twenty grand under. The other deal was eighty-four thou; this one's

sixty-four. Maybe I can fix you up with something to make up the difference."

"Like?"

"Like Quaaludes. You handle them?"

"There's Ludes and there's Ludes, man. What are you talking about?"

"Seven-fourteen RORs, mint condition. I got some at my place. I'll
show you. First-rate, genuine stuff. They're going in Atlanta for two bucks
a pop on the streets. We had a million, I got fifty or sixty thousand left,
let you have them for fifty cents apiece. Maybe we can get you a little bit
of coke, too."

"Can you deliver now?"

"Uh, now? The Ludes, I don't know. Maybe on the coke. How long are
you going to be in Atlanta?"

"We get the grass, we split."

"Well, that's a problem. Look, I've got six thousand pounds coming in
in a day or two. Get back to me. If we can deal on that, I'll throw in the
Ludes then."

"Let's see what the grass is, right? Like I ain't done business with you
before, mister. Ain't done business with you yet."

"Sure, sure. What about film? I can get you some eight-millimeter
hard-core. First-rate stuff."

"What the fuck is this, a department store?"

"Just a suggestion."

"Some other time, man. Why don't we just shut up and deal?"

Gordon paid for lunch, and the four men crossed through the lobby to
the outside staircase leading to the second-floor rooms. Larry knocked at
the door of 202, the corner room. A television set inside clicked off, and
the door opened as far as the chain lock would permit. Agent Wally
Brooks, all 220 pounds of him, filled the space like a war veteran crammed
into his old infantry uniform. He swung the door closed to take off the
chain, then opened it wide. Larry, Newman, and the two subjects stepped
in.

At the office Brooks was a gentle enough giant, low-keyed almost to the
point of indolence. But with a day's stubble on his chin, his face wore a
look of surly, rumpled ferocity that made him perfect for the part of the
armed goon hired to protect Newman's end of the deal. He eyed Gordon
and Harrel malevolently, as though he were considering jumping them
just as a matter of principle, then hung back by the door, where he
managed to fail totally at making himself unobtrusive.

"All right," Gordon said. "Let's have a look at what you've got."

With a toss of his head, Newman signaled Brooks to get the money. Brooks stepped out on the walkway and closed the door behind him. "The money's in the next room," Newman explained.

A minute later Brooks returned, carrying a small metal strongbox secured with a padlock. He handed the box to Newman and remained by his shoulder, obviously ready to earn his pay if there were any signs of trouble. Newman took his wallet from his pocket, unfolded it, and plucked out a key, with which he unlocked the box.

Gordon sat on the bed to count the money. He went through it twice, riffling the packets of twenties, fifties, and hundreds, counting through perhaps a dozen of them. It took him almost fifteen minutes, and when he was done, he asked, "Where can I make a phone call?"

On a signal from Newman, Brooks tossed him the key to the next room. The drug seller ordered Harrel to stay with the money while he went next door to call his connection. In three minutes he was back. "He'll be here in fifteen minutes," he said.

Fifteen minutes were more like forty-five. At a knock on the door, Brooks and Harrel, the two opposing bodyguards, leaped to their feet and headed for the door on courses calculated to produce a collision. Brooks roughly shouldered the smaller man aside, put on the chain lock, and opened the door a few inches. He found himself looking at a kid in blue jeans and a denim jacket. "Yeah?" he growled.

The kid asked for Dan, and Gordon came forward to check out the visitor, peering around Brooks's shoulder like a man peeking down the street from around the corner of a building. "Let him in," he said.

The kid was no more than twenty-two or twenty-three years old. He had short hair and the well-scrubbed look of a clean-cut college student. Larry got the feeling looking at him that he never went to class dressed that way; he wore pressed slacks and a jacket and probably thought of himself as the height of cool because he didn't wear a tie. Larry sized him up as a business school type who undoubtedly despised the screwed-up "hippies" who smoked the pot and snorted the coke he sold.

Gordon made no introductions. He took the kid to the next room for a conference and returned in five minutes. He looked badly shaken. "We've got problems," he said. "There's not even the four hundred pounds. There's just one hundred."

Newman blew up, berating Gordon for his incompetence and insisting he wouldn't have come all the way down from Virginia for a lousy hundred pounds of fifth-rate marijuana. He turned his anger on Larry, shouting that he was holding him responsible for this fiasco.

Larry fell into the role of peacemaker. "Look, it's not his fault. I've dealt with him before, and he's straight. Things happen, that's all. You're already here, you might as well take what you can get or the whole thing's a total loss."

Newman said he would have to check with his people in Virginia to see whether they wanted him to deal for the hundred pounds. Ordering Brooks to stay with the money, he took Larry with him to the vacant room next door. As soon as they were alone, he asked, "What do you think? Is this all he's good for?"

Larry didn't know. He was convinced Gordon could deal in quantity, but he had no firsthand knowledge. Everything he had ever done with the man had fallen through. "But he says he's getting a six-thousand-pound load in a couple of days. Maybe we ought to just pull out now and come back for that. I hate taking a guy like him down on a lousy hundred-pound bust. I'd rather stick him good."

Newman had his doubts. He was certain Inspector Peters wouldn't consent to taking the whole thing apart and putting it back together just so Larry could tie up Gordon in a prettier package. He called Peters and got exactly the answer he had expected: "Take him down."

Newman managed to look simultaneously annoyed and sheepish when he returned to the corner room. "Fuck it, get the stuff," he said. "It's a horseshit waste of time, but the time's already wasted."

The business school kid turned to Newman. "What are you driving?" he asked.

"Got a van. Why?"

"Give me the keys. I'll take your wheels to pick up the stuff, save loading and unloading."

Newman had to think fast. GBI had taken the precaution of sending up to Virginia to borrow a set of plates for the van, but no one had contemplated letting the drug dealers drive it themselves. There was a GBI radio in the glove compartment.

"Are you fucking nuts?" he exploded. "Nobody takes my wheels. If you wanna make it easy, I'll go with you."

The kid would have gone for the idea, but Gordon didn't like letting Newman learn the location of the stash. When he raised the point, Newman laughed at him. "You guys are crazy," he snorted derisively. "A fucking hundred pounds, and you act like it's the goddamn French Con-

206

nection. I got eighty-four grand in that tin box, and I'm not worried. All you guys got is that lousy hundred pounds, so what are you sweating? If you wanna use the van to pick it up, I go with it. If not, let's forget the whole thing."

Gordon was in no position to call the bluff. The kid and Newman went out together, leaving Larry and Brooks alone with Gordon and Harrel. Gordon muttered a few self-serving apologies for the way the deal was going, blaming everyone but himself. Larry cut him off with a question about the Quaaludes. He said he didn't know that Newman would go for another deal, but he thought he knew a man who could handle them if he could give his personal assurance they were genuine pharmacy-grade tablets. Gordon offered to go home for the samples, promising to be back in half an hour.

With Gordon out of the room, Larry had his chance to work on Harrel. He snapped his fingers as though he suddenly remembered something. "Shit," he said, talking aloud to himself, "I should have asked him if he's got a sample of the coke." He turned to Harrel. "Johnny, see if you can catch him. Tell him to bring back some of the coke if he's got any."

Harrel looked confused. He knew he was supposed to stay with the money. "Uh, he must be gone already," he mumbled stupidly.

"And maybe he isn't," Larry shot back. "If you move your ass a little, maybe you'll catch him. We've had about as much stalling around from you guys as we're gonna take."

"Awright, I'll check," Harrel whined, backing to the door as though he expected Larry to come after him if he turned his back.

The moment he was out of the room, Larry turned to Brooks. "Quick, the radio."

Brooks reached under the pillow and pulled out a small walkie-talkie. He handed it to Larry, who flipped the switch on and depressed the mike button.

"Listen, you've got to move fast," he whispered urgently. "Gordon just left, and I sent Harrel after him. Grab Harrel, detain him, don't let him back upstairs. But whatever you do, make sure you don't let Gordon see you do it. I'll explain later."

The voice that came back from the command post was Clardy's. "That's a hell of an order, man. Are you guys okay in there?"

Clardy sounded uncomfortable. Newman had been wearing the only wire, and when he left with the kid, the command post lost its monitoring capability on Larry and Brooks.

"Cool as hell," Larry radioed back with a convincing ring of confidence.

A few minutes later Brooks said, "Someone's coming up the stairs."

Larry smoothed the bedclothes over the walkie-talkie. He didn't know whether the assignment he gave Clardy had been carried out, but he decided to take a chance and assume it was.

Gordon stepped into the room, mumbling a vague apology about not being able to get his hands on the Quaaludes. It took him a few seconds to realize something was wrong. He looked around the room quickly. The bathroom door was open, and he could see there was no one in there.

"Where's Johnny?" he asked, troubled.

"He split."

"What do you mean, split?" Gordon exploded. "What the fuck's going on?"

Larry shrugged, as if he couldn't understand it himself. "He said it looked like everything was under control here, he'd catch up with you later."

Gordon sat heavily on the bed. Something wasn't right here, and he didn't know what. "C'mon, Larry, tell me just what happened," he pleaded, as though he thought Larry had been holding something back on him.

Larry acted reluctant. "Look, it's none of my business, what can I tell you? He made a phone call. He said he was tied up, it was taking longer than he expected. I wasn't really listening. He said a couple of other things. Then he said he'd be right over. That's all I know."

"Who the fuck was he talking to?" Gordon demanded rhetorically. He didn't expect an answer.

"I don't know; it sounded like a chick. Tell you the truth, Dan, we're better off without him. You know I never liked that guy."

Gordon muttered some dark threats addressed to his absent henchman.

An hour and a half passed, with Gordon getting edgier and edgier by the minute, his mood foul, the quality of the revenge he would exact on Harrel improving with each tense minute. Brooks stayed by the picture window next to the front door, peeking from behind the drawn curtains for a glimpse of Newman and the kid. Finally, he spotted them coming out the lobby door and heading for the staircase.

Gordon leaped from the bed and raced to let them in, impatiently shouldering Brooks out of the way and throwing open the door. A third man was with them. Gordon seemed to know him.

"Where the hell have you guys been?" he demanded, his voice combining relief and frustrated annoyance, exactly like a parent waiting up for a daughter three hours past curfew.

Newman shrugged, passing the question back to the college kid.

"We had a couple of beers," the kid answered. "Then there was this chopper hanging around; we had to cool it a while."

Larry glanced apprehensively at Newman, who was studiously indifferent. He knew the helicopter was the DeKalb County unit borrowed for surveillance. Someone must have botched the job, but no harm seemed to have been done. Gordon, though, wanted reassurance. He questioned the kid closely until he was satisfied the deal hadn't been compromised. Larry listened attentively, his admiration for Newman's skills growing with each word.

Apparently what had happened was that the helicopter moved in too close as the kid was directing Newman to the marijuana stash. With his superb instincts as an undercover agent, Newman sensed that the kid had spotted it and was about to say something. He got the drop on him by pointing it out himself. "Shit, I think we've got company," he said. "That chopper's been on our tail the last twenty minutes."

The DeKalb County deputies in the helicopter were monitoring the conversation in the car from the transmitter under Newman's belt and realized immediately they had to back off. For the next few minutes Newman drove a randomly zigzagging course while the helicopter played out its role by wandering off in a different direction, hovering from time to time as though it were looking for something. Newman, though, refused to be satisfied, leaving it up to the kid to convince him it had been a false alarm.

Gordon was satisfied with the kid's account. "Okay, okay," he mumbled, only then realizing he hadn't introduced Larry to the third man, a paunchy dentist in his mid-thirties named Olin Douglas. The flabby little stranger hadn't moved since he had come into the room. Like a curious but well-mannered child, he stood off by himself, his eyes wandering about the room. Larry crossed to him and shook his soft, moist hand.

Douglas, it turned out, had known Gordon since their undergraduate days at Auburn and had been investing in his drug deals for more than a year. The marijuana had been stashed in the two-car garage attached to his $80,000 home in Chamblee, a fashionable north Atlanta suburb. Douglas had been so impressed with Newman and the thought of $84,000 sitting in a tin box just a few minutes' drive away that he insisted on being present when the deal went down. Just fine, Larry thought wryly. His first arrest was suddenly turning into a party, with the bad guys lining up to go to jail. Okay, the more the merrier.

Newman had inspected the drugs and professed to be satisfied with the quality. It had been weighed in batches on a bathroom scale at the dentist's house after Newman first had taken the precaution of verifying the scale by stepping on it himself. The total weight of the marijuana came to 101 pounds, plus a few ounces. Gordon graciously agreed to call it 100 even as a token of friendship. Newman nodded glumly, unimpressed by Gordon's generosity. With Brooks standing over him, he opened the strongbox and counted out $16,000.

Gordon had to restrain himself from re-counting it, but he was going out of his way to impress Newman with a show of good faith. As he slipped the banded packets of money into his jacket pockets, a look of gross satisfaction crossed his face.

Larry watched the money disappear with a feeling of relief at least as great as Gordon's. The buy was over, and his first GBI case was just about to be wrapped up. He knew the arrests were probably the most dangerous part of the process, but for a few seconds he could afford to put that out of his mind in the carefully concealed euphoria of having accomplished what he had set out to do. Besides, he didn't expect trouble, especially with Harrel taken out of the picture. He doubted Gordon was even armed.

For the next two minutes time stood completely still while the drug dealers and the undercover agents shook hands all around, congratulating each other. Finally, Gordon, the kid, and the dentist moved to the door, Newman accompanying them as they stepped out onto the second-floor walkway. There was a last round of handshakes, and Larry heard Newman amiably agreeing he would be getting back in touch for another buy. "I can't hold it against you, man," he conceded graciously. "These kind of fuck-ups happen. But you're a good man to do business with. Looks like we got ourselves a righteous deal."

Larry's nerves sparked like live wires. "Righteous deal" was the preset code phrase to signal the backups to move in for the arrests.

From inside the room, he could see only Newman's back in the doorway, but within seconds he heard the heavy thudding of footsteps pounding down the walkway toward the room. Gordon heard it, too, and managed to sidestep past Newman back into the room, where he froze in his tracks like an animal at bay.

Wally Brooks had his gun leveled at Gordon's chest, his badge in his left hand. "Georgia Bureau of Investigation," he barked. "You're under arrest."

At just that instant half a dozen GBI agents led by George Clardy charged into the room, guns drawn. Gordon wheeled to look, only his upper body turning, his legs rooted to the spot. His hands already were reaching up in surrender as he turned to Larry, a look of utter hurt and betrayal in his eyes. Larry stared back at him with the same look, his hands raised by his shoulders. Clardy caught on instantly and cuffed Larry while Brooks did the honors for Gordon. They were taken to separate rooms in the motel for questioning.

For an undercover agent, the trickiest part of any deal is to get past the arrests without his own escape arousing suspicion. In planning the Gordon case, GBI had been willing to risk exposing Larry as an agent, on the assumption that Gordon didn't have any lines of communication to the other targets of Larry's investigations—Farnum in Virginia and Agee in Florida. But when Gordon showed up with Johnny Harrel, Larry came up with a brilliant ad-lib ploy that solved all his problems at once.

"I knew what you were thinking as soon as I heard you wanted Harrel out of the picture," Eason explained. "There was nothing to it. We just badged that little monkey as soon as he made it down the stairs and asked if he'd mind answering a few questions. We didn't have to take him anywhere. The only thing he could think of was getting us out of the lobby. With a deal going down just a few feet away and those dudes coming back any minute with a hundred pounds of grass, the last thing in the world he wanted was for us to be jawing there with him when the grass showed up. So we asked him what he knew about Spivey. Stuff like that. You should have been there, Larry. Funny as hell. We buy a little time, tell him thanks, and he beats it the hell out of there. Couldn't get away fast enough. He's pretty shook, but happy as a pig in shit just to be out of there without giving the cops a thing."

After being interrogated in the motel, Larry, Gordon, and the two other suspects were taken to the DeKalb County jail to be fingerprinted and booked. For a few hours Larry and Gordon shared a cell, with Larry enjoying every minute of Gordon's fully predictable diatribe against Harrel. The wheel had come full circle, as Larry remembered his first meeting with Harrel, Gus McClellan, and Jack Winter at least a lifetime ago. Now Harrel's ominous prophecies about what lay in store for anyone who crossed his boss were coming true, with Harrel himself the target.

With the one phone call each was allowed, Gordon called his lawyer, and Larry called Jerri, who quickly came to the jail to go through the charade of posting bond. When Larry got to Jerri's apartment, the phone was ringing. It was Harrel, who had been afraid to call his boss and had been trying to reach Larry for hours. With a few deft sentences Larry completed the destruction of his most cherished enemy.

He told Harrel, accurately enough, that Gordon was planning to have him killed. When the whining gunman protested his innocence, explaining how he had been detained by the cops, Larry advised him to forget that ridiculous story. "I don't know if he'll listen to you," Larry advised, "but if I were you, I'd just get in touch with him, lay it out to him why you did it, and just pray your ass off he forgives you. What was it, were you jammed up or something? He's known you a long time, maybe he'll understand."

Harrel sniveled that he hadn't been jammed up, that he hadn't sold out to the cops. "I wouldn't even have left the room if you didn't tell me to. Please, Larry, do me a favor, call him up and tell him that."

Larry hung up on him.

It was the last time Larry spoke to Harrel, who went into hiding that night and surreptitiously left the country in the morning.

Seventeen

"**Y**our wife called," Jerri grumbled as Larry climbed in bed beside her.

"You mean my ex-wife," Larry corrected.

She was in no mood for quibbles. "Wife, ex-wife, I don't give a damn. She called three times."

It was after midnight, and Larry didn't have the energy to concern himself with what Charlene wanted. Besides, he was sure he knew. Money. She had probably made herself a New Year's resolution to put the screws on tight. He lay awake a long time and then slept fitfully, finally falling into a deep sleep toward morning. By the time he dragged himself through a shower and down to the office, Mike Eason had already heard from Charlene. "Spivey, how the hell did you ever get mixed up with that woman?" he demanded in lieu of a greeting.

"She called here?" Larry asked incredulously.

"Better believe it."

"What did she want?"

"Six hundred bucks."

"I hope you told her how much I'm getting paid."

"I did, brother. And she laughed. Then she said if you're so goddamned important to us, we'd find a way to come up with the money or she makes a few phone calls and tells people you're a narcotics agent."

"Jesus Christ."

"Precisely."

Eason hadn't given her any satisfaction, so she called Billy Shepherd, and when she got nowhere with him, she tried Inspector Peters. "She went through this office like a scythe," Eason said, a note of grudging admiration in his voice. "Something's gotta be done about that lady, or she's gonna do what she says."

There was a decidedly humorous aspect to the situation, although no one at GBI appreciated it properly at the time. Unless Charlene was handled right, an elaborate and expensive investigation into drug rings smuggling literally hundreds of millions of dollars' worth of narcotics was about to become unglued for lack of $600. Peters, Eason, Clardy, Shepherd, and Larry met around the conference table to discuss Charlene's demands as seriously as if they had been laying strategy on a two-ton buy. In the end, the only conclusion they could reach was that Charlene would have to be bought off. As much as it hurt him to do so, Peters authorized Eason to draw $600 from the informants' fund. "Let's try and think of her as a kind of negative informant," he joked balefully. "We're paying her for information we don't want her to give."

Larry called Charlene and arranged to meet her for lunch at a Howard Johnson's in Sandy Springs. Eason and Clardy went with him, playfully suggesting he wear a wire. When they got to the restaurant, Charlene was already waiting at a booth by the window, her bright peach fingernails drumming impatiently on the tabletop as though she were counting the seconds they were late. As Larry stepped through the first of the double glass doors at the front of the restaurant, Eason grabbed his arm.

"You sit next to George and let me handle this," he pleaded. "Whatever you do, don't argue with her."

Charlene smiled radiantly as Eason slid into the booth beside her. A beautiful woman at all times, she looked as if she had invested at least an extra half hour at the makeup mirror for this meeting, and the results were well worth it. Her skin shone like a child's, and her hair flowed over her shoulders to her breasts. She was wearing a dark blue mini-dress with a scarf tied at her throat. She extended her hand daintily toward Eason and then Clardy, both of whom she greeted with her heaviest magnolia-blossom accent. She made a point of ignoring Larry as completely as if he hadn't walked in with them.

Eason wanted to order lunch before getting down to business, but Charlene wouldn't hear of it. "Ah just hate like the dickens imposing on you fellas like this," she purred. "But y'all just cain't believe how *absolutely* desperate Ah am for money right about now. Ah really don' wanna take more of yoah time than Ah *absolutely* have to."

Larry bit his lip. Two *absolutelys* in two sentences were a lot, even for

Charlene. Eason said he could appreciate her difficulties, but he hoped she could appreciate Larry's. "Not to mention ours," he added. "Naturally, all this has nothing at all to do with the bureau, but we were kind of hoping we could come in as sort of impartial outsiders and help settle this thing amicably."

"Well, Ah certainly hope y'all are right about that," Charlene agreed. She was being very agreeable. "Ah just never in mah life would have imagined there'd be so much hootin' and hollerin' about six hundred l'il ol' dollars. Ah've just absolutely got to get down to Daytona for the races. Ah always go, y'know. In fact, Ah haven't missed a race in five years— Ah mean, except foah las' year, when Ah was married to that no-good son of a bitch."

For the first time she looked at Larry, who returned her venomous smile in kind. He felt Clardy nudge him under the table. Just then the waitress came up to take their orders. Charlene cocked her head toward Larry and asked the waitress if she thought he was good-looking.

The waitress didn't want to get caught up in the middle of anything. She studied Larry as though he were an abstract painting she had been asked to comment on. "Yeah, I reckon he's a good-lookin' boy," she said at last. "Why?"

" 'Cause he's a son of a bitch, that's why."

"That's enough of that!" Eason said sharply, sending the confused waitress away.

Charlene's eyes looked as if there were a fire behind them. "I know you boys all stick together," she hissed. "But it just isn't fair the way you're all comin' down on a girl that only wants the teeniest little bit of what's hers. I don't know if this undependable son of a bitch told you, but I've got a court order against him for five thousand dollars. For the life of me, I can't see why you're making such a fuss. I'm trying to be nice, believe me I am. If I had a mind to, I could go back to that nice little old judge and have sweetheart over there put in jail for contempt until I get my five thousand dollars. Now you boys don't want that to happen, do you?"

Eason managed to get in a few words, but there was no stopping Charlene. She stared straight at Larry and said, "Don't sit there so smug, Mr. Ex-husband. You think you can scare me by looking so mean, with that big gun under your jacket, but believe me I'm not scared of you. I've got a gun, too, you know. I'd shoot the whole pack of you right here if I thought I could get away with it."

Eason's eyes lit up. "Did you say you have a gun?" he asked hopefully.

Charlene smiled coyly. "Yes, I do."

"What kind of gun is it?"

"It's a thirty-eight, automatic or something. Larry knows. He gave it to me. He probably still owes for it."

"It's a three-eighty," Larry said, speaking for the first time.

"Do you have a permit for it?" Eason asked.

"Why, Mistah Eason, you don't think I'd carry a gun without a permit," Charlene purred, reaching into her handbag. "I suppose you want to see it?"

"Please, ma'am."

She slid the permit from her billfold and handed it to him. His face fell when he saw it was perfectly valid. "How did you get this?" he asked.

"Oh, it was easy. I just went up to a judge and tol' him I had this real mean ex-husband that wouldn't pay me what he owed me and was threatening me and trying to kill me an' all. An' the judge just wrote me out a pistol-totin' license right on the spot. May I have my permit back, please?"

Eason decided it was time to make a tactical withdrawal, if not a full-scale retreat. He offered Charlene $300.

"Six."

"Four."

"Five."

"You got yourself a deal, lady," Eason said. "But all I've got is four hundred. You must have something, don't you, Larry?"

Before they went into the restaurant, Eason had given Larry $200 of the $600 from the informants' fund so it would look as if he were coughing up something personally. Larry took $100 out of his wallet and handed it to Charlene, along with the four from Eason. She left before lunch came.

At the office later that afternoon, Inspector Peters was happy to be out of it with $100 change, although he didn't delude himself that he had heard the last from the former Mrs. Spivey. He congratulated all three agents on a successful engagement with the enemy.

Floyd Farnum had a new angle. "Call my cousin," he told Larry. "His name is Tommie Mullins. I'll give you his number, but tell him you filched the number from me, that I don't know you're calling, and you'd like to deal straight with him. He liked the color of your money, he'll go for it. When the time's right, I'll let him know I'm in the deal."

Larry placed the call and got a warm reception from Mullins, who asked him to come to Roanoke the following Wednesday.

Mullins met Larry at the airport on January 7. A tall, slender man in his mid-twenties, he sported a Fu Manchu mustache that accentuated the naturally sorrowful look of his sullen gray eyes. There was a listless nervousness about him, the hallmark of the chronic small-timer. He seemed to be looking over his shoulder all the time, more out of habit than real watchfulness, and Larry felt confident there was no chance he would spot the surveillance team the Virginia State Police's intelligence unit had agreed to provide.

Larry and Mullins drove to the Roanoke Holiday Inn in Mullins's green Bonneville. Leaving Larry to check in and relax for a few minutes, Mullins went off to get a friend he said Larry had to meet. Shortly after six o'clock Larry went downstairs to the restaurant, took a corner table, and ordered a drink. Twenty minutes later Mullins came in, accompanied by a slightly paunchy and very pale young man in a beige leisure suit and an anemic blond with bobbed hair. Mullins introduced the man as Cotton Andrews and the girl simply as Fred. According to Mullins, Cotton Andrews was an expert on every kind of narcotic and the right-hand man of the Virginia mob's top drug merchant.

Andrews apologized for his boss's absence. "He wanted to meet you himself," he said, his voice surprisingly high and adolescent, "but he's not back in town yet. I suppose Tommie told you, there's a big meeting in Vegas. He was supposed to be back last night. He's heard some nice things about you, so he asked me to pinch-hit. If there's anything you need, give a holler."

Larry didn't think he needed anything.

"Maybe a girl," Andrews suggested.

Larry couldn't tell if he was being offered an evening with Fred but didn't want to take the chance. "Thanks anyway, but are we going to do business or not?" he asked, trying to sound no more surly than impatience would account for.

"I don't want to string you along," Andrews said. "I could tell you he'll be back tomorrow, but I don't know for sure."

Larry vowed to mark the date on his calendar. It was, as best he could recollect, the first time a drug dealer evinced any proclivity for the kind of straight talk that is taken for granted in every other line of work. For months he had been in a world of bluff and braggadocio, where every moment is spent running a number on someone and trying to add up the numbers coming in from the other side. Larry thanked Andrews for his candor and explained that he wanted to get started immediately. "Can we talk?" he asked.

"You mean Fred? She's okay. Sure."

Larry explained the agreement he had reached with Agee in Florida, identifying Agee only as a pilot with a long record of successful drug runs. "We worked out some figures on a ten-ton deal," he said. "And what it comes to is we need two hundred grand front money, which gets us the grass and a DC-Four to fly it in. You take that to your boss and find out if he's interested. No sense my wasting my time if you people aren't up for it."

Andrews didn't bat an eyelash. "If that's all you're worried about, don't sweat it," he said. "We've got the two hundred; we're just looking for some ways to put it to use. And I know the man is interested. He wouldn't have sent me here if he wasn't. All he wants is for me to get the picture from you and brief him when he gets back, probably no later than Sunday. As soon as I feed him the story, we're ready to roll. Won't take but a day or two to clean up all the corners."

Larry jotted down all the figures he had worked out with Agee, breaking it down into a detailed prospectus. He folded the note and handed it to Andrews, who slipped it into his breast pocket.

Andrews and Fred excused themselves immediately after dinner, leaving Larry in the restaurant with Mullins, who stretched out his long legs and leaned back as contented as a well-fed cat. It took three scotches and almost two hours before Larry could pry himself away from the suddenly flush but implacably minor-league middleman. He saw Mullins off, walking him to the parking lot, then went up to his room, where he put on the chain lock, opened his side of the double door leading to the adjoining room, and knocked three times on the knobless door facing him. Virginia agent Barry Keessee swung it open.

"Did you get it all?" Larry asked.

"We was just playin' the tapes back, ol' buddy," Keessee drawled. "Cain't say for sure it's gonna be a hit, but some of them tunes is mighty catchy."

In the morning Larry flew back to Atlanta to await word from Andrews's boss.

Monday afternoon while Larry was at headquarters and Jerri was at work, her twelve-year-old son Mark spent the rainy afternoon at home with three schoolmates. The boy worshiped Larry, about whom all he knew was that he was a cop of some kind, but not a regular cop, that he carried a gun and traveled a great deal. In the boy's mind, this made him some sort of romantic James Bond type of figure, a bearded, turtlenecked father figure on whom he could pin the luridly violent fantasies that can inflame even a healthy twelve-year-old's imagination.

Through the afternoon Mark regaled his friends with wholly made-up tales of Larry's exploits, most of them involving spies. When the other boys reacted skeptically, Mark tried to prove his point by showing them Larry's gun. He ransacked the apartment in a futile search for it, but all he could come up with was a box of .38 caliber ammunition. Luckily he didn't find the loaded .45 automatic Larry kept hidden in the tiny boiler room behind the closet under the stairs.

By the time Jerri got home from work Mark's friends had gone, and the boy had replaced the ammunition; but his hasty efforts to cover up the traces of his search hadn't done much good. She knew at once what he had been looking for but didn't want to say anything about it until she had a chance to discuss it with Larry. After dinner, while Mark watched television in the living room, Jerri took Larry into the bedroom for an urgent, whispered discussion.

She was deeply upset, perhaps more than she should have been. Larry tried to put the problem in perspective. To some extent she had been spoiled by Mark's unusual gentleness; growing up fatherless, the boy had only his mother as a role model and had shown no signs of normal boyish experimentation with violence. The sudden appearance of guns in his world simply gave him a chance to let off some pent-up hostility. In the end Larry agreed to have a long and serious talk with Mark.

He waited until the boy had been in bed a few minutes and then tiptoed into his room, carrying a pack of cigarettes and a lighter in one hand, an ashtray in the other. "Mark, are you still up?" he whispered.

"Yeah, sure," the boy answered, his voice wide awake.

Larry sat on the bed and lit a cigarette. Mark rolled onto his side and raised his head from the pillow, supporting himself with his hand, the pose touchingly mature, the way kids can be when they try being grown-up. For a moment Larry ached with an awareness of the boy's vulnerability. It was difficult to talk when he knew that the keenness with which the boy fastened himself on this unexpected moment of intimacy was itself a product of the same hero worship Larry was going to try to reduce to more manageable proportions.

He put his hand on Mark's shoulder and started to talk, explaining more about his work than he had ever told anyone. Even a twelve-year-old in today's society knows far more about drugs than he should. When Larry told Mark he was a narcotics investigator, the boy tried to sidetrack him with a distracting barrage of questions. With some effort, Larry got himself moving in the right direction again. He showed Mark his gun, hoping that familiarity would reduce its magical potency, and told him he had never had to use it and hoped he never would.

The boy seemed disappointed. "Aren't you going to catch these guys?" he asked, pouting.

"I hope so," Larry said matter-of-factly. "But I'm not going to shoot them."

He painted a picture of narcotics work as mostly meetings in offices and in restaurants that left the boy bored and dissatisfied. When he saw that Mark was struggling to keep awake, he leaned over and kissed him on the cheek. Mark squirmed uncomfortably, embarrassed at being treated like a child.

When Larry came out of the bedroom, Jerri was on the couch crying. He had always felt awkward in the presence of a woman's tears, unable to communicate his feelings of gentleness with the same assurance as he expressed other emotions. But he held her to him and comforted her, forcing himself to overcome his impatience. He realized that she was crying for him as much as for her son, that she was afraid he would get hurt or killed, afraid the undercover work would damage him in other, less physical ways. But he wasn't a man who could apologize to others for the risks he chose to run. When the phone rang, it was almost with a feeling of relief that he got up from the couch to answer it. Cotton Andrews told him the boss was back from Vegas.

"Spivey?" The voice at the other end was low and gravelly, probably a man in his fifties.

"Yeah."

"I just talked to Cotton. He likes the way you put things together. I got no problems going for the two hundred. You and Cotton make the arrangements. He'll call you back in an hour."

The phone went dead. The man had been careful not to identify himself, but the way he talked told Larry a lot. The voice was street tough, experienced. Larry guessed that whereas Floyd Farnum always referred to his associates as the organization, the man he had just spoken to would call them the mob. He wasn't fancy.

Larry quickly called Ron Agee in Fort Lauderdale and told him to make hotel reservations. When Cotton Andrews called back exactly one hour later, Larry was able to tell him the arrangements had been made.

220

On Wednesday, January 14, Larry and Cotton checked into the Pier 66, Fort Lauderdale's plushest hotel. Agee came over, and they ordered lunch in Larry's room. After less than an hour of detailed negotiations, a deal was struck. Andrews would put up $170,000 in cash, $90,000 of which would be front money for ten tons of marijuana. The rest was for the aircraft, $70,000 for purchase of the DC-4, $10,000 for miscellaneous expenses such as fuel and maintenance. Agee had jockeyed things around so that they would be able to use the airstrip in Colombia he had used for the Polk County deal. They would be buying from the Indians, from whom Agee could get higher-grade marijuana at a better price. With a selling price of $200 a pound, the load would bring $4 million to be split three ways after expenses. Agee's cut was 40 percent of the $3.15 million profit, which he would split with an unnamed associate. Larry figured he meant Ehrlichman, but the name didn't come up. Andrews's boss would take the same cut Agee was getting, $1.26 million. That would leave Farnum and Larry to split $600,000 as their commission for putting the deal together. Farnum's cousin Tommie Mullins was out, his only reward a nominal fee for getting Larry in contact with Andrews. Agee had lined up a broker in Michigan who guaranteed the selling price on the understanding he would be allowed to pocket the difference between $200 a pound and any higher price he was actually able to get.

In the morning Larry returned to Atlanta, where he checked in at headquarters and learned that GBI and the Virginia intelligence unit had been working overtime during his absence. They had done a thorough work-up on Cotton Andrews, who had a yellow sheet a criminal twice his age could have been proud of. There were at least eleven arrests but only one conviction. All the arrests were drug-related. He had just finished a thirty-month stretch in a Virginia prison. Through undercover sources, they also had been able to identify his boss, the gruff-voiced older man Larry had spoken with briefly on the telephone.

His name was Horace Shawkey, and he was everything his terse conversation had led Larry to suspect. He couldn't have been more mob-connected if his name had ended in a vowel. Fifty-four years of age, he was, quite simply, an old-time gangster. Over the years, he had been arrested for armed robbery, gambling, truck hijacking, pimping, loan sharking, and murder. The only one that had ever stuck was the hijacking, for the record showed he had done time for boosting a $3 million load of furs. There were no narcotics arrests or convictions, but the man was so crooked that even the front he maintained to cover his illegal income was illegitimate. He owned and operated a string of whorehouse massage parlors located in just about every town in Virginia large enough to have its own post office.

That evening Shawkey called Larry at Jerri's apartment. "Cotton tells me you're ready to go," he growled. "He'll let you know as soon as we've got the money."

For the next few days the phone lines between Atlanta, Fort Lauderdale, Roanoke, and Bassett Forks were kept busy with a steady stream of updates on the latest developments. On Tuesday, January 20, Cotton finally reported that everything was set. Larry called Farnum, who immediately sent Roger Sorenson down in the Skymaster to pick up Larry and fly him to Virginia.

"That guy we were dealing with, are you still in touch with him?" Sorenson asked when Larry met him at the airport.

Larry didn't know what he was talking about. "What guy?" he asked.

"You know the one I mean," Sorenson said, fishing for the name and finding it. "George."

"Oh, him. Yeah, off and on. Why?"

Sorenson shrugged indifferently, playing the role of the big mover who occasionally found it convenient to get involved in deals that were really beneath him "Nothing really. I was talking to him a while back about getting him some coke samples. Floyd wanted me to check if he's still interested."

"I'll give him a call, find out."

Larry called Clardy from a pay phone at the airport. They waited twenty minutes for Clardy to drive out to meet them. The agent paid Sorenson $1,200 for the sample, then drove back to town with an ounce of cocaine and one additional narcotics charge against both Sorenson and Farnum.

That evening Farnum took Larry, Sorenson, and Cotton Andrews to dinner in Martinsville. Cotton's girlfriend Fred and Farnum's wife Tracy rounded out the party. Over drinks, Andrews confessed that his boss was having a little trouble raising the entire $170,000. "He'll be coming with us when we go down to Fort Lauderdale in the morning. He'll have a hundred grand and a couple of guys with him. He's got a friend down there in Key Biscayne or somewhere that's supposed to kick in the other seventy."

Farnum did a few lightning fast calculations and said, "Tell him not to bother. As soon as we get down to Lauderdale, I'll run over to Grand Cayman and pull seventy grand out of one of my accounts there. No sense bringing in some guy we don't even know."

Andrews said, "Suit yourself."

As easily as that, with just a couple of sentences over drinks, Farnum cut himself into the deal two ways. Now he was down for a major share of the backers' commission in addition to the 20 percent he would be splitting with Larry.

After dinner Larry asked Andrews about the two men Shawkey would be bringing. At first Cotton was evasive, describing them merely as "friends." Then he identified them as bodyguards, and finally he admitted they were a pair of hit men who traveled everywhere with the boss.

"Well, I think he's in for a disappointment," Larry said. "The plane we're going in only seats six. What happens to him if he has to appear in public with only one cannon?"

Andrews laughed. "I guess he can handle it. He'll take Donnie. Donnie's filled sixteen contracts. The other guy's pretty new at it, runs a barbershop on the side. I don't figure he's done more than five hits, six tops."

"No, of course. You wouldn't want him. Have him take Donnie by all means," Larry agreed grimly.

Eighteen

orace Shawkey lived with his mistress, a retired hooker named
Lynne, in an apartment behind one of his massage parlors in
Roanoke. A heavily muscled man, he had the thick neck, the
close-cropped graying hair, and the bullish swagger of an aging but still
formidable barroom brawler. Born and reared in California, he had come
to manhood in Raymond Chandler's Los Angeles but had somehow ended
up in Virginia, as out of place as a prizefighter at a duchess's wedding. One
look at him was enough to show he didn't fit in with the college-educated
smoothies running the drug industry in the South. But if Shawkey was a
square peg, he left no doubt he would, as the old joke had it, make his own
hole. Although he was rarely seen out of the company of his garishly
violent bodyguards, he gave the impression that he wasn't above settling
differences with his own fists—or his own guns, if that was what seemed
called for.

While Roger Sorenson readied the Skymaster for the flight to Fort
Lauderdale, Larry and Floyd Farnum drove to pick up Shawkey at his
apartment. Lynne opened the door for them but didn't stick around long
enough for Larry to get much of an impression of her, beyond the orange-
red hair and the overstated curviness of her body. "Horace will be out in
a minute," she announced with slightly comic formality before leaving
them alone in the living room.

Shawkey was reputedly a wealthy man, but his home was decorated like
a second-rate motel. There was a seascape print on the wall above the

couch, and Larry half expected he would find the same print in each of the other rooms in the apartment.

After ten minutes Shawkey came out, tucking his shirt into his pants. "Which one is Spivey?" he demanded.

Larry acknowledged that he was Spivey.

"Then who's this?"

"Floyd Farnum," Farnum said, reaching out his hand.

Shawkey nodded. "I've heard of him," he said, as though speaking of someone not there. "Supposed to be pretty smart is what I hear."

"I try to take care of myself," Farnum said, trying to accept the compliment and sound tough at the same time.

"Yeah, I'll bet," Shawkey growled. "Look, why don't you sit down or something? I'll be ready to go as soon as my man gets here."

He turned and walked back to the bedroom area, leaving his guests alone. Too intimidated to talk, Larry and Floyd found chairs and settled in to await the arrival of Shawkey's man—apparently the bodyguard Cotton Andrews had mentioned at dinner. Both of them felt a little like fans hoping to catch a glimpse of a movie star, for they were curious to see what a real hit man looked like.

When he showed up a half hour later, Larry felt a little of what Jerri's son Mark must have felt a few nights before, when Larry had told him undercover narcotics work was mostly writing reports and attending meetings. Swanson was a disappointment from top to bottom. He had medium-length blond hair and a boyish look that completely belied his profession. In manner, he was as deferential and courteous as a headwaiter greeting a steady customer.

Farnum drove them to the airport, where the Skymaster had long been ready for takeoff. Cotton Andrews met them there. On the flight to Fort Lauderdale, Swanson began to live up to his billing, scaring Farnum silly by engaging in an elaborate ritual with his gun, which he checked out as ostentatiously as a muscle man flexing himself into a state of preparedness. As soon as they landed, Farnum rushed to the car rental desk to put some distance between himself and the smiling killer. He drove Larry and Sorenson to the Pier 66 in a rented car, while Shawkey, Andrews, and Swanson were left to catch up in a cab.

Larry and Cotton were booked into one large room, Shawkey and his bodyguard in another, Farnum and Sorenson in the third. Agee drove over for a meeting and closeted himself immediately with Larry and Farnum. They had barely shaken hands when he hit Farnum with an unexpected proposal that threatened to blow all of Larry's carefully laid plans out of the water.

Agee said he had a friend who went by the name Dean Nations. A slick operator who sometimes moved so fast he couldn't keep up with himself, Nations had just bought three thousand pounds of Colombian marijuana, concluding the deal so quickly that he found himself the owner of a ton and a half of contraband that he had no way of picking up. "It's just sitting on a runway in Ríohacha, Colombia, and it's costing Dean money every minute it's out there," Agee said.

He suggested that since the Skymaster already was in Fort Lauderdale, Farnum could pick up a piece of change by sending his pilot down to Ríohacha for part of the load. Agee, who knew everything worth knowing about aircraft, calculated that with the seats out, the Skymaster could carry a thousand-pound payload. For such a run, the "piece of change" Nations had in mind came to $90,000—thirty to Farnum for the use of his aircraft, thirty to Sorenson for making the flight, and thirty for providing a suitable field and hiring an unloading crew.

The moment Larry heard the proposition, he knew it meant trouble. When the spirit moved him, Farnum could be as cautious as a cat burglar; but he was just as likely to go off half-cocked, and Agee's suggestion was just the sort of thing that would appeal to him. Larry knew Farnum well enough to realize that the young Virginia entrepreneur couldn't pass up a spur-of-the-moment mission with a pretty price tag on it.

The problem was that if Farnum decided to take the job, Larry was locked in. He would have no choice but to have the run interdicted, for the one inviolable rule no narcotics agent could afford to ignore was that he couldn't let a load get through. Occasionally tactics demanded that a dealer be let free, as Larry had done with Johnny Harrel after the Gordon bust. But to stand back and let a drug shipment hit the streets in order to bust a bigger load would be to put the Georgia Bureau of Investigation into the smuggling business and to make every agent on the case an accessory.

Desperately Larry looked for a way out, something he could say that would convince Farnum not to do the deal. But all he could come up with was a whispered aside that he knew perfectly well wouldn't do any good. "Jesus, Floyd, maybe we oughta take it a little easy. Who the hell is this Dean Nations anyway? I never heard of him."

Farnum shrugged laconically, a couldn't-be-bothered gesture, and opened the door to the adjoining room, where Roger Sorenson was lounging on the bed with his ankles crossed.

"Rog, get your ass in here," Farnum barked playfully. "It's about time you started earning your keep."

Sorenson bounded into the room like a child into the schoolyard, delighted at the prospect of becoming useful. Farnum caught his arm and literally dragged him out onto the balcony for a two-minute conference.

"He says he'll do it," Farnum announced to Agee. "How soon can Nations be here?"

The lanky smuggler unfolded himself from an upholstered chair and crossed to the phone. He dialed an Atlanta area number. "I got some dudes'll do it. . . . Skymaster, we figure it's good for half a ton. . . . I told them ninety. When can you be here?"

He hung up the phone and turned to Farnum. "He says tomorrow. You'll have your money twenty-four hours after his people take delivery."

Farnum wasn't sure he liked the idea. "How well do you know this cat?" he asked.

"Nations? Known him for years. I trust him, if that's what you mean. But that's no reason you ought to. Make up your own mind; you're a big boy."

Farnum wasn't sure whether he was being condescended to or whether that was just Agee's style. "I've got to have some money up front," he said. "Forty-five before we go, forty-five when we deliver."

Agee's heavy-lidded eyes lowered a notch. "How well does he know you?" he asked pointedly. "A man doesn't hand someone he's just met forty-five grand to take a trip in an airplane. It could be you'd go the wrong way."

A clear point for Agee. But even from across the room, Larry could see the wheels behind Farnum's eyes turning. Without missing a beat Farnum said, "Then let's do it this way. When we get back, we give him half the load. He gets the other half when we get paid."

"What good does that do you?"

"Say he gets popped after we deliver the stuff. Then I'm out ninety thousand dollars."

"Say he gets popped after you give him half the load and he leads the narcs back to where you're sitting on the other half. Then you're out twenty years."

Floyd Farnum was a hard man to figure. In his own way, he was as egotistical as a prom queen, but he never minded backing down because he never put his ego on the line in anything he did. Being outwitted didn't particularly bother him because he had the capacity to admire the skill it took to outwit him.

"Fine," he said, "no problem. I'm not investing anything except Rog and some gasoline. If the guy stiffs me, he stiffs me."

"Good," Agee grunted. "That's taken care of. Now let's talk about the DC-Four. Did Shawkey bring the money?"

Larry and Farnum answered simultaneously. Larry said, "Yeah, more or less." Farnum said, "Not really."

"Okay, let's split the difference. Not really more or less," Agee answered, amused and annoyed. "What the fuck does that mean?"

" 'Yeah' means he's got a hundred grand in a paper sack he carries around like it was groceries," Farnum explained. " 'Not really' means a hundred isn't a hundred seventy."

Agee turned crisp. "Well it takes one-seventy. You were supposed to know that."

Judging by the speed with which he reacted, Farnum had been waiting for just such an opening. He was through it as quickly as a 185-pound halfback. "Just the point I was going to make," he said, speaking rapidly. "I told his boy I would kick in whatever he's short. Now I'm wondering what we need his hundred for. He's halfway out the door already. No sense leaving him standing there letting in the draft. Let Rog make the run for Nations. We get the ninety grand, plow it right back into the DC-Four job, and cut Shawkey out completely. I don't figure we need him and his cowboy."

It was a dazzling move. Only a few hours earlier Floyd had cut himself in for a good percentage of Shawkey's share of the deal. Now he was taking over entirely. It took Larry a moment to get his bearings, to figure out how much damage had been done to his case or, in fact, whether it had been damaged at all. And he came to the surprising conclusion it hadn't. What clarified the situation for Larry was the sight of Roger Sorenson, still on the balcony where Farnum had left him, grinning in through the plate-glass door like a floor lamp someone had forgotten to turn off. Sorenson was the fall guy. He was going to jail, directly to jail, the moment he tried to land the Skymaster with half a ton of Dean Nations's marijuana. If Shawkey was still on the scene, he would immediately turn tail and run, making Larry's artfully forged ticket of admission into the Virginia syndicate instantly worthless. Farnum's new scam at least had the advantage of sending the burly Virginia gangster and his cheerful hired gun home before the shit hit the fan.

In the two or three seconds it took Larry to go through this elaborate doublethink, he almost missed Ron Agee's curious reply to Farnum's proposal. The idea of capriciously altering the entire financial structure of what promised to be a $4 million deal didn't faze him in the least. The only question he asked was: "What do you mean, cowboy?"

Farnum gave him a terse and harrowing verbal image of Donnie Swanson, adding that Shawkey himself apparently was armed to the teeth.

That settled it. Although Ron Agee had time and again demonstrated his utter fearlessness in the air, he was deathly afraid of guns. As many times as he had been down the road, Agee still believed that the illegal importation of narcotics was, or at least should be, a gentleman's trade.

Farnum himself handled the expulsion of Horace Shawkey. He never explained exactly what it was he told the syndicate chieftain, but from what Larry was able to piece together from a few casually dropped hints over the next few days, apparently the gist of it was that he felt uncomfortable about Agee, that he was willing to run the risk himself by testing the waters with a small deal, and that he'd get back to Shawkey later if everything worked out. Shawkey not only bought it but was deeply appreciative. Less than an hour after Farnum had spoken to him, he checked out of the Pier 66, taking Donnie Swanson and Cotton Andrews with him.

With Shawkey out of the picture, Farnum inherited his financial responsibilities, including $30,000 due immediately on the DC-4. He telephoned Tracy in Bassett Forks and instructed her to collect $10,000 from the cash reserves he kept squirreled in the safes in the offices of each of his skating rinks. He wanted her to join him in Fort Lauderdale but suggested that for her own safety she wire the money down first. Farnum offered to pay the other $20,000 due on the airplane by check, as long as the owner had no objection to a draft on a bank in the Cayman Islands. Agee didn't expect it would be a problem.

They shook hands all around, Farnum collected Sorenson from the balcony, and the four new partners repaired to the glass-walled restaurant overlooking the pool, where they dined on filets and lobsters while toasting each other as liberally as diplomats. Spirits were high, the euphoria of the moment combining with the liquor to strip bare something of the character of each of the men around the table. Sorenson postured ridiculously, playing a part out of "Terry and the Pirates" so intently that his jaw actually seemed to get squarer with each sip from his scotch and soda. Farnum was giggling like a child, while Agee, haughty and arrogant, studied them both as though they were curiously hairless pets.

Larry watched them with an uncomfortable sense of detachment. In the course of the evening he realized that, with the exception of Sorenson, these were men he would have liked, perhaps admired, if he had met them in any other capacity. In fact, he did like them. Agee's absolute self-command, his adventurer's approach to smuggling appealed to the adventurer in Larry, in much the same way that Farnum's adolescent innocence struck a response from another side of his own personality. That was what made it so damned hard to drink their liquor, eat their food, and laugh at their jokes while planning to have them arrested.

Alone in his room later that night, Larry called GBI to give an update on the strange twists the case had taken. George Clardy promised to work up a tactical plan for bringing down as many of the smugglers as possible. Customs would be brought into the case; its air surveillance team would pick up Sorenson's return flight from Ríohacha when the pilot touched down to refuel at Grand Turk Island. He would be tailed into Florida. Meanwhile, Larry should attempt to learn the location of the landing field so that GBI and Customs could stake it out.

In the morning Larry drove Farnum to the Miami airport, where he caught a flight for the Caymans to get the $70,000 he needed for the deal. On his way back from the airport, Larry picked up the $10,000 draft Farnum's wife had wired down. Returning to the Pier 66, he met Agee and handed the money over to him. Accompanied by Sorenson, Larry and Agee drove to the Fort Lauderdale airport to inspect the DC-4 and meet Tracy Farnum's flight from Roanoke. She arrived around noon, having spent the entire night racing from one roller rink to another to round up the money. Leaving Sorenson at the airport so that he could take the seats out of the Skymaster and make some adjustments in the autopilot, Larry drove Tracy to the hotel. Sorenson's gear was moved into Larry's room, and Tracy went to take a nap in the room her ex-husband would be returning to that night.

Toward evening Farnum called from Grand Cayman to say he wouldn't be back until the next morning at ten.

On Wednesday, January 28, Larry and Tracy drove to the Miami airport to meet Floyd's flight. "Did you get the money?" Larry asked as soon as Farnum had cleared customs.

"Better," Farnum answered enigmatically, refusing to elaborate. In his room an hour later, he threw his suitcase on the bed, unlocked it, and lifted out a small, squarish package wrapped in brown paper and tied with nylon string. When he sliced the string with his pocket knife and folded back the paper, about fifty tiny parcels, each wrapped in an individual square of newspaper, tumbled onto the bedspread. The thought flashed through Larry's mind that Farnum must have done some kind of drug deal in the Caymans, but before he had a chance to figure out if that made any sense, Farnum unwrapped one of the packets and held up a small bar of gold about an inch and a half long, an inch wide, and three-eighths of an inch thick. He passed it to Larry, who studied the lettering stamped into the surface of the metal. It said the bar weighed ten tolas, which meant nothing to Larry.

Farnum, who never liked to proceed in a straight line if he could find any angles to play, had come up with a scheme for multiplying his profit on the deal. He took back the bar and rewrapped it, stacked the parcels, folded the brown paper around them, slid them back into his suitcase, and began to explain. He started at the elementary level, with the fact that a tola was an Indian unit of measure equivalent to three-eighths of a troy ounce. The gold in his suitcase weighed five hundred tolas and was worth "a shade under thirty-one thousand dollars." The United States government had recently lifted the prohibition on the private ownership of gold, but in Colombia, where citizens still were not permitted to own the precious metal, it sold at black-market prices from three to four times the legal trading price.

What Farnum had in mind was a simple two-way smuggle that would multiply his profit on the marijuana deal at least threefold. He was sure the Indians with whom Agee dealt would accept $30,000 in gold as the full equivalent of the $90,000 they wanted for the marijuana. "No sense making money in just one direction when you can make it in both," he said.

Dean Nations arrived at the hotel exactly at six o'clock, as promised, a punctuality totally at variance with the mores of the drug-dealing community. In other regards, though, he was an almost-too-perfect specimen of the breed. With shoulder-length blond hair, in blue jeans and a loosely woven cotton shirt, his belt secured with a large American Indian silver-and-turquoise buckle, he was the stereotypically perfect doper. He wore an expensive-looking digital alarm watch on his wrist, a reminder that although his style of dress suggested hip informality, he was in reality a man with a busy schedule.

The planning meeting for the Ríohacha run took place in Larry's room, with all the principals except Farnum in attendance. Sorenson would be leaving the Fort Lauderdale international airport Thursday evening at six. He was to fly to Grand Turk, where he would be refueled by one of

Nations's associates. He was then to take off and fly directly south over Haiti to Ríohacha, Colombia, arriving at dawn of the thirtieth. The Indians there would help him remove the fuel drums he was carrying in the cargo area. After refueling him from the drums, the Indians would load on a thousand pounds of marijuana. He was to take off immediately and return to Grand Turk, where Nations's associates would again refuel him, having already bribed the airport line boy.

Before he left Grand Turk, he would be given his landing destination in code, either A, B, or C. Larry knew that one of the letters referred to a farm about thirty miles south of Gainesville owned by Farnum and operated by Roger Sorenson's brother. He assumed the other two possible sites had been selected by either Nations or Agee, since the Virginians hadn't done any scouting in the area.

At this point in the discussion, Sorenson unexpectedly asked Larry to leave the room for security reasons, so that only he and the men he was working for would possess certain vital details about the flight. Concealing his annoyance to avoid seeming suspiciously curious about matters that were none of his business, Larry went next door and pounded on Farnum's door until he woke Tracy. She left him standing in the hallway while she put on some clothes and woke Floyd. The two men then went down to the bar to talk.

Ultrasophisticated in the financial intricacies of high-level smuggling, Farnum knew surprisingly little about the nuts and bolts of an operation like the one he was now into up to his eyeballs. It took two drinks before he got up the nerve to ask the question that had been preying on his mind.

"Say, Larry, I was wondering," he began sheepishly. "We told them we'd supply the unloading crew, didn't we?"

"Right."

"Right." He nodded. "So I guess we gotta do that, right?"

Larry didn't answer.

"No problem. We'll just hire the people. We shouldn't have much trouble finding enough people, huh?"

"Enough?" Larry asked.

"Yeah, I mean, like, however many it takes." There was a pause, and then he took the bull by the horns. "How many guys is it going to take?"

Larry laughed. Farnum had never done a day's work in his life; a thousand pounds, hand-carried from one place to another, probably struck him as an unimaginable quantity. "Two," Larry said flatly.

"Two?"

"That's right. Me and you."

"Well, yeah, I don't know, I mean maybe there's going to be other things I should be doing. What do you say I hire another guy to help you out? What do you think of that kid that was here?"

"Cotton?"

"Right, Cotton. Say I pay him a grand. Would he do it?"

Larry suggested they call him and find out. He stood next to Farnum at a phone booth in the lobby while Farnum placed the call. Andrews sounded surprised to hear from them.

"What are you cats up to? Is the deal really going to go down?" he asked.

"Sure. I thought you understood that."

"No, no. All I knew was you split just after we split. I figured it all fell apart."

"I didn't split," Farnum said, feeling slightly insulted. "I just had to run down to Cayman to pick up some gold."

"No shit. What kind of Gold?"

"Gold, regular gold."

"You mean Colombian Gold?"

"No, man, gold. Gold-gold."

"From Cayman. Cayman Gold? I never heard of it. You sure you don't mean Jamaica Gold?"

"I don't mean any kind of Gold. I mean gold. Like in gold bars, see?"

"Bricks, right?"

"Jesus Christ, will you listen a minute. Not bricks. Not Cayman Gold. Just gold. Like they make coins out of."

"Oh, fuck," Andrews groaned. "Whaddya want with that?"

He knew everything there was to know about narcotics but didn't understand the first thing about money, whereas Farnum was just the opposite. But the diametric difference between them gave them something in common, for they shared a mutual inability to understand each other. Andrews readily agreed to fly down to Florida to work on the unloading crew for $1,000.

"Nice kid," Farnum said when he hung up the phone.

Larry headed back to his room expecting trouble from Sorenson. Whenever Farnum's pilot had nothing to do, he was as servile as a spaniel, but the moment anyone gave him a role to play he metamorphosed into Little Caesar. As Larry turned the key in the lock, his antennas were tuned for the slightest vibration of hostility. He was resolved to put a stop to it immediately, before it got dangerous. Sorenson greeted him coldly, saying nothing about the conclusion of his meeting with Agee. Neither spoke as Larry got ready for bed. Then Sorenson said, "I hope you didn't mind my asking you to leave, but it had to be that way. You really didn't have any business being there in the first place."

Larry turned on him. "How's that again?"

"I said you didn't have any business there anyway," Sorenson repeated.

Larry took a step toward him, challenging. "Don't tell me what's my business and what's not. Don't ever do that," he growled, his anger genuine now.

Like a fighter throwing jabs while in retreat, Sorenson backed off slightly but tried to get in another shot. "Jesus, Larry, it's nothing personal," he purred. "But I just can't help wondering what you're doing here. Floyd's putting up the money, these guys have got the grass, and I'm doing the flying, taking all the risks. Where do you come in?"

That was exactly what Larry wanted to hear. It was a dangerous question, and if Sorenson ever asked it when any of the others were around, it could get them wondering the same thing. The fact was Larry had no business being there. He had put Farnum and Sorenson together with Agee and Nations, and for that he would expect to get paid. But he would have no reason to stay on the scene and every reason in the world to want some distance between himself and the dealers. Here was the double-pronged dilemma Inspector Peters had warned him about at the very beginning of his career: He could never be essential to the operation, or the smugglers would be able to charge entrapment when they were arrested; but he had to appear essential, or they would start wondering why he was there. Already Sorenson was starting to see through Larry's act, although still without any understanding of its significance. If anyone with more brains than Sorenson started asking the same question, it could cost Larry his life.

Larry took two steps toward the pilot, who was just a foot or so from the bathroom door. With a quick move, Larry was on top of him, grabbing him by the collar and flinging him against the door. It gave way, and Sorenson tumbled into the bathroom, crumpling to the tile. Larry stood over him and pulled him to his feet. "Where do I come in!" he shouted. "I come in because this is my deal, motherfucker. If you say anything like that to me again, you're going to be carrying your nuts around in your hand."

He slapped him hard across the face and stalked back to the bedroom.

At breakfast in the morning Farnum said he thought he had heard shouts from the next room during the night. He asked if anything was wrong. Larry pointedly declined to answer. Sorenson said, "No, nothing's the matter. Larry and I were discussing the deal, that's all. We had a difference of opinion, but we've come to an understanding."

After breakfast Farnum rented a car and set off with Tracy on the three-hundred-mile drive to the farm in Gainesville that was penciled in as one of the three possible landing sites. He asked Larry to fly up to Atlanta to meet Cotton Andrews, who would have to make a connection there since there were no direct flights from Roanoke to Gainesville. This assignment gave Larry a chance to sit down face to face with his colleagues at GBI and work out some detailed planning for the arrest. Except for a few furtive phone calls, he had been out of contact for what felt like a very long time, and he wanted to make sure all bases would be covered.

At GBI headquarters he found Inspector Peters, Agents Clardy, Eason, and Shepherd, and two patrol officers from the customs air branch waiting for him. Inspector Peters announced that GBI planned to begin its surveillance at the Atlanta airport the moment Larry met Cotton Andrews. The undercover agent and the drug expert would be photographed in the airport and boarding the flight to Gainesville in order to bulk out the case file with complete documentation of the connection. At the Gainesville end of the flight the surveillance would be picked up by a GBI team working in liaison with Florida authorities, whom Eason had already contacted.

Larry carefully detailed everything he knew about the upcoming run, including his best estimate of Sorenson's departure time from Grand Turk on his return flight with the drugs. He had to confess he had only a vague idea of the location of the farm that was one of the possible landing sites and knew absolutely nothing about the other two coded destinations. The customs agents were confident they would be able to pick up Sorenson out of Grand Turk and tail him from there. But unless they knew where he was going, they would have to force him down and arrest him rather than risk losing the load. On the other hand, if they learned the location of the landing field and had time enough to stake it out, arrests wouldn't be made until after Dean Nations took delivery.

At the conclusion of the lengthy meeting, Larry returned to Hartsfield International Airport, just two blocks from GBI headquarters. He met Cotton Andrews's 11:15 flight from Roanoke, and forty-five minutes later he and Andrews were en route to Gainesville, where they were met by

Floyd and Tracy Farnum. They had driven only a half mile down the two-lane boulevard from the terminal to the intersection with State Highway 24 when Farnum announced that he thought he was being followed.

Larry, who knew perfectly well they were being followed, cursed to himself but showed no outward reaction. "Are you sure?" he asked.

Farnum turned at the next intersection to find out. The car behind him turned with him. Farnum made three lefts in a row to confirm what he already knew. "No sweat," he said. "Let's take them for a ride."

He drove down Florida 24 into Gainesville, where he picked up I-75 heading north. When they eased out onto the expressway just outside town, three cars followed them up the ramp in close formation. By this time it was obvious to the agents behind Farnum that he knew they were there, so there was no reason for them to disguise their presence. There was also no reason for them to be there since it was utterly inconceivable Farnum would lead them anywhere interesting. But the charade went on, the agents carrying out their futile assignment with no more flexibility than a windup toy running itself down in a toy chest.

Larry was all for checking into the nearest motel and getting some sleep, but Farnum was determined to inconvenience himself as much as he was inconveniencing the men behind him. He drove all the way to Valdosta, Georgia, about 150 miles north of Gainesville, before calling it a night. He paid for two rooms, one for himself and Tracy, one for Larry and Andrews, then ordered breakfast in the motel coffee shop. The sun was coming up when Larry and Cotton Andrews finally got to their beds.

Farnum let them sleep until ten, then called their room and told them to meet him by the car in fifteen minutes. He had already checked them out. In daylight, with traffic on the road, the tail was harder to pick up, but it was still there. After stopping for another breakfast, the smugglers drove to the Valdosta airport, where Farnum visited the field manager's office to ask questions about when the airport closed, what night security precautions were taken, and so forth. He figured the agents tailing him would interrogate the manager as soon as he left, and he wanted to plant the idea that he was planning an after-hours landing there. The foursome drove around for a few hours, returning to the airport two or three times before heading north on I-75. Farnum wasn't in the least bothered by the tail, for he knew the cops wouldn't be following him if they had any idea where they ought to be going. Like a mother quail protecting her nest, he was leading them away from the actual landing site.

"Might as well drive on up to Atlanta," he said cheerfully. "There's nothing doing down here."

"In that case I ought to call my girl, tell her I'm coming," Larry said, grabbing for an excuse to get to a telephone.

When they pulled up at a gas station, Farnum accompanied Larry to the phone. He trusted Larry, but it was perfectly in character for him to make sure his trust was deserved. He waited long enough to satisfy himself it was a woman on the other end of the line and then stepped into the men's room a few feet from the phone booth.

As soon as the men's room door closed behind him, Larry cupped his hand over the receiver and gave Jerri whispered instructions to call Phil Peters immediately and inform him that Farnum was leading his men on a wild-goose chase.

Farnum stepped out the men's room and said, "Let me talk to her."

With a heightened appreciation of his partner's deviousness, Larry handed over the phone.

"Hi there. Are you this no-good character's girl friend?" Farnum asked, thickening his accent under the illusion it made him more charming. "What's your name? Jerri. Well, listen, Jerri, why don't you just give me the name of the nicest restaurant you know in Atlanta, get yourself all dolled up, and come out and meet us there around six? Jesus Christ, what kind of a name is that? Admiral who? Admiral Benbow Inn? Got it. See you at six, lookin' forward to it."

He hung up, put in a dime, and placed a collect call to a number with a central Florida area code. "We won't be down," he said tersely. "String the lights yourself. You and Rog are going to have to do the unloading. No, no problems, I'll explain later. Tell Rog to make sure and vacuum out the plane when you're finished. Then have him fly it on up to Gainesville and check into the hotel. Call me in Atlanta at the Admiral Benbow Inn as soon as Roger gets there. We'll be in the dining room."

Larry bit his lip at the near miss. If Farnum had placed his call before Larry called Jerri, he could have had her tell GBI to trace the number Farnum had called. Then they would have had the location of the farm. Now, unless he could get free in the next hour or so, it would be too late. Customs would have to force Sorenson down and arrest him before he could make his delivery to Dean Nations.

And that is exactly what happened. Roger Sorenson thought he spotted a tail just as he came over American waters about twelve miles off Melbourne, halfway up Florida's east coast. As he banked into a short clearing turn to check the traffic behind him before turning northwest toward Gainesville, he noticed a big twin-engine Commander hanging like a gull out his portside window. A Twin-Beech D-18 seemed to be hovering off the Commander's starboard wing, with another Commander behind it, making a loose formation. Sorenson had dropped the Skymaster down to about a thousand feet when he was still well out to sea, and there would be no reason for the three aircraft to be coming up on top of him unless they wanted to make trouble.

Customs, he thought grimly, wiping his dry tongue across his lips. For a moment he lost them as he took up the 320-degree heading he had been planning before he spotted them. For a minute or two he flew mindlessly, fretting unproductively while cold balls of sweat rolled down his sides. Like a slow winter sunrise, it finally dawned on him that the worst possible thing he could do was to lead them to Gainesville, and he banked around to the right so sharply it cost him almost four hundred feet before he could get the nose back up enough for the overloaded Skymaster to keep its altitude. Above him, the three Customs aircraft—he was sure of it now—drifted by like balloons in the wind.

Suddenly the frightened smuggler decided to make a run for it. It was a spur-of-the-moment notion, but it gripped him like an obsession even though he had been flying long enough to know there was nowhere for him to go. Yet even with half a ton of marijuana to slow it down, his Skymaster could dance like a water bug. He vaulted back up to a thousand feet to give himself enough altitude for another trick and saw both Commanders wheeling around behind him in big, open circles. He cut to the west and realized at once he had made a mistake, the turn bringing him a couple of hundred yards closer to the Commander out his starboard window.

Not that it mattered. He could outfly them, but he couldn't outrun them. He tried a portside turn, but now they had him boxed, the second Commander closing on his port wing as though it wouldn't mind sheering it off. His only consolation was the fact he had lost the ponderous low-wing Beechcraft, which was probably a good three or four miles back now, trying to figure it all out. If they had sent up three Beeches, he could have screwed them into the ground, he thought fatuously. If they had sent up a flock of geese, he could have made Christmas dinner.

With a reckless desperation he recognized unconsciously as the prelude to surrender, he dropped down to five hundred feet, the swampland under him speeding by inhospitably. If he could find a dry spot big enough to touch down, he thought he would be willing to take his chances in the swamp. But he either couldn't find one or was too frightened to try.

Rejecting fields as fast as they flew by, he ran out of chances to escape when he ran out of swamp. The Commander on his left pulled up so tight he could see the stubble on the copilot's chin. The man held up a foot-square placard with a large U.S. Customs shield emblazoned on it; stenciled below the emblem were the numerals 122.9, the air-to-air radio frequency they wanted him to call them on.

They instructed him to proceed to Sebring, park the airplane on the runway, and get out with his hands above his head. Leaving the Beechcraft in the air in case he tried a touch-and-go at Sebring, the two Commanders followed him down, taking him into custody without a struggle.

Three and a half hours later Roger Sorenson was in the DEA office in West Palm Beach, Florida, drafting a five-page handwritten confession in which he stated that Larry Spivey had approached him "to pick up a small load of marijuana and fly it back to the States." The confession, which went on to picture Larry as the architect of the drug-smuggling plot, also implicated Floyd Farnum, Ron Agee, and Dean Nations. Sorenson's trip to Colombia was described in considerable detail:

I departed from Fort Lauderdale at 1815 on Jan. 29, 1976 and refueled at Gran Turk Island. I flew thru the night and arrived at dawn at the setup in Columbia. Numerous indians appeared out of the bushes followed by a contact named Franco who oversaw the loading of the plane from an old pickup truck. The truck was guarded by nine men with rifles. I refueled the airplane while the indians loaded the marijuana. I spread a bed spread over the sacks and started to start engines.

One of the guards brought over two black packages tied together with twine saying "this needs to go too." I was busy holding the plane from moving (the rear engine was started) and didn't stop to argue with the armed native. I did not know what was contained in the packages and had agreed to carry marijuana only, but due to the circumstances went ahead and took off.

At Sebring Airport two plane loads of agents landed behind my aircraft and I surrendered myself to them. An agent asked if only marijuana was on the plane and I pointed out the two black packages. The agent analysed the material and pronounced it to be cocaine.

The setup [in Colombia] was located by flying along the coast from the Riohaca beacon to a small town, notable by a large cemetery before the town, and then flying inland toward the desert 7 kilometers along a major dirt road. Note: the setup is the second runway from town.

Arraigned on two counts of smuggling, Roger Sorenson was held in a federal house of detention in West Palm Beach from January 30 to February 3, when Floyd Farnum wired a bail bondsman $1,500 to cover his $10,000 bond. During his stay in jail, Sorenson tried desperately to buy leniency by selling out his friends. His offer of information against Larry put the Florida DEA agents in a rather awkward position, for they were reluctant to make any deals in which all they got was an on-the-job evaluation of a GBI agent. On the other hand, they couldn't show their disinterest without giving away Larry's identity as an undercover agent.

They had no choice but to listen studiously, their pencils flying over their note pads, while Sorenson painted an increasingly garish picture of Larry Spivey's career as a major drug importer with connections in Virginia, Georgia, Florida, Mexico, and Guatemala.

The moment Sorenson was released from jail, he got the bail bondsman to drive him to the Palm Beach airport, where he called Floyd Farnum at home in Bassett Forks. Unwilling to hang around until the next flight to Roanoke later that afternoon, he booked himself onto a flight to Greensboro, North Carolina, after first getting Farnum's assurance he would meet him at the airport. At the time Sorenson's call came through, Larry was in Farnum's living room, having flown up from Atlanta the day before because Floyd wanted him there when Sorenson was debriefed. Larry made himself at home in the empty house while Farnum drove down to Greensboro in his XKE to pick up the pilot.

Four days of expecting a visit from drug agents any minute hadn't done Farnum's disposition any good. His silver Jag sped away from the Greensboro airport even before Sorenson had time to get his backside settled against the leather upholstery.

"Jesus, it's good to be here," Sorenson sighed, trying to make it sound as if his troubles were all behind him.

Farnum eyed him malevolently. "I want to hear every fucking word you told them and every fucking thing they told you. Mainly what you told them. Then I'll tell you whether you're lucky to be here."

Sorenson assured him he hadn't said a thing, but Farnum knew him better than that. By the time they reached the Virginia state line about forty-five minutes later Sorenson realized he had a credibility problem and chose a particularly idiotic way to solve it. "You gotta believe me, Floyd. They didn't get a thing out of me," he whined. "I had to give them a statement. Look, I'll show you."

Farnum pulled to the shoulder and grabbed the five photocopied pages Sorenson had taken out of his jacket pocket. He saw his own name in the first paragraph, scanned down until he saw it again, and didn't read further.

"You fucking bastard," he screamed, flinging the pages back at Sorenson. "You gave me up, you son of a bitch. I'll kill you."

Sorenson looked hurt. "No, I didn't," he pleaded, pointing to the offending sentence with a shaky forefinger. "Look, all it says is 'Floyd Farnum and I were approached by Larry Spivey,' see? It doesn't really say you *did* anything."

"It says plenty."

"Not about you, not really, Floyd. All I told them was what I had to. Honest. I mean, it was your plane, they kept asking about you. I had to tell them something, to get them off the track. You didn't read the whole thing. Read it, you'll see."

"I don't have to read it."

"Read it, please. You'll see. I hardly said anything about you. It's mostly Larry. I told them Larry was in back of it."

"Great. If I don't kill you, he will."

"You won't tell him, will you, Floyd? Please, promise me you won't tell him. The thing is, I had a lot of time to think down there, all alone in the cell, right? And I think I figured it out. Someone must have told them where I was coming in. How else did they get there? It must have been Larry. It couldn't have been anyone else. The guy's a fucking stool pigeon, Floyd. He's got it coming."

Farnum said, "He'll definitely kill you."

He threw the car into gear and popped out the clutch, spewing gravel behind him as he raced the last twenty miles to his house. Neither he nor Sorenson spoke the rest of the way. When they pulled into the driveway, Floyd had to order Sorenson out of the car. He led the way into the house. Roger turned white when he saw Larry waiting in the living room. He excused himself to go to the bathroom.

"Larry, we've got problems. That guy's not right," Farnum whispered urgently. "He's making a lot of trouble."

"Talking?" Larry asked.

"A lot of talking."

"Jesus. Who'd he name? Me and you?"

"Mostly you. Me too."

"It figures," Larry said flatly, because it did figure. Sorenson and he hadn't liked each other since the day they met. "Look, don't let on that you told me. I want to find out exactly what that bastard said. Then we can take care of him."

"You're not going to kill him, are you?" Floyd asked.

Before Larry had a chance to answer, they heard the toilet flush. Both men turned to face the corridor Sorenson would be coming down. Half a minute passed, then more. The bathroom door didn't open. Then Larry heard footsteps outside on the driveway and bolted for the front door with Farnum following on his heels.

They got to the driveway seconds too late, just in time to see Farnum's sleek Jaguar careening backward away from them, spinning out onto the road, and then plunging from sight. Farnum let out a long volley of expletives that came to a sudden stop when he realized Larry was laughing.

"I think Roger just saved everyone a lot of grief," Larry explained, in answer to Farnum's quizzical look. "That was just about the last anyone's going to see of him. And without him to testify, there's no way they can use anything he told them."

Stuck without a car, Larry and Floyd went back into the house to wait until Tracy came home. When she got there a few hours later, they took her Pinto and drove the three hours to the UltraSkate rink in Charlotte, where Sorenson had converted part of the office into a small apartment. Floyd's Jaguar was parked in the lot, the keys considerately left on the desk in the office. The safe and the till had been emptied, and there was evidence of hasty packing in the apartment.

"He said he thought you were a stool pigeon," Farnum confided, standing over the pathetic assortment of abandoned belongings.

Larry smiled ruefully. "Good riddance," he said, marveling to himself that so far only Sorenson had figured it out.

Nineteen

Instead of hightailing it to South America, as Larry had expected him to do, Roger Sorenson caught a flight from Charlotte, North Carolina, to Palm Beach, Florida, where he showed up at the offices of the Drug Enforcement Administration in an obviously distraught condition. He was wild-eyed, ranting, making insane accusations. He said Larry had threatened to kill him. He demanded protection, demanded that Larry be arrested as a drug dealer and prosecuted.

The DEA agents had enough perspicacity to realize at once he was utterly uncontrollable. They instructed him to go into hiding at Farnum's farm outside Gainesville, which was operated by Sorenson's brother. They told him to lie low until a solution for his problems could be worked out. The agents then contacted Larry in Atlanta and brought him up to date on the situation.

Within a matter of days, two Central Intelligence Agency case officers reportedly showed up at the farm, identified themselves to Sorenson, and asked if he still felt he needed protection. When he said he did, they asked if he would consider relocating. Sorenson was then told to get in touch with a gentleman named Drew Furst at the Valley Tool and Die Company in Fort Lauderdale. Furst would be expecting to hear from him.

A few days later Furst apparently offered the desperate drug smuggler a job as a bush pilot flying small observation aircraft for the Rhodesian government at a salary of $4,000 a month. Sorenson accepted. Sometime before the end of February he was whisked out of the United States to begin his new career as soldier of fortune.

While Sorenson's disappearance was being orchestrated in Florida, events on other fronts were moving with the same breathtaking rapidity. On February 3, the very night Roger Sorenson stole Floyd Farnum's silver Jaguar and fled to the protection of the Palm Beach DEA, an undercover Dade County narcotics agent was shot to death in Miami while doing a marijuana buy. The incident had no apparent connection with Larry's GBI investigation, but a few days later, over coffee with Ron Agee at the Miami airport, Larry got another reminder that in the drug dealers' underworld everything connects. According to Agee, Geoff Logan, the young smuggler being held in Miami on the murder charge, was in fact an employee of Dean Nations. The marijuana he had been trying to sell to the Dade County agent he ended up killing had come off Sorenson's Skymaster. As Agee explained it, Logan had been sent to Grand Turk to refuel Sorenson on both the inbound and outbound legs of his flight. "You were probably wondering how come the newspaper stories all said Sorenson was busted with only six hundred pounds of grass?" Agee asked rhetorically. "Well, first off, my people in Colombia tell me he never loaded on the full thousand pounds. He was in such a god-awful hurry to get out of there, he just split before the full load was on. All he had with him was eight hundred pounds. Then when he got to Grand Turk, Logan gave him the signal to proceed to landing site A, the farm. While the plane was being refueled, Logan opened up the belly pod and took out the two hundred pounds stored there."

"What about the coke?" Larry asked. "Whose was it?"

"Nations."

"Did you know about it?"

"Nobody did. It was just a one-kilo sample. They had two hundred pounds of it sitting down there, waiting for a taker. Probably still do, for all I know. When I first heard there was coke on board, I figured Nations and Sorenson had worked out a separate side deal. But my man down there tells me Sorenson went white when they handed it on."

"That still leaves one question. Why did Logan take the two hundred pounds?"

"Two possibilities," Agee answered. "One, Nations was running a scam on his backers. He ordered Logan to do it, figured Logan could sell it himself and they'd split the profits. Or, two, the kid did it on his own, just a simple rip-off. Personally, I like the second one better."

"Why?"

"Just a hunch. Not that I'd put it past Nations to try a stunt like that. He's a sneaky little mother. Just look at the way he got Sorenson to fly a load of coke up for nothing. But not this time. The reason I think it's the kid is that Sorenson got popped. Now how did that happen? Someone must have tipped the narcs."

Larry held his breath. Sorenson had accused him of being the informant, and Agee was a lot smarter than Sorenson.

"So I say to myself, who's the stool, and I run down the list of candidates," Agee went on. "I know it wasn't me, and I know it wasn't Nations because no one rats out his own load. It sure as hell wasn't Sorenson because he took the fall. I figure it can't be you or Farnum because you knew where the load was coming in, and Customs apparently didn't, or they wouldn't have forced him down. So who does that leave? Geoff Logan. And it fits perfectly. He loads off two hundred pounds. Then he calls up the feds and tips them Sorenson's on the way loaded to the gunwales with marry-whana. While they get everything that flies chasing off after Sorenson, Logan's got a free ride in with two hundred pounds of grass that didn't cost him a nickel. It's a perfect rip-off because no one's ever going to know he did it. When Sorenson gets busted with a couple hundred pounds less than he's supposed to have, everyone figures the narcs are rolling joints with the difference. It would have worked, too, except something went sour in Miami and Logan ended up icing a cop. Too bad for Logan."

Yes, Larry thought, and too bad for the cop. The chain of circumstance linking his death to Larry's work was a long one, with many branches. But the connection was there, stretching from McClellan to Gordon to Farnum to Agee to Nations before it reached Geoff Logan's finger on the trigger of a gun that killed a young policeman whose name Larry never even learned. He died trying to stop the sale of narcotics lifted from a shipment Larry had helped arrange. There were nine dead in Mexico, their bodies ranked like a ghostly parade before Larry's eyes on some of the bad, sleepless nights; there was Customs Agent George Singleton, dead after a shoot-out with unarmed smugglers; and now there was a Miami cop taking his position at the end of the line. Too bad for all of them, Larry thought bitterly. And for all of us.

Early in February the Palm Beach office of the DEA began laying plans for a massive raid on the Ríohacha drug depot Sorenson's statement had pinpointed for them. At the same time, agents in Guatemala were continuing their efforts to build a case against former Chief of National Detectives Quintana, whose representatives had tried to sell Larry 250 pounds of pure cocaine.

Quintana had been kept under surveillance ever since Larry's meeting with his brother-in-law Agustín had provided positive proof of the existence of the cocaine stash. A few abortive attempts were made to deal with Agustín, but the agents on the case weren't able to approach him with the right introductions, and nothing ever came of the venture. Even before the end of 1975, Rick Taveras and the other DEA personnel on the scene had settled into a grim routine of tailing Quintana everywhere while doing nothing else to further their investigation. Like primitive Indians awaiting the return of the Spaniards they regarded as gods, they apparently were content to cool their heels until the unspecified day when Larry would return to conclude the deal with Agustín. Undercover operatives were set up all around Quintana's home, including one agent who spent two months posing as a vegetable seller operating out of a pushcart at the corner of Quintana's street.

Through December and January the investigation stayed in limbo. Then, on February 4, 1976, a violent and savage act of God brought it to a sudden end.

At exactly 3:02 A.M., Wednesday, February 4, the earth began to rupture in the Sierra de las Minas northeast of Guatemala City. The shock, which measured 7.5 on the Richter scale, lasted for thirty seconds and could be felt all the way from Mexico to Costa Rica. Racing the length of the Motagua Fault, which follows the base of the range Larry had crossed with Jefferson Juárez on his first trip to Cobán, the quake next exploded under the village of San Pedro, just fifteen miles outside the capital. Within seconds, San Pedro had ceased to exist.

In Guatemala City itself, the first homes to go were the expensive residences perched on the hillsides of the suburban districts at the north end of the city. Tumbling like coal down a chute, they left no survivors. By 3:35 Guatemala City was in a state of chaos that brings out the worst and best in people. Even with all electrical power off—electricity in the city automatically disconnects in severe quakes—rescue efforts began while buildings were still falling all around.

Acting instinctively, too confused to assess their priorities, half a dozen DEA agents converged at once on Quintana's home, knowing that the drug-dealing chief would make his way at once to his multimillion-dollar horde. Exactly as they expected, Quintana emerged from the darkness of his house to the darkness of the street shortly before four o'clock. Accompanied by two armed bodyguards, he picked his way through the ruined and turbulent city toward the now-useless refrigeration units where the drugs were stored. With injured and homeless people thronging the streets, with looters scattering like roaches before him, the man who only a few months before had headed his nation's top law enforcement agency pushed on, as heedless of the desolation around him as he was of the narcotics agents following close behind.

It was almost five o'clock when Quintana and his two bodyguards entered a two-story cement factory in an industrial section of the capital. The walls showed hairline cracks in a few places but looked as if they would hold. Three DEA agents followed them inside and stopped, listening, their flashlights pointed at their feet. They heard voices from below, found a staircase, and started down.

The basement was littered with boxes in storage. Proceeding carefully, the agents fanned out to circle in toward the back wall, where the sounds had come from. The first agent to make his way to the back of the building found himself on the apron of a cleared area facing the steel door of a giant cold-storage locker. Quintana and the two bodyguards were directly ahead of him, no more than fifteen feet away, their backs to him as they studied the dials on the refrigerator.

He waited until he was sure his partners were in position, then barked the order to freeze. One of the bodyguards wheeled toward him, reaching for the pistol on his hip. The guns of all three agents blazed instantly, leaving Quintana and both his men dead on the basement floor.

Two days later, on February 6, a third quake rocked Guatemala, followed by three more on the eighth, ninth, and tenth. When the toll was finally assessed, more than a million people were homeless, seventy-seven thousand had been injured, and twenty-three thousand were dead. In that context, the three who died defending $75 million worth of drugs counted for less than nothing.

On February 26, 1976, a 125-man commando team consisting of DEA agents and Colombian troops raided a marijuana dump in Dibulla, Colombia, a few miles from Ríohacha. Following the directions provided by Roger Sorenson, the raiders closed in from all sides, positioning themselves around the two prefabricated metal buildings that made up the depot before announcing their presence. Because of the size of the raiding party, resistance was minimal. A few shots were exchanged, but there were no injuries. Within a matter of minutes all the occupants of the two large sheds had surrendered. Thirteen Colombians and one American, a thirty-two-year-old Miamian, were taken into custody.

DEA agents immediately moved in to inspect the sheds. They were literally staggered by the mountain of marijuana spread out before their eyes. There were numberless bales of tightly pressed marijuana, each about fifty pounds; there were sacks of uncompacted dried plants piled almost to the ceilings. Along the walls of one of the sheds stood a bank of Sears trash mashers, which the drug dealers had been using to compress the marijuana into bales.

When the agents finally finished the laborious task of weighing and cataloging their take, they were practically numb from fatigue and excitement. If they hadn't seen the stash with their own eyes, the numbers would have been scarcely credible. The confiscated marijuana weighed out at exactly 163,800 pounds, a shade under 82 tons. Conservative estimates put the street value of the haul somewhere over $91 million, making it far and away the largest marijuana seizure in history, in size and value more than twice the haul from any previous raid.

Larry Spivey, whose undercover work had produced the information that made the raid possible, learned of the seizure the same way thousands of other Americans did—through the newspapers.

Twenty

"I t's not a chess game," Larry sighed. "That's kind of what I thought this job was going to be. Matching wits with the bad guys. I wish it was, but it's not. It took me a long time to figure it out, and what it looks like now is a great big slot machine. You pull the handle and see what comes up. Sometimes it's a whole row of horseshoes, sometimes zip. And each time you yank on that handle, you're starting from scratch."

He slid his glass away from him and waited for George Clardy to say something. It was still early February, two days after Roger Sorenson had fled to the protective custody of the DEA in Florida, the day after Quintana had died while Guatemala City was tumbling around him. Neither Larry nor Clardy had any idea what use the federal drug agents would be making of Sorenson's tip about a marijuana depot in Colombia. The situation at the moment looked bleak.

"I know," Clardy commiserated. "We got no case against Shawkey; we got shit against Agee; we can't touch Nations unless Sorenson testifies. Looks like we got ourselves one cherry and a bunch of lemons. I reckon it's time to put in another silver dollar and go for the jackpot."

The jackpot this time was going to be Agee and Shawkey. Shaking off his doubts about whether any of what he was doing made sense, Larry agreed to give Agee a few more days to cool off and then get in touch with him to set the wheels turning again on the ten-ton DC-4 deal that had been put on a back burner when Sorenson was arrested. If at all possible, he would try to swing it so that Shawkey would be dealt back in. He let Clardy pay for the drinks and went home.

Jerri greeted him with two messages. The first was from Charlene, who had been to the Daytona races and was out of money again. She was threatening to send the sheriff after Larry with a contempt-of-court citation unless he came up with $5,000 to pay the judgment she had against him.

"Please tell that woman if she's got some kind of problem with you, I don't want to hear about it," Jerri pleaded. "She had me on the phone forty-five minutes."

"Better you than me," Larry joked grimly, but Jerri didn't think it was funny.

The second call was from a man who left an area code 305 number where he could be reached. Larry figured the call was from Agee. The fact that the first digit after the exchange in the number he left was a 9, indicating a pay phone, suggested he had something important to talk about.

"We got something hot down here, Larry," Agee said genially. "You interested?"

"Does the sun come up in the morning?"

"How soon can you get here?"

"First flight tomorrow."

"Not good enough. I'm at the airport now. I've already made you a reservation on the next flight down, leaves Atlanta in about forty-five minutes."

"I'll be on it," Larry promised. "What airport are you at? Fort Lauderdale?"

"Miami."

Larry just had time to call Clardy and report that he was back in business. He made it to the airport two minutes before boarding time and was in Miami by half past seven. Agee met him at the gate and led him to a restaurant on the airport's main concourse. When they were seated, he pointed out a couple a few tables away.

"Those are the people we're going to be dealing with," he said. "I just wanted to talk to you privately first." He ordered two cups of coffee and two muffins from the waitress, then turned back to Larry. "Hope you like muffins. Look, what kind of a problem is Sorenson going to be?"

Larry had been expecting the question. "No kind of problem. He's a stand-up guy," he lied glibly.

Agee shrugged. "You sure? He struck me as a turkey."

"He is. But he's more scared of Farnum than he is of the fuzz. If he makes trouble for Floyd, Floyd tells Shawkey, and Shawkey sends his people out to make sure Sorenson gets his whole body air-conditioned in plenty of time for summer. Did you get a look at that animal Shawkey travels with?"

"No, but I heard," Agee said, smiling now at the recollection. His attitude toward torpedoes like Donnie Swanson was the same as what honest citizens feel about the cops: You wouldn't want them camped on your porch, but it was comforting to know you could find one when you needed him.

"As long as you think he's cool, that's all I need to know," Agee said. He left two dollars on the table and led the way to the couple seated a few yards away. The man was in his fifties, overweight and prosperous-looking. Agee introduced him as George Strayer. The woman was in her early thirties, well tailored and well tanned, with light brown hair she wore short and wavy, very suburban. She had a discreetly attractive figure and a pretty, slightly Irish-looking face. Agee introduced her as Phyllis Laine. "Let me give you the picture," Agee said.

The picture was that Phyllis Laine was the mistress of a man named Stan Eccles, who was at that very moment cruising off the coast of Jamaica in a rented forty-one-foot power sailboat. He and two friends, one of them a former *Penthouse* Pet of the Month named Christine Snow, had put a down payment on a thousand pounds of Jamaican marijuana. The marijuana had been delivered to a remote beach, where it was awaiting pickup. Unfortunately Eccles and his colleagues had come up $9,000 short, and they needed a backer who could bring them the money fast enough to allow them to complete the deal.

Larry looked skeptical. "I don't mean to cast any aspersions on your old man, ma'am," he said, with a nod to Phyllis, "but I've got to know. Why do I want to get mixed up with a man who orders a thousand pounds of grass he can't pay for?"

She had a deep, throaty voice that dripped sincerity. "Of course, I understand," she said. "I assure you, Stan knows what he is doing. They rented the boat they're using in Florida, and it developed engine trouble off Haiti. Parts had to be flown in, and that tied them up three weeks. They couldn't very well turn to the owners without raising a lot of questions about why they were in Haiti when they were supposed to be sailing around the Bahamas, now, could they? Between the boat, which is costing us eight hundred dollars a week, and lodgings, and the cost of the repairs, we're broke."

Larry liked the way she talked. He turned to Agee and asked him what he wanted him to do.

"That's up to you," Agee said. "This Jamaican *primo* can be wholesaled at three hundred a pound. Stan's willing to give anybody who backs him half the load, five hundred pounds. If you have any friends who'd like to turn a quick buck, they can make an easy hundred and a half for a nine-thousand-dollar investment—figure ten thousand if you throw in some expenses. I assume you know some people like that?"

Larry suggested Shawkey, and Agee countered by suggesting Farnum. Neither was exactly what Larry had had in mind when he flew down from Atlanta, for there was a big difference between a thousand pounds and the ten-ton DC-4 deal he had been hoping Agee wanted to talk to him about. He masked his disappointment and tried to swing the discussion in the direction he wanted it to go. "I don't think Farnum's interested," he said. "It was his plane Sorenson got busted in, so he's expecting a knock on his door any minute. He's got his head pulled in like a turtle. But Shawkey's going crazy looking for some action after the way Farnum cut him out of the last one. He'll do it in a minute. He can take the money he makes on this one and plow it back into the DC-Four deal."

Agee liked the idea. "Call him," he said. "It's about time we got moving in some direction."

"He's going to want to talk to you," Larry countered, knowing that if it were he who proposed the deal to Shawkey, it would constitute entrapment. He fished a dime from his pocket and excused himself to use the pay phone, taking Agee with him. When he got Shawkey on the line, he gave only the sketchiest outline of the plan.

"Is the fly-boy vouching for this clown in Jamaica?" the grizzled gangster growled.

"Which fly-boy?"

"Well, not the one in the can, Spivey. Use your head. A. C., or whatever his name is."

"Agee."

"Awright, A. G. What the fuck is that guy's right name anyway? I don't like dealing with guys that won't come up front with their right names."

"That is his name. Here, talk to him yourself."

He put Agee on the line, and Shawkey barked a few surly questions. "Okay, mister, you've got yourself a partner," he conceded suddenly. "I'll have Cotton on the next plane down. How much is this going to cost me?"

"Nine thousand for the merchandise, a thousand for expenses."

"He'll have eleven with him, that ought to cover it," Shawkey said tersely. "Just tell Spivey he's got to go down to Jamaica with him. I want both of them to look it over and come back with my money if everything doesn't have a nice clean feel."

"Well?" Larry asked as Agee stepped out of the booth. "Is he in?"

"He's in, and so are you. He says you've got to go down there with Andrews. That's okay, isn't it?"

It made it more complicated, but Larry was sure he could handle it. He would have to get word to Jamaica that he was coming, because he refused to take the chance of getting arrested in a foreign country with no proof of who he was. And he would have to find a way to keep GBI and Customs posted about the smugglers' plans, or there would be no one to meet Stan Eccles's boat when it came in. Larry said he had to make a few phone calls to Atlanta to straighten out his affairs, and Agee discreetly withdrew to check out the flight board in the main concourse to see when the next flight from Roanoke was scheduled.

As soon as Agee was out of sight, Larry called the reaction center at GBI and had his call patched through to George Clardy. He quickly outlined the evening's developments, expecting to get swift congratulations on having sprung a new trap for Shawkey. Clardy was anything but ecstatic.

"Slow it down a little, Spivey. You're moving too fast," he said, trying to put it as gently as possible. "You've got to look all the way down to the end of the road. What kind of a case is this going to give you against Shawkey? Or Agee for that matter?"

"Smuggling. A thousand pounds," Larry said doubtfully, knowing Clardy had spotted a catch.

"No way. Eccles, yeah. And anybody else on the Jamaica end. Maybe Andrews, too, since he's going with you. But all we'd have on Agee is your testimony about some conversations. No tapes, no nothing. It's conspiracy at best, and we'd have to burn you to get it."

"But we'd get Shawkey. It's his money."

"Who says? You? He didn't tell you that, he told Agee. And I doubt he's paying by check."

"Then what do I do?"

"You get out of it, best way you can."

"Too late. I said I'd go. Besides, I have to stay in tight with them to set up the DC-Four thing."

"Suit yourself. But cover your ass. Remember, the last deal you were in was popped. This is going to make it two in a row. With a track record like that, Agee and Shawkey are going to treat you like you've got a social disease, and then we're absolutely back to zero. Do not pass Go, do not collect two hundred dollars."

Through the glass door of the booth Larry saw Agee coming down the corridor. He told Clardy to call Jerri and tell her he'd be home in a few days.

"Get it straightened out?" Agee asked.

"Almost. My girl's going to make some of the arrangements. I've got another call to make."

"Sure, sure," Agee said agreeably, starting to move off toward the restaurant. "Andrews's plane comes in at nine. There won't be another flight to Jamaica until the morning. We'll have to stay here tonight. I'll go tell Phyllis."

Larry dialed the overseas operator and asked to be put through to the Jamaican Ministry of Justice. He got a clerk on the night desk, identified himself as an American narcotics agent, and explained that a large marijuana deal was scheduled to take place in Jamaica soon, possibly as early as the next morning. Unlike many other Caribbean countries, Jamaica takes narcotics violations seriously. After repeating his message to two more functionaries, he was put through to the chief justice of Cornwall Province. The magistrate listened without interrupting while Larry told him everything he knew about the plans.

"Mr. Spivey, how can I satisfy myself that you are who you say you are?" he asked.

"Call Inspector Peters at the Georgia Bureau of Investigation."

"I shall do that. Now, assuming that your information is correct, what do you wish of us?"

"We want your people to seize the narcotics before they leave your country. Make whatever arrests are necessary. It is essential that the load not get through. If it makes it here, we will have to seize it, and that would interfere with a major investigation."

"I see," the chief justice said, and from the tone of his voice it sounded as if he did. He gave Larry two phone numbers where he could be reached at any time and wished him luck.

Returning to the restaurant, Larry slid into the booth next to Phyllis Laine and announced that he was in. They ordered a round of drinks to toast their venture, then another to kill some of the time until Cotton Andrews arrived with the money. George Strayer, the third man at the table, turned out to be an interesting character who claimed to be making money hand over fist with what he described as a rather elaborate scheme involving computer-programmed prostitution. For curiosity, if for no other reason, Larry would have liked to have learned more about him, but nine o'clock got there in a hurry. Together, they trooped off to the debarkation gate to meet Andrews.

The boyish-looking drug expert had brought his equally boyish-looking girl friend Fred. In the car, Strayer announced that he knew an "interesting" X-rated motel halfway between Miami and Fort Lauderdale. It featured water beds, hard-core porn on television, mirrors everywhere, and closed-circuit cameras set up so that one room could monitor another. Only Andrews and Fred were interested, so Strayer dropped them there, let Agee and Phyllis Laine off at a Fort Lauderdale parking lot where Agee had left his car, and offered to put Larry up for the night.

In the next few hours Larry managed to find out a little bit more about Strayer's business, which was both more legitimate and more fascinating than he had at first implied. Essentially, it was a computerized credit barter system which made it possible for businessmen to trade their products or services for the products and services of others without money changing hands. Strayer's company levied a small percentage for each transaction, which his clients were more than willing to pay because of the tremendous tax advantages of doing business through him. On a whim, a call girl friend of Strayer's had asked to be included and had done so well by it she signed up twenty-five of her colleagues. But the bulk of Strayer's business concerned more mundane occupations.

Larry wondered why a man who was making so much honest money would want to get mixed up with smugglers. The answer had something to do with the streak of restless dissatisfaction he sensed in so many of the brightest men of his generation, a restlessness that was spreading like an infection to an older generation that only a few years ago would have found plenty of reason for smugness in the mere fact of an annual six-figure income. Now even fat and wealthy men like George Strayer wanted adventure.

In the morning, Larry and Strayer picked up Phyllis Laine at her home and Cotton Andrews and Fred at their motel. At the airport Larry, Andrews, and Fred split up Horace Shawkey's $11,000 so that none of them would be in violation of the U.S. federal law prohibiting any individual from taking more than $5,000 in cash out of the country. Their Eastern Airlines flight landed at Montego Bay's single-runway airport shortly before noon. After clearing customs and sampling the planter's punch distributed free by a local rum manufacturer, Phyllis bought everyone lunch at the cafeteria on the second floor of the terminal building. Andrews went off to make arrangements for an afternoon flight to Port Antonio, where Phyllis said they were most likely to catch up with Eccles. He managed to book seats on a single-engine flight that took off whenever the charter airline got enough people to fill its six-seater airplanes. A tall black-skinned young man with an almost impenetrable reggae accent was the only other passenger.

They took off around two o'clock, flying along the coast for about twenty minutes to Ocho Rios, where the West Indian got off. Another twenty-minute hop over glittering water got them to Port Antonio, where a Volkswagen minibus, one-third of the town's entire taxi fleet, drove them to the Bonnie View Hotel, perched high on the wooded hill that rose sharply from the shore. On the way to the hotel, Phyllis spotted an aluminum mast on a ship tied up out of sight on the other side of a pier. "I guess Stan's in town," she said.

While Phyllis and the Virginia couple went to their rooms to deposit their luggage, Larry surveyed the scene from the hotel veranda. Below him, the village lay torpid in the sun, its one-street shopping district as depopulated as the tile and tin-roofed residential areas that stretched around it toward the harbor.

The taxi had been asked to wait. Larry suggested they would attract less attention if Cotton and Fred stayed at the hotel while he and Phyllis went off in search of Stan Eccles.

The taxi threaded its way down the cobblestoned hillside and came out suddenly at the foot of the blunt peninsula that formed one side of Port Antonio Harbor. At the yacht basin, Phyllis asked after the crew of the aluminum-masted sailboat and learned that the ship had been tied up there two or three days. Someone suggested they look for the Americans in town. Saying she wanted to walk, Phyllis dismissed the cab. Automatically Larry filed away the information that she didn't seem in much of a hurry to find her lover.

It was a warm afternoon, with the sunlight thick as syrup in the air. The pleasant warmth of a gentle, nuzzling offshore breeze filled Larry with a sense of well-being that acted on him almost like a narcotic, although he couldn't afford to do more with it than make a mental note to come back here someday when he wasn't working. "I thought you said Eccles was cruising offshore," he said.

Phyllis tossed her head, dismissing the faint note of accusation in his voice. "I imagine they needed supplies," she said coldly. In certain moods she was a particularly attractive woman.

"Could be, but there'd be less people noticing them out on the ocean," Larry answered matter-of-factly.

They had walked no more than five minutes, past picturesquely splintered wood houses and into the sprawling lane of shops and restaurants that constituted downtown Port Antonio, when they were almost run down by a maroon Renault careening around a corner, its horn blaring.

The driver braked quickly, leaped from the car, ran up to Phyllis, and threw his arms around her. It was Stan Eccles. He was in his mid-forties at best and would have looked considerably older if it weren't for his deeply tanned skin and the adolescent shagginess of his slightly graying hair. Apparently he had gone native, for he was wearing a bright, tight-fitting striped T-shirt, a strand of amber beads around his neck, tattered jeans, and sandals. It wasn't the kind of footwear a man would wear on a boat, and Larry wondered how long he had been ashore. He also wondered whether any of the other things Phyllis had told him about the deal were true.

While Eccles and his mistress remained locked in an embarrassingly long embrace, two people climbed from the front seat of the Renault. The first, whom Larry hardly noticed, was a man in his late fifties dressed in sneakers, jeans, and T-shirt. The second was an absolutely gorgeous blonde wearing almost nothing at all. Her tawny orange shorts were little more than a flash of flame licking at her honey-colored skin, and her breasts seemed to be struggling to get out of the tiny halter top that held them. She smiled at Larry, her pale lips parting to show perfect teeth, and offered her hand, needlessly introducing herself as Christine Snow. She introduced her companion as Bill Jones.

Eccles broke away from Phyllis long enough to greet Larry. "Are you the guy who brought the money?" he asked.

"I brought the man who brought the money."

"Good enough," Eccles laughed with the mechanical good humor of a salesman. He turned back to Phyllis, but she had walked off and was already seated in the passenger seat of the Renault. Eccles shrugged and climbed back in behind the wheel, while Larry, Christine, and Bill Jones slid into the back seat, Christine in the middle, where both men could enjoy the feel of her next to them.

They drove to the hotel, where they split up long enough for everyone to shower and dress before they met on the veranda for drinks. Larry was the first one down, joined after a few minutes by Christine. She had changed to a pale sundress in which she looked every bit as stunning as when Larry had first seen her. They ordered drinks and watched the sun go down in flames over the ocean, the thick tropical night closing in on it like the sea swallowing a ship. The mere fact of their having watched it together seemed to give them something in common, like the bond formed between two strangers who happened to have been next to each other when they heard that the war was over or that the president had died.

The intimacy of the moment was shattered by the arrival of Jones, who showed up with a drink in his hand. "I hope I'm not intruding," he said, laughing exactly the way Eccles had laughed on the street in Port Antonio. He sat down, noticed a star, and launched into a monologue on astrology that both Larry and Christine declined to interrupt.

Eccles and Phyllis showed up to rescue them after what seemed a long time. Larry remembered that no one had bothered to tell Andrews to join them. He pointed out the oversight and excused himself to go fetch the man with the money that was making all this possible.

A half hour later Cotton and Fred joined the party on the veranda, and they all moved inside for dinner. Not one for beating around the bush, Cotton asked immediately, "How far away is the beach where the stuff is stored? I'd like to check it out."

Eccles cleared his throat and said, "Well, it's not exactly on the beach."

"I was told it was," Cotton said, trying to sound tough and not doing a bad job of it.

"That's right, the last time I talked to Phyllis it was on the beach. The beach is just about ten miles west of here, a perfectly secure place, believe me. I tried to tell them that, but there's no talking to these people. Natives, you know."

"No, I don't know," Andrews sneered. "I know I came out here to check out some grass. Now is there some grass or isn't there?"

Cotton was at least a dozen years younger than Eccles and looked even younger, but Eccles didn't seem capable of preventing himself from being bullied. "Yes, yes, of course there is," he stammered. "They took it back into the mountains, that's all. For security. It's an inconvenience, but it doesn't change anything."

Apparently Cotton had played the tough guy long enough to satisfy himself he had done what Shawkey sent him to do. "Okay," he said, suddenly agreeable. "How long will it take them to get it back down to the beach?"

Before Eccles could answer, Larry stood up and said, "Cotton, I want to talk to you."

Andrews looked surprised, but he followed Larry into a corner of the lobby beyond the reception desk, where they could talk privately.

"What the hell's the matter with you, Cotton?" Larry asked sharply. "The way you were talking, I thought you were going to tell the guy to go to hell."

The young drug dealer smiled sheepishly. "Oh, that," he said. "That was just to let him know he can't mess around with us."

"No, Cotton, you don't seem to understand. That part was okay. These people don't have their act together. They're supposed to be on their boat, where nobody will notice them, and instead, they're tooling around this little hamlet like it's the Grand Prix of Monaco. There can't be anybody down here who's not wondering who the hell they are. If you had looked around like you were supposed to, instead of spending the whole afternoon balling what's-her-name, you would have known that. The grass isn't even where it's supposed to be."

Cotton didn't seem worried. "So what?" he said. "Who said it had to be on the beach?"

Larry's exasperation was real, even though it didn't matter one way or the other what Andrews decided to do. All Larry wanted to do was get it on the record that he didn't like the setup. He had to divert suspicion from himself when Eccles and his friends were arrested. "Listen, Cotton," he said, speaking slowly. "These people are fixin' to get popped, no two ways about it. They'll get all of us popped. And the government down here doesn't fool around. They'll put us away for so long it'll be six years till they let us see the exercise yard. You do what you want, but I'm getting out of here in the morning. If you're smart, that's what you'll do, too. Horace will fucking kill you if you throw out his money on a load that's not going to make it."

The change that came over Andrews was sudden and dramatic. As Larry looked into the young man's eyes, he saw an unmistakable glint of fear there. "I've got to do it, Larry," Andrews said, pleading. "I'm broke, bad broke. There's people I owe money to looking for me. Horace said anything over three-hundred-a-pound on this deal is mine. Don't worry, it'll go through. I know it will."

This time Larry did walk away—a move he would later regret.

Andrews returned to the table a few minutes after Larry did. "I think I had just asked you how long it would take to get the grass ready for loading," he said awkwardly, as though there had been no interruption in the conversation.

Apparently, while Cotton and Larry were out of the room, a decision had been reached to let Christine Snow do the talking. "It can be delivered tomorrow," she said. "They demand half payment in advance. Forty-five hundred dollars must be taken to them tonight."

"Taken where?" Larry asked.

"In the mountains," Christine said, her voice like a rock. "There are guerrillas there. You have to know where you're going. I do. I've made the trip a dozen times."

There was no further discussion of the deal. After dinner Andrews went to his room for the money and returned with a white envelope, which he handed to Christine. She set it on the tablecloth in front of her without comment. Andrews hovered over her shoulder for a few seconds, then left with Fred. A few minutes later they were followed by Eccles and Phyllis, who made a point of taking Jones with them.

"Maybe I should go with you," Larry said when they were alone. "Your luck can't hold out forever with these guerrillas."

Christine's long fingers played with the corners of the envelope. "I can take care of myself," she said.

Larry studied her without answering. "How long have you known Stan Eccles?" he asked at last.

"I thought you were going to ask how long I've known Mr. Jones. You're more tactful than I would have expected."

It was clear she was trying to keep him at arm's length, but he didn't know why. "You didn't answer my question," he said.

"It's none of your business."

"I don't think he knows what he's doing, Christine. I think there's going to be trouble, and I'm not staying around for it. I'm leaving in the morning."

Christine looked at him hard, examining his face as though she knew he wasn't guessing and were trying to figure out why he was warning her.

"I'm leaving in the morning, too. My boyfriend is being tried for murder in Florida. I have to be there to testify." Her voice was flat, the way another woman might have said she had to be back for a friend's wedding.

She didn't seem to want to talk about it, so Larry suggested they move out to the veranda for a drink.

There was a flattering note of regret in her voice. "No," she said, "I really can't. It will take me all night to get up into the mountains and back. I said I'd go by myself, and I will."

Larry said nothing, made no move to stop her as she walked out of the dining room. He was still at the table ten minutes later, when he saw her again, looking incredibly hard and at the same time incredibly feminine in Levi's and an army campaign shirt. She crossed the lobby without looking into the restaurant and went outside, where she got into Stan Eccles's Renault and drove off. When the sound of the engine had faded into the still tropical night, Larry went out to the veranda himself and ordered the drink he would have had with her.

The next thing he knew, Christine was standing over him with a cup of coffee in her hand. "I told you I'd be all right," she said.

Barely awake, he had only a vague recollection that she was supposed to go somewhere, but he couldn't quite get it straight. Then the fog lifted slightly, and he realized it was morning and she was back already. He sat up enough to take the cup from her hand and sip on the searing brew, then handed the cup back to her and closed his eyes. He heard the faint click of the cup being set on a table and the soft hissing sound of fabrics on flesh, and then he felt her body beside him in the bed.

"Did you tell them why you're leaving?" Christine asked, taking her eye off the road to glance across at Larry. She was pushing the Renault over the mountains as though the devil himself were chasing it.

"I told Cotton last night," Larry said, watching the road more intently than she did. "He didn't want to listen to me; it's his headache. I couldn't see any percentage in telling Eccles. If he hasn't figured out what an ass he is by now, he never will."

Eccles had given them the car to return to the rental agent in Kingston, and he wouldn't have done that if he had had any feeling that Larry was running out on him. He probably hadn't expected Larry to stay for the loading anyway since Cotton could handle that job perfectly well himself.

Shortly before noon they reached the Kingston airport, where they learned they had a few hours to kill before the next flight. They made reservations, ate a quick lunch, and decided to do some sight-seeing, driving down the peninsula to the old church at Port Royal. Built by Morgan the pirate three centuries ago, at what had once been the tip of the peninsula, the tiny wood and stone church seemed to beckon them with a promise of coolness, silence, and rest.

Larry went to study the tombstones in the neatly kept cemetery beside the church while Christine tied her scarf over her head and went inside to pray. The tombstones, many of them indecipherable, recorded the deaths of pirates, of seamen, of women in childbirth. While he was still contemplating them, Christine came running out of the church, her eyes wet but her face radiantly happy, the scarf still knotted under her chin like a babushka.

"Larry, Larry," she called excitedly. "They've got a guest register inside. It must be a thousand years old. Come and sign it with me!"

Feeling a little like a reluctant father being dragged off to see something his small child has built, Larry followed her inside. They leafed through the book, laughing as they tried to conjure up the people responsible for the vast collection of signatures tumbling all over the crowded pages. Larry took the pen and signed, then Christine signed below him, writing a name Larry couldn't read that was much longer than Snow. She drew a bracket joining their names and in large, careful script wrote the word *Smugglers* next to it. They both agreed it was a gesture the long-dead buccaneer who had built the church would have enjoyed.

The first thing Larry did when he got home was call Horace Shawkey. "I told your man to get his ass and your bread out of there," he said. "But it looked good to him. There was no talking to the guy. Don't hold your breath, Horace. If those turkeys make it out of Jamaica, it'll be a miracle."

Having absolved himself of responsibility for the inevitable loss of Shawkey's payload, he hung up the phone, which immediately rang.

"Larry, it's Christine. I need your help."

"What's the matter?"

"How soon can you get here? I'm in Fort Lauderdale," she said, without answering his question.

He left without explaining to Jerri because he didn't have an explanation. It was possible it was just a trick to get him back, but he doubted it. Christine sounded deeply upset.

When she met him at the airport, she had a newspaper in her hand. "Confessed Drug Addict Tells of Slaying," the headline read. Christine asked him to read the accompanying article, which dealt with the performance of a twenty-five-year-old witness named Lucille Brody at a Fort Lauderdale murder trial:

The trial of Carl M. Parent opened today in Broward Circuit Court with the defense attorney trying to discredit the key witness, a confessed heroin addict who said she saw Parent shoot her boyfriend,

Steven O'Neill, at 5 A.M., Oct. 1, 1975. Miss Brody originally told police she was in another room of the house when the shooting took place. But today she said she had lied because she was afraid of Parent. Miss Brody testified she heard a blast and "hit the deck." She heard O'Neill say, "Oh, my God," and saw him clutch his chest. She said Parent then pointed the gun at her, but Christine Snow, with whom the defendant was living at the time, stopped Parent from killing her. She then testified Parent took a pistol from a wicker table in the room, fired a shot into the ceiling, and dropped the weapon near O'Neill's body. On cross-examination, Miss Brody was questioned at length about her history of using illegal drugs, which began with marijuana at age seventeen.

"Parent is the boyfriend you were telling me about?" Larry asked, handing the newspaper back to her.

She nodded dumbly, her face twisted by a confused mixture of fear and anger she couldn't seem to sort out. She clearly didn't want to talk there, so Larry followed her to the car, letting her take her own time to explain. She drove out of the attended parking lot without saying anything, then pulled into the metered parking area only a few hundred feet down the airport boulevard and turned off the engine. She turned in her seat to face Larry and said, "I'm scared, Larry. I don't know what to do. Where should I start?"

"At the beginning," he suggested unhelpfully.

She said she was in love with Carl Parent. He was thirty-two years old, a dealer in heroin and cocaine. He had made plans to do a two-pound cocaine deal with O'Neill. "Actually," she explained, "Carl didn't have the coke. A lot of things had happened, and he was desperately broke. He was planning to rip Steve off. If it didn't turn out so horribly, it would be funny because Steve didn't have the money. He was planning to rip off Carl for the coke. That is funny, isn't it?"

"Not very. What happened?"

"Steve showed up around five o'clock in the morning. That was when the deal was supposed to go down. We had two dogs, Weimaraners, and they always barked when anyone came to the door. So they started barking when Steve knocked on the back door. I grabbed them and was taking them down the hall to the bedroom, like I always did when anyone came over. Carl went to open the door. I noticed he had his shotgun with him, but that didn't surprise me because he always had it when he was doing a deal.

"Steve had his girl with him. That's Lucille, the girl in the newspaper. They were both higher than kites. They had been shooting heroin and snorting coke all night. I heard them come in, and I heard Carl say, 'Do you have the bread?' Steve said he did, and the next thing I heard was an explosion."

"A shot?"

"A shot, yes. But it sounded more like an explosion. I shoved the dogs into the bedroom and ran back to the kitchen. Steve was lying on the floor; there was blood all around. Lucille was leaning over him, and Carl was right on top of her with his shotgun at her head. He was yelling at her, and I think he wanted to kill her, too. I ran up and pulled him off her. She was hysterical, mostly about Steve. I don't think she even realized Carl wanted to kill her. It took a couple of minutes to calm both of them down a little.

"Then Carl got a gun, just like Lucille said. It actually was Steve's gun, he had loaned it to Carl. So Carl fired a shot and put the gun on the floor next to Steve. He told Lucille he was going to call the police, and when they came, she was going to tell them Steve drew first.

"But we both could see it wasn't going to work. She was so coked up, so completely out of it she'd never be able to tell it straight. The police would crack her in a minute. Then I had a better idea. Lucille and I would both say we were in the bedroom. It would just be Carl's word, and since Steve's gun was there and it had been fired, the police wouldn't have any choice but to believe him. And that's what we did. Carl called his lawyer, and his lawyer called the police. Lucille gave a statement that she was in the bedroom with me. They could tell she was stoned, and she wasn't very coherent, but at least she said she was sure where she was. And I said the same thing. I said I heard two shots, one right after the other. First a pistol shot, then a shotgun. There was nothing the cops could do. They took a statement from Carl and they went away."

"And now you're sticking to your story, but Lucille isn't?" Larry asked.

"I never thought she would be so strong. I figured it would be my word against hers, and Carl's lawyer would tear her apart. But it doesn't sound like he did. Larry, I'm scared."

Larry was in a bind. A heavy dealer such as he was supposed to be would never advise her to testify for the prosecution. Yet if he failed to talk her out of testifying for Parent, he would have to notify the court in Florida. He would have to take the stand and testify that Parent's star witness had confessed to him she intended to perjure herself. And he would have to testify against her in the perjury trial that would follow. "I don't know what to tell you, Christine. You're in deep shit. What you need is a lawyer," he suggested.

If she withdrew her false statement to the police, the defense would not call her. With a voluntary recantation, a good lawyer with good connections in the prosecutor's office probably could save her from being prosecuted for the false statements she had already made. And once Parent learned she wouldn't be testifying for him, he might have no choice but to plead guilty. It would all work out perfectly. No one would get hurt except the killer.

Larry asked Christine to drive him to a phone booth where he would call a friend who could recommend a lawyer. He called GBI. Mike Eason listened to what he had to say and told him, "Spivey, you don't need a lawyer, you need a psychiatrist. You're supposed to be home in the sack with your lady, and instead, you're off in another state with some *Penthouse* bunny that's going to commit perjury. Man, you're crazy."

"Pet," Larry corrected.

"How's that?"

"Pet. They don't call them bunnies. They call them pets. It's a different magazine."

"Spivey, a naked lady is a naked lady. Now tell me again what it is you want."

"The name of a lawyer down here I can send her to."

Eason said he would have to do some checking and would call him back. Larry waited by the car, talking to Christine through the open window. Twenty minutes later the phone rang, and Larry answered it. Eason had a couple of names for him, all of whom he said had excellent reputations. Larry picked the one who had been a prosecutor only a few years earlier and had won convictions in some Florida cases Eason had been involved in.

In the morning Larry and Christine drove to the offices of Carmichael and Gould in an unpretentious professional building in Hollywood. They sat in the waiting room without speaking until Charles Gould, the lawyer Eason had recommended, was free. It was Christine's idea that Larry should talk to him first.

Seated in a straight-backed chair opposite Gould's large mahogany desk, Larry played the role of the big-money drug dealer looking for legal aid for a friend. "This chick out there's got a problem," he said, "and some people gave me your name. She's mixed up in this murder case they're trying in town here, and she's in over her head. She and this other chick gave statements, right? Only the other one flipped."

"Miss Brody. Yes, I know about her testimony."

"You in this case or something? Maybe you're not the guy we should be talking to?"

"Only what I read in the papers and hear around the courthouse. It's a small town and a big case, Mr. Spivey."

"Right. So anyway, with Brody flipping, it leaves Christine where she's going to get it either way. If she keeps going the way she's going, she's gonna take it on the chin, and if she turns around, they're gonna stick it up her ass. Pardon the terminology, counselor, but you get the picture."

"I get the picture," Gould said. He pressed the button on his intercom and asked the receptionist to show in Miss Snow.

For two hours Larry fretted over business magazines in Gould's waiting room until Christine came out. She was as ebullient as a kid just let out of school. "He get you fixed up?" Larry asked.

"He sure did," she beamed with satisfaction. "I have to come back next Monday, that's all."

They walked together out of the office and around to the side of the building, where Christine had parked her brother's car.

"What do you have to come back for?" Larry asked, hardly able to credit what he suspected had happened.

"To go over my testimony. He said it would be no problem."

He stopped her before she got into the car and made her explain it to him right there in the parking lot.

Gould had listened to her story, hearing her all the way out without interruption. When she was finished, he had asked her what she wanted to do.

"Well," she had answered, "Larry says I'm in trouble. That's why he brought me here to see you."

"Never mind what Larry says," Gould had answered. "What do you want to do?"

"I want to help Carl."

Gould then told her she could. "What it comes down to is your word against the other girl's. If you do a good job, there's no way anyone can prove you're lying. There should be no risk to you. And from what I hear about the other girl's record, you should have no problem convincing the jury you're the one who's telling the truth. You don't have a record, do you?"

266

"Not in the States," Christine had said.

"Where?"

"Bahamas. I got a suspended sentence. It was a smuggling thing."

"It shouldn't be a problem. Ever used narcotics?"

"Grass, sure. And some coke."

"Heroin?"

"Never."

"Ever hospitalized for narcotics?"

"No."

"Ever arrested? Other than the Bahamas thing. I don't mean convicted, I mean just arrested. For trafficking or anything else?"

"No, never."

"Then you're home free."

That had been the first forty-five minutes of their conversation. For the next hour and a quarter, Gould carefully rehearsed her in her perjured testimony. The meeting scheduled for next Monday was to be the dress rehearsal for her performance before a live audience the next day. Gould wanted $500 for helping her, payable Monday.

Larry needed time to think, and he needed to be away from her so he would be free to take whatever steps were necessary. He had sent her to a lawyer in order to prevent her from committing perjury and a murderer from going free. But the lawyer Eason had sent him to turned out to be as crooked as any of the people Larry was investigating. Instead of preventing the perjury, he had suborned it, leaving Larry in the position of having helped Parent secure his freedom.

"I hope he knows what he's talking about," Larry said. "For your sake, Christine."

He asked her to drive him to the airport, explaining he had left some deals brewing in Atlanta and had to get back to them. She dropped him in front of the terminal, and when he leaned over to kiss her, she offered her hand. Then she asked him if he could lend her $500 to pay the lawyer. Larry said he didn't have it on him but would try to get it for her.

The agents convened around the conference table at GBI headquarters didn't know whether to laugh or cry. "Spivey, I don't understand it," Inspector Peters groaned. "We were running a nice shop here, investigating crimes while you still thought drugs were something you got at a drugstore. We take you in, and inside of four months you put us all in the perjury business."

"It's not even our case," Billy Shepherd chimed in. "It's outside our jurisdiction; it's got no connection with any of our investigations. Will somebody please explain to me what our man is doing in the middle of it?"

Larry tried to defend himself, pointing out accurately enough that it wasn't he who had come up with the name of a crooked lawyer. Whatever ground he gained with that comment, though, was lost immediately when he announced that Gould was expecting $500 on Monday, and Larry, posing as a well-heeled smuggler, was expected to pay it.

"Oh, Jesus Christ, no," Mike Eason cried, burying his head in his arms. "We'll all go to jail!"

"Don't be so hard on the boy," George Clardy said lightly. "Larry can't help it if he can't get laid without uncovering a crime. 'I've got to send you over, sweetheart, because all of me says not to. I'll have some rotten nights, but that will pass. I won't play the sap for you.' "

He ended with a first-class Bogart sneer that even Larry thought was funny. The jokes went on for another five minutes, until everybody had worked that side of the situation out of his system. Then it was time to face the fact that they all had a very serious problem here. It went without saying that the Broward County authorities would have to be notified about Christine's intentions immediately.

Larry called the police department in Pembroke Park, Florida, the Fort Lauderdale suburb where the murder had taken place, and asked to speak to the investigating officer in charge of the case. His call was put through to Captain Ronald Gaetinello, who made no effort to conceal his excitement as he listened to Larry's story.

"This ought to make all the difference in the world, Mr. Spivey," Gaetinello said. "But the case is already on trial. It's out of my hands. The man you should be talking to is the prosecutor. Stay where you are, and he'll call you back inside of five minutes."

In less than half that time Larry was on the phone with Walt LeGraves, a special investigator in the state prosecutor's office. For the third time in an hour, Larry ran through everything he knew about Christine Snow's role in the murder of Steven O'Neill. LeGraves said that the prosecutor would be in touch as soon as he got out of court.

Shortly before five o'clock, Assistant State Attorney Gene Garrett called GBI and had Larry retell the story for what finally promised to be the last time. Gaetinello and LeGraves listened in on extensions.

"Mr. Spivey, I can't thank you enough," Garrett declared. "Your testimony will assure that man's conviction."

268

"Well, that's the problem right there," Larry said. "If it's not absolutely necessary, I'd rather not testify."

Garrett sounded shocked. "You are in law enforcement, aren't you?" he asked, not to be snide but because he genuinely couldn't believe that a cop would have any hesitation about appearing in court.

"Yes, I thought I had explained it," Larry answered patiently. "I'm working in an undercover capacity. If I go into court, it's going to blow my cover completely. You can appreciate that."

"Sorry, but I can't," LeGraves shot back. "We're not dealing with smugglers here, Mr. Spivey. This is the big casino. Murder one. You can't weigh one against the other."

They haggled for half an hour, at the end of which a compromise was worked out. Larry would spend the weekend with the prosecutor, meticulously going over everything Christine Snow had told him, everything that could be used to shake her on the witness stand. When she took the stand, Larry would follow the trial from the prosecutor's office, feeding back information that could be used against her. "You do that for me," Garrett said, "and I give you my word I'll do everything I can to make your testimony unnecessary."

Larry told him he had a deal, and Garrett promised to have someone from the sheriff's office meet him at the airport when he flew in Saturday morning.

On that note the meeting broke up, and Larry went home, hoping this time he'd get a chance to stay awhile. He stretched out on the couch while Jerri, her legs curled under her, sat on the floor beside him, cradling her head on his chest. He had been gone only a few days, but it felt like forever.

And for Jerri it felt longer. For some reason, the Jamaica trip had scared her in a way none of his other disappearances in the company of drug dealers had. Perhaps it was simply because she hadn't been around when he had gone to Guatemala and Mexico, so that this was the first time she had had to sit home and worry while he was out of the country. Larry hadn't made it any easier for her by telling her about some of his close calls in Latin America. At the time she had enjoyed hearing about them, vicariously sharing in the excitement. But when she was alone in the house, those stories came back to haunt her, replaying themselves in her mind with less happy endings.

"When is it going to end, Larry?" she asked, regretting the question as soon as it was said. She had vowed to herself she wouldn't add to the strain he was under by laying her difficulties on him. And she didn't like the melodramatic way she had said it. But she couldn't help herself.

For a few minutes he played absently with her hair, letting the softness and scent of it bathe his face. "Don't ask me that, Jerri," he whispered back, not as a rebuke but as a plea. It was a question he had been asking himself.

She sat up and lit two cigarettes, offering him one. "You know, Larry, that's what doesn't make sense about it."

"It does make sense," he protested mildly, not fully out of conviction. "I just can't explain it to you."

"Because I wouldn't understand?"

"No. Because I can't explain it."

She shook her head sorrowfully, her blond hair swaying like water lapping a shore. "It doesn't make sense because it doesn't have an ending," she said thoughtfully. "Nothing without an ending makes sense."

They talked past midnight. Jerri reminded him this wasn't what he had ever wanted for himself, and all Larry could say was that he had to see it through.

"But you have seen it through, Larry. Don't you know that?" she demanded. "You started this to keep Gus McClellan and the others from dragging you into their plans. Gordon's been arrested; the book is closed. You keep opening it. If you weren't working undercover, it wouldn't be so bad. But a man can't go on fooling everybody forever."

"Is that what I'm doing?"

"Of course it is. And sooner or later they'll see through it. They'll kill you when they do."

"Nobody's going to kill me."

"Then what? You'll kill them? How many deaths do there have to be?"

Her words brought him back to places he didn't want to be. "I haven't killed anyone, Jerri," he said weakly.

"Because it hasn't come to that," she said. "It will."

Twenty-One

Phil Peters gave Larry Friday off. That turned out to mean only Friday morning, and only the first part of Friday morning at that. The inspector called him a little after ten and "asked" him to come to the office.

Forty-five minutes later Larry was being congratulated by his boss for having "hit the big time."

"It can't be worse than it is already," Larry said, assuming Peters was being facetious. But it turned out he wasn't.

Peters led Larry into his office, where David Hallman, a young agent who specialized in conspiracy law, was sitting at a small table next to a stack of folders reaching exactly to his eyebrows. Peters explained that Hallman had just been assigned to the smuggling detail, giving Larry, Eason, and Clardy a fourth teammate. The folders behind which Hallman was hiding were the thirty-seven case files opened to date on the subjects of the smuggling detail's investigations. Except for the few concerning individuals already deceased, there wasn't one of them that wasn't at least a week or two out of date. It would be Hallman's job to keep on top of the cases, to evaluate them, and to provide up-to-the-minute shopping lists of what was still needed to develop them to the point where they could be successfully prosecuted.

Larry wanted to know what the smuggling detail had done to earn a thirty-three percent increase in manpower. Peters triumphantly held up a small sheaf of papers, all of which had arrived on his desk that morning. The Alcohol, Tobacco, and Firearms division of the U.S. Treasury Department had run a check on the German machine gun Floyd Farnum had given Larry and discovered to its dismay that it wasn't hot. Since ownership of such a weapon could not be legally transferred without the transaction's being registered with ATF, this meant Farnum had access to a crooked gun dealer with enough clout to handle such an exotic weapon. ATF then ran a check on Farnum's long-distance telephone tolls and discovered that he had spoken repeatedly with an arms broker in Houston who was known to be supplying weapons to insurgents in Angola. They wanted to know more.

The FBI was keenly interested in Mike Thevis, a prosperous Atlantan they had long known to be the undisputed pornography king of the entire country. Dan Gordon, whom Larry had busted on New Year's Day, once bragged that his own smuggling ventures were backed by Thevis. The bureau wanted Larry to parlay his now-defunct connection with Gordon into a connection with Thevis.

The Secret Service had filed a request for additional help with the counterfeiter Floyd Farnum had mentioned the first time he met Larry; Internal Revenue wanted Larry to find out more about Farnum's money-laundering operation; and Customs wanted more information about the proposed route of Stan Eccles's sailboat, which didn't seem to have been seized in Jamaica and should have been well on its way to Florida.

"All of a sudden there's a lot of folks think you can help them out," Peters concluded, inexplicably lapsing into his thickest down-home drawl. "I already called Garrett and put him on notice he was gonna have to bust his ass to put your little bunny's boyfriend away without your help because he just might find himself at the end of a very long line."

Larry asked if that meant he wasn't going to Fort Lauderdale Saturday as planned. Peters told him to go ahead but instructed him not to compromise his undercover position in any way and not to take the stand without personal authorization from Peters. If Garrett tried to have him served with a subpoena, he was to get back to Georgia immediately so that a decision could be reached on whether he was to honor it.

On Friday night the question U.S. Customs had asked Larry to look into was answered for him. Ron Agee called him at home, getting him out of bed, to tell him he had just heard from Phyllis Laine. Eccles and Jones had been arrested in Jamaican waters five days earlier and held incommunicado by the Jamaican police. Cotton Andrews had already returned to the States and so escaped capture.

"Does he know about the arrests yet?" Larry asked.

"I just found out myself. I tried to call him, but I can't reach him. That's why I called you. I can't reach Shawkey either. Man, he's gonna be pissed. Who do you figure sold out the load?"

"Are you crazy?" Larry shot back. "I already told you, nobody sold it out. Just Eccles's stupidity. He did everything but take out ads in the papers. Why do you think I got the hell out of there?"

"Yeah," Agee said. "I forgot."

Larry hung up the phone with uneasy feelings. This wasn't the sort of information Agee would forget, so his question about an informant must have been some kind of test, which Larry had no way of knowing if he had passed. He made a few phone calls trying to track down Andrews and Shawkey, but neither could be reached, so he rolled over and went back to sleep, figuring Agee would catch up with them sooner or later.

In the morning Larry called the office and asked them to tell Customs to stop looking for Eccles's boat. Then Jerri and Mark drove him to the airport, dropping him off at the terminal door. She couldn't wait around to see him off because she had to deliver her son to his father for his regular every-other-weekend visit. Larry had a half hour to kill before his flight, so he went into the coffee shop for breakfast.

The first thing he saw as he walked in was Cotton Andrews, standing at the register paying his check. Hiding his surprise, he called Andrews's name and hurried up to him. "Cotton, I've got to talk to you," he said urgently. "Have you got a minute?"

"I've got to catch a plane, but it's not for another half hour," Andrews said.

"Yeah, me too. C'mon, have a cup of coffee."

As they walked to a table, Andrews asked Larry where he was going. When Larry told him Fort Lauderdale, Andrews said, "Great, so am I. We can sit together."

Sure, Larry thought. I can introduce him to the sheriff's deputies who are meeting me there. But what he said was: "I've got bad news for you. Did Agee call you last night?"

"No. Haven't heard from him since I got back. What's up?"

"Eccles got popped."

Andrews went white, and he actually looked as if he were going to throw up. "That can't be," he stammered, his voice choked. "Even with good winds he can't get here till Tuesday, Monday at the earliest."

"Not here. They busted him in Jamaica."

There was a long silence, during which Larry could read with excruciating clarity everything Cotton Andrews was thinking. Finally, Andrews voiced the question that was on his mind. "You didn't tell Horace what you told me, did you?" he asked, pleading for the right answer.

"That Eccles was running a loose shop? Yeah, I told him."

"Oh, shit," Andrews whined. "You didn't have to, did you?"

"Hey, Cotton. He didn't send me down there to get a tan. He wanted to know."

"Christ, you could have stood up for me."

Larry felt sorry for the frightened but personable young drug expert, who a few weeks earlier hadn't remembered that gold was the name of a metal as well as of a strain of marijuana. But he had no choice but to be hard on him. "Look, I could see it coming a mile off. If you didn't have your head up your ass, you would have seen it, too. It's not like I didn't warn you, y'know, but I've got to look out for me. What are you going to do?"

Andrews shrugged helplessly. "Go back and tell the boss, I guess. No sense going to Lauderdale now. I was supposed to line up a truck to take the load. Jesus, he's gonna fucking kill me, you know that."

He stood up, his coffee untouched, and turned to walk from the restaurant.

"Take care of yourself, Cotton," Larry called after him.

Andrews looked back over his shoulder. "How am I gonna do that?" he asked.

Cotton's departure solved Larry's problem about being met in Fort Lauderdale by sheriff's deputies, but at a very steep price. It was the last time Larry ever saw Cotton Andrews. Two weeks later Roanoke police came to Andrews's house because of a complaint from neighbors about the noise his dog was making. Andrews's car was in the driveway, but there was no sign of either Andrews or Frederika Keats, the woman with whom he had been living. From the condition of the animal, the occupants appeared to have been away at least a week, although it did not seem they had taken any belongings with them. The dog was turned over to the humane society, where it was never claimed. Neither Cotton nor Fred has ever been heard from again. They are officially presumed dead.

Larry was met as promised in Fort Lauderdale and whisked away in an unmarked car to the Broward County courthouse, which he entered through a side door, even though it was Saturday and there was no one inside except the prosecutor and his staff.

Garrett didn't seem happy to see him. "I got a call from your boss," he said glumly. "Apparently, if I put you on the stand, I've got to answer to him, the Secret Service, Customs, the FBI, and for all I know the B'nai B'rith and the Roman Catholic Church. I don't know who the hell you are, Spivey, but from the way it sounds, if you testify, the whole government goes out of business."

"Not really," Larry answered, looking for the right words to mollify him. "We've got a lot of man-hours invested in some very big cases, that's all. I'm here to do everything I can to help you out so that we don't have to jeopardize all that."

Garrett nodded gratefully. He had a square face and candid gray eyes that suggested he held few illusions about where he stood. "Fine. Then let's get to work," he said, forcing enthusiasm into his voice.

The entire afternoon was spent going over Christine Snow's expected testimony in meticulous detail. It wouldn't be easy to punch holes in her story, but it might be possible to shake her by hinting that the prosecution knew a lot more than she could account for. She was obviously frightened about the consequences of committing perjury, or she wouldn't have asked for Larry's help after she had read about the other witness's performance on the stand. Garrett wanted to play on that fear to unnerve her.

In the evening Larry had dinner with Garrett and LeGraves at Garrett's house. Captain Gaetinello stopped by around ten to pick up Larry and deliver him to an apartment maintained by the Pembroke Park police for undercover purposes. Gaetinello gave him the keys to an unmarked police car that was being placed at his disposal during his stay in Fort Lauderdale.

Sunday was an exact replay of Saturday. On Monday Larry drove to the airport and parked in the metered lot, then called Christine from the terminal and told her he had just flown into town.

"You should have told me what time you were coming. I would have met you," she said.

She picked him up twenty minutes later, greeting him warmly. But after he gave her the money for the lawyer and they had talked for a few minutes, he detected an unmistakable coldness in her manner, as though he had fulfilled his usefulness for her. She looked tired and drawn, her eyes hollow and tinged with fear, like the eyes of a small child left in a strange place too long. She asked Larry if he wanted a lift into town.

"No, thanks anyway," he said. "I've got some people to see. We're not going in the same direction." He wished her luck.

"I'm going to need it," she said.

"Don't worry," Larry answered, maneuvering to plant seeds of doubt in her mind. "You've got nothing to worry about. It's like the lawyer said. As long as they can't prove O'Neill didn't fire a gun, there's no way they can touch you."

He saw the tiny twitch of her mouth that told him he had hit home. He guessed that as soon as she could get to a telephone, she would call Parent's lawyer to find out what Larry had meant. When she found out that a paraffin test done on the victim's hands had turned out negative, it would give her something to think about.

He watched her drive off with only the dimmest sense of loss. In the course of a man's life he meets few women to whom he is powerfully attracted and a great many to whom it is easy to say good-bye. Unless he is very unlucky, he won't run across more than one who falls into both categories.

Monday evening Larry ate a TV dinner alone in the Pembroke Park PD's safe house. Around ten o'clock he went out to make a few phone calls. He wanted to touch base with Agee in order to convince him not to let Eccles's arrest in Jamaica slow down the planning for the DC-4 deal. And he wanted to talk to Jerri.

He drove to a nearby shopping center in Hollywood and pulled into the empty parking lot to use the booth near the front of the store. He hadn't even opened his car door when the burglar alarm in the store went off. It took him only a second to realize where the sudden sound was coming from.

He wheeled his car around to face the store and stepped on the high-beam button, illuminating a good portion of the storefront. He grabbed for the police radio that conveniently came with the car and called in the alarm, then drew his gun and scrambled to the pavement. Figuring that whoever was inside probably wouldn't come out the front with a pair of headlights illuminating the place like a fairground, he raced toward the back.

Running at full speed along the side of the building, he heard a door latch click not twenty feet in front of him and put on the brakes so hard he had to windmill his arms to keep from falling. He stepped to the side, flattening himself against the building wall, just in time to see two men emerge from the darkened building. They checked out the scene in both directions but failed to see him.

Larry didn't want them scooting back into the building, where the police might have a problem getting them out, so he let them walk a few steps from the door before moving in behind them.

"Hands up, don't turn, and don't move," he barked, startling them as effectively as the burglar alarm had startled him a few minutes earlier. Their hands went up.

"Turn to the wall nice and slow. Now lean, legs apart, you won't get hurt."

He had to hold them there for only a minute or two before a pair of uniformed officers arrived in a squad car. They were approaching very slowly, so he called to them. "This way, please. These gentlemen were on their way out."

While one of the patrolmen cuffed the prisoners, the other asked Larry who he was. For some reason it seemed a difficult question, so Larry simply gave his name and suggested that if the officer had any questions he should contact Captain Gaetinello. The patrolman shrugged, not giving much of a damn either way, and Larry walked back to his car conscious of an almost embarrassing feeling of petty satisfaction. He had been an officer of the law a little more than four months, and he had just made his first arrest.

Still shaking his head over the incident, he put off making his phone calls and drove to the nearest bar, which turned out to be an unpretentious blue-collar watering spot with color pictures of University of Miami Hurricanes taped to the mirror behind the bar. He took a stool next to an inoffensive-looking little man in a plaid sport jacket and asked the girl behind the bar for a scotch and soda.

A plain girl with limp hair and very small teeth, she mixed the drink and came around the bar to deliver it, smiling as woodenly as an airline stewardess at the end of a very long flight. "Here you go, honey," she crooned as she handed him the glass. "Long time no see."

Larry was about to remind her they had never met when she threw her arm around his neck, leaned as close to him as she could, and gave him the bad news.

"The guy next to you has a gun," she whispered. "He's fixing to make trouble. Don't do anything to annoy him. The cops are on the way."

"Sweetie, you're looking terrific," Larry responded aloud. "Taking good care of yourself, huh?"

They hugged each other playfully, and then she returned to her station behind the bar. Larry watched her go, thinking this just wasn't his night.

He swung around so he could watch the small man in the plaid jacket out of the corner of his eye. After a minute the man took out a pack of matches and a cigarette. Larry observed that he was right-handed. He bided his time, wondering how many cops there were in Hollywood, Florida, and regretting having sent two of them away with the department store burglars.

Almost five minutes passed before two uniformed cops walked into the bar. Larry spotted them over his shoulder and turned on his stool to face the man in the plaid jacket.

"Hi, I'm Larry Spivey," he announced loudly, smiling broadly as he offered his hand.

The little fellow, taken by surprise, hesitated a second before extending his own hand. With the bluff effusiveness of a used-car salesman greeting a customer, Larry clamped his right hand around the little man's and his left hand on the man's forearm, which he pumped unmercifully. Meanwhile, the girl behind the bar was gesturing frantically for the police, who were scanning the room as though they would be expected to testify about the exact location of everyone in it. The guy in the plaid jacket finally caught on to what was happening and tried to wrench free, but Larry had too good a grip on him. One of the cops pulled back the man's jacket and drew an automatic weapon from his waistband. Larry let go so the cop could cuff him.

"Thanks," the cop said as he dragged the man from the stool and led him to the door.

"Not at all," Larry replied.

The barmaid wouldn't let him pay for his drink. Well, Larry thought, so it goes in the life of a crime fighter. He wondered how Hollywood, Florida, would manage to get along without him.

Captain Gaetinello picked Larry up at his apartment in the morning and drove him to the courthouse, parking at the side of the building. They hurried inside and took the stairs to Walt LeGraves's office on the second floor. It was only a thirty-foot walk from the staircase to the office door; but when they were halfway there, a door down the hallway opened and Charles Gould, Christine Snow's attorney, stepped out.

Gaetinello saw him first and reacted quickly. Grabbing Larry by the elbow and shoving him on ahead the way he might drag a prisoner in for questioning, he pushed Larry the last few steps to LeGraves's office. "Damn, that was a close one," he sighed when the door had closed behind him.

The problem was that neither he nor Larry could be sure it hadn't been too close. Larry couldn't afford to take the chance Gould had spotted him, so he had to come up with a cover story in a hurry. "What kind of unsolved crimes do you have that are recent?" he asked. "Like yesterday."

"I'll check for you," the captain said. "But this office only handles homicides."

"I'm not fussy."

Gaetinello conferred briefly with LeGraves, who then reported to Larry. "Try this one on for size. We had a young lady, call girl actually, got herself pistol-whipped last night. Her head's in little pieces, like a busted plate. No way she's gonna make it."

"Any connection with drugs?"

"Cocaine user."

"That'll do," Larry said. "Tell me about her."

LeGraves produced a photograph of the victim. He gave Larry all the information he had on her and on the crime, and Larry memorized it before reaching for the phone to call Gould's office. The receptionist said Mr. Gould was out and was not expected back until later that afternoon.

"Well, this is Larry Spivey. I've been picked up by the police. I have to talk to him."

"Certainly, Mr. Spivey. He should be calling in. Are you in custody now?"

"Yes."

"Where?"

"State attorney's office."

"Oh, that's perfect," she said unthinkingly. "Mr. Gould is in the court-house right now. I'll give him your message as soon as I hear from him, and he'll be right over."

Less than five minutes later the lawyer stepped into the prosecutor's office and announced that he represented Mr. Spivey and wished to speak with his client. LeGraves went through the expected motions of stalling out a lawyer while the prosecutor gets in a few more questions, and then Larry was brought out. Garrett said that he did not intend to charge Spivey with the crime "at this time."

On his way back to Gould's office in Gould's telephone-equipped Cadillac Brougham, Larry protested his innocence. "I mean I knew her, but what the hell. I didn't even see her last night."

Gould told him not to worry about it. "I'm sure they believe that or they wouldn't have let you go now. I doubt very much that they'll charge you, but if they do, that will be time enough for us to concern ourselves."

"Anything you say, Counselor," Larry answered sullenly.

Gould said he was just stopping by the office to pick up messages before going for lunch. He invited Larry to join him. "My club okay?" he asked.

"Beats me. I've never been to your club. Who the hell eats lunch at eleven o'clock anyway?" Larry snarled, obviously a man who had had more than enough hassles for one morning.

"I have to eat whenever I get a chance," Gould boasted, gloating over the size of his practice. "Besides, the dining room will be empty at this hour. It will give us a chance to talk."

Larry had adopted a surly mood in order to get rid of Gould quickly so he could sneak back to Garrett's office to be there when Christine testified. But Gould's suggestion that they had something to talk about was too tempting to pass up. "Your club it is," Larry said.

Gould ordered a tartar steak and seemed offended when Larry opted for a simple sandwich. When the immaculately liveried waiter had served their meals and withdrawn to the kitchen, they were indeed alone in the immense and dimly lit oak-paneled room. "You said you wanted to talk?" Larry demanded, letting Gould know at once he didn't like pussyfooting around.

"You're an interesting man, Mr. Spivey," Gould began.

"Yeah, I know that," Larry cut him off. "You're not buying me lunch so you can tell me how interesting I am."

"Of course not," Gould said, recovering quickly. "I enjoy talking to interesting people because sometimes it develops that we have interests in common."

"Is that the only word you know, *interesting?*"

"Forgive me, but I'm trying to be discreet. Perhaps you should know a little bit more about me. My firm has tended to get rather specialized in recent years. We have had a great deal of success handling narcotics cases, and I daresay there is no one in the Southeast who can do a better job disposing of such charges than my partner and I. Naturally, over a long period of time we've made a certain number of friends and have gathered large amounts of information. Don't you agree we might have interests in common that would be worth talking about?"

"You don't hear me saying anything, Counselor," Larry said. "Just keep going the way you're going."

Gould swallowed a small square of raw meat before continuing. After a few sentences, he dropped out of the heavily coded vernacular he had been using and began to speak openly, explicitly offering Larry a chance to buy drugs. Larry showed only minimal interest. He said he was well supplied as it was and had no need to look elsewhere unless Gould had something special to offer.

"Indeed, I do, sir," Gould announced grandly. "Christine informs me you were expecting complications for your friends in Jamaica. How did that turn out?"

Larry hesitated a long time before answering, as though he were considering whether he should ignore the question. "The people she was talking about got popped," he said at last.

"Ah," Gould sighed. "That's just my point. These matters can be so difficult at times, especially when it involves the necessity of smuggling something out of one country before you can smuggle it into another."

"And you've figured out a way to grow grass in the clouds?"

"Not quite, Mr. Spivey. But very close. I have a contact with the freighter *Don Emilio.* I trust you've heard of the *Don Emilio?*"

For many months, drug enforcement agencies up and down the eastern seaboard had known of the existence of a large freighter that regularly plied the Atlantic coast, remaining in international waters and off-loading large quantities of marijuana and cocaine to smaller smuggling vessels. The shrimp boat seized at Southern's Bluff, Georgia, in the summer of 1975, was assumed to have picked up its eighteen-ton load from this phantom freighter, as was the sailboat *Odessa,* seized in Savannah a few weeks later, after its crew had unloaded three tons of marijuana into a fleet of waiting trucks. So far no drug agency had been able to come up with a line on the freighter or a clue to its identity. All those arrested with narcotics taken from the ship had refused to divulge its name, perhaps out of fear, perhaps because they genuinely didn't know it.

"I've heard lots of things," Larry said indifferently. "We're well taken care of."

Gould wasn't ready to give up yet. "Just keep us in mind, Mr. Spivey," he said. "When other people have difficulties keeping themselves supplied, we never have any. I can get you any quantity you might want of any commodity. As often as you want. The *Don Emilio* makes a run every three weeks. Think it over."

Larry promised to pass the information on to his associates. After lunch, he told Gould he was going back to Atlanta, and the lawyer offered to drop him at the airport. From the airport Larry had to take a taxi back to the courthouse, where he made it up to Garrett's office without incident. Garrett was in court, cross-examining Christine Snow.

"Where the hell have you been?" Walt LeGraves demanded.

It was too long a story for Larry to go into, so he simply said it had taken longer than he had expected to extricate himself from Gould. His lunchtime conversation had convinced him that testifying against Carl Parent was now absolutely out of the question. The door to a mammoth international drug operation had just been opened for him, and there was no way GBI or Customs would let a single homicide case close it.

Fortunately the reports he got from the courtroom indicated his problems in Pembroke Park would soon be over. Gene Garrett was enjoying his finest hour as a prosecutor, at the expense of Christine Snow. He unnerved her when he asked why Steve O'Neill had fired wildly into the ceiling since it was he who had got off the first shot. Even though the question raised an objection and she wasn't allowed to answer it, she obviously saw the inconsistency and knew the jury saw it, too. She was looking for a way out when Garrett suggested that perhaps he had been reaching for his gun but that Parent had outdrawn him. Perhaps O'Neill had been hit when he was shot?

Christine's mind was a jumble as she tried to sort out the consequences of every statement she made, both for herself and for Parent. She clutched at this straw, assuming it would leave her lover's self-defense claim intact. Yes, she conceded, it was possible O'Neill had been hit.

The moment she said it, the trial was over for her. On direct testimony she had sworn she didn't hear the fatal shotgun blast until a second or two after O'Neill's handgun went off. Now she was admitting she might have been mistaken about the sequence of shots. Her credibility before the jury was entirely destroyed. The damage had been so thorough that Parent's attorney couldn't risk questioning her again on redirect for fear she would only make it worse.

She didn't move when the judge told her she could step down, and she had to be told again. The defense then asked for a short recess, during which Garrett went upstairs to his office and told Larry he would be free to return to Atlanta as soon as the judge had concluded his charge to the jury later that afternoon.

The name of a ship may not seem like much to go on, but Larry was a former navy man who knew it actually gave him a lot. He couldn't even wait to get back to the office to begin checking whether there was any truth at all in what Charles Gould had told him. He immediately called the intelligence section of the U.S. Customs office in Miami and passed on the information. He asked the desk officer there to contact him at GBI as soon as he learned anything.

Larry then flew back to Atlanta. By the time he got to the office in the early evening Customs had called to inform him that there was indeed such a ship and that it was of Panamanian registry. It would take them only a matter of days to research ship registries, which would produce pictures of the vessel that could be used to locate it on the high seas. Port records would also be checked to find out what ports of call the *Don Emilio* had made, and this information might make it possible to deduce something about its routes.

Phil Peters had stayed late in the office to wait for Larry so he could congratulate him on his work. Larry asked Peters if he should get in touch with Gould after a suitable interval and arrange to buy a load off the ship.

"Oh, shoot," Peters groaned. "Don't you think you've done enough for a day? Whaddya say we give those boys at Customs a chance to have a little fun?"

Twenty-two

E arly Wednesday evening Gene Garrett called to report that after
only three hours of deliberation his jury had returned, claiming it
was deadlocked at six to six. The judge then re-charged them,
detailing the elements necessary for finding the defendant guilty of second-
degree murder if they found insufficient proof of premeditation to warrant
a conviction for first-degree murder. After another four hours of deliberation the jury came back with a verdict. Carl Parent was guilty of murder
in the second degree. A sentencing date was set for early April. Garrett
said he was satisfied with the result, and if Garrett was satisfied, so was
Larry.

Over the next week, Customs continued to call back with additional
information on the *Don Emilio*. Ownership of the vessel was traced to a
Panamanian corporation, one of the principal stockholders of which was
Moisés Torrijos, the brother of Panamanian President Omar Torrijos.
Port records failed to disclose a single port of call for the vessel over the
past two years, indicating that if the *Don Emilio* wasn't engaged in some
sort of illegal enterprise, then Torrijos's corporation was inexplicably
listing a nonexistent ship on its records.

Descriptions of the ship and pictures of its silhouette were being disseminated among all naval units capable of taking part in a search for it.
Navy submarines, surface vessels, and aircraft all had been alerted to be
on the lookout for the *Don Emilio,* and Customs had even convinced the
National Security Administration to throw its satellite network into the

sea hunt. Because the ship was of foreign registry, the State Department had come into the case, with Secretary of State Henry Kissinger insisting that he be notified the moment the drug-laden mother ship was located. In return he promised to get back to Customs within twenty minutes with permission to board. Customs agents explained to Larry that under the Hovering Vessels Act, an antibootlegging statute dating back to Prohibition, the Coast Guard had authority to board foreign ships outside U.S. territorial waters if those ships were engaged in acts that violated American law.

While U.S. Customs was busy searching for a four-hundred-foot freighter, the pilot of the small sailboat seized by Jamaican police made it back to his home in Fort Lauderdale. Stan Eccles considered himself lucky to get off as lightly as he did. He and Bill Jones had managed to jettison their precious cargo of marijuana before their sailboat was boarded by Jamaican cops, but in the rush to get the bulky bales of incriminating evidence over the gunwales, Jones had forgotten the single joint in his shirt pocket. The Jamaicans, frustrated at having lost the large haul they had expected to seize, used this one joint as a pretext for towing the sailboat into Port Antonio Harbor and arresting both men on board. Eccles and Jones were held incommunicado for six days, during which time they were questioned none too gently by their captors. They persisted in denying they had been carrying marijuana and refused to name their Jamaican suppliers. Finally, the police had no choice but to release them with a wrist-slap fine.

After almost a week of heavy interrogation in a country where no one had ever heard of Miranda and Escobedo, Stan Eccles figured the toughest part of his ordeal lay behind him. He had lost $10,000 and thrown a thousand pounds of marijuana into the ocean, but he had come out of it all right. It was Horace Shawkey's grass, so it was Horace Shawkey's problem.

Shawkey didn't see it quite the same way. He was sitting in Eccles's living room when a taxi dropped Eccles off directly from the Fort Lauderdale marina. Shawkey's legs were trailing along the expensive upholstery of Eccles's crushed velvet sofa for all the world like the legs of a man in his own home. Seated in the two matching chairs were Donnie Swanson, Shawkey's personal hit man, and Greg Stein, a young dark-haired apprentice Swanson was inducting into the business. Eccles had never met Shawkey before, but the moment he unlocked his front door he knew who his uninvited guests were. He made an effort to remember what being cheerful felt like in order to pretend nothing was wrong. But playing before such a small and unappreciative audience, he couldn't keep up the performance for more than a minute or two. "You must be wondering what happened to the load?" he asked.

Shawkey nodded. He hadn't spoken since Eccles had walked in.

Eccles figured this was a good time to offer his guests drinks, but Shawkey declined with a simple scowl. Swanson and Stein didn't even change expressions when he turned to them.

"Mind if I get myself one?" Eccles asked.

"I was wondering what happened to the load," Shawkey answered.

Slowly Eccles began to tell the story. At every point he stopped to emphasize that the deal was going down beautifully, that everything was going according to plan, that it was the perfect smuggle.

"That's not the way Spivey tells it," Shawkey growled.

The little wheels behind Stan Eccles's eyes spun faster than they had ever spun in his life. "Oh, Spivey," he said. "I figured he'd try something like that. To tell you the truth, that guy was absolutely impossible to work with. We just couldn't believe he'd ever done a deal before. Maybe he hasn't, I don't know. What do you think, Horace? You must have checked him out. You did, didn't you? Well, anyway, I can't tell you how glad we were when he finally pulled out. We were afraid he'd get us all busted. That's what Bill and I were thinking; only I didn't want to say so. There are some guys like to lay the blame all around, but you know me, Horace. It's not my style."

"I don't know you," Shawkey reminded him. "Are you telling me what happened is Spivey's fault?"

"I didn't say it, Horace. You didn't hear it from me. But look, if he's trying to lay it all on me, then I've got to look out for myself, don't I?"

Shawkey turned to the blond hit man. "Get Spivey on the phone," he ordered.

Swanson crossed to the telephone and dialed Larry's number in Atlanta. "Spivey, someone wants to talk to you," he said, handing the phone to his boss.

In two pithy sentences, Shawkey ordered Larry to get to Fort Lauderdale on the next flight. When he hung up the phone, Eccles tried to go on with his explanation, but Shawkey cut him off. "Save it till Spivey gets here," he snapped.

For the next three hours the four men sat in Stan Eccles's living room without speaking.

Larry didn't know why Horace Shawkey wanted to see him, but he knew it wasn't to buy him dinner. He called George Clardy and told him he felt he had to go, but he wanted to be armed. In the past he had always packed his gun in his suitcase, but if this trip turned out to be anything like what he thought it might be, he didn't want to have to ask permission to unpack when Shawkey's man pulled a gun on him.

Clardy tried to talk him out of going, but when it was clear he was losing the argument, he told him to go ahead to the airport and promised to meet him there. Twenty minutes after Larry got to the airport, Mike Eason came racing into the terminal.

Clardy, it turned out, had called Inspector Peters to ask his advice on how to get Larry aboard an aircraft with a gun. The inspector replied that nothing less than a letter from him would do. Eason got the job of running over to his house to pick it up simply because he lived closer to the inspector.

Armed with Eason's GBI identification and the letter from Inspector Peters stating that Mr. Spivey was a GBI agent traveling on GBI business under extremely dangerous circumstances, they were able to convince the chief of airport security to let Larry board the airliner with his weapon. The security chief, who seemed to be acting under the impression Larry was an explosive device that might go off at any minute, personally escorted him onto the airplane and to his seat, remaining in the aisle until he had buckled himself in.

Larry had no trouble spotting his one-man welcoming committee in the reception area inside the gate at Fort Lauderdale. Approaching the scowling young heavy with the bulging sports jacket, he asked bluntly if Shawkey had sent him. The bodyguard, taken by surprise, seemed about to tell him to mind his business but quickly got hold of himself and remembered why he was there. "Mr. Shawkey wants to see you," he said needlessly, leading the way to the car he had left illegally parked just outside the terminal.

There was no point asking the gunman where they were going since it was obviously an important part of his self-image not to answer such questions, so Larry simply sat back to enjoy the ride. The car pulled up in front of a large home in an extremely wealthy suburb, and Larry followed the bodyguard up the flagstone walkway to the front door. He noticed the house was dark except for a single light downstairs.

He was surprised to see Stan Eccles standing about ten feet from Horace Shawkey in the middle of the beam-ceilinged living room. Not pleased, but surprised. "How the hell did you get here?" Larry demanded. "Agee said you ran into trouble."

Eccles shook his head glumly, studying the floor. "It was nothing, just a little misunderstanding with some of the locals," he said softly. "Agee exaggerates."

Shawkey had seen enough of this happy reunion to satisfy himself. "Stan tells me you made an ass of yourself down there, Spivey. He says he thinks you got them busted."

Larry went into an immediate rage. "You fucking bastard," he shouted, wheeling to face Eccles. "Where do you come off with a bullshit story like that?" He turned to Shawkey and reminded him that the first thing he had done when he got off the plane from Jamaica was call Roanoke to let Shawkey know how badly things were going. Gesturing toward Eccles, he said, "That's the fucking truth, and he knows it. I took your boy Cotton aside and told him this flamingo here was drawing too damn much attention to himself. I told him not to do the deal. But he wouldn't listen; he thought it was all cool. I practically had to work him over. Ask him yourself."

"Ah, that's the problem," Shawkey sighed. "Cotton is no longer available."

Larry took in the meaning of his words instantly but pretended not to. "I think Stan and I have got to talk this over," he said flatly, motioning for Eccles to join him in the kitchen. Donnie Swanson stood up to stop them but backed off when his boss signaled his consent.

"What's the fucking idea?" Larry demanded as soon as he and Eccles were alone. The kitchen was separated from the living room by a chest-high countertop, but they had gone all the way toward the back of it, where they were out of sight from the three gangsters who had subsided back into the crushed velvet furniture.

"I guess it was just an honest misunderstanding," Eccles said weakly.

Larry's left fist caught Eccles just above his silver-and-turquoise belt buckle, and the air went out of him with a loud whoosh clearly audible in the living room. In the moment of silence that followed, Larry heard the click of Horace Shawkey's cigarette lighter.

"I mean, I figured maybe the way you and that girl were carrying on, maybe it attracted some attention," Eccles gasped.

The second punch got him in exactly the same place.

"Aw, shit, it was probably just her. She's a goddamned good-looking piece," Eccles tried again.

Larry pulled back his arm for a third punch, but Eccles quickly remembered some things he had done wrong himself in Jamaica.

"Tell him, don't tell me," Larry snarled, shoving Eccles ahead of him into the living room.

Eccles took a few seconds to compose himself. "Larry reminded me of some things I forgot," he announced sheepishly.

Shawkey nodded his approval. "That's kind of what I figured, Spivey. I just thought you'd want to set the record straight yourself," he said. "Greg here will take you wherever you want to go, but stick around town. We've got some business to talk about as soon as I'm finished here."

While Greg drove Larry to a modest Fort Lauderdale motel, Horace Shawkey and Donnie Swanson remained behind with Eccles. Shawkey made himself comfortable, waiting for the sound of Greg's car to fade into the night before lighting a cigar and commencing to speak.

"It's safe to conclude you fucked up, isn't it?" he asked.

Eccles raised his eyebrows and tossed his head, trying to make light of what he knew was a desperate situation. "I wouldn't put it that way," he said.

"I didn't ask how you'd put it. I'm telling you how I put it. I thought Spivey clarified the whole situation, but if there are still doubts, I can get him back here again."

Eccles was having trouble keeping his dinner down. "That won't be necessary," he said.

"Perhaps not. Donnie can make his point just as convincingly as Spivey. Can't you, Donnie?"

Swanson didn't even acknowledge his boss's question. He simply regarded Eccles steadily, like a leopard sizing up dinner.

"We don't want to hurt you, Stan," Shawkey said unctuously, his sudden solicitousness more ominous than his threats. "We just want to give you a chance to unfuck up. We think you deserve it."

It took Eccles almost half a minute to get up enough nerve to ask what that meant.

Shawkey gestured to Swanson, who reached into his pocket and came out with a white business envelope, which he handed to Eccles.

"There's ten grand in there," Shawkey said coldly. "Why don't you count it?"

"If you say so, Horace, it's okay with me. I trust you."

"Count it."

Eccles counted it, then looked up, at a loss to know what he was expected to do with it.

"This is the chance of a lifetime, Stan. You took my money and you were supposed to come back with a load. I expected that load. But you brought me nothing, Stan. Now I'm giving you another chance; only this time you're going to do it right."

"Sure, anything you say. But look, if you want your money back, sure, it goes without saying. First thing in the morning, as soon as the bank opens—"

"I don't want the money. I want the load. If I wanted the money, I wouldn't have invested it in our little arrangement. You can understand that, can't you?"

"Of course, whatever you say, Horace. It's just got to take me a little time to set up a new connection."

"What's the matter with your old connection? Did you rat on them? Did they get busted, too? You didn't tell me about that part, Stan."

"No, no, nothing like that. We didn't say a thing. They weren't busted. It's just that I'm hot down there. They caught me dealing. If I show up again, this time I'm going to wind up in the joint."

Shawkey stood up, straightened his pants, and brushed some imaginary lint off his sleeves. The lit end of his cigar gestured toward Eccles as he spoke. "Listen to me closely, Stan, because a man doesn't offer another man a second chance very often. You're going back to Jamaica in the morning, and you're coming back with a load, the same load you were supposed to bring me last time. See, Stan, when I give a man money to buy something for me, I expect one of three things. The first is that he buys it. And the other two are that he's dead or he's in jail. And you're not either of those other things yet. I think the police in Jamaica gave you a little taste of what it feels like to be in jail. Now I'm going out to my car, and Donnie here is going to give you a little taste of what it feels like to be dead. Then it's up to you. You make your own decision, Stan. Nobody's telling you what to do."

He turned and walked to the front door. Fifteen minutes later Donnie Swanson slid in behind the wheel of Shawkey's tomato red Caddie and drove his boss to meet Larry.

When Shawkey's junior bodyguard dropped him at a motel, the first thing Larry did was stash his gun. If Shawkey spotted it, there would be no way to explain how he had gotten it down with him on the flight from Atlanta, and the only choices open to him would be to arrest Shawkey on the spot or take a bite out of the gun to prove it was licorice. Neither seemed a desirable move.

It was almost eleven o'clock when Shawkey arrived, knocking on Larry's door. "Agee's coming over here to meet us," he announced. "We've been playing with ourselves too goddamned long already."

Shawkey was ready to reopen discussions of the plan to fly in a DC-4 loaded with ten tons of Colombia's highest grade of marijuana, which had been aborted when Roger Sorenson's arrest forced everyone to pull in his horns temporarily. In fact, Larry learned now that during his brief absence in Jamaica, Shawkey, who had been ostensibly cut out of the original plan, had made contact with Agee and indicated his desire to be cut back in.

Larry and Shawkey went downstairs to the motel's coffee shop to wait for Agee. A dingy room where the air itself was grease-stained and the inked-in prices on the floppy cardboard menus charted the course of inflation more tellingly than an economic report, it was supposed to close at eleven. But Horace Shawkey laid a $50 bill on the short-order cook, who happened to own the place, and he agreed to stay open, waiting on Shawkey's table himself because he wouldn't split the fifty with his waitress.

The party was on its second order of pie and third round of coffee when Agee joined the group. Donnie Swanson and his assistant hit man discreetly got up and moved to a nearby table, perhaps on a signal from Shawkey, but if so a subtle one, for Larry saw nothing.

The talk for the first half hour or so was a rehash of the plans left hanging from the deal that had never come off. Except for a commitment to meet again in the morning, intentions were left unspecified. Shawkey indicated he had lined up $200,000, more than enough to bankroll the deal. Yet when Larry reminded him that Floyd Farnum already had invested $30,000 in the airplane that would be used, Shawkey graciously agreed that there was room enough in the scheme for Farnum.

At the meeting the next morning, Larry tried to pin Shawkey down more closely. He definitely wanted Farnum in on this deal, which would be the capstone of his undercover career, the one venture that sealed all the smugglers into a solid, airtight package. Acting as Farnum's representative, he pointed out that the thirty thousand Floyd had already invested constituted just under 16 percent of the capital needed to finance the first flight. In addition, Farnum deserved credit for putting the package together in the first place.

For some reason, Shawkey was in an expansive mood—perhaps because by the time the meeting took place he had already heard that a badly battered Stan Eccles had set sail for Jamaica at dawn. Larry, of course, had no way of knowing of Shawkey's arrangement with Eccles or of Eccles's departure and, therefore, no way of accounting for the Virginia gangster's sudden generosity. Shawkey simply said, "I've got no quarrel with Floyd. He tried to cut me out before, but he didn't try to fuck me over. Does twenty percent seem fair?"

"Plenty fair," Larry agreed.

"But you take your cut out of that," Shawkey added shrewdly.

"Understood," Larry said.

"Then get him down here," Shawkey ordered gruffly. "If he's in this thing, I want him here."

Moving carefully, because of the ever-present entrapment problem, Larry suggested that Farnum didn't know whether there were any hard feelings and would feel more comfortable about the invitation if it came from Shawkey himself. Shawkey agreed, withdrew to call Bassett Forks, and returned five minutes later to report that Floyd Farnum would be arriving on the first flight the next morning.

The meeting broke up at that point. It was clear to Larry that Shawkey and Agee were constitutionally incapable of devoting more than an hour or two at a stretch to working out the arrangements that still needed to be made. They played a grind-'em-out game, marching down the field four yards on each play, never moving on to the next topic until the last one had been fully resolved. At this rate, the meetings would drag out for days.

Left to himself for the afternoon, Larry called GBI to check in. "Unless you can figure out some way to send me some of my clothes," he told Mike Eason, "I'm buying me some shirts and some underwear and putting it on my expense vouchers."

Eason laughed. "I don't think the boss is gonna go for that," he drawled. "But give it a try. Just make damn sure you don't get any bullet holes in any GBI shirts."

With Floyd Farnum in attendance at the next day's meeting, the discussion turned to the question of a landing site. Shawkey wanted Larry and Farnum to make the arrangements; that meant securing a suitable field and hiring a landing crew. This was a service which should have entitled them to a small cut in the deal, but Shawkey felt they had already been well taken care of in the 20 percent share they were down for.

Larry suggested he knew a man who could handle it.

"Who are you thinking of?" Farnum asked.

"George," Larry said. He was thinking that if he pulled off this gambit, he would have engineered the smoothest arrest in narcotics enforcement history. The unloading crew would consist entirely of undercover narcotics agents.

Farnum jumped at the idea. "George is cooler than hell," he said. "We won't even have to pay him. Just let his people pull out a chunk of the grass. It shouldn't cost us more than five hundred pounds, right?"

"Who's this George?" Shawkey demanded. He was willing to delegate responsibilities, but he clearly wanted to be on top of every aspect of the deal and was slowly putting himself in command of the entire scheme. Agee, who usually did most of the talking, already had taken a back seat to him.

Larry hesitated, hoping Floyd would answer Shawkey's question. "George is all right," Farnum said. "I've been dealing with him for years."

That was a lie; Farnum and Clardy had done only two small deals together and had worked on a few more that never came off. But it was a lie that suited Larry's purposes perfectly. When it turned out Clardy was an agent, it wouldn't have been Larry who had recommended him.

"Get him down here," Shawkey ordered, exactly as he had ordered Farnum's appearance at what was quickly turning into a royal court.

Everything stopped for another day until Clardy could be summoned. Since Larry was the one who knew Clardy best, it was naturally his job to place the call, utterly simplifying the task of briefing him on what was expected. For the first time, Larry let himself slip into the delusion that this undercover business was nowhere near as complicated as he had imagined. The dopers were practically racing each other to jail.

Clardy was met at the airport by Greg Stein and driven to Larry's motel. In twenty years of doing business, the owner of the coffee shop had never had so few customers or made so much money. Shawkey paid well for his privacy.

Clardy listened to Ron Agee's explanation of what was wanted. Since Agee would be landing with a full load and taking off empty a few minutes later, he wouldn't need more than a three-thousand-foot runway, preferably lighted. It had to be in a relatively untraveled section of rural Georgia, but with good highway connections to the interstates to cut down truck travel time with the illegal cargo. The unloading crew should consist of about eight or ten men so that the entire unloading and vacuuming of the aircraft could be accomplished in under half an hour.

"How much are you bringing in?" Clardy asked.

"Ten tons," Agee answered with impressive casualness. "We'll supply all the equipment. All you've got to do is get the stuff into the trucks at the airfield and off the trucks at the warehouses."

"Where are the warehouses?"

"It's your job to arrange that. Rent enough space somewhere near the airfield, that's all. We'll want four separate warehouses, not too close to each other."

Clardy put on a brief show of haggling over the price for his services, and in the end negotiated Farnum all the way up to the five hundred pounds the Virginian had assumed it would cost. The undercover agent shook hands all around and was driven back to the airport, where he caught a flight to Atlanta to begin scouting for a field.

Meeting followed meeting with numbing succession, a process as tedious but as necessary as the general staff planning sessions to work out the logistics for a landing operation in enemy-held territory. Agee located and put a down payment on four surplus airline catering trucks with elevating beds, so that the marijuana could be wheeled straight from the cargo hold of the DC-4 onto the trucks with hand dollies.

In private meetings between Agee and Clardy, who shuttled back and forth between Atlanta and Fort Lauderdale half a dozen times over the next ten days, a deal was worked out to leave Clardy in permanent possession of the trucks, thus simplifying the planning for all subsequent runs of the Marijuana Express. The trucks were to be owned by a Georgia corporation established expressly for this purpose and boasting no other assets. The Georgia corporation was in turn owned by a Cayman corporation owned by a Cayman attorney retained by Floyd Farnum. If any of the trucks ran into trouble en route, drug authorities would have a hell of a time figuring out whom to go after.

As originally planned, the entire load would be brokered through a grass merchant Agee knew in Kalamazoo, Michigan. Agee made the preliminary phone call to him. "That load of carpet you wanted to bid on is coming in," he said. "Are you still interested?"

"How many yards?"

"Twenty thousand."

"No problem. When can I take delivery?"

"In two weeks, the usual day. Shall I send our salesman up?"

The usual day was Sunday, the day Agee always brought his flights in. And the salesman turned out to be Larry, who was immediately put on a plane for Detroit. Before he left, Shawkey gave orders that once initial contact was established, the broker was to deal only with him.

Larry's trip to Michigan lasted no more than six hours, including two hours' flying time each way. The broker, a wiry young man in his middle thirties dressed from head to toe in leather, had driven straight from Kalamazoo to meet Larry's flight. They talked in the airport lounge.

The broker quickly agreed to guarantee a price of $250 a pound, up fifty from when the deal originally had been proposed to him. When the load came in, he would have sixty buyers from all over the country ready to inspect it at the warehouses and take delivery. He would collect from them, cash on the barrelhead, with an understanding that he would be entitled to keep the difference between $250 and whatever prices he could negotiate. Larry was to secure rooms in each of five different motels to house the marijuana buyers' convention that would be suddenly descending on an unwitting Georgia town.

Larry and the broker shook hands, and then Larry retraced his steps to the gate he had just left to board a return flight to Fort Lauderdale.

With the buyers now lined up, it was time for Horace Shawkey to make his down payment on the marijuana. The deal with the Colombian suppliers required that $90,000 be paid ten days in advance of delivery, the balance not due until the load was sold and the DC-4 returned to South America for its next load. To simplify the handling of the money, an arrangement had been made with a high-ranking officer in the Colombian air force stationed in Fort Lauderdale with the air force's procurement office. Shawkey himself personally delivered the $90,000 to the Colombian colonel, who would put it on that day's air shuttle to Bogotá, where it would find its way into the hands of the suppliers. Shawkey then left for Roanoke, intending to return on Saturday, March 13, the eve of the flight.

Planning in Atlanta ran exactly parallel to the planning in Fort Lauderdale, except that the Georgia Bureau of Investigation had to be infinitely more careful. For George Clardy, the first order of business was to line up an airfield for the smugglers. It took him four days of scouring the Georgia countryside before he found the right place, a private air park in Turner County just ten miles by state highway from I-75 and a little more than an hour south of Macon. The field boasted a forty-six-hundred-foot lighted runway, greatly exceeding Agee's specifications. Clardy identified himself to the owner of the field as a GBI agent, explained the purpose for which he wanted the man's property, and negotiated terms. The owner and his wife were asked to stay away from the field the weekend the flight was supposed to come in, for there was always a possibility of gunfire. The unloading crew of agents would have the smugglers outnumbered, but the men on the aircraft might want to make it a contest. The chances were very good that Horace Shawkey, who liked to play it safe with his own property, would have Donnie Swanson or someone very much like him riding shotgun on the DC-4.

Once the owner of the airstrip had given his consent, Larry was called upon to dust off his long-unused experience in real estate dealing to draw up a suitable lease. In order to have something to show Shawkey and Agee, neither of whom knew that the airfield would be needed only once, the lease was written for a year. In a rider, which the drug dealers wouldn't be shown, both the Georgia Bureau of Investigation and the owner were authorized to cancel the arrangement at any time on seventy-two hours' notice.

With the airfield secure, Clardy then drove to Macon, where he rented four mini-warehouses for storing the goods. Larry accompanied him, using the occasion to put deposits on the motel rooms the Michigan broker had asked him to arrange.

In all, more than a hundred law enforcement personnel would be involved in the wave of arrests that was expected to follow Ron Agee's arrival. Phil Peters assigned twenty-six agents to the case, every man and woman he had, except for a few whose commitment to ongoing cases made them unavailable. Agents George Clardy, Paul Carter, Gary Newman, Glenn Longino, David Hallman, Tom Davis, Bob Sprayberry, Tony Gaylee, Paul Music, and Wally Brooks would serve as the unloading gang. Customs was donating thirty men to the operation, including two pilots and two airplanes for aerial surveillance of Agee's arrival. The Georgia State Police put about fifty men on the case, and on D day would have a fleet of aircraft and helicopters monitoring the movements of the buyers. Virginia sent five men to take part, including undercover Agents Barry Keessee and Wayne Oyler. Finally, the U.S. attorney's office for the Southern District of Georgia and the attorney general's office were sending observers to make sure the case was airtight from a prosecutorial point of view.

The entire operation would be personally orchestrated by Inspector Phil Peters, working out of a command post set up in the Macon National Guard armory, which had been commandeered to bivouac the army of narcotics agents brought in for what everybody was hoping would turn into a one-day hunting season.

With eight days to go until Agee's flight, both teams were fully deployed on both sides of the scrimmage line that only one team knew existed. It was a time for waiting.

Twenty-three

L arry had played his part perfectly, following to the letter the advice Phil Peters had given him six months earlier, before he had taken his first undercover assignment. He had put the deal together so seamlessly that each member in the smuggling partnership rolled along on the course set for him as automatically as a train rolling down the tracks. The cases against Shawkey, Agee, and Farnum were airtight, and there wasn't the slightest possibility any of them could successfully contend he had been entrapped. Indeed, by the weekend before the flight, Larry's role in the venture had been reduced to absolute zero. He had been given responsibility for the airfield and the unloading crew, but Clardy now was handling that and reporting directly to Shawkey. He had made the arrangements with the broker in Michigan, but the broker now was communicating directly with Shawkey. He had brought Farnum into the deal and was ostensibly his agent, but Farnum had now withdrawn to Bassett Forks with nothing further to do than await the arrival of the messenger bearing his and Larry's share of the proceeds.

If anything, it was too perfect a job. Because Horace Shawkey could add up a column of numbers as well as another man, and it didn't take him longer than it took Larry to add it all up and realize that Larry and Farnum were getting a good percentage of the profits and had nothing further to contribute. It was then that he elected to save himself the difference between 20 percent of ten tons of grass and the price of two teams of button men.

Larry had no knowledge of what was coming. Barring unexpected animosities, he always figured he was safe unless his cover got burned, and he knew he was still safe on that score. He was so deep into the dual identity of an agent and a smuggler that he always assumed danger lay on the interface where his two identities met. That a smuggler would kill him simply as another smuggler, to save money, had never been a prominent part of his nightmares.

What was on his mind toward the beginning of March was keeping up with the constantly evolving situation and staying away from the sheriff. The last time he had spoken with Charlene, she had hung up on him, and he was sure she was finally going to carry through on her threat of having him arrested on a civil contempt warrant. He had promised himself to have the matter taken care of as soon as Shawkey and Co. had been put out of business.

On Saturday evening, March 6, Larry had just gotten off the phone with Horace Shawkey when he and Jerri were surprised by a knock on the door. "Bitch," Larry muttered, meaning the epithet for his ex-wife. "Take care of it, will ya, honey?" he whispered, getting up from the couch and heading for the utility closet under the stairway.

They had discussed this before, and Jerri knew her part. She was to tell the deputies simply that he was out and wasn't expected back for a day or two.

The two tall young men at the door showed no identification. "Police, ma'am," one of them said deferentially. "Is Larry Spivey here?"

"No, I'm sorry. He's not," Jerri lied, perhaps less than glibly.

The two men exchanged glances. One of them stepped deftly past her. "It's important, ma'am," he said. "Mind if we wait?"

Jerri turned helplessly after him, and the second man took advantage of the opportunity to follow the first inside. "Well, no," she stammered. "I don't mind. But I'm not expecting him back tonight. I—I've got plans. I was just leaving."

"That's all right, ma'am. This won't take long," the first man said. He was wearing a three-piece suit, had medium-length hair that looked like it was done by a stylist rather than a barber. His partner was smaller, squarer, and carried a cheap imitation leather briefcase.

In the closet under the stairwell, Larry knew at once who they were and wondered if Jerri had picked up on the mistake they already had made. Saying it wouldn't take long didn't make sense. In the darkness, he reached silently for the door cut into the false closet back, behind which

298

the apartment's boiler was housed. He kept his .45 hanging from a nail driven into one of the unfinished stairway supports.

The fiberboard door swung noiselessly under the gentle pressure of the palm of his hand, and he stepped into the tiny overheated recess. Groping blindly, he found the gun in its hiding place and slid it from the holster, then picked his way back to the closet. He could hear Jerri speaking and didn't know what he had missed. "Then it's not about the warrant?" she was saying.

"No, ma'am," the same voice Larry had heard before said.

"I'm sorry," Jerri apologized, trying to understand. "You're working with GBI, aren't you?"

There was no answer, and Larry could imagine the expressions on the faces of Horace Shawkey's two hired killers as they tried to digest this latest piece of intelligence. They would quickly conclude that the only difference it made was that they were doing Shawkey more of a favor than he had paid them for.

Jerri, too, immediately realized she had blundered. "I really don't know when he'll be back. I'm sure it won't be tonight. He went away for the weekend," she blurted out, lying transparently now.

"Sit tight, lady. We've got all the time in the world," a new voice said.

The masks were off now, and Larry doubled his concentration as he eavesdropped on the scene that was supposed to have been his own murder. He was listening for clues, tiny indications of intention that would tell him when he should make his move. In the stillness that followed, he heard two small snapping sounds that were the smaller man's briefcase being opened. There was a short gasp from Jerri, as she saw the sawed-off shotgun inside.

"Who are you?" she demanded, the slightest quaver of hysteria audible in her voice.

"Don't sweat it. Our business ain't with you," the second voice said.

"I wouldn't mind doing some business with you, honey," the one who had spoken first said, his voice a contemptible sneer.

Jerri must have moved or gestured something in response because the same man muttered a sexual obscenity. "Cover for me, man. I'm gonna have me a little fun. Spivey ain' gonna have no use for her, tha's for sure."

He laughed. The other man said, "Hey, man, we got work to do."

"Ain't no work here till the pigeon flies back into the coop, boy. Do what I tell ya," he commanded. "Git upstairs," he barked to Jerri.

There was no response for a moment. "You hear me, bitch," he snarled. "Don' ac' like you're too fuckin' good for me, cunt, 'cause I'm fixin' to show you."

"Get your hands off me," Jerri cried.

In the closet, Larry had to restrain himself from coming through the door with his .45 blazing. But he couldn't shoot without risking hitting Jerri. He had no choice but to bide his time. The sickening reality was that his best chance would come when Jerri's agony left him one-on-one with the hired gun who remained downstairs.

Above his head, Larry heard the irregular thudding of footsteps echoing through the staircase as riotously as if he were inside a pealing bell. The killer's steps, heavy and slow, thud, pause, thud, thud, pause; Jerri's steps lighter, staggering, obviously resisting. Twice she tripped, off-balance from the shoving, but her captor kept forcing her on. Larry guessed he had his gun in his hand. He could hear her protests, or the sounds of her protests, for her words were as indistinguishable as their meaning was clear. The man apparently was saying nothing or else muttering so low his voice didn't carry. With each second that passed, Larry's grip on himself slipped, like a frayed rope surrendering strand by strand. And with each second, the price Shawkey's hit men would pay went up, for the bill would include Jerri's shame as well as his own.

Larry tried to put the sounds from upstairs out of his mind as he concentrated on the man in the living room. He heard sobs and cries, the cries stifled in the sobbing, but he made himself not listen. Downstairs the professional killer in the living room was pacing slowly, his footfalls almost inaudible except for the rhythmic scraping of his shoes along the carpet.

Barely a minute passed, and Larry heard the footsteps sharpen as the killer moved out of the living room and into the tiled hallway, right past the door behind which Larry crouched, holding his breath. It would have been easy then to step free and shoot the man in the back, except that Jerri was upstairs alone with an armed man who would kill her before he came downstairs to investigate the shots. So Larry held back, believing, as he always believed, that there would be a right moment to act, but only one.

He drew back the hammer of his .45, knowing he would have to be ready to kill in an instant. He held the gun by his ear, waiting. The footsteps moved off a few feet farther to Larry's left and modulated ever so slightly. The kitchen or the bathroom. Memories of subtle sounds he never would have guessed his brain had stored away suddenly came back to him, and he decided the man was in the bathroom. This was going to be his chance, he told himself, waiting the smallest fraction of a second to be sure.

Then, as incongruently comic as a fart at a funeral, he heard the man urinating. His left hand twisted carefully at the doorknob while his right thumb gently lowered the hammer of the gun. He leaned out enough to see straight down the hallway in front of him to the bathroom door. Closed. The prissy bastard had closed the door to take a leak, and it was going to cost him his life.

Like a ghost in his own house, Larry inched silently toward the bathroom door, waiting for the sound of the toilet flushing that would tell him he had only three or four more seconds for the one act in his life he would have to do absolutely perfectly. Above him, Jerri was crying, her voice clearer now that the closet no longer insulated him from it. The urinating stopped just as Larry slid into position by the left-hand side of the doorframe, his whole body coiled like a snake, his right arm tensed to throbbing.

The toilet flushed, three seconds passed, four, certainly not much more than that, and the doorknob turned before his eyes and the door swung slowly away from him.

He never saw the man's face before he hit him, and afterward there wasn't enough left of it to see. His fist, reinforced with almost two pounds of steel, came down overhand so hard it sliced through the man's skull like a knife through putty, the edge of his hand and the stock of his gun dividing the face in front of him, the barrel of the gun following like a needle through the hole in a button. Oddly, the man sagged to the floor slowly, like a lady in a faint, and Larry reached back to hit him again, then stopped himself, assured the man was only a few minutes' worth of dying short of being dead.

He slipped his shoes off and tiptoed back down the hallway and past the closet, stopping at the foot of the stairs to plan what he had to do. Pressed almost flat to the wall, he inched sideways up the stairs, using no more of each step than the width of his shoe, knowing that a single creak could cost Jerri her life. The hammer of his .45 was drawn back again, and as his finger coaxed at the trigger, he felt a crawling sensation in his hand from the dead man's blood drying.

At the landing at the top of the stairs, he paused to get his bearings, expecting to find them in the master bedroom. For the first time he realized how close they had all come to an even worse disaster. A week earlier or a week later Jerri's boy would have been at home. From where he stood, he could see into Mark's room. It was empty, as he knew it would be.

Their room was to his right, the door opening off the corridor on the left. It was a moment when all the details of one's surroundings suddenly take on an intense purposefulness, as though the simple amenities of life all had been designed, either well or badly, for survival—the carpet laid down on the hallway floor only to deaden the sound of footsteps, the hallway light switch outside the bedroom door installed only to offer concealment on a night like this.

Moving quickly, without making a sound audible even to himself, he reached the doorway and readied himself. He raised his gore-soaked gun to his cheek and positioned his left hand on the light switch. Then, in one absolutely decisive move, he stepped into the open doorway and commenced firing as he switched off the light behind him, his eyes taking in everything in the fraction of a second between the inception of the act and the moment a rain of bullets poured irrevocably from the barrel of his gun.

Jerri lay on the bed, naked, the killer astride her. His pants were around his ankles, his bare buttocks no more than fifteen feet from the doorway where Larry stood. Apparently he had heard something, or sensed something, because just before Larry opened fire, he had pulled himself to his knees, turning his upper body toward the doorway while his hand reached reflexively for the shotgun he had laid on the bed beside him.

The first shot caught him in the ribs, hitting with an impact that actually lifted his soft, fleshy body half an inch from the mattress and carried it toward the wall. Each successive shot—there were four—bounced him on the bed, like a child on its father's knee, until finally the horrible string of explosions ended and he pitched forward across the woman under him.

For the briefest second Larry closed his eyes, then lowered his gun and hurried to Jerri, who still lay under the dead man who had been raping her. Larry had to roll the corpse off her.

Jerri's eyes were closed tightly, her face frozen in terror. She was sobbing convulsively, but so silently it seemed impossible she was breathing. As Larry reached out to her, she cried, "Don't touch me, don't touch me."

Yet he couldn't leave her there. She was screaming now, wave after wave of unintelligible cries. He pulled her from the bed and drew her toward her son's room. "Get away from me, don't come near me," she was shrieking, and he had no choice but to obey. Wrapping the bedspread over her nakedness, he left her alone with her waking nightmares and returned downstairs.

Incredibly, the man he had left on the bathroom floor was still alive, his breath blowing bubbles of blood in the gaping cavity at the front of his face. Larry kicked at the side of his head, and the breathing stopped. He went to the kitchen and reached for the phone, only then realizing he still held his gun in his hand.

The dispatcher at GBI patched him through to Mike Eason.

"Mike, listen. Shawkey sent two guys to hit me. I had to kill both of them. Get someone over here right away. And get a doctor here for Jerri."

"She hurt bad?"

"She's hysterical. In shock, I guess. She may have been raped."

"Oh, Jesus."

"For Chrissakes, Mike, hurry."

The first person to arrive at Jerri's apartment was a sergeant with the DeKalb County police. Larry opened the door for him. "Everything under control?" he asked, standing in the doorway.

"I think so. Come in," Larry said.

The sergeant shook his head. "Can't. We got orders to protect the scene, give you any assistance you need. But no one goes in till your people get here."

That was only a minute or two later, first Eason, then Clardy, then Inspector Peters himself. Somewhere in the middle a doctor arrived and sedated Jerri. He saw no reason to hospitalize her if the sedative put her to sleep.

Larry tried to go up to see her after the doctor left, but the sight of him sent her into a new wave of hysteria. "You have to be patient with her, Larry," Eason counseled. "After what she's been through, it's gotta take her time to get over it."

Eason went up to her and came back a half hour later to report she was finally asleep. He had been crying, and he didn't try to hide it.

While Eason was caring for Jerri and Clardy was getting a full report on the incident from Larry, Inspector Peters had been busy barking orders and pulling strings to salvage the situation. The first priority was to get Larry and Jerri out of the apartment, in case Horace Shawkey had any more surprises in store. A DeKalb County patrol team was sent to secure a pair of motel rooms, one for Larry and Jerri, the second for a GBI team that would bodyguard them through the night.

With a few phone calls to the highest echelon of the DeKalb County Police Department and the coroner's office, Peters imposed a total news blackout on the killings to keep Shawkey from learning his hired guns had failed.

While Inspector Peters was momentarily off the phone, Larry found time to sneak off to the kitchen and place a call to Floyd Farnum, who was in exactly the same position as he with regard to Shawkey. It stood to reason that the double-dealing gangster had taken contracts on both of them, and Larry wasn't going to stand by and let Farnum get killed.

"Floyd, Larry. I've got to talk to you."

"Jesus, I'm glad you called. I was just thinking of giving you a call. Found out some interesting news. And I'm worried. I don't know how to tell you this, but remember all that shit I told you about the organization up here? It's not the Mafia or anything like that. It's just a bunch of guys, right? Well, I guess that doesn't go for Horace. He's about as connected as a guy can get."

As distraught as he was, Larry almost laughed at the grotesque irrelevance of Farnum's discovery. "Hey, that's no bulletin, Floyd," he said. "We knew that, didn't we?"

"Man, we didn't know half of it. I'm talking about heavy Mafia, as heavy as it comes. And he's got us in it, too. Listen, I gotta tell you what I heard. You wanna know where Horace got the two hundred grand for this deal? From some sharkskin suit out in the Midwest that's on the fucking national council. Larry, we just became honorary Eye-talians, and I'm not sure I like it."

Larry let out a low whistle of surprise that caught the ear of the inspector and the other agents in the living room. In less than half a minute Peters was standing over his shoulder as Farnum went on talking.

"Now the thing that started me asking around was he doesn't need any two hundred thou for this deal, right? I'm paying for the fucking plane, so he can't need much over a hundred. Then why the heavy bread? Because he's doing a number on us, Larry. Some people I know who know say even Agee doesn't know it, but when he takes off in Colombia, he's gonna have two hundred pounds of A-number-one coke tucked in back somewhere. Horace is getting it flown in free."

"Okay, Floyd," Larry said, cutting him off. "Listen to me a minute, and then do whatever you've got to do. Two guys just came after me. Horace sent them. If I'm on the list, you're on the list."

On the other end of the line, Farnum gasped but said nothing. For a moment, Larry felt a crazy impulse to make the warning clearer, to say to him, *Floyd, get out of this, get all the way out. Shawkey is fixing to kill you, and I'm a narc. If he doesn't get you, I will.* But he stopped himself, and the silence on the line lasted a long time. Then Farnum said, "Shit, Larry, this isn't the way we planned it, is it?"

"It's not the way I planned it," Larry said. "Take care of yourself, Floyd."

He hung up and turned away from the phone, stepping around Inspector Peters, who reached out a hand to detain him.

"I don't reckon we'll ever catch up with Mr. Farnum now," Peters said softly. "You had to call him, didn't you?"

"Wouldn't you have?"

The inspector nodded. "Just don't forget which side you're on, son. Don't go thinking about any of this too much. You leave Shawkey to us."

Larry walked away from him. In a few minutes Eason came downstairs with Jerri on his shoulder. She had a robe on, and she was walking in her sleep, drugged insensible. Larry opened the door for them, and Eason led her out to a waiting police car and helped her into the back seat. Larry and Clardy slid into the front, and they drove to the motel without speaking.

For the next week Larry worked side by side with Inspector Peters, perhaps because Peters felt he needed him there, perhaps because the inspector wanted to keep an eye on him. The large battalion of law enforcement personnel from four separate agencies and two states had to be drilled into a smoothly running unit, had to be carefully rehearsed until each man could play his part to perfection. A thousand contingencies had to be planned for, yet the operation had to be left flexible enough to respond appropriately if Sunday brought the thousand and first, which nobody had foreseen.

Because Clardy was meeting with Shawkey constantly, GBI was never more than a few hours behind the smuggler's latest thinking. In fact, Phil Peters knew more about the plans than even Ron Agee, who was being told nothing about the location of the airfield and would be told nothing until the last minute before his takeoff. When he returned with the drugs, he would wait on the ground only long enough for Clardy's crew to unload him and vacuum out the interior. Then he would take off and fly to Fort Lauderdale, where he would have no further contact with anyone connected with the smuggling operation until a messenger arrived with his share of the payoff.

When the marijuana had been unloaded into the trucks, Clardy's crew would drive it to the four warehouses Clardy had rented. Only Clardy and Shawkey would know the locations of all four warehouses, for each team of workers would be told only its own destination. Shawkey himself would possess the only set of keys to all four warehouses. He would give the broker one key and the address of one warehouse. The broker would schedule buyers to appear at the warehouse at ten- to thirty-minute intervals, depending on the size of the load they were taking. When the first warehouse was empty, the broker would pay Shawkey in full for the marijuana he had sold before being given the key and the address of the next warehouse.

Shawkey figured that if everyone moved expeditiously, all ten tons of grass could be on their way out of Georgia in less than eight hours after Agee's touchdown. Sometime between midnight, when Agee was expected to land, and 8:00 A.M. Monday, when the warehouses would be empty, Horace Shawkey would have personally taken in $5 million in cash. Floyd Farnum's share of the take would have come to exactly half a million dollars, Larry's share a few thousand less since Farnum was taking his expenses off the top.

Once, in the course of the week, Shawkey asked Clardy, in passing, "What do you hear from Spivey?"

Clardy knew what the question meant but didn't even look up from what he was doing. "Haven't talked to him," he said laconically. He guessed Shawkey was getting nervous about not having heard from the men he had sent out with the contract.

The GBI plan was based point for point on the smugglers' method of operation. Agee and anyone else on the plane with him could be arrested at the airfield while the unloading was going on. The DC-4 then would be flown to Fort Lauderdale by a Georgia State Police pilot, in case Shawkey was watching for it to take off.

Helicopter, airplane, and ground surveillance would be used to monitor each of the warehouses. Each buyer who left with drugs would be followed for at least ten miles before being arrested, to prevent word of the arrest from leaking back to those still in line. They would be permitted no phone calls until the roundup was over. Only when the last of the buyers was in custody would Shawkey himself be taken down.

Police in Virginia could safely be sent to pick up Floyd Farnum any time after the DC-4 touched down, but the GBI team was putting even money that Farnum wouldn't be found. If the prospect of half a million dollars foolishly tempted him to disregard Larry's warning and stick around for the payoff, the chances were that Shawkey's hit men would have caught up with him. If he did the smart thing, the Virginia troopers would find no trace of him when they showed up at his house with a warrant for his arrest on Sunday. Peters in particular regretted seeing him escape prosecution but consoled himself with the reflection that a man like Farnum couldn't stay underground for long. Sooner or later he would turn up behind some kind of crooked scam somewhere. His escape was, in any case, a small price to pay for a ten-ton seizure and a roundup of heavy dealers from all across the country.

For everyone connected with the investigation, the tension during the last week of waiting mounted excruciatingly. But for Larry in particular the situation had become almost unbearable. Jerri didn't recover after a night's sleep, as the doctor had hoped she might. He had warned Larry that rape victims often go through periods of depression that may last for weeks, but nothing he said prepared Larry for the severity of her reaction. From what she was able to communicate of her sleeping and waking nightmares, it was clear that the rape itself was only a part of the horror that replayed itself over and over in her mind.

On the first morning he was awakened from a light and troubled sleep by the sound of her sobbing in the bed next to his. When he tried to comfort her, she recoiled, as though it were he who had tormented her. The next three or four days ran him through a stupefying maze of ambivalent feelings, as he alternately told himself that she needed his support and that the best thing he could do for her was to stay away. Twice he went to the doctor for advice but was told only that there were no hard-and-fast rules, that he would have to play it by ear.

By Thursday, five days after the incident, the intensity of her reaction to him hadn't abated in the least, and he was forced to acknowledge that it would be better if he went away. He felt she blamed him not only for drawing those men to her house, not only for his impotence in letting them degrade her, but also for his brutality in killing them. He asked Mike Eason to arrange psychiatric care for her and reluctantly moved out of the motel where GBI had been keeping them. It was the bitterest night of his life. He knew in time she would recover, for she was a strong woman, but he knew also she would never stop hating him.

On Saturday evening Horace Shawkey, Ron Agee, and George Clardy held their last meeting in Shawkey's motel room in Fort Lauderdale. They tied up some loose ends and talked their way through the whole next day, then split up shortly after eight o'clock. Sometime between ten and eleven o'clock, Shawkey received a telephone call from one of the goons he had staked out around Stan Eccles's home. Eccles was back.

Accompanied by Donnie Swanson and another hired gun, Shawkey drove to the home of an associate who had been slated to accept delivery of the thousand pounds of marijuana Eccles was supposed to pick up in Jamaica. He asked the man if Eccles had brought in the load. He was told he had, but that it was almost two hundred pounds light. Eccles had said that was all he could get.

Shawkey and his bodyguards then drove to the Fort Lauderdale marina, where they succeeded in boarding Eccles's sailboat. They had no difficulty at all finding the four bales of marijuana stowed under the deck.

"Get yourselves a cab back to my place," Shawkey ordered the bodyguards. "I'll catch up with you later."

Swanson volunteered to go with him, but Shawkey shook his head. This was something he wanted to take care of himself.

He drove to Eccles's house alone, arriving after midnight, probably closer to 1:00 A.M. There were lights on in the living room and kitchen. Phyllis Laine opened the door when he knocked. "Good to see you, Phyllis," he said curtly, stepping past her. "Stan here?"

"He just got back," she answered quickly, a twinge of apprehension in her voice. "He was going to call you first thing in the morning."

Shawkey smiled. "It's a good thing I stopped by. I'm leaving first thing in the morning. He would have missed me."

His tone reassured her, and she went inside to fetch Eccles. They whispered together in the bedroom for a few minutes. Then Eccles came out alone. He was wearing slacks, slippers, and a short dressing jacket with satin trim.

"Horace, I made it!" he called cheerfully, leading his partner into the living room. "I would have sworn it couldn't be done, but I did it."

They talked amiably for a few minutes, Eccles leading the way to the long sofa in the middle of the room, where they sat side by side. After a while Phyllis joined them and asked if they would like coffee or drinks. Shawkey opted for coffee, so she went into the kitchen to put on the electric drip machine.

Although separated from the two men only by the counter between the kitchen and the living room, she could hear little of what was being said. There was obvious tension between them, but they both seemed to be in good moods, trying to mask it. She knew, of course, of the beating Shawkey's man had given her lover, and she attributed the subtle undercurrent of hostility she sensed to residual animosity both men were trying to put behind them.

In retrospect, she could not pinpoint exactly when she noticed that voices were being raised. For a few seconds she tried to watch and listen, then gave up in frustration and focused her concentration on arranging something to serve with the coffee.

The violence of what followed was sudden, shocking, brutal, and fast. One of the men—no one will ever know which—drew a gun, and the other matched his move. Without even moving from where they sat, they blasted away at each from point-blank range, no more than three feet of space between them. In the kitchen Phyllis Laine, fearing for her life, threw a chair through the window and dived out after it. She ran to the house next door and called the police.

When the police got to the house, Stan Eccles was still on the couch, hit two times, once directly in the center of the forehead. Horace Shawkey was seated next to him, slumped forward, four bullets in his chest and abdomen. Eccles was dead; Shawkey wasn't expected to make it through the night.

Franklin Jameson, a veteran investigator in the Broward County prosecutor's office, arrived on the scene less than an hour after the police. Shawkey had already been taken to the hospital, but Eccles's body remained on the couch until cops from the forensic division had finished photographing it from all angles. Jameson spent ten minutes getting briefed on the case by the ranking detective, then began looking around for himself. Because of the hour and because there weren't expected to be any prosecutions—the two men had obviously shot each other, and both would be dead by morning—the special investigator was drowsily going through the motions of an investigation, fully expecting to find nothing, when he was startled by a name scrawled on the back of a slip of paper taken from Shawkey's pocket. Spivey, it said, followed by a phone number. Recognizing the name from the Parent murder case, he reached for the telephone and dialed the number. There was no answer. He pressed down the button, got a dial tone, and dialed the operator, identifying himself and asking to be put through to the Georgia Bureau of Investigation.

At the GBI reaction center, there was an understandable reluctance to put anyone through to Larry, who was then living at the command post in the Macon National Guard armory. With the biggest drug haul of GBI history only hours away, the control center was treating the very existence of the Macon bivouac as top secret. Jameson had to tell his story three times before he finally got someone willing to authorize the connection.

It was still an hour shy of dawn. Unable to sleep, Larry had wandered into the unoccupied communications center to await Phil Peters's arrival. Peters wanted him around but insisted on keeping him inside the armory through the whole operation, where he could monitor all the action but would have no contact with any of the subjects. Even at this stage, when his undercover status no longer mattered, he didn't want Larry in on the arrests, in part because he believed that men in custody become hostile, bitter, and less talkative in the presence of the undercover man who betrayed them, in part also because he wasn't sure what Larry would do in a face-to-face confrontation with Shawkey. Larry was pacing the floor, planning how he would phrase his appeal to Peters, when the phone rang.

A man's voice asked for him by name. "Who's calling?" he asked.

"Franklin Jameson, Broward County prosecutor's office. We met in Garrett's office on the Carl Parent thing."

"Sure, right. How the hell did you get me here?"

"It wasn't easy. Look, we had a shooting here last night, got a couple of stiffs on our hands, figure you might know something about them. Actually, only one of them's croaked, but the other should be joining him later today. You know a man named Stanley Eccles?"

"Eccles, sure. That was the guy in Jamaica. Who's the other one? Jones?"

"No. Fellow by the name of Shawkey. Horace Shawkey. Know him?"

Larry went white, the telephone almost falling from his hand. He felt cheated, robbed. He knew instantly that there was no possible ending now that would satisfy him, no way to make sense out of any of it. Because what was there left to do? Arrest Ron Agee? What did it matter? Agee was a crazy, amoral adventurer who smuggled drugs because it was the most dangerous thing he could think of to do in an airplane. A month ago busting the legendary pot plane pilot of Polk County would have been a triumph worth all the blood it cost, a wonderful story to tell and retell endlessly over beers with Clardy and Eason, a case that would have agents all over the country licking their lips. But now he didn't give a damn about Ron Agee.

It was Shawkey he wanted, because destroying Shawkey was the only part of it that made sense anymore. He had wanted to test himself by making the arrest himself. He had earned the right to find out whether he could draw his gun on Shawkey without killing him, and that was what he had wanted to tell Phil Peters. Instead, Stan Eccles, who God knew had less reason than Larry to kill the man, turned out in the end to have had reason enough. The poor bastard, at least he did what he had to. It was a hell of an epitaph. Here lies Stan Eccles, who couldn't do anything right but did what he had to.

Without even realizing he was talking, Larry told Jameson what he wanted to know about Shawkey and hung up the phone. He looked around the room and realized he was no longer alone. Half a dozen agents had come in while he was speaking and had begun tuning in the radios that grew like wild mushrooms on all the lamplit surfaces of the windowless room. They were getting reports from Clardy, already at the Turner County airfield making last-minute preparations for Agee's landing. They were getting reports from agents deployed around the motels where the buyers were camped, reports from agents moving into position around the four warehouses. From the agent in the tower at the Fort Lauderdale airport, word came in that Agee's DC-4 was on the runway, cleared for takeoff.

Now there were sixteen hours to kill.

Epilogue

The shooting of Horace Shawkey queered the great Turner County marijuana sale. George Clardy attempted to step into Shawkey's shoes, delivering the warehouse keys to the Michigan broker with an explanation that Shawkey had been detained. "No sweat, I'll wait for Horace," the broker answered wisely. By late afternoon it was clear to him Shawkey wasn't going to show, and he pulled out of town. In the course of the evening the sixty buyers he had gathered in Macon began to disperse, drifting away in ones, twos, and threes to take their business elsewhere.

Only Ron Agee and a friend flying copilot were arrested in the case. Agee was tried, convicted, and sentenced to thirty years in prison for smuggling marijuana. His sentence was later cut in half after he testified before a House of Representatives subcommittee investigating drug smuggling.

Floyd Farnum disappeared as predicted. He is still under indictment in Virginia, but his whereabouts are unknown.

Horace Shawkey not only managed to survive four shots from Stan Eccles's gun, but pulled through ten hours of surgery, recovering sufficiently to be discharged from the hospital. Within a few weeks, however, he suffered a relapse, diagnosed as peritonitis resulting from his wounds. He was readmitted to the hospital, where he died only a few days later.

In October 1976, eight months after Larry first learned the name of the *Don Emilio,* an American submarine spotted the Panamanian freighter loading drugs off the coast of El Pájaro, Colombia. The ship was followed on its northward course, while the secretary of state was notified that the long search had come to an end. Rather than wait for the vessel to violate the Hovering Vessels Act by off-loading a portion of its cargo to an American ship, the secretary negotiated a deal with the Panamanian government. The *Don Emilio* was boarded by the coast guard in international waters just north of the Bahamas. On board were 100 tons of marijuana and 440 pounds of pure cocaine, a drug haul valued in the hundreds of millions of dollars.

The *Don Emilio* was then towed to Miami, the coast guard turning it over to the DEA as soon as it reached American waters. By the time it docked all the cocaine and one of the crewmen had disappeared. To this day, the DEA does not officially acknowledge there was cocaine aboard. According to the deal worked out with the Panamanian government, the marijuana was confiscated and burned, while the ship and its entire crew were returned to Panama. Because the seizure had been made in international waters, the U.S. attorney had no choice but to decline to prosecute.

In 1978 the dope ship was seized again. Again it was carrying a cargo of more than one hundred tons of narcotics; again it was released; again there were no prosecutions.

Larry Spivey is no longer a member of the Georgia Bureau of Investigation. He retired from the life of an undercover agent as soon as the Turner County case was closed. In his brief six-month career, he had developed information leading to the seizure of $521 million worth of drugs. Eighteen homicides had happened around him, including two men he killed himself. It was enough.